On New Shores

On New Shores

Understanding Immigrant Fathers in North America

Edited by Susan S. Chuang
and Robert P. Moreno

LEXINGTON BOOKS

A division of
ROWMAN & LITTLEFIELD PUBLISHERS, INC.
Lanham • Boulder • New York • Toronto • Plymouth, UK

LEXINGTON BOOKS

A division of Rowman & Littlefield Publishers, Inc.
A wholly owned subsidary of The Rowman & Littlefield Publishing Group, Inc.
4501 Forbes Boulevard, Suite 200
Lanham, MD 20706

Estover Road
Plymouth PL6 7PY
United Kingdom

British Library Cataloguing in Publication Information Available

Library of Congress Cataloging-in-Publication Data

On new shores : understanding immigrant fathers in North America / edited by
Susan S. Chuang and Robert P. Moreno.
    p. cm.
  Includes bibliographical references and index.
  ISBN-13: 978-0-7391-1880-1 (cloth : alk. paper)
  ISBN-10: 0-7391-1880-3 (cloth : alk. paper)
  ISBN-13: 978-0-7391-3007-0 (electronic)
  ISBN-10: 0-7391-3007-2 (electronic)
  1. Fathers—North America—Social conditions. 2. Immigrants—North America—
Social conditions. 3. Emigration and immigration—North America. I. Chuang,
Susan S., 1969– II. Moreno, Robert P., 1962–
  HQ756.O57 2008
  306.874'20869120973—dc22   2008021817

Printed in the United States of America

♾ ™ The paper used in this publication meets the minimum requirements of
American National Standard for Information Sciences—Permanence of Paper
for Printed Library Materials, ANSI/NISO Z39.48-1992.

DEDICATION

To my lovely and darling parents who have encouraged and supported me in every step of my life.

—Susan S. Chuang

To my family for their support and patience.

—Robert P. Moreno

To all the fathers around the world who have moved to build a better life for their children and families.

—Susan S. Chuang and Robert P. Moreno

Contents

Figures and Tables

LIST OF FIGURES

TABLES

Foreword

During the last few decades, psychosocial research on fathers both in North America and elsewhere has made considerable progress. We have learned that in a broad variety of societies, fathers tend to be of crucial importance in their children's lives. This holds true not only when they act in their traditional roles as breadwinners, disciplinarians, and authority figures, but also when they serve as sources of guidance and emotional support for their children. For instance, in their cross-cultural research on the effects of parental acceptance and rejection on children's personality development and mental health, Ronald Rohner, Robert Veneziano, Abdul Khaleque, and others have found that the effects of perceived paternal behavior at times outweighed those of the related maternal behavior. In other words, children with responsible and responsive fathers tend to be happier and better adjusted, enjoy more stable self-esteem, and view the world, and their place in it, in more positive terms.

In spite of these important and encouraging findings, we know far too little about the fathers of immigrant families. Indeed, the book that you are about to read, *On New Shores: Understanding Immigrant Fathers in North America*, is the first one to focus specifically on this important and ever-growing group. Prepared by a team of social scientists representing a veritable "Who's Who among Father Researchers," this volume provides a first map of scientific *terra incognito*. The map includes new theories and hypotheses, research findings on a broad range of immigrant fathers from non-European backgrounds, methodological advice by veteran researchers, suggestions for further scientific expeditions into uncharted territories, and useful suggestions for policymaking.

Many of the authors suggest that research on immigrant fathers is most likely to be valid if it is conceived in the context of several levels of theoretical analysis, employs a wide variety of methods, and is conducted by representatives of a broad range of disciplines. As in other areas of social scientific research, the era of simple and sovereign theories has come to an end. Instead, we need more detailed and intricate scientific maps that can fully represent the complex economic, cultural, and psychosocial realities shaping the outer and inner lives of immigrant fathers.

In addition to the usual challenges of fatherhood, immigrant fathers frequently must face an array of unique and difficult circumstances. Most of them have come to Canada or the United States because they want to improve the lives of their families; they want their children to have the education and the type of life that they could not secure for themselves. In this quest they frequently need to make great sacrifices, as I learned in my research on Chinese immigrants residing in New York City: a former manager of more than thirty workers had metamorphosed into a waiter in a restaurant who saw few chances for having a substantive career, another Chinese father had spent several lonely years "on new shores" before he could find the means to bring his young children and wife from their homeland, and a third father saw his son grow into a successful but rather Americanized academic whose inner world he could no longer share.

To be an immigrant father, then, can be a most difficult experience, and we as academics need to acknowledge this in our publications. Nevertheless, I also learned that most immigrant fathers are a hardy lot, whose struggles with uninspiring occupational options, linguistic handicaps, and difficult-to-understand cultural mazes are seen by them as worthwhile as long as their children can look forward to a brighter future. Other, more highly educated and trained immigrant fathers may have it easier: living in a world of multicultural corporations, hi-tech companies, and sophisticated academic institutions, they may be able to transmit their superior occupational skills and privileged positions to their offspring, whose sustained exposure to a multicultural world may later be of great advantage to them in their own careers.

In cities as varied as Los Angeles, New York, and Toronto, children from immigrant families make up an ever-increasing percentage of the school population. It would seem obvious that we need to know much more about these families than we do now—and that includes increasingly comprehensive knowledge about the role of fathers in the lives of their children with whom they may or may not live. We need this knowledge in order to create and sustain more effective social and educational institutions and policies that can support and nourish these families. If we fail in this task, we mortgage our future.

Adopting such a perspective, this volume takes a crucial first step toward gaining a better understanding of immigrant fathers and the roles they play in their families. I congratulate the editors and authors on their significant achievement. If I may, I would also like to thank them on behalf of all those fathers whose lives they are trying to capture with objectivity, but also with compassion.

Uwe P. Gielen

Acknowledgments

We wish to first acknowledge the College of Human Ecology (formerly known as the College of Human Services and Health Professions) and the Office of Research at Syracuse University for their generous financial support of the first On New Shores Conference in 2005. The conference inspired the collaborative effort of this edited book. We also thank Ambika Krishnakumar and Jaipaul Roopnarine for their contributions at the conference and Diana Biro for assisting us in editing the chapters. Most importantly, we are grateful to all the immigrant fathers who devoted their time so that we would have a greater understanding of fathering among immigrant families.

1

Multidisciplinary and Multi-Methodological Approaches on Fathering in Immigrant Families

Susan S. Chuang and Robert P. Moreno

Over the past few decades, researchers, social policymakers, and educators have come to understand the importance that fathers play in children's lives. Social and cultural changes such as women's participation in the work force and changes in family structure have led to heightened interest in the role of fathers in family life and children's development. We have come to understand that a father's role in the family is not limited to providing economic resources, but also in the care and nurturing of their children. Fathers' participation in their children's lives has been linked to children's cognitive development, motivation, social competency, and school achievement (Lamb, 2004; Lamb, Chuang, and Cabrera, 2003).

Unfortunately, the vast majority of the research on fathering has been conducted among Euro-American families in North America. This is problematic given the rapid demographic changes that are occurring in North America. In countries such as Canada and the United States, the immigrant populations are among the highest in the world. For example, according to Statistics Canada 2006, the immigrant population rose from 17.9 percent in 2001 to 19.8 percent in 2006, the highest increase in seventy-five years. This was four times the growth rate (3.3 percent) as compared to native Canadians (Statistics Canada, 2006). Similarly, in the last decade, the foreign-born population increased from 7.9 percent of the total population to 11.1 percent in the United States. Today in the United States, one child in five is from an immigrant family (Van Hook and Fix, 2000). Despite these demographic shifts, the vast majority of research on families is drawn from non-immigrants. As a result, our conceptual and theoretical frameworks regarding fathers specifically, and families in general, may be increasingly less relevant for a rapidly growing segment of the North American population.

This volume is loosely divided into four sections. Chapters 2–5 lay the foundation for our discussion on immigrant fathers. In chapter 2 ("The Many Faces of Fatherhood: Some Thoughts about Fatherhood and Immigration"), Michael E. Lamb provides us with an overview of fathering and the social construction of fatherhood over the last several decades. In doing so, he discusses variations in fathering across cultures and examines the influence of the social and physical ecologies. Lamb points out that variability, change, adaptability, and opportunism are key features when examining fathering. He then turns his attention to the issue of immigration and its contribution to our understanding of fathers, although conceding that immigration is likely to have a major impact on individual migrants. Lamb questions immigration's universal and direct effect on fatherhood.

In chapter 3 ("Family Acculturation and Change: Recent Comparative Research"), John W. Berry discusses the sociocultural and psychological processes involved in adaptation that are relevant to the immigrant experience. Using his ecocultural framework, Berry provides a "road map" for the types of cultural adaptation that occur among immigrants (integration, separation, assimilation, and marginalization) and challenges the unidimensional and unidirectional concept of acculturation held by many researchers and policymakers. Drawing from his thirty-country study, Berry argues that structural aspects of families are not randomly distributed, but follow predictable arrangements. By understanding the ecocultural settings of immigrants, we can better understand where families "are coming from" and thereby facilitate the acculturation of immigrants.

In chapter 4 ("Immigrant Fathers: A Demographic Portrait"), Donald J. Hernandez, Nancy A. Denton, and Suzanne E. Macartney point to the dramatic increase in the proportion of children in immigrant families over recent decades (immigrant fathers account for about one in five fathers with children ages zero to seventeen in the home). Using results based on new analyses of the U.S. Census 2000, the authors lead us through a comprehensive examination of the demographic characteristics of immigrant fathers in the United States. Their chapter addresses current gaps in our knowledge regarding immigrant fathers.

Given that employment is often cited as a primary reason for relocating to a new country and "breadwinning" is central to fathering, it is important to understand immigrant fathers' participation in the work force and its impact on their families. In chapter 5 ("Immigrant Fathers' Labor Market Activity and Its Consequences for the Family"), Roberto M. De Anda and James D. Bachmeier address these issues. Using the 2000 Integrated Public Use Microdata Series, the authors discuss employment patterns among immigrant fathers from Latin America and Asia as compared to their U.S.-born co-ethnics and non-Hispanic white fathers. Their findings indicate that the economic outcomes for immigrants vary based on national origin, and reveal a stark dichotomy between the economic mobility and incorporation of persons originating from Europe, the Middle East, and India, and a delayed pattern (or even a downward mobility) of those from Latin America.

The next three chapters focus more specifically on Asians in Canada and the United States. A prevalent theme in these chapters is questioning the uni-dimensional portrayal of Asian parenting with respect to fathers. In chapter 6 ("Transcending Confucian Teachings on Fathering: A Sign of the Times or Acculturation?"), Susan S. Chuang and Yanjie Su use a multi-methodological approach that takes a critical look at the role of Confucianism in contemporary Chinese and Chinese Canadian fathers. Drawing from their findings, the authors caution researchers against over-relying on traditional views of Chinese parenting ("strict father, kind mother") and family functioning (father as "master of the family"). They present evidence to support their view that contemporary Chinese and Chinese Canadian fathers view themselves as active and engaged as playmates, educators, and caregivers of their children.

In chapter 7 ("Asian Immigrant Fathers as Primary Caregivers of Adolescents"), Akira Kanatsu and Ruth K. Chao focus on Asian immigrants and investigate the characteristics most associated with adolescents' identification of their fathers as primary caregivers. Their findings indicate, as with previous studies, that parents' employment status is one of the strongest determinants of fathers' involvement in parenting. In addition, immigrant youth may be more impacted when fathers assume non-traditional roles as caregivers than their U.S.-born counterparts. For example, although monitoring and warmth were related to adolescents' adjustment outcomes among first-generation adolescents, these parental practices were not related to adjustment outcomes among second-generation adolescents.

In chapter 8 ("Korean Immigrant Fathering: Dealing with Two Cultures"), Eunjung Kim provides an overview of fathering among Korean families. Kim first presents the historical and cultural account of Korean families and contrasts these families with Euro-American families. She also focuses on issues of parenting practices and verbal communication and how these factors may impact the quality of relationships that fathers have with their children. Kim brings to our attention the unique challenges that immigrant Korean families may face and provides practitioners and community leaders with critical information about these families.

The next two chapters focus on Latino immigrant fathers and their construction of fatherhood. In chapter 9 ("Acculturation via Creolization: Constructing Latino American Fathering Identities"), Carl F. Auerbach, Louise Bordeaux Silverstein, Carrie Zlotnick-Woldenberg, Aris Peguero, and Sara Tacher-Rosse provide a critique of current understandings of acculturation as a model for the cultural adaptation of immigrants. Instead, they draw from linguistics and offer an alternative conception of cultural adaptation—*creolization*. Using Latino fathers as an example, they argue that immigrant fathers are not simply taking on U.S. cultural norms, or living simultaneously in two cultures. Rather they are constructing entirely new Latino American fathering identities. The authors go on to argue how their notion of creolization can also be equally useful to understand changes in fathering among white middle-class families.

In chapter 10 ("Immigration and Latino Fatherhood: A Preliminary Look at Latino Immigrant and Non-Immigrant Fathers"), Alfredo Mirandé offers us an examination of immigrant Latino men's construction of masculinity and fatherhood. With the use of provocative questions such as "What is the worst or lowest thing that a man can do?" Mirandé reveals that a Latino man's portrait of a "good man" and "good father" is far from stereotypical notions of the uninvolved macho male preoccupied with sexual conquest, but rather that of the primary provider concerned with responsibility, selflessness, and moral character.

In chapter 11 ("Breaking New Ground: Dominican, Mexican, and Chinese Fathers and Families"), Catherine S. Tamis-LeMonda, Erika Y. Niwa, Ronit Kahana-Kalman, and Hirokazu Yoshikawa present preliminary findings from their longitudinal study of infants of immigrant low-income families from Mexico, the Dominican Republic, and China living in New York City. The authors argue that father involvement in immigrant families is tied to family relationships and resources and to the extent that these change, so does fathering. However, they also suggest three pathways that apply to fathers from all backgrounds: 1) father involvement might affect children through fathers' influence on mothers, 2) father engagement might directly promote children's developing skills, and 3) economic investments by fathers might influence children's access to learning materials and resources, thus bolstering development.

The final section of the book focuses on methodological issues and future directions. In chapter 12 ("Studying Immigrant Fathering: Methodological and Conceptual Challenges"), Joseph H. Pleck presents a comprehensive review of the methods for assessing existing and emerging fathering-related constructs and the relevance of each construct. Pleck critically addresses the argument of the cultural validity of our current constructs that were based on Euro-American, middle-class fathers' experiences and its relevance to minority-ethnic, lower socioeconomic status (SES), and (implicitly) immigrant fathers. Pleck also stresses the importance of including influential factors on fathering such as paternal residence, paternal warmth-responsiveness, social fathering, paternal identity, and so on as we investigate fathering among immigrant families. Innovative methods such as narrative interviewing and "pie chart" instruments are also considered in this chapter.

In the concluding chapter ("Imagining the Future of Immigrant Fathers"), Ross D. Parke, Eric Vega, Jeffrey Cookston, Norma Perez-Brena, and Scott Coltrane delve into immigrant fathering by focusing on a multilevel framework which includes individual, dyadic, familial, societal, and cultural levels of analysis which are critical for understanding and imagining the future of immigrant fathers. Topics such as disciplines of researchers, the process and dynamics of acculturation, and issues that host countries may face with the immigrant population are examined. Parke and colleagues stress the importance of understanding the changing demography for different ethnic groups since some immigrant groups in the future will be entering a North America in which some ethnicities, such as Latinos, are no longer viewed as minorities. This underscores the need to recognize not only intra-ethnic group variability but between–ethnic group differences in immigration experience. This shift in demographic representation will have profound implications for economic opportunities, political and social policy influence, and socioemotional adjustment of fathers and their families. Parke and his colleagues provide suggestions for future research on immigrant fathers so that we can gain a greater understanding of the ever-changing and evolving context of immigrant fathers in North America.

This book is our attempt at assembling the leading scholars in the field of fathering to help us better understand the nature of the fairly uncharted realm of immigrant families. By turning our attention to immigrant fathers, we are forced to scrutinize our prevailing models of fathering and assess their applicability to families in the process of change and adaptation. Immigrant fathers bring with them their cultural values, beliefs, and behaviors from their country of origin, and engage and negotiate a new sociocultural terrain.

REFERENCES

Lamb, M. E. (2004). *The role of the father in child development* (fourth ed.). Hoboken, NJ: Wiley.

Lamb, M. E., Chuang, S. S., and Cabrera, N. (2003). Promoting child adjustment by fostering positive paternal involvement. In R. M. Lerner, F. Jacobs, and D. Wertlieb (Eds.), *Handbook of applied developmental science*, Vol. 1 (211–32). Thousand Oaks, CA: Sage.

Statistics Canada (2006). The Daily: 2006 Census: Immigration, citizenship, language, mobility and migration. Retrieved January 14, 2008, from http://www.statcan.ca/Daily/English/071204/d071204a.htm.

Van Hook, J., and Fix, M. (2000). A profile of the immigrant student population. In J. R. DeVelasco, M. Fix, and T. Clowell (Eds.), *Overlooked and underserved: Immigrant children in U.S. secondary schools* (9–33). Washington, DC: Urban Institute Press.

2

The Many Faces of Fatherhood: Some Thoughts about Fatherhood and Immigration

Michael E. Lamb

Any analysis of immigration and fatherhood draws our attention to two concepts that have been considered by numerous researchers and policymakers. My goal here is to see whether examination of the intersection of these two concepts adds to our understanding of fatherhood. I begin with a discussion of fatherhood and its social construction, with an emphasis on cross-cultural variation and secular changes over the last few decades. I then turn attention to the multiple forms that migration can take in the course of asking how the conceptions and practice of fatherhood may change in response to migration. For a variety of reasons, I conclude that there are too many unanswered questions at this stage for us to speak with any confidence about likely and general effects of immigration on fatherhood.

FATHERHOOD

Let us begin by examining the concept of fatherhood. Although, as Mead (1950) famously observed, fatherhood is a biological necessity and a social accident, social scientists have explored the ways in which fatherhood can be defined and characterized extensively for the last three decades. For most of this period, and for most social scientists, the goal has been to identify the unique features of fatherhood, those that distinguish it from the related concepts of motherhood and parenthood, and this quest thus gives shape to this section.

Historically, social scientists and commentators around the world have placed much emphasis on the concept of breadwinning, the provisioning of women and children by fathers and father figures. Women have assumed increasing responsibility for provisioning themselves and their families in the last four decades, however, and thus the tight identification of fathers with breadwinning has been attenuated. Nevertheless, when asked to identify the features of parental roles that they most closely identified with, many fathers still listed financial provision as the most central aspect of their role (Warin, Solomon, Lewis, and Langford, 1999). Policymakers, too, have maintained a focus on paternal breadwinning as a key role demand.

Other more psychological roles have also been emphasized recently in affluent postmodern societies—notably nurturance, emotional support, companionship, play, and tutelage (Lamb and Lewis, 2004)—and in those Western societies most enamoured of post-Freudian analysis, fathers have been assigned special responsibility for the development of sex roles and gender identity, especially in sons (Biller, 1994).

Research conducted in the 1970s and 1980s showed that, even in the first trimester of their children's lives, fathers and mothers appeared to interact differently with their infants. When videotaped in face-to-face interaction with their two- to twenty-five-week-old infants, for example, fathers tended to provide staccato bursts of both physical and social stimulation, whereas mothers tended to be more rhythmic and containing (Yogman, 1981). Mothers addressed their babies with soft, repetitive, imitative sounds, whereas fathers touched their infants with rhythmic pats. During visits to hospitalized premature infants, mothers were responsive to social cues, fathers to gross motor cues (Marton and Minde, 1980). Similarly, Israeli fathers of hospitalized preterm infants were consistently more likely to stimulate and play with their infants than mothers were, although they were less likely to engage in caretaking (Levy-Shiff, Sharir, and Mogilner, 1989).

When observed with infants and toddlers, American fathers tended to engage in more physically stimulating and unpredictable play than mothers did (Clarke-Stewart, 1978; Crawley and Sherrod, 1984; Dickson, Walker, and Fogel, 1997; Lamb, 1977a, 1977c; Power and Parke, 1983; Teti, Bond, and Gibbs, 1988), although rough physical play became less prominent as children grew older (Crawley and Sherrod, 1984). Since these types of play elicit more positive responses from infants, young children often preferred to play with their fathers when they had the choice (Clarke-Stewart, 1978; Lamb, 1977c). Similarly, fathers were more likely to hold their seven- to thirteen-month-old infants while playing or in response to the infants' requests to be held, whereas mothers were more likely to do so in the course of caretaking (Belsky, 1979; Lamb, 1976, 1977c). It was thus not surprising that infants responded more positively to being held by their fathers than by their mothers (Lamb, 1976, 1977c).

Fathers and mothers did not simply play differently; play was often an especially salient component of father-infant relationships. According to

Kotelchuck's (1976) informants, mothers spent an average of eighty-five minutes per day feeding their six- to twenty-one-month-olds, fifty-five minutes per day cleaning them, and 140 minutes playing with them. The comparable figures for fathers were fifteen, nine, and seventy-two minutes. According to parental diaries (Yarrow, MacTurk, Vietze, McCarthy, Klein, and McQuiston, 1984), similarly, the average father spent 6 and 7.3 hours per week playing with his six- and twelve-month-old, respectively (43 percent and 44 percent of the time spent alone with the infant), compared with 17.5 and 16.4 hours by the average mother (16 percent and 19 percent, respectively, of the time she spent alone with the infant).

It was not only affluent Euro-American fathers who appeared to specialize in play: middle-class African American (Hossain, Field, Pickens, Malphurs, and Del Valle, 1997; Hossain and Roopnarine, 1994) and Hispanic American (Hossain et al., 1997) fathers were also more likely to play with their infants than to feed or clean them despite claiming (like many Euro-American fathers) that parents should share childcare responsibilities (Hyde and Texidor, 1988). English fathers were also more likely than mothers to play with, rather than care for, infants and toddlers (McConachie, 1989), and similar differences were evident in India (Roopnarine, Talukder, Jain, Joshi, and Srivastav, 1992), as well as in France, Switzerland, and Italy (Best, House, Barnard, and Spicker, 1994; Frascarolo-Moutinot, 1994; Labrell, 1996). By contrast, Taiwanese fathers reported that they rarely played with their children (Sun and Roopnarine, 1996), and fathers on Israeli kibbutzim did not play with their eight- and sixteen-month-olds more than mothers did, although the mothers were much more actively involved in caretaking and other forms of interaction than the fathers were (Sagi, Lamb, Shoham, Dvir, and Lewkowicz, 1985). Likewise, German (Best et al., 1994), Swedish (Lamb, Frodi, Hwang, and Frodi, 1983; Frodi, Lamb, Hwang, and Frodi, 1983; Lamb, Frodi, Hwang, and Frodi, 1982), and Aka (hunter-gatherer) (Hewlett, 1987, 1991) fathers were not notably more playful than mothers.

Although mothers and fathers both adjusted their speech characteristics when speaking to young children, maternal and paternal communicative styles differed. For example, Gleason (1975) and Rondal (1980) suggested that, because fathers used more imperatives and attention-getting utterances, and utter more complex sentences than mothers did, they contributed in unique, though still poorly understood, ways to linguistic development. Similarly, Rondal's (1980) research suggested that the different communicative styles adopted by mothers and fathers forced children to learn a greater variety of linguistic conventions. For example, the Belgian two-year-olds he studied addressed their mothers using the informal "tu," whereas they addressed their fathers using the more formal "vous."

Research conducted during this same period also suggested that patterns of parental behavior differed when both parents worked full-time during the day (Pedersen, Cain, Zaslow, and Anderson, 1982). As expected, fathers with nonworking wives played with their infants more than mothers did, but this pattern was reversed in families with working mothers. Likewise, Field, Vega-Lahr, Goldstein, and Scafidi (1987) reported that employed mothers were much more interactive in face-to-face contact with their infants than employed fathers were. Maternal employment did not necessarily change the nature of father-child relationships, however. The relationship between employment and the quality of child-father interaction was moderated by the fathers' attitudes and ages in the large NICHD Early Child Care Study (2000), with younger men and those committed to equal parenting more sensitive in their play styles. Such belief systems are very important. In New Delhi, for example, a strong "traditional" culture is maintained and fathers in dual earner families were indistinguishable from men in single earner families (Suppal and Roopnarine, 1999).

What happened when fathers were highly involved in infant care? Field (1978) reported that primary caretaking fathers and mothers behaved more similarly than primary and secondary caretaking fathers, although fathers engaged in more playful and non-containing interactions than mothers did regardless of their involvement in childcare. Pruett (1985; Pruett and Litzenberger, 1992) only studied fathers who were highly involved in infant care but repeatedly remarked on the distinctive playfulness of these fathers. Frascarolo-Moutinot (1994) reported no differences in playfulness between "new fathers" (i.e., more involved fathers) and "traditional" French fathers, although the wives of the new fathers were less intrusive and controlling than the wives of traditional fathers. However, we found that Swedish mothers were more likely than fathers to vocalize, display affection to, touch, tend to, and hold their infants whether or not their partners took a month or more of paternity leave (Lamb, Frodi, Frodi, and Hwang, 1982; Lamb, Frodi, Hwang, Frodi, and Steinberg, 1982a, 1982b).

Beyond the infancy period, mothers and fathers appear to adopt quite similar interaction styles, although they may do so for very different reasons. Social learning theorists have long assumed that the different interactional styles of mothers and fathers must somehow help boys and girls acquire gender-appropriate behavioral repertoires (e.g., Block, 1976). Consistent differences between parents have been hard to identify, however (Lytton and Romney, 1991; Russell and Saebel, 1997; Siegal, 1987). For example, Lytton and Romney's meta-analysis of 172 studies involving over twenty-seven thousand children revealed only one consistent difference between mothers and fathers—a small but significant tendency for fathers to encourage the use of sex-typed toys more than mothers did. Otherwise, there were insufficient data to support the claim that mothers and fathers differentially affect their children's sex role development. In one recent study, however, Lindsey and Mize (2001) examined parent-child and child-peer dyads in "pretence" and "physical play" sessions. Not only did mothers engage in more pretend play with their daughters while father-son dyads specialized in physical play, but patterns of parent-child pretence and physical play also predicted the amounts of the same type of play with peers. Lytton and Romney further reported that, beyond the preschool years, the similarities between the behavior of mothers and fathers increased. For example, Labrell, Deleau, and Juhel's (2000) more recent research suggests that, by forty-two months, French fathers were no longer more challenging than mothers. Similarly, each parent's language came to resemble the other's, especially when they interacted in mother-father-child triads (Pellegrini, Brody, and Stoneman, 1987), and the communicative balance between parent and child appeared comparable for mothers and fathers (Welkowitz, Bond, Feldman, and Tota, 1990).

Interestingly, children in a variety of cultures clearly differentiated between the roles of mothers and fathers. For example, Raag and Rackliff (1998) introduced preschoolers to a laboratory play room in which a range of sex-neutral and sex-stereotyped toys were laid out and then asked the children which toys they and their parents thought it was appropriate to play with. Many boys, particularly those who had chosen sex-stereotypical toys, stated that their fathers would consider cross-sex toy play to be "bad." Thus fathers were believed by sons but not daughters to have more restrictive rules of conduct than mothers did. By the time of their entry into school, furthermore, children appeared to have highly stereotyped views of parental roles. Domestic work was widely described as the mother's prerogative while breadwinning was seen as the province of fathers throughout the school years (Hartley, 1960; Langford, Lewis, Solomon, and Warin, 2001; Williams, Bennett, and Best, 1975), and interviews with over eight hundred five- to fifteen-year-olds in four societies revealed that these beliefs persisted into middle childhood and adolescence (Goldman and Goldman, 1983).

Researchers have also described comparable differences in the ways in which mothers and fathers relate to their adolescent sons and daughters (Collins and Russell, 1991; Steinberg, 1987, 1990). As in infancy, middle-class mothers appeared to engage in more frequent interaction with children in middle childhood and adolescence (especially interactions involving caretaking and routine family tasks) than fathers did, whereas most father-child interactions during this developmental period involved play, recreation, and goal-oriented actions and tasks (see also Lamb, 1997; Montemayor and Brownlee, 1987; Russell and Russell, 1987). However, mothers and fathers were equivalently involved in activities related to their children's and adolescents' scholastic and extracurricular performance and achievement (Youniss and Smollar, 1985), and both parents frequently engaged in nurturant caretaking in middle childhood (Russell and Russell, 1987).

Overall, these findings suggested that the distinctive maternal and paternal styles were quite robust and were still evident when fathers are highly involved in childcare. Fathers tended to adopt a more playful interaction style than mothers did when interacting with their infants, especially in cultures or subcultures with clear divisions of labor. These patterns were not ubiquitous, however, as noted above, and there were cultures (e.g., Northern Thailand) with a clear division of labor in which fathers and mothers did not differ with respect to playfulness or sensitivity (Tulananda and Roopnarine, 2001). In addition, the differences between maternal and paternal interaction styles tended to be quite small, although they may be important: Zaouche-Gaudron, Ricaud, and Beaumatin (1998) argued that French fathers who differentiated between maternal and paternal roles tended to have a more positive impact on their children's development than those whose roles were less distinctive. Whether or not differentiated maternal and paternal roles reflected enduring and longstanding features of these cultures or were the product of shared literatures and media is unclear, and researchers have not undertaken enough comparative studies to identify cross-cultural differences, let alone understand their origins and possible significance.

In any event, dramatic changes have taken place over the last three to four decades in most developed countries. Everywhere, contemporary fathers are participating in basic child care much more extensively than their own fathers did, even though it has proven enormously difficult to define and measure paternal involvement (Pleck, 1997), not least because one has to take into account mothers' and fathers' commitments to other activities, notably employment and the changing nature of parenting as children grow older.

Despite debate about the scope of fatherhood (Hawkins and Dollahite, 1997; Palkovitz, 2002), research has been dominated for the last two decades by a conceptual framework (Lamb, Pleck, Charnov, and Levine, 1985, 1987) in which three components of father involvement are distinguished: 1) engagement: the dynamic between the father and the child, usually through caregiving or interaction (e.g., through play or instruction); 2) accessibility or availability to the child; and 3) responsibility for the care of the child.

The literature suggests that, in all known societies, men have lower levels of engagement than women, and tend to engage in relatively little caregiving. In the largest survey of two-parent households in the United States (the Panel Study of Income Dynamics, or PSID), for example, fathers were available daily for three and a half hours to their children under the age of twelve and interacted with them for 1.8 hours, of which 39 percent was spent in play or "companionship" while only 28 percent (i.e., just over half an hour) involved caregiving (Yeung, Sandberg, Davis-Kean, and Hofferth, 2001). Fathers spent about 73 percent as much time as mothers did engaged with their children, according to this survey and another conducted at about the same time in Canada, but some other surveys reviewed by Pleck and Masciadrelli (2004) suggested that men spent as little as 44 percent as much time in such activities as mothers did (a Dutch survey). Unfortunately, detailed time diary studies have not been conducted in most European countries, so comparable data are not available. However, Smith (2002) has compiled statistics from the European Community Household Panel data set on the proportions of men who reported spending fourteen or more hours per week in unpaid childcare activities: the proportions ranged from nearly 41 percent in Denmark to 13 percent in Portugal, underscoring the enormous variability among these countries. In general, northern European countries appear to have more involved fathers than do countries in the south, but there are several deviations from this general pattern (see O'Brien, 2004, for a more extensive discussion of paternal involvement in European countries).

There is consistent evidence that patterns of paternal involvement have been changing in Western Europe and North America, in any event. Time budget studies in the 1980s and the 1990s (most conducted in the United States) suggested that men's accessibility to children increased by 66 percent, while their engagement increased by 43 percent (Pleck, 1997). These increases continued into the turn of the century. As Pleck and Masciadrelli (2004) concluded:

> Overall, the data suggest that average levels of paternal engagement and accessibility have increased in the United States over the last several decades, both in absolute and relative terms. Sandberg and Hofferth's (2001) analysis is particularly strong because it controls for maternal employment status, and shows that paternal involvement has increased in two-earner families over this period. There are also good data showing increases in paternal engagement in Canada and the Netherlands between the 1980s and the 1990s and in Finland and Norway in earlier decades. (240)

Parental responsibility is harder to assess, but secular increases appear to be taking place in this regard, too. Again, in the words of Pleck and Masciadrelli (2004, 242): "Overall, the relative rate of primary paternal care in dual-earner families suggests that for a significant portion of the workweek, a substantial minority of fathers have a high level of responsibility. In addition, the rate of fathers being the primary child care arrangement has gradually increased since 1977."

In the member countries of the European Union, there is evidence of increased male participation in childcare as well, albeit over a shorter period of time (1994–1996). Statistics compiled by Smith (2002) showed increases in the numbers of men who spent fourteen or more hours per week in unpaid childcare activities in almost all of the thirteen countries sampled, although these parallel changes have not obliterated the international differences in paternal participation that preceded them.

Recent increases in male domestic involvement largely reflect changes in their own and, particularly, their partners' engagement in paid employment (Presser, 1989). Enormous individual variation is ubiquitous, however, and the sources of these variations, beyond cultural norms, are legion. They range from demographic factors such as family structure, parental work patterns and schedules, ages, gender, and number of children, and family socioeconomic status to factors in the individuals' backgrounds and motivational structures that make them more or less eager to participate actively in the day-to-day care of their children (Pleck and Masciadrelli, 2004).

Whatever factors influence fathers' tendencies to be more or less involved in interactions with their children, there appears to be substantial stability, at least during the period from birth through the first thirty months (Hwang and Lamb, 1997; Lamb, Hwang, Broberg, Bookstein, Hult, and Frodi, 1988; Nugent, 1987; Pruett and Litzenberger, 1992), although stability in our sample of Swedish fathers was quite low over a fifteen-year period (Lamb, Chuang, and Hwang, 2004).

In any event, it is clear that sharply defined differences between maternal and paternal roles are being softened by these secular changes as men become increasingly involved in the types of activities—feeding, cleaning, nurturing, soothing—and behaviors that were previously seen as the exclusive province of women and mothers. In an earlier era, as noted above, men were predominantly viewed in many cultures as playmates, sources of stimulation and excitement. These role definitions almost certainly reflected the absence of clearly defined paternal responsibilities (apart from breadwinning) and the limited amount of time that fathers spent with their children rather than the parameters of a clearly defined paternal role. Differences between maternal and paternal roles in that era were clearly secondary to culturally defined male and female roles. Furthermore, the better defined those roles, the clearer the distinction between maternal and paternal roles and, in almost every case, the more poorly defined—almost by negation—the relevant paternal roles. In light of the changes taking place, however, there is less and less justification for viewing the identification of fatherhood with play and companionship as something with unique psychological significance (say, to foster gender identification and sex role adoption), as I once thought (Lamb, 1976, 1977b). But if paternal playfulness is epiphenomenal, it may still have its uses: it allows children and fathers to discover the pleasures of meaningful relationships and it increases the affective salience of relatively small amounts of time in mutual interaction (e.g., Lamb, Frodi, Hwang, and Frodi, 1982), both factors that foster the formation of the bonds that instantiate parents, both mothers and fathers, as the most significant psychological forces in their children's lives (Lamb and Lewis, 2004).

It is also worth noting that the assumptions and presumptions that kept fathers from greater involvement in their children's care until recently were and still are rooted in differentiated male and female roles more generally. The sharper the perceived line between men and women, the sharper the lines between maternal and paternal roles, the smaller the role fathers are expected to play in the direct care and nurture of their children, and the greater the expectation that they will assume primary responsibility for provisioning both women and children. In many ways, paternal roles are mere decorative features, like tail fins on automobiles in the 1950s, on the broader roles of men in given cultures.

Although their numbers are tiny and they do not feature in contemporary discussions of migration in the industrialized world, it is instructive to examine the roles played by men in contemporary hunter-gatherer societies, not least because their lifestyles are believed to resemble those in which humans first evolved as a species (Hewlett, 1987, 1991, 1992; Hewlett and Lamb, 2005; Konner, 1990). Among the Aka hunter-gatherers of the Central African Republic and Congo, women hold their infants more than mothers in other societies, but these children are still held and cared for by their fathers more than infants in other societies because they are nearly constantly held or in physical contact with others, even when asleep (Hewlett, 1991; Hewlett, Lamb, Leyendecker, and Schölmerich, 2000; Hewlett, Lamb, Shannon, Leyendecker, and Schölmerich, 1998). Aka do not question these practices or offer elaborate explanation or justifications; that is just the way things are. Babies clearly need to be held, and they are held by their mothers, fathers, grandparents, siblings, and others who live with their families. This simple aphorism encapsulates the broader and perhaps more universal lesson—namely, that humans are both incredibly adaptable and incredibly opportunistic. Other hunter-gatherers, such as the !Kung, do not hold their babies as much, for example, perhaps because the savannah ecology they inhabit does not make physical contact as necessary as does the dense forest ecology in which the Aka live (Konner, 2005). In both groups, as among the forest-dwelling Bofi, however, the amount that fathers do for their children varies depending on the availability of other care providers. More generally, Hrdy (2005a, 2005b; see also Lamb, 1998; Lamb and Ahnert, 2006) has recently explored the widespread reliance on "allo-mothering" among diverse animal species, including humans, and an examination of hunter-gatherer child care underscores not only the extent to which allo-mothering is nearly universal but also how the identity of "allo-mothers" varies as individuals opportunistically exploit the human resources available to them.

Forest-dwelling hunter-gatherers like the Aka and the Bofi are characterized by extremely egalitarian norms and minimal gender differentiation,
whereas hunter-gatherers like the Hadza of East Africa are more gender
stratified and, not coincidentally, not characterized by equivalently high
levels of paternal participation in childcare (Marlowe, 2005). Paternal participation in infant care is also lower among agricultural groups in Africa
than among the forest hunter-gatherers like the Aka and Bofi, although fathers in these cultures begin providing care, guidance, and tutelage to their
offspring much earlier in their development than Western fathers became
involved in childcare in the middle part of the twentieth century.

The physical and social ecologies occupied by these African groups and
by parents in industrialized societies are dramatically different, but this
brief discussion underscores several key concepts that are highly relevant
to our analysis of modern fatherhood. These are broad brushstrokes, but
the colors are clear: variability, change, adaptability, and opportunism are
key features when we examine parenting (perhaps especially fathering) and
childcare in cross-cultural and/or historical perspective. Indeed, the variability within cultures and subcultures is much more impressive than the
cross-cultural differences, especially when these are specified in terms of
mean differences, and I suspect these findings will increasingly be true as
the effects of globalization, widespread travel, and immigration proceed.

MIGRATION

The concept of migration is an increasingly common phenomenon in this
age of globalization (e.g., Adams and Kirova, 2006; Antonucci, 2006; Booth,
Crouter, and Landale, 1997). Migration in search of a better life or, at worst,
flight from persecution, famine, or hopelessness has characterized human
behavior since time immemorial, but the pace has quickened as increased
knowledge of the opportunities elsewhere has drawn the adventurous and
the ambitious into competition with the desperate and the destitute. Unfortunately, as indicated earlier, we know little about either the conception
of fatherhood or the behavior of immigrant fathers (Shimoni, Este, and
Clark, 2003; Roer-Strier, Strier, Este, Shimoni, and Clark, 2005), or about
these constructs in the cultures from which most immigrants come. Further,
the few extant studies in those cultures-of-origin have in any event focused
on the least representative, most Westernized, and most privileged strata of
these cultures. There is every reason to believe that the behavior of men (or
women, for that matter) in these privileged groups tends to resemble that
of individuals in the more privileged strata of other societies more than
would the behavior of their less fortunate compatriots, although similarities are likely to deepen as globalization proceeds. Many of the migrants

to industrialized countries are indeed drawn from these privileged strata: less encumbered, more adventurous, better educated, and more desirable to their hosts than most of their former compatriots. While we focus on them in our analyses, it is thus important to remember the ways in which they differ from their compatriots, for the very characteristics that make them more likely to migrate make them not only less representative of their native cultures but also less wedded to many of their native mores and practices and more open to incorporation of practices and beliefs characteristic of the cultures into which they move. In addition, of course, their privileged status gives such immigrants license to behave as they choose. By contrast, those who are forced to migrate to avoid persecution or poverty may come from marginalized groups in their native countries but, because their migration is involuntary, they may be less eager to adopt the mores of their host countries and more eager to maintain those with which they are most familiar.

The immigrant experience also differs depending on the attitudes and responses of the host community (Adams and Kirova, 2006; Roer-Strier et al., 2005). Receiving cultures differ with respect to the pervasiveness of expectations that immigrants will be assimilated into the mainstream rather than cherished or tolerated as a subgroup. Immigrants, in turn, are likely to accommodate novel practices and expectations with varying degrees of enthusiasm depending on the extent to which they are being respected, tolerated, or reformed.

Links to the country of origin can also be important (Booth et al., 1997). Mexican migrants to the United States, like many South Asian immigrants to the United Kingdom, remain closely tied to their home regions by emotional and financial responsibilities and thus tend to remain deeply rooted in their native cultures, often viewing themselves not as immigrants, but as temporary economic sojourners who intend to return home when (and if) that becomes possible. In such cases, assimilation is likely to be minimal.

Even in these cases, however, different dynamics become prominent when members of a new generation grow up in the host country, often schooled (formally and informally) in the language and norms of a culture that may remain quite alien to their parents (Booth et al., 1997). For these individuals, the country of origin is not home, and it is common to find divided loyalties and values, with individuals picking and choosing from the models and practices they have observed in their own families as well as in the broader culture in which they have grown up. In addition, of course, the parents of these children are likely to be better adapted and assimilated than compatriots who have not raised children in the host country because their children are able to act as interpreters of the culture and language. For this reason, countries like Israel have long sought to assimilate and incorporate successive waves of immigrants by teaching the children to speak Hebrew and socializing them into the national norms and customs (Roer-Strier and Strier, 2006). They, in turn, socialize the older generation.

Overall, it is clear that immigration is likely to have a major impact on individual migrants but is unlikely to have a universal and direct effect on fatherhood. Rather, immigrants need to evaluate the costs and benefits of maintaining features of their native cultures (like patterns of child rearing) relative to the costs and benefits of assimilating and adapting those of the new host country. Those assessments are not straightforward and the individual resolutions vary depending on the migrants, their native cultures, their receiving or host cultures, and their motivations for migration. As noted earlier, furthermore, most of the cultures that have been studied are characterized, not by clear and universal paternal roles, but by a diverse array of practices, themselves in flux, even when there are cultural scripts which appear to prescribe certain modes of behavior. To complicate matters further, it is important to remember that the behavior of mothers and fathers tends to be driven by necessity more than by ideology or even custom whether or not migration has taken place. Just as it is simplistic to speak of specific roles that characterize fathers in any particular cultural niche, therefore, so is it unrealistic to expect immigration to have universal effects on fathers in general, or even on fathers from particular regions or cultures. Instead, our understanding of roles as important as parental roles demands a much more nuanced appreciation for the conditional nature of human roles and relationships. Unfortunately, we are only now embarking on the types of scholarship and research that might prove fruitful while stimulating further analysis of these important topics.

REFERENCES

Adams, L. D., and Kirova, A. (Eds.). (2006). *Global migration and education.* Mahwah, NJ: Erlbaum.

Antonucci, T. C. (Ed.). (2006). *Immigration, adaptability, and well-being across the life-span.* Mahwah, NJ: Erlbaum.

Belsky, J. (1979). Mother-father-infant interaction: A naturalistic observational study. *Developmental Psychology, 15,* 601–7.

Best, D. L., House, A. S., Barnard, A. L., and Spicker, B. S. (1994). Parent-child interactions in France, Germany, and Italy—The effects of gender and culture. *Journal of Cross-Cultural Psychology, 25,* 181–93.

Biller, H. B. (1994). *The father factor.* New York: Pocket Books.

Block, J. (1976). Issues, problems and pitfalls in assessing sex differences: A critical review of "The psychology of sex differences." *Merrill Palmer Quarterly, 22,* 283–340.

Booth, A., Crouter, A. C., and Landale, N. S. (Eds.). (1997). *Immigration and the family.* Mahwah, NJ: Erlbaum.

Clarke-Stewart, K. A. (1978). And daddy makes three: The father's impact on mother and young child. *Child Development, 49,* 466–78.

Collins, W. A., and Russell, G. (1991). Mother-child and father-child relationships in middle childhood and adolescence: A developmental analysis. *Developmental Review, 11,* 99–136.

Crawley, S. B., and Sherrod, R. B. (1984). Parent-infant play during the first year of life. *Infant Behavior and Development, 7,* 65–75.

Dickson, K. L., Walker, H., and Fogel, A. (1997). The relationship between smile type and play type during parent-infant play. *Developmental Psychology, 33,* 925–33.

Field, T. (1978). Interaction behaviors of primary versus secondary caretaker fathers. *Developmental Psychology, 14,* 183–84.

Field, T., Vega-Lahr, N., Goldstein, S., and Scafidi, F. (1987). Interaction behavior of infants and their dual-career parents. *Infant Behavior and Development, 10,* 371–77.

Frascarolo-Moutinot, F. (1994). *Engagement paternal quotidien et relations parents-enfant* [Daily paternal involvement and parent-child relationships]. Unpublished doctoral dissertation, Universite de Geneve, Geneve, Switzerland.

Frodi, A. M., Lamb, M. E., Hwang, C. P., and Frodi, M. (1983). Father-mother-infant interaction in traditional and nontraditional Swedish families: A longitudinal study. *Alternative Lifestyles, 5,* 142–63.

Gleason, J. B. (1975). Fathers and other strangers: Men's speech to young children. In D. P. Dato (Ed.), *Language and linguistics* (289–97). Washington, DC: Georgetown University Press.

Goldman, J. D. G., and Goldman, R. J. (1983). Children's perceptions of parents and their roles: A cross-national study in Australia, England, North America and Sweden. *Sex Roles, 9,* 791–812.

Hartley, R. (1960). Children's concepts of male and female roles. *Merrill Palmer Quarterly, 6,* 83–91.

Hawkins, A. J., and Dollahite, D. C. (Eds.). (1997). *Generative fathering: Beyond deficit perspectives.* London: Sage.

Hewlett, B. S. (1987). Intimate fathers: Patterns of paternal holding among Aka pygmies. In M. E. Lamb (Ed.), *The father's role: Cross-cultural perspectives* (295–330). Hillsdale, NJ: Erlbaum.

———. (1991). *Intimate fathers: The nature and context of Aka pygmy paternal infant care.* Ann Arbor: University of Michigan Press.

——— (Ed.). (1992). *Father-child relations: Cultural and biosocial contexts.* New York: Aldine De Gruyter.

Hewlett, B. S., and Lamb, M. E. (Eds.). (2005). *Hunter-gatherer childhoods.* New Brunswick, NJ: Transaction/Aldine.

Hewlett, B. S., Lamb, M. E., Leyendecker, B., and Schölmerich, A. (2000). Internal working models, trust, and sharing among foragers. *Current Anthropology, 41,* 287–97.

Hewlett, B. S., Lamb, M. E., Shannon, D., Leyendecker, B., and Schölmerich, A. (1998). Culture and early infancy among Central African foragers and farmers. *Developmental Psychology, 34,* 653–61.

Hossain, Z., Field, T., Pickens, J., Malphurs, J., and Del Valle C. (1997). Fathers' caregiving in low-income African-American and Hispanic American families. *Early Development and Parenting, 6*, 73–82.

Hossain, Z., and Roopnarine, J. L. (1994). African-American fathers' involvement with infants: Relationship to their functional style, support, education, and income. *Infant Behavior and Development, 17*, 175–84.

Hrdy, S. B. (2005a). Comes the child before man: How cooperative breeding and prolonged post weaning dependence shaped human potential. In B. S. Hewlett and M. E. Lamb (Eds.), *Hunter-gatherer childhoods* (65–91). New Brunswick, NJ: Transaction/Aldine.

———. (2005b). Evolutionary context of human development: The cooperative breeding model. In S. C. Carter, L. Ahnert, K. Grossmann, S. B. Hrdy, M. E. Lamb, S. W. Porges, and N. Sachser (Eds.), *Attachment and bonding: A new synthesis* (Dahlem Workshop Report 92, 9–32). Cambridge, MA: MIT Press.

Hwang, C. P., and Lamb, M. E. (1997). Father involvement in Sweden: A longitudinal study of its stability and correlates. *International Journal of Behavioral Development, 21*, 621–32.

Hyde, B. L., and Texidor, M. S. (1988). A description of the fathering experience among black fathers. *Journal of Black Nurses Association, 2*, 67–78.

Konner, M. (1990). *The tangled wing: Biological constraints on the human spirit*. New York: Henry Holt.

———. (2005). Hunter-gatherer infancy and childhood: The !Kung and others. In B. S. Hewlett and M. E. Lamb (Eds.), *Hunter-gatherer childhoods* (19–64). New Brunswick, NJ: Transaction/Aldine.

Kotelchuck, M. (1976). The infant's relationship to the father: Experimental evidence. In M. E. Lamb (Ed.), *The role of the father in child development* (329–44). New York: Wiley.

Labrell, F. (1996). Paternal play with toddlers: Recreation and creation. *European Journal of Psychology of Education, 11*, 43–54.

Labrell, F., Deleau, M., and Juhel, J. (2000). Fathers' and mothers' distancing strategies towards toddlers. *International Journal of Behavioral Development, 24*, 356–61.

Lamb, M. E. (1976). Interactions between eight-month-old children and their fathers and mothers. In M. E. Lamb (Ed.), *The role of the father in child development* (307–27). New York: Wiley.

———. (1977a). The development of mother-infant and father-infant attachments in the second year of life. *Developmental Psychology, 13*, 637–48.

———. (1977b). The development of parental preferences in the first two years of life. *Sex Roles, 3*, 495–97.

———. (1977c). Father-infant and mother-infant interaction in the first year of life. *Child Development, 48*, 167–81.

———. (1997). Fathers and child development: An introductory overview and guide. In M. E. Lamb (Ed.), *The role of the father in child development* (third ed., 1–18, 309–13). New York: Wiley.

———. (1998). Nonparental child care: Context, quality, correlates, and consequences. In W. Damon, I. E. Sigel, and K. A. Renninger (Eds.), *Handbook of child psychology* (Vol. 4), *Child psychology in practice* (fifth edition, 73–133). New York: Wiley.

Lamb, M. E., and Ahnert, L. (2006). Nonparental child care: Context, concepts, correlates, and consequences. In W. Damon, R. M. Lerner, K. A. Renninger, and I. E. Sigel (Eds.), *Handbook of child psychology* (Vol. 4), *Child psychology in practice* (sixth ed., 950–1016). Hoboken, NJ: Wiley.

Lamb, M. E., Chuang, S. S., and Hwang, C. P. (2004). Internal reliability, temporal stability, and correlates of individual differences in paternal involvement: A 14-year longitudinal study in Sweden. In R. D. Day and M. E. Lamb (Eds.), *Conceptualizing and measuring father involvement* (129–48). Mahwah, NJ: Erlbaum.

Lamb, M. E., Frodi, A. M., Frodi, M., and Hwang, C. P. (1982). Characteristics of maternal and paternal behavior in traditional and nontraditional Swedish families. *International Journal of Behavioral Development, 5,* 131–41.

Lamb, M. E., Frodi, A. M., Hwang, C. P., and Frodi, M. (1982). Varying degrees of paternal involvement in infant care: Attitudinal and behavioral correlates. In M. E. Lamb (Ed.), *Nontraditional families: Parenting and child development* (117–37). Hillsdale, NJ: Erlbaum.

Lamb, M. E., Frodi, A. M., Hwang, C. P., Frodi, M., and Steinberg, J. (1982a). Effects of gender and caretaking role on parent-infant interaction. In R. N. Emde and R. J. Harmon (Eds.), *Development of attachment and affiliative systems* (109–18). New York: Plenum.

———. (1982b). Mother- and father-infant interaction involving play and holding in traditional and nontraditional Swedish families. *Developmental Psychology, 18,* 215–21.

Lamb, M. E., Frodi, M., Hwang, C. P., and Frodi, A. M. (1983). Effects of paternal involvement on infant preferences for mothers and fathers. *Child Development, 54,* 450–58.

Lamb, M. E., Hwang, C. P., Broberg, A., Bookstein, F. L., Hult, G., and Frodi, M. (1988). The determinants of paternal involvement in primiparous Swedish families. *International Journal of Behavioral Development, 11,* 433–49.

Lamb, M. E., and Lewis, C. (2004). The development and significance of father-child relationships in two-parent families. In M. E. Lamb, *The role of the father in child development* (fourth ed.). Hoboken, NJ: Wiley.

Lamb, M. E., Pleck, J. H., Charnov, E. L., and Levine, J. A. (1985). Paternal behavior in humans. *American Zoologist, 25,* 883–94.

———. (1987). A biosocial perspective on paternal behavior and involvement. In J. B. Lancaster, J. Altmann, A. S. Rossi, and L. R. Sherrod (Eds.), *Parenting across the lifespan: Biosocial dimensions* (111–42). Hawthorne, NY: Aldine.

Langford, W., Lewis, C., Solomon, Y., and Warin, J. (2001). *Family understandings: Closeness and authority in families with a teenage child.* London: Family Policy Studies Centre.

Levy-Shiff, R., Sharir, H., and Mogilner, M. B. (1989). Mother- and father-preterm infant relationship in the hospital preterm nursery. *Child Development, 60,* 93–102.

Lindsey, E. W., and Mize, J. (2001). Contextual differences in parent-child play: Implications for children's gender role development. *Sex Roles, 44,* 155–76.

Lytton, H., and Romney, D. M. (1991). Parents' differential socialization of boys and girls: A meta-analysis. *Psychological Bulletin, 109,* 267–96.

Marlowe, F. W. (2005). Who tends Hadza children? In B. S. Hewlett and M. E. Lamb (Eds.), *Hunter-gatherer childhoods* (177–90). New Brunswick, NJ: Transaction/ Aldine.

Marton, P. L., and Minde, K. (1980, April). *Paternal and maternal behavior with premature infants.* Paper presented at the meeting of the American Orthopsychiatric Association, Toronto.

McConachie, H. (1989). Mothers' and fathers' interaction with their young mentally handicapped children. *International Journal of Behavioral Development, 12,* 239–55.

Mead, M. (1950). *Male and female.* Harmondsworth, UK: Penguin.

Montemayor, R., and Brownlee, J. (1987). Fathers, mothers, and adolescents: Gender-based differences in parental roles during adolescence. *Journal of Youth and Adolescence, 16,* 281–91.

NICHD Early Child Care Research Network. (2000). Factors associated with fathers' caregiving activities and sensitivity with young children. *Journal of Family Psychology, 14,* 200–219.

Nugent, J. K. (1987). The father's role in early Irish socialization: Historical and empirical perspectives. In M. E. Lamb (Ed.), *The father's role: Cross-cultural perspectives* (169–93). Hillsdale, NJ: Erlbaum.

O'Brien, M. (2004). Social science and public policy perspectives on fatherhood in the European Union. In M. E. Lamb (Ed.), *The role of the father in child development* (fourth ed., 121–45). Hoboken, NJ: Wiley.

Palkovitz, R. (2002). *Involved fathering and men's adult development.* Mahwah, NJ: Erlbaum.

Pedersen, F. A., Cain, R., Zaslow, M., and Anderson, B. (1982). Variation in infant experience associated with alternative family roles. In L. Laosa and I. Sigel (Eds.), *Families as learning environments for children* (203–21). New York: Plenum.

Pellegrini, A. D., Brody, G. H., and Stoneman, Z. (1987). Children's conversational competence with their parents. *Discourse Processes, 10,* 93–106.

Pleck, J. H. (1997). Paternal involvement: Levels, sources, and consequences. In M. E. Lamb (Ed.), *The role of the father in child development* (third ed., 66–103, 325–32). New York: Wiley.

Pleck, J. H., and Masciadrelli, B. P. (2004). Paternal involvement by U.S. residential fathers: Levels, sources and consequences. In M. E. Lamb (Ed.), *The role of the father in child development* (fourth ed., 222–70). New York: Wiley.

Power, T. G., and Parke, R. D. (1983). Patterns of mother and father play with their 8-month-old infant: A multiple analyses approach. *Infant Behavior and Development, 6,* 453–59.

Presser, H. B. (1989). Can we make time for children? The economy, work schedules, and child care. *Demography, 26,* 523–43.

Pruett, K. (1985). Oedipal configurations in young father-raised children. *Psychoanalytic study of the child, 40,* 435–60.

Pruett, K., and Litzenberger, B. (1992). Latency development in children of primary nurturing fathers: Eight-year follow up. *Psychoanalytic Study of the Child, 4,* 85–101.

Raag, T., and Rackliff, C. L. (1998). Preschoolers' awareness of social expectations of gender: Relationships to toy choices. *Sex Roles, 38,* 685–700.

Roer-Strier, D., and Strier, R. (2006). Role of home and school in the socialization of children in Israel: Fathers' views. In L. D. Adams and A. Kirova (Eds.), *Global migration and education* (103–19). Mahwah, NJ: Erlbaum.

Roer-Strier, D., Strier, R., Este, D., Shimoni, R., and Clark, D. (2005). Fatherhood and immigration: Challenging the deficit theory. *Child and Family Social Work, 10,* 315–29.

Rondal, J. A. (1980). Fathers' and mothers' speech in early language development. *Journal of Child Language, 7,* 353–69.

Roopnarine, J. L., Talukder, E., Jain, D., Joshi, P., and Srivastav, P. (1992). Personal well-being, kinship ties, and mother-infant and father-infant interactions in single-wage and dual-wage families in New Delhi, India. *Journal of Marriage and the Family, 54,* 293–301.

Russell, A., and Saebel, J. (1997). Mother-son, mother-daughter, father-son, and father-daughter: Are they distinct relationships? *Developmental Review, 17,* 111–47.

Russell, G., and Russell, A. (1987). Mother-child and father-child relationships in middle childhood. *Child Development, 58,* 1573–85.

Sagi, A., Lamb, M. E., Shoham, R., Dvir, R., and Lewkowicz, K. S. (1985). Parent-infant interaction in families on Israeli kibbutzim. *International Journal of Behavioral Development, 8,* 273–84.

Sandberg, J. F., and Hofferth, S. L. (2001). Changes in children's time with parents: United States, 1981–1997. *Demography, 38,* 423–36.

Shimoni, R., Este, D., and Clark, D. E. (2003). Paternal engagement in immigrant and refugee families. *Journal of Comparative Family Studies, 34,* 555–68.

Siegal, A. U. (1987). Are sons and daughters more differently treated by fathers than by mothers? *Developmental Review, 7,* 183–209.

Smith, A. (2002). *The role of the state in encouraging male parenting: Lessons from Europe.* Paper presented to a conference on Women in Politics, Birkbeck College, London.

Steinberg, L. (1987). Impact of puberty on family relations: Effects of pubertal status and pubertal timing. *Developmental Psychology, 23,* 451–60.

———. (1990). Interdependence in the family: Autonomy, conflict, and harmony in the parent-adolescent relationship. In S. S. Feldman and G. Elliott (Eds.), *At the threshold: The developing adolescent* (255–76). Cambridge, MA: Harvard University Press.

Sun, L. C., and Roopnarine, J. L. (1996). Mother-infant, father-infant interaction and involvement in childcare and household labor among Taiwanese families. *Infant Behavior and Development, 19,* 121–29.

Suppal, P., and Roopnarine, J. L. (1999). Paternal involvement in child care as a function of maternal employment in nuclear and extended families in India. *Sex Roles, 40,* 731–44.

Teti, D. M., Bond, L. A., and Gibbs, E. D. (1988). Mothers, fathers, and siblings: A comparison of play styles and their influence upon infant cognitive level. *International Journal of Behavioral Development, 11,* 415–32.

Tulananda, O., and Roopnarine, J. L. (2001). Mothers' and fathers' interactions with preschoolers in the home in northern Thailand: Relationships to teachers' assessments of children's social skills. *Journal of Family Psychology, 15,* 676–87.

Warin, J., Solomon, Y., Lewis, C., and Langford, W. (1999). *Fathers, work and family life.* London: Family Policy Research Centre.

Welkowitz, J., Bond, R. N., Feldman, L., and Tota, M. E. (1990). Conversational time patterns and mutual influence in parent-child interactions: A time series approach. *Journal of Psycholinguistic Research, 19,* 221–43.

Williams, J., Bennett, S., and Best, D. (1975). Awareness and expression of sex stereotypes in young children. *Developmental Psychology, 11,* 635–42.

Yarrow, L. J., MacTurk, R. H., Vietze, P. M., McCarthy, M. E., Klein, R. P., and McQuiston, S. (1984). Developmental course of parental stimulation and its relationship to mastery motivation during infancy. *Developmental Psychology, 20,* 492—503.

Yeung, W. J., Sandberg, J. F., Davis-Kean, P. E., and Hofferth, S. L. (2001). Children's time with fathers in intact families. *Journal of Marriage and Family, 63,* 136–54.

Yogman, M. (1981). Games fathers and mothers play with their infants. *Infant Mental Health Journal, 2,* 241–48.

Youniss, J., and Smollar, J. (1985). *Adolescent relations with mothers, fathers, and friends.* Chicago: University of Chicago Press.

Zaouche-Gaudron, C., Ricaud, H., and Beaumatin, A. (1998). Father-child play interaction and subjectivity. *European Journal of Psychology of Education, 13,* 447–60.

3

Family Acculturation and Change: Recent Comparative Research

John W. Berry

When families and individuals migrate from one society to another, they carry with them cultural and psychological attributes that set the stage for how they will deal with the process of acculturation. This chapter provides a general framework for understanding these background factors, taking an *ecocultural* perspective; it also provides a second framework that proposes a way to understand variations in how they negotiate their new lives, using the concept of *acculturation strategies*.

The chapter has four parts. First, I present my ideas regarding how a society's ecological context provides conditions for the development of collective cultural practices and individual behavioral repertoires. Understanding these ecocultural settings allows us to (literally) know where families and individuals "are coming from" as they immigrate to societies of settlement, and engage in the process of acculturation. Second, I outline the various acculturation strategies that groups and individuals use following their immigration. These strategies (integration, separation, assimilation, and marginalization) now have considerable empirical support. These variations challenge the unidimensional and unidirectional concept of acculturation that has long been held by researchers and policymakers. Third, I review an international comparative research project that deals with families in thirty countries. Results show remarkable similarities across groups and countries in the structure and function of families. Within this pattern of universality, there are also important variations according to gender (fathers/mothers; boys/girls), and generation (parents/children) in many of the phenomena under study. The fourth part draws some conclusions and proposes some implications of the findings, particularly with respect to immigrant settlement and changing community and educational institutions.

ECOCULTURAL FRAMEWORK

Over the years, I have attempted to develop a working framework for cross-cultural psychological research. This ecocultural framework is a kind of map that lays out the categories of variables that need to be examined in research that seeks to understand human behavioral diversity in its cultural context.

This ecocultural perspective has evolved through a series of research studies devoted to understanding similarities and differences in perception, cognition, and social behavior (Berry, 1976; Berry, Van de Koppel, Sénéchal, Annis, Bahuchet, Cavalli-Sforza, and Witkin, 1986; Mishra, Sinha, and Berry, 1996) within a broad and general approach to understanding human diversity. The core ideas have a long history (Jahoda, 1995) and have become assembled into conceptual frameworks (Berry, 1975, 1995) used in empirical research, and in coordinating textbooks in cross-cultural psychology (Berry, Poortinga, Segall, and Dasen, 2002; Segall, Dasen, Berry, and Poortinga, 1999). Similar ideas and frameworks have been advanced by both anthropologists (e.g., Whiting, 1974) and psychologists (e.g., Bronfenbrenner, 1979) who share the view that human activity, both cultural and individual, can only be understood within the ecological context within which it develops and takes place.

The ecocultural perspective is rooted in two basic assumptions. The first (the universalist assumption) is that all human societies exhibit commonalities, both cultural (cultural universals) and psychological (psychological universals). This latter perspective holds that basic psychological processes are shared, species-common characteristics of all human beings on which culture plays variations during the course of development and daily activity. The second assumption (the adaptation assumption) is that, on the basis of these common processes, behavior is differentially developed and expressed in response to ecological, sociopolitical, and cultural contexts. This view allows for comparisons across cultures (on the basis of common underlying processes), and makes comparison worthwhile (using the surface variation as basic evidence).

In the social sciences, such as cultural anthropology (e.g., Murdock, 1975) or sociology (e.g., Aberle et al., 1950), there is substantial evidence that groups everywhere possess shared social and cultural attributes. For example, all societies have language, tools, social structures (e.g., norms, roles), and social institutions (e.g., marriage, family, justice). It is also evident that groups express such commonalities in different ways from one time and place to another. Similarly, there is parallel evidence, at the individual psychological level, for both underlying similarity and surface variation (Berry, Poortinga, Pandey, Dasen, Saraswathi, Segall, and Kagitcibasi, 1997). For example, all individuals have the competence to develop, learn and perform speech, create and use technology, engage in role-playing, and construct and abide by norms. At the same time, there are obviously group and individual differences in the extent and style of expression of these shared underlying psychological processes.

This combination of underlying similarity with surface expressive variation has given rise to the conceptual orientation in cross-cultural psychology called "universalism" by Berry et al. (2002) to distinguish it both from absolutism (which tends to ignore cultural influence on behavioral development and expression) and from relativism (which tends to ignore the existence of common underlying psychological processes). Paradoxically, this search for our common humanity can only be pursued by observing our diversity, and this dual task is the essence of cross-cultural psychology (Berry, 1969, 2000).

Following is an outline of our current ecocultural thinking about how people adapt culturally (as a group) to their longstanding ecological and sociopolitical settings. To begin, one continuing theme in cultural anthropology is that cultural variations may be understood as adaptations to differing ecological settings or contexts (Boyd and Richerson, 1983). This line of thinking, usually known as "cultural ecology" (Vayda and Rappoport, 1968), or "ecological anthropology" (Moran, 1982), has a long history in the discipline (see Feldman, 1975). Its roots go back to Forde's (1934) classic analysis of relationships between physical habitat and societal features in Africa, and Kroeber's (1939) early demonstration that cultural areas and natural areas co-vary in Aboriginal North America. Unlike earlier simplistic assertions by the school of "environmental determinism," the ecological school of thought has ranged from "possibilism" (where the environment provides opportunities, and sets some constraints or limits on the range of possible cultural forms that may emerge) to an emphasis on "resource utilization" (where active and interactive relationships between human populations and their habitat are examined). Of particular interest to psychologists was Steward's (1955) concept of the "cognized environment." This concept refers to the features of the environment that are perceived as being of greatest relevance to a population's subsistence. With this notion, ecological thinking moved simultaneously away from any links to earlier deterministic views, and toward the more psychological idea of individuals actively perceiving, appraising, and changing their environments.

The earlier ecological approaches have tended to view cultures as relatively stable (even permanent) adaptations (as a state), largely ignoring adaptation (as a process), or adaptability (as a system change characteristic) of cultural populations (Bennett, 1976). However, it is clear that cultures evolve over time, sometimes in response to changing ecological circumstances, and sometimes due to contact with other cultures. This fact has required the addition of a more dynamic conception of ecological adaptation as a continuous as well as an interactive process (between ecological, cultural, and psychological variables). It is from this most recent position that I have developed my ecocultural framework. This is a view that is consistent with more recent general changes in anthropology, away from a "museum" orientation to culture (collecting and organizing static artifacts in cases along a wall) to one that emphasizes cultures as constantly changing, and being concerned with creation, metamorphosis, and re-creation.

The current version of the ecocultural framework (see figure 3.1) proposes to account for human psychological diversity (both individual and group similarities and differences) by taking into account two fundamental sources of influence—ecological and sociopolitical—and two features of human populations that are adapted to them—cultural and biological characteristics. These population variables are transmitted to individuals by various "transmission variables" such as cultural transmission (enculturation, socialization), genetics, and acculturation. Our understanding of both cultural and genetic transmission has been greatly advanced by recent work on culture learning (e.g., Tomasello, Kruger, and Ratner, 1993) and genetic factors (Keller, 1997). The essence of both these domains is the fundamental similarity of all human beings at a deep level, combined with variation in the expression of these shared attributes at the surface level, which is an example of the concept of universalism mentioned above.

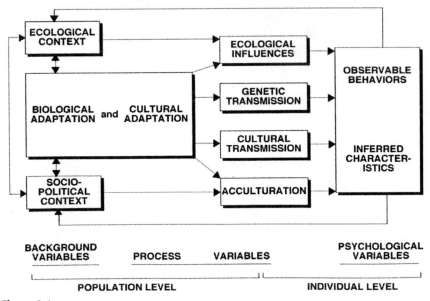

Figure 3.1.

At the sociopolitical level of the framework, research on the processes and outcomes of acculturation has also been advancing (e.g., Chun, Balls-Organista, and Marin, 2003; Sam and Berry, 2006), necessitated by the dramatic increase in intercultural contact. This sociopolitical context brings about contact among cultures so that individuals have to adapt to more than one context. When many cultural contexts are involved (as in situations of culture contact and acculturation that follow migration of individuals and families), psychological phenomena can be viewed as attempts to deal simultaneously with two, sometimes inconsistent, sometimes conflicting, cultural contexts (Berry, 2003).

To summarize, the ecocultural framework considers human diversity, both cultural and psychological, to be a set of collective and individual adaptations to the contexts in which they develop and operate. Within this general perspective, it views cultures as evolving adaptations to ecological and sociopolitical influences and views individual psychological characteristics in a population as adaptive to their ecological and cultural contexts. It also views (group) culture and (individual) behavior as distinct phenomena at their own levels that need to be examined independently in order to be able to examine their systematic relationships.

Place of Family within the Ecocultural Framework

While most use of the ecocultural framework has been in the study of perception and cognition, it equally applies to the exploration of social behavior. Recent work (Georgas and Berry, 1995; Georgas, van de Vijver, and Berry, 2004) has extended this interest in the social aspects of behavior. Georgas and Berry (1995) sought to discover ecological and social indicators that might allow societies to be clustered according to their similarities and differences on six dimensions: ecology, education, economy, mass communications, population, and religion. A number of cultural zones were distinguishable on the basis of these indicators. Georgas et al. (2004) further examined ecosocial indicators across cultures and then sought evidence for their relationships with a number of psychological variables (such as values and subjective well-being). Results showed that many of the ecosocial indicators came together to form a single economic dimension, termed "affluence"; this dimension was distinct from another major indicator, "religion," in the pattern of relationships they had with the psychological variables. Specifically, across cultures, a high placement on affluence (along with Protestant religion) was associated with more emphasis on individualism, utilitarianism, and personal well-being. In contrast, for other religions, together with low affluence, there was an emphasis on power relationships, loyalty, and hierarchy value.

As a cultural institution, the family may be seen as adaptive to its eco-cultural context. The family thus occupies a central place in the ecocultural approach, serving to link background contexts to individual behavioral development. It is well established that features of family and marriage are closely related to ecocultural features of a society, especially to settlement pattern, role differentiation, and social stratification. The anthropologist Tylor already noted these relationships in the 1880s. He proposed that no-madic societies (mainly hunting and gathering–based peoples) tended to have nuclear families and monogamous marriages, in contrast to sedentary societies (mainly agricultural peoples), who tended to have extended fami-lies and polygamous marriages. Tylor suggested that these family and mar-riage types allowed for efficient economic functioning in their respective habitats: hunters operate best in small units, with symbiotic relationships between two spouses and their direct offspring; agriculturalists require larger working units, facilitated by multiple spouses and a larger network of kin and offspring. In these agricultural societies, hierarchical relationships predominate within the family, and there is generally a higher degree of social stratification in society at large (Nimkoff and Middleton, 1960).

As explained further below, families migrating from rural/agricultural settings to urban/industrial ones (which is probably the most common transition during contemporary migrations) will bring with them ways of engaging each other within the family, and members of their new society, that entail the acceptance of authority and hierarchy. This usually takes the form of parental control over children and fathers' control over all other members of the family.

Families are particularly engaged in the process of cultural transmission to their offspring. Within this concept, a distinction is commonly made between enculturation and socialization. The first, enculturation, refers to a general, pervasive "enfolding" of developing individuals, leading to their adoption of the norms and values of their society, and their incorporation into the cultural group. The second, socialization, is a more specific process involving deliberate teaching and reinforcement so that particular charac-teristics and skills are acquired by developing individuals. Both these forms of cultural transmission have been proposed as adaptive to the ecological context. Specifically, Barry, Child, and Bacon (1959) were able to demon-strate a clear relationship between type of ecological (exploitive) pattern and socialization. More specifically, training of children for "responsibil-ity" and "obedience" appeared more in agricultural and pastoral societies, whereas training for "achievement," "self-reliance," and "independence" was more frequent in hunting and gathering societies. Thus, we have evi-dence that an exploitive subsistence pattern is a reasonably good predictor of socialization emphases on the basis of their study.

In summary, there is a broad ecological dimension running from agricultural to hunting and gathering interactions with the environment. Associated with the agricultural end of the dimension are a sedentary lifestyle, high population density, high sociocultural stratification, polygamy, extended families, and socialization emphases on compliance. In contrast, associated with the hunting end of the dimension are a nomadic lifestyle, low population density, low stratification, monogamy, nuclear families, and practices emphasizing assertion. Societies that range along this ecological dimension also vary concomitantly on these other ecological and cultural variables. Knowledge about these cross-cultural variations in the way families are structured and how they operate is essential if we are to understand families as they immigrate to their new societies.

When this ecological dimension is extended to include contemporary industrial and postindustrial societies, a more complex pattern becomes apparent (Berry, 1993; Lomax and Berkowitz, 1972). With the increasing high density of cities, we observe a reduction in pressures toward compliance as a result of a loss of community cohesion and the increase in anonymity afforded by these large cities. There is also a reduction in the frequency of extended families and a parallel increase in the proportion of nuclear families, which is accompanied by a further reduction in pressures toward compliance. Thus, an increase in stratification, compliance, and conformity from hunting to agrarian societies changes course to become a decrease in these features as societies move from agrarian to industrial and postindustrial arrangements.

However, it is likely that some of the cultural institutions and practices that were established over centuries as adaptations to earlier ecological contexts will persist into industrial and postindustrial times, even as social change takes place in their home countries. Most important for our current focus on immigrant families is that these practices are also likely to continue as part of family life in their new societies. This phenomenon of *cultural lag* may also be accompanied by the individual-level phenomenon of *behavioral lag*. Just as customs do not change overnight in response to changing ecological circumstances, so too individual behaviors do not change overnight following engagement with the new society. Thus, in addition to the role of the ecological context, the sociopolitical context has played an important role in shaping both the cultural and the transmission features of families. Particularly, the colonization of Asia by Indian and Chinese societies, and of Africa and the Americas by European societies, has brought about societal changes that have altered cultural patterns, including family arrangements and emphases in cultural transmission practices. Colonization also introduced new religions and forms of education (particularly formal schooling) in most of these societies. And, more recently, much increased availability of telemedia continues to promote change from outside by portraying alternative lifestyles and consumer goods. Their impact has led to an apparent increase in nuclear families and monogamous marriage in previously polygamous societies with extended families. Associated changes, such as delayed marriage, fewer children, and increased divorce rates, have also been assigned to acculturative influences, mainly emanating from contemporary Western domination of the "Majority World." Sociopolitical impacts on cultural transmission have also been discerned, including increased pressures toward "assertion" and a decline in "compliance" during socialization.

Thus, the study of family and of family change that is guided by the ecocultural framework needs to take into account both the ecological bases of the institutions, communities, and families, and the changes introduced by sociopolitical features of their contemporary lives. To repeat, we need to understand all these features of families, prior to their immigration, if we are to have any chance of understanding how they enter into, and deal with, the process of acculturation following their settlement in our societies.

GENERAL ACCULTURATION FRAMEWORK

The initial interest in acculturation grew out of a concern for the effects of European domination of colonial and indigenous peoples. Later, it focused on how immigrants (both voluntary and involuntary) changed following their entry and settlement into receiving societies. More recently, much of the work has been involved with how ethnocultural groups relate to each other and how they change as a result of their attempts to live together in culturally plural societies. Nowadays, all three foci are important as globalization results in ever-larger trading and political relations: indigenous national populations experience neo-colonization; new waves of immigrants, sojourners, and refugees flow from these economic and political changes; and large ethnocultural populations become established in most countries (see Chun, Balls-Organista, and Marin, 2003; Sam and Berry, 2006, for overviews).

The concept of acculturation has been elaborated by Redfield, Linton, and Herskovits (1936), and by the Social Science Research Council (1954). In essence, acculturation is a process of cultural change that results from the contact and continuing interaction between two cultural groups. As for cross-cultural psychology (Berry et al., 2002), it is imperative that we base our work on acculturation by examining its cultural contexts. We need to understand, in ethnographic terms, both cultures that are in contact if we are to understand the individuals that are in contact.

At the individual level, Graves (1967) introduced the concept of "psychological acculturation." This concept refers to changes in an individual who is a participant in a culture contact situation, being influenced directly by both the external culture, and by the changing culture of which the individual is a member. There are two reasons for keeping these two levels distinct. The first is that our field insists that we view individual human behavior as interacting with the cultural context within which it occurs; hence separate conceptions and measurements are required at the two levels. The second is that not every individual enters into, and participates in, or changes in the same way. There are vast individual differences in psychological acculturation, even among individuals who live in the same acculturative arena.

Berry (2003) developed a framework that outlines and links cultural and psychological acculturation and identifies the two (or more) groups in contact. This framework serves as a map of those phenomena that I believe need to be conceptualized and measured during acculturation research. At the cultural level, we need to understand key features of the two original cultural groups prior to their major contact, the nature of their contact relationships, and the resulting cultural changes in both groups and in the emergent ethnocultural groups during the process of acculturation. The gathering of this information requires extensive ethnographic, community-level work. These changes can be minor or substantial, and range from being easily accomplished to being a source of major cultural disruption.

At the individual level, we need to consider the psychological changes that individuals in all groups undergo and their eventual adaptation to their new situations. Identifying these changes requires sampling a population and studying individuals who are variably involved in the process of acculturation. These changes can be a set of rather easily accomplished behavioral shifts (e.g., in ways of speaking, dressing, eating, and in one's cultural identity) or they can be more problematic, producing acculturative stress as manifested by uncertainty, anxiety, and depression (Berry, 1976). Adaptations can be primarily internal or psychological (e.g., sense of well-being, of self-esteem) or sociocultural, linking the individual to others in the new society, as manifested for example in competence in the activities of daily intercultural living. General overviews of this process and these specific features can be found in the literature (e.g., Berry, 1980, 1990, 1997; Berry and Sam, 1997; Birman, 1994; Ward, 1996).

While only two general domains (cultural and individual) are included in the framework, all these concepts apply equally to social institutions, including the family. For example, the structural and functional features of the family as a collective enterprise, both prior to contact, and with respect to changes following contact, need to be studied as cultural components. Individual members of the family can be examined with respect to behavioral changes, stress experiences, and their eventual adaptations. Within families, it is also important to consider the acculturation of spousal dyads (Ataca and Berry, 2002) and of parent-child dyads (Berry,

Phinney, Sam, and Vedder, 2006), particularly the possible contribution of differential acculturation among members to the character of family life following immigration.

Not all groups and individuals undergo acculturation in the same way; there are large variations in how people seek to engage in the process. In much of the earlier research, it was assumed that individuals changed from being "traditional" in their attitudes and behaviors to becoming more like the dominant society that was influencing them (e.g., Gordon, 1964). This assimilationist view of how people changed served the purposes of those who considered that the goal of acculturation was to achieve a "melting pot," in which all peoples would come to share one language, one identity, and one set of values. However, beginning in the 1980s (see Berry, 1980), this unidimensional conception of acculturation began to change and yielded to more complex and multidimensional views (Ryder, Alden, and Paulhus, 2000). These various orientations are termed acculturation attitudes (see Berry et al., 1989) or acculturation strategies (Berry, 2005). Which strategies are used depends on a variety of antecedent factors (both cultural and psychological) and there are variable consequences (again both cultural and psychological) of these different strategies. These strategies consist of two (usually related) components: attitudes and behaviors (that is, the preferences and actual outcomes) that are exhibited in day-to-day intercultural encounters.

Four acculturation strategies have been derived from two basic issues facing all acculturating peoples. These issues are based on the distinction between orientations toward one's own group and those towards other groups (Berry, 1970, 1974, 1980). This distinction is rendered as a relative preference for maintaining one's heritage culture and identity and a relative preference for having contact with and participating in the larger society along with other ethnocultural groups.

These two issues can be responded to on attitudinal dimensions, with generally positive or negative responses at each end. These two dimensions intersect to define four acculturation strategies, which carry different names, depending on which ethnocultural group (the dominant or non-dominant) is being considered. From the point of view of non-dominant groups, when individuals do not wish to maintain their cultural identity and seek daily interaction with other cultures, the assimilation strategy is defined. In contrast, when individuals place a value on holding on to their original culture, and at the same time wish to avoid interaction with others, then the separation alternative is defined.

When there is an interest in maintaining one's original culture while also engaging in daily interactions with other groups, integration is the option. In this case, immigrants maintain some degree of cultural integrity, while at the same time seeking, as a member of an ethnocultural group, to participate as an integral part of the larger social network. Integration can take a number of forms. One is similar to how a bilingual person switches between languages, depending on the linguistic context, speaking either language in the appropriate setting. Another is when there is a blending, in which features of both cultures are merged into a new behavioral repertoire that is distinct from both original cultures. This may be compared to a "joint venture" in which practices of one corporation are adapted to better fit the requirements of working with another corporation in their home setting.

Finally, when there is little possibility or interest in cultural maintenance (often for reasons of enforced cultural loss) and little interest in having relations with others (often for reasons of having experienced exclusion or discrimination), then marginalization is defined. This situation is characterized by confusion, uncertainty, and frequent signs of social and psychological problems (such as substance or family abuse, school failure, or inability to keep a job).

THIRTY-COUNTRY STUDY OF FAMILY ROLES AND VALUES

In this section we use our work on the thirty countries study to illustrate the value of the ecological model for understanding family adaptation and cultural change. The thirty-country study is a comparative examination of family structure, family roles, and some related family and personal values (Georgas, Berry, van de Vijver, Kagitcibasi, and Poortinga, 2006). Guided by the ecocultural framework (Berry, 1976), and by a model of family change (Kagitcibasi, 1996), this project sought to understand contemporary families in thirty countries, representing most cultural regions of the world. Colleagues in these thirty countries provided ethnographic and demographic portrayals of the family and of recent and ongoing changes in family life. These colleagues also collected data from university students, who served as "cultural reporters." Their information provided data on a number of features of family life, including family structure, roles, relationships, and values. Total sample size was 5469 (60 percent females). The significance of this study for understanding immigrant families is that it provides country-level descriptions of a number of cultural and psychological variables that are often considered to be important during the acculturation process. This information provides the ethnographic background that was mentioned earlier as being an essential basis for any cross-cultural study.

Various ecological and cultural (and some sociopolitical) variables were employed, guided by earlier research (Georgas and Berry, 1995; Georgas, van de Vijver, and Berry, 2004), including the percentage of the population engaged in agriculture, per capita gross domestic product, and level of education. These indicators were factor analyzed, producing an index that is called affluence. This variable was also used to produce three clusters (high, medium, low), into which all countries could be placed. In addition, based on the same earlier research, a second index, religion, was created by assigning a society to a category based on their dominant religious denomination (Roman Catholic; Protestant; Christian Orthodox; Muslim; Buddhist/Hindu/Traditional beliefs). Each society was given a score on these two indicators, and they were employed as input or background variables in the ecocultural framework. The societies in the study, and their scores on the affluence and religion variables, are provided in table 3.1.

Table 3.1. Affluence Index Scores, Affluence Cluster, and Religious Denomination for Thirty Countries

Country	Ecology		Sociopolitical Religion[a]
	Affluence	Affluence Cluster	
Algeria	−1.06	3	4
Brazil	−0.55	2	1
Bulgaria	−0.37	2	3
Canada	1.62	1	1
Chile	−0.40	2	1
Cyprus	−0.44	2	3
France	0.99	1	1
Georgia	−0.74	2	3
Germany	1.28	1	2
Ghana	−1.34	3	5
Greece	0.05	2	3
Hong Kong	0.71	1	5
India	−1.03	3	5
Indonesia	-0.89	3	4
Iran	−0.68	2	4
Japan	1.08	1	5
Mexico	−0.22	2	1
Nigeria	−1.36	3	4
Pakistan	−0.92	3	4
Saudi Arabia	0.04	2	4
South Korea	0.32	1	5
Spain	0.29	1	1
The Netherlands	0.78	1	1
Turkey	−0.67	2	4
UK	0.78	1	4
Ukraine	−0.09	2	3
USA	2.81	1	2

Note. [a]1 = Roman Catholic; 2 = Protestant; 3 = Christian Orthodox; 4 = Muslim; 5 = Buddhist/Hindu/Traditional Beliefs. Religion refers to the dominant religion in each society.

Source: J. Georgas, J. W. Berry, F. van de Vijver, C. Kagitcibasi, and Y. H. Poortinga. (2006). *Family across cultures: A 30 nation psychological study.* Cambridge: Cambridge University Press.

Individual respondents provided information on a number of family and psychological variables; only two of these (family roles and family relationship values) are reported here. The questionnaire requested ratings of a number of family roles for each member of the extended family, including mother, father, siblings, and grandparents; only responses for mother and father are reported here. These responses were factor analyzed separately for both mothers and fathers. Three factors emerged: "expressive," "financial," and "childcare." Differences in these roles are likely sources of discord between generations within migrating families, and between immigrant families and the role preferences found in their societies of settlement.

These three factors resemble those found in previous research, except that the usual "instrumental" role is now divided into two distinct roles in our data ("financial" and "childcare"). In this study, the expressive factor included items such as: (mother/father) "provides emotional support to children," "provides emotional support to spouse," and "keeps the family united."

The financial factor was carried by items such as (mother/father) "contributes financially," "manages finances," and "gives pocket money to children." The childcare factor was based on items such as (mother/father) "takes children to school," "plays with children," and "helps children with homework."

Participants also provided responses to a scale on family relationship values (Georgas et al., 1996). Factor analysis of the fourteen items produced two factors, which we call "hierarchy" and "kin relationships" (see table 3.2). Hierarchy refers to the general dominance of fathers over others in the family (e.g., "The father should be the head of the family," and "The mother's place is in the home"). Kin relations refers to the quality of interpersonal relationships within the family (e.g., "Children should respect their grandparents," and "Children should help with chores in the house").

Our core interest is in the relationships between the ecocultural context variables, and the family roles and the family relationship values. Table 3.3 presents the correlations across the thirty countries between these two background variables and family roles for mother and father. There is a clear pattern of relationships between both context variables (affluence and percentage in agriculture), and many of the roles of fathers and mothers, and family relationship values. As expected, low affluence and high percentage engaged in agriculture were strongly related to high father's expressive and financial roles in the family, and to mother's expressive role (but not to mother's financial role). Also as expected, education relates to these roles and values in a parallel way to that of affluence. Of particular interest is the finding that all three context variables (affluence, agriculture, and education) are related to the father's financial role, but not to the mother's financial role. There is very little variation on mother's financial role across these

Table 3.2.   Factor Loadings of Family Relationship Values

Construct/Item	Factor Loadings
Hierarchy	
Father should handle money	.75
Father is breadwinner	.72
Mother should accept father's decisions	.70
Father is head of family	.69
Mother's place is at home	.69
Mother is go-between	.59
Kin Relationships	
Children should respect grandparents	.69
Honor family's reputation	.63
Children should obey parents	.62
Parents teach behavior	.60
Problems are solved within the family	.60
Children take care of old parents	.58
Good relationships with relatives	.56

Note. The two factors explained 44.36% of the variance.

Source: J. Georgas, J. W. Berry, F. van de Vijver, C. Kagitcibasi, and Y. H. Poortinga. (2006). *Family across cultures: A 30 nation psychological study.* Cambridge: Cambridge University Press.

three variables. For example, across the three levels of affluence, means for mother's financial role are 4.61, 4.61, and 4.58, compared to those for fathers (5.16, 4.85, and 4.32).

There are also clear relationships between these three context variables and both the hierarchy and kin relationships values for both fathers and mothers. High affluence predicts low hierarchy and low kinship relationships scores (see table 3.3).

Religious denomination was also an important predictor of roles and family relationship values, but in a more variable way. These relationships exist mainly for Catholics and Muslims. For fathers, being a Catholic was related to having a lower expressive role and lower hierarchy values; being a Muslim father was related to having higher expressive and financial roles, and to higher hierarchy and kinship relations values. For mothers, there were no relationships for Catholics with any family role, but for Muslim mothers, there were positive relationships for all three roles. For values, both Catholics and Protestants had lower hierarchy values, but Muslims had higher hierarchy and kin relations values.

To further explore the relationships between affluence, religion, and the two family relationship values, figure 3.2 presents the mean scores according to the affluence clusters and religious denomination categories. On the

Table 3.3. Correlations of the Family Roles for Each Family Position and Family Relationship Values with Affluence, Education, and Religious Domination

| | Family Roles | | | | | | Family Relationship Values | |
| | Father | | | Mother | | | | |
Variables	Exp.	Fin.	Care	Exp.	Fin.	Care	Hier.	Kin
Affluence	−65	−58	11	−61	11	16	−68	−64
% working in agriculture	71	67	14	71	3	1	69	64
Sociopolitical								
Education	−55	−45	3	−54	15	22	−59	−60
Religion Catholic	−56	−34	22	−32	24	32	−49	−21
Protestant	−31	−21	32	−19	17	25	−41	−25
Orthodox	13	24	15	16	34	49	7	−1
Muslim	73	53	−25	58	−47	−51	62	56

Note. Exp. = Expressive; Fin. = Financial; Hier. = Hierarchical; Kin = Kinship relationship.

Source: J. Georgas, J. W. Berry, F. van de Vijver, C. Kagitcibasi, and Y. H. Poortinga. (2006). *Family across cultures: A 30 nation psychological study.* Cambridge: Cambridge University Press.

John W. Berry

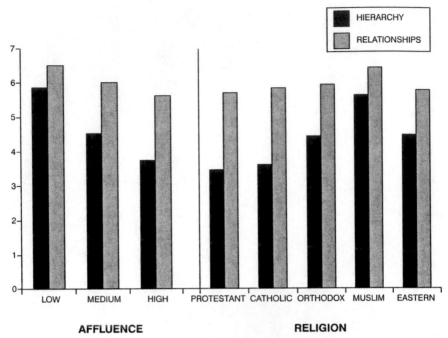

Figure 3.2.

left are the three affluence clusters, and on the right are the five religious de-
nominations. Here, it is evident that both values decline in a linear way with
increasing affluence. As we have noted, the pattern for religion is more variable, but there is evidence for linear variation of both values over the range
from Protestant, to Catholic, to Orthodox, to Muslim societies. The values in
countries with Eastern religions resembled those in Orthodox societies.

To summarize, when we examine the relationships between ecological
and sociopolitical variables that were drawn from the ecocultural framework
and cross-cultural features of family life, we find that there are predicable
patterns, rather than random links. These patterns are consistent with the anthropological literature dealing with economic practices, and with religious
belief systems. They are also consistent with, and were predicted from, previous psychological research carried out within the ecocultural tradition.

RESEARCH IMPLICATIONS

The approach to studying family and acculturation taken in this chapter
is broadly ecological and comparative. The ecological perspective has two
important aspects. First, social institutions and individual behavior are

seen as collective and personal adaptations to the contexts in which they developed and now exist. From my perspective, too often in psychology, the minute preconditions of human activity are given more attention than these broad features of the habitat that provide the very foundations for the phenomena that we study. With this ecocultural approach, some structural features of the family and some psychological features of individual members and their family relationships have been linked to some broad contextual factors.

A second important aspect of this ecological approach is that features of the context are assessed independently of features of families and of individuals. In this sense, they can be considered as "independent" variables in a complex network of relationships. In much contemporary cross-cultural psychological research, features of the background context are generated from individual data (such as giving a country or society a score on a variable based on the mean scores of individuals), so that it is difficult to establish relationships between the two levels in the absence of independent measurement.

The comparative perspective allows for the examination of broad patterns of relationships among ecological, cultural, and psychological factors. When only one or a few instances are taken into consideration, premature conclusions can be drawn based on only a small portion of the evidence. The nuclear, monogamous, highly affluent, and predominantly Christian-based societies and families of the Euro-American world are surely no basis for understanding cultural or psychological phenomena of the vast array of people in the "Majority World."

Building on these advantages of the ecocultural and comparative approaches, societies, families, and individuals within them have been examined here. The study focused on the cultural, social, and psychological qualities that are developed in differing ecocultural contexts, which are brought by immigrants as part of their personal and collective baggage to their new societies. Probably the most important lesson to come from this study is the degree of consistency in patterns of relationships among ecological, cultural, social, and psychological factors. The examination of families across cultures showed that structural aspects of families are not randomly distributed around the world, but follow predictable arrangements linked to agricultural and educational features of the societies, and to their levels of affluence and the religious denomination that has largely shaped their social institutions. Moreover, some personal qualities (such as values) fit into this pattern with a high degree of consistency.

With respect to acculturation, this chapter has outlined the need to examine the cultural and psychological features that groups, families, and individuals carry with them when they migrate to their societies of settlement. There are clear variations in parental roles and family relationship values across cultural groups. When these features of family life differ between immigrant and receiving societies, they are likely to be a source of difficulty, both between parents and their children, and between immigrant families and those in their new society. These difficulties may then contribute to less than optimal adaptation of immigrant children as they attempt to make sense of the differences they find between their own families' ways and those of their settled peers. This possibility is supported by current research on the importance of such role and value differences (Berry, Vedder, Georgas, Sam, and Sabatier, 2007) in contributing to the adaptation of immigrant youth. That study found that the greater the country differences in the ways that fathers and mothers deal with the common tasks of daily life, the less the children are oriented to their new society (i.e., they pursue assimilation to a lesser extent), and the less well their children adapt psychologically and socioculturally to their new society.

The frameworks and findings regarding variations in families across cultures presented in this chapter, and the recent analyses of the importance of these variations in the acculturation process, suggest that knowing about features of the family in the societies of origin allows for a better understanding of how immigrant youth will acculturate, and how well they will adapt, to their new society.

I believe that family research that is both ecological in perspective and comparative in scope provides a basis for producing some generalizations that may be useful in guiding the development of public policy and in guiding immigrant families and individuals through the sometimes difficult process of acculturation.

AUTHOR NOTE

My research program on acculturation with indigenous and immigrant populations and members of the larger society over thirty-five years has been supported by the Social Sciences and Humanities Research Council of Canada, and the Canadian Ethnic Studies Programme of the Ministry of Multiculturalism, Ottawa. My thanks also go to the many students and colleagues with whom I have enjoyed working.

REFERENCES

Aberle, D. F., et al. (1950). Functional prerequisites of society. *Ethics, 60*, 100–111.
Ataca, B. and Berry, J. W. (2002). Psychological, sociocultural, and marital adaptation of Turkish immigrants in Canada. *International Journal of Psychology, 37*, 13–26.
Barry, H., Child, I., and Bacon, M. (1959). Relations of child training to subsistence economy. *American Anthropologist, 61*, 51–63.
Bennett, J. (1976). *The ecological transition*. London: Pergamon.

Berry, J. W. (1969). On cross-cultural comparability. *International Journal of Psychology, 4,* 119–28.

———. (1970). Marginality, stress and ethnic identification in an acculturated Aboriginal community. *Journal of Cross-Cultural Psychology, 1,* 239–52.

———. (1974). Psychological aspects of cultural pluralism: Unity and identity reconsidered. *Topics in Culture Learning, 2,* 17–22.

———. (1975). An ecological approach to cross-cultural psychology. *Nederlands Tijdschrift voor de Psychologie, 30,* 51–84.

———. (1976). *Human ecology and cognitive style: Comparative studies in cultural and psychological adaptation.* New York: Sage/Halsted.

———. (1980). Acculturation as varieties of adaptation. In A. Padilla (Ed.), *Acculturation: Theory, models and findings* (9–25). Boulder, CO: Westview.

———. (1990). Psychology of acculturation. In J. Berman (Ed.), *Cross-cultural perspectives: Nebraska symposium on motivation* (201–34). Lincoln: University of Nebraska Press.

———. (1993). Ecology of individualism and collectivism. In U. Kim et al. (Eds.), *Individualism and collectivism* (77–84). London: Sage.

———. (1995). The descendants of a model. *Culture and Psychology, 1,* 373–80.

———. (1997). Immigration, acculturation and adaptation. *Applied Psychology: An International Review, 46,* 5–68.

———. (2000). Cross-cultural psychology: A symbiosis of cultural and comparative approaches. *Asian Journal of Social Psychology. Special Issue: Indigenous, cultural, and cross-cultural psychologies, 3,* 197–205.

———. (2003). Conceptual approaches to acculturation. In K. Chun, P. Balls-Organista, and G. Marin (Eds.), *Acculturation* (17–37). Washington, DC: APA Press.

———. (2005). Acculturation: Living successfully in two cultures. *International Journal of Intercultural Relations, 29,* 697–712.

Berry, J. W., Kim, U., Power, S., Young, M., and Bujaki, M. (1989). Acculturation attitudes in plural societies. *Applied Psychology, 38,* 185–206.

Berry, J. W., Phinney, J. S., Sam, D. L., and Vedder, P. (Eds). (2006). *Immigrant youth in cultural transition: Acculturation, identity and adaptation across nations.* Mahwah, NJ: Lawrence Erlbaum Associates.

Berry, J. W., Poortinga, Y. H, Pandey, J., Dasen, P. R., Saraswathi, T. S., Segall, M. H., and Kagitcibasi, C. (Eds.). (1997). *Handbook of cross-cultural psychology* (three volumes). Boston: Allyn & Bacon.

Berry, J. W., Poortinga, Y. H., Segall, M. H., and Dasen, P. R. (2002). *Cross-cultural psychology: Research and applications.* Second ed. New York: Cambridge University Press.

Berry, J. W., and Sam, D. L. (1997). Acculturation and adaptation. In J. W. Berry, M. H. Segall, and C. Kagitcibasi (Eds.), *Handbook of cross-cultural psychology. Vol. 3: Social behaviour and applications,* second edition (291–326). Boston: Allyn & Bacon.

Berry, J. W., van de Koppel, J. M. H., Sénéchal, C., Annis, R. C., Bahuchet, S., Cavalli-Sforza, L. L., and Witkin, H. A. (1986). *On the edge of the forest: Cultural adaptation and cognitive development in Central Africa.* Lisse: Swets and Zeitlinger.

Berry, J. W., Vedder, P. , Georgas, J., Sam, D. L., and Sabatier, C. (2007). Ecological and cultural background, parental roles and the acculturation and adaptation of immigrant youth. Unpublished paper.

Birman, D. (1994). Acculturation and human diversity in a multicultural society. In E. Trickett, R. Watts, and D. Birman (Eds.), *Human diversity* (261–84). San Francisco: Jossey-Bass.

Boyd, R., and Richerson, P. (1983). Why is culture adaptive? *Quarterly Review of Biology, 58,* 209–14.

Bronfenbrenner, U. (1979). *The ecology of human development.* Cambridge, MA: Harvard University Press.

Chun, K., Balls-Organista, P., and Marin, G. (2003). *Acculturation: Advances in theory, measurement and applied research.* Washington, DC: APA Books.

Feldman, D. A. (1975). The history of the relationship between environment and culture in ethnological thought. *Journal of the History of the Behavioural Sciences, 110,* 67–81.

Forde, D. (1934). *Habitat, economy and society.* New York: Dutton.

Georgas, J., and Berry, J. W. (1995). An ecocultural taxonomy for cross-cultural psychology. *Cross-Cultural Research, 29,* 121–57.

Georgas, J., Berry, J. W., van de Vijver, F., Kagitcibasi, C., and Poortinga, Y. H. (2006). *Family across cultures: A 30 nation psychological study.* Cambridge: Cambridge University Press.

Georgas, J., Berry, J. W., Shaw, A., Christakopoulou, S., and Mylonas, S. (1996). Acculturation of Greek family values. *Journal of Cross-Cultural Psychology, 27,* 329–38.

Georgas, J., van de Vijver, F. J. R., and Berry, J. W. (2004). The ecocultural framework, ecosocial indicators and psychological variables in cross-cultural research. *Journal of Cross-Cultural Psychology, 35,* 74–96.

Graves, T. (1967). Psychological acculturation in a tri-ethnic community. *South-Western Journal of Anthropology, 23,* 337–50.

Gordon, M. (1964). *Assimilation in American life.* New York: Oxford University Press.

Jahoda, G. (1995). The ancestry of a model. *Culture & Psychology, 1,* 11–24.

Kagitcibasi, C. (1996). *Family and human development across cultures: A view from the other side.* Hillsdale, NJ: Erlbaum.

Keller, H. (1997). Evolutionary approaches. In J. W. Berry, Y. H. Poortinga, and J. Pandey (Eds.), *Handbook of cross-cultural psychology, Vol. 1* (215–55). Boston: Allyn & Bacon.

Kroeber, A. (1939). *Cultural and natural areas of native North America.* Berkeley: University of California Press.

Lomax, A., and Berkowitz, W. (1972). The evolutionary taxonomy of culture. *Science, 177,* 228–39.

Mishra, R. C., Sinha, D., and Berry, J. W. (1996). *Ecology, acculturation and psychological adaptation: A study of Advasi in Bihar.* Delhi: Sage.

Moran, E. (1982). *Human adaptability: An introduction to ecological anthropology.* Boulder, CO: Westview Press.

Murdock, G. P. (1975). *Outline of cultural materials.* New Haven, CT: Human Relations Area Files.

Nimkoff, M. F., and Middleton, R. (1960). Types of family and types of economy. *American Journal of Sociology, 66,* 215–25.

Redfield, R., Linton, R., and Herskovits, M. (1936). Memorandum on the study of acculturation. *American Anthropologist, 38,* 149–52.

Ryder, A., Alden, L., and Paulhus, D. (2000). Is acculturation unidimensional or bidimensional? *Journal of Personality and Social Psychology, 79,* 49–65.

Sam, D. L., and Berry, J. W. (Eds.). (2006). *Cambridge handbook of acculturation psychology.* Cambridge: Cambridge University Press.

Segall, M. H., Dasen, P. R., Berry, J. W., and Poortinga, Y. H. (1999). *Human behavior in global perspective.* Second ed. Boston: Allyn & Bacon.

Social Science Research Council (1954). Acculturation: An exploratory formulation. *American Anthropologist, 56,* 973–1002.

Steward, J. (1955). *The concept and method of cultural ecology: Theory of culture change.* Urbana: University of Illinois Press.

Tomasello, M., Kruger, A., and Ratner, H. (1993). Culture learning. *Behavioral and Brain Sciences, 16,* 495–552.

Vayda, A. P., and Rappoport, R. (1968). Ecology, cultural and non-cultural. In J. Clifton (Ed.), *Cultural anthropology* (477–97). Boston: Houghton Mifflin.

Ward, C. (1996). Acculturation. In D. Landis and R. Bhagat (Eds.), *Handbook of intercultural training,* second ed. (124–47). Newbury Park, CA: Sage.

Whiting, J. W. M. (1974). *A model for psychocultural research.* Annual Report, Washington, DC: American Anthropological Association.

4

Immigrant Fathers:
A Demographic Portrait

Donald J. Hernandez, Nancy A. Denton,
and Suzanne E. Macartney

Fathers are important because, along with mothers, they bear immediate and direct responsibility for rearing children, for creating and nurturing the next generation of parents, workers, and citizens. The dramatic increase during recent decades in the proportion of children in immigrant families calls, therefore, for increasing attention to immigrant fathers. The first national demographic portrait to distinguish fathers by immigrant family circumstances was published only recently, and it presented information by race-ethnicity for fathers in immigrant and native-born families, but not by country/region of origin for the foreign-born (Hernandez and Brandon, 2002). This chapter is intended to help the fill the gap in knowledge about immigrant fathers by presenting results based on new analyses of U.S. Census 2000 using the Integrated Public Use Microdata Series (IPUMS) 5 percent microdata file prepared by Ruggles et al. (2004). (For additional information regarding fathers not presented here go to www.albany.edu/csda/children).

The wide-ranging social and economic circumstances measured in Census 2000, combined with the large sample size, provide uniquely rich data for a demographic overview of immigrant fathers that is both broad in coverage and detailed in the number of origin countries for which estimates can be presented. Census 2000 also is limited, however, in one important respect. Because the census does not ask men the number of children they have fathered, it is possible to identify only those fathers who currently are living with their children. Since many children move away from home beginning about age eighteen years of age, and insofar as much public interest focuses on fathers with children in the dependent ages who live at home, this chapter presents a demographic portrait of fathers in families with at least one child ages zero to seventeen years old in the home.

Thus, the focus is on the 27 percent of men age fifteen years and over who have a child under age eighteen living at home, not the remaining 73 percent who do not live with a dependent child. In this chapter, men are included in the analysis as fathers if the child in the home is a biological, step, or adopted child, or if the child is the biological, step, or adopted child of the woman with whom the man is living as a cohabiting partner.

THE DEMOGRAPHIC TRANSFORMATION OF AMERICA

Because our interest in fathers derives from the fact that they are providing and caring for their children, the chapter begins by highlighting the profound demographic transformation that is leading to a new race-ethnic majority among children in America, and the implications of this transformation for all Americans. U.S. Census Bureau projections indicate that the proportion of children who are white, non-Hispanic will drop below 50 percent after 2030, less than twenty-five years from now (U.S. Census Bureau, 2004). The corresponding rise of the new American majority does not, however, reflect the emergence of one numerically dominant group, but instead a mosaic of diverse race-ethnic groups from around the world. By 2030, Census Bureau projections indicate for children that the proportions will be 26 percent Hispanic, 16 percent black, 5 percent Asian, and 4 percent Native American, Hawaiian, or other Pacific Islander.

This historic transformation is being driven by immigration and births to immigrants and their descendants. Following the previous enormous wave of immigration to the United States, by 1910 more than one-fourth of children (28 percent) had at least one foreign-born parent. Of these children in immigrant families, nearly all (97 percent) had parents with origins in Europe (87 percent) or Canada (10 percent) (Hernandez and Darke, 1999). Immigration then dropped sharply with the coming of the world wars and the Great Depression, and by 1960 only 6 percent of children lived in immigrant families.

Immigration rebounded again sharply beginning around 1965, bringing large numbers of immigrants to the United States, and the proportion of children in immigrant families climbed to 13 percent in 1990 and then 20 percent in 2000. In fact, between 1990 and 1997 alone, there was an increase of 47 percent in the number of children in immigrant families, compared to only 7 percent for children with U.S.-born parents (Hernandez and Charney, 1998). The most recent wave of immigration brought not only large numbers but also an enormous shift in the global origins of immigrants, and by 2000, only 14 percent of children in immigrant families had parents from Europe or Canada, while the vast majority (86 percent) had origins in Latin America (62 percent), Asia (22 percent), or Africa (2 percent).

The immigration-driven emergence of race-ethnic minorities as the majority population is occurring at all ages, but will occur first among children. In 2030, the baby-boom generation, which was born between 1946 and 1964, will be in the retirement ages of sixty-six to eighty-four years old. The Census Bureau projects that by 2030, 72 percent of these older adults will be non-Hispanic white compared to only 56 percent for working-age adults and 50 percent for children. Consequently, as the growing elderly population of the predominantly white baby-boom generation reaches retirement, it will become increasingly dependent for economic support on the productive activities and civic participation (e.g., voting) of working-age adults who are members of racial and ethnic minorities, many of whom as children will have grown up with immigrant fathers. The year 2030 may seem rather distant, but children ages zero to seventeen in 2008 will be in the prime working ages of twenty-two to thirty-nine in 2030. Thus, current immigrant and race-ethnic minority children will provide essential economic resources in support of the mainly non-Hispanic white baby boomers throughout their retirement years. The care and nurturing provided by immigrant fathers to their children is, therefore, important not only to these fathers and children, but also to the soon-to-retire baby-boom generation.

IMMIGRANT FATHERS ARE FROM AROUND THE WORLD

Insofar as one in five children (20 percent) lived in immigrant families in 2000, it is not surprising that a similarly high proportion of fathers in Census 2000 (18 percent) are immigrants, that is, men who were born in countries other than the United States. Among immigrant fathers, 36 percent were born in Mexico, while 7 percent were born in Central America, and 5 percent in South America, for a total of 48 percent from Latin America (see table 4.1). The Caribbean accounts for 8.8 percent of immigrant fathers, with roughly equal proportions from Cuba (2.2 percent), the Dominican Republic (2.0 percent), Haiti (1.4 percent), Jamaica (1.5 percent), and other English-speaking islands (1.7 percent). All together, then, nearly six in ten (56 percent) immigrant fathers were born in Latin America or the Caribbean.

Men born in Africa account for 3 percent of immigrant fathers, and of these three in five (1.8 percent) are black, and two in five (1.2 percent) are white or Asian. A similar proportion of fathers (1.9 percent) were born in the former Soviet Union, while other European countries, Canada, Australia, and New Zealand account for a total of 13.2 percent of immigrant fathers. Nearly twice as large is the proportion (25 percent) from Asia. About one-fifth of the immigrant fathers from Asia were born in Indochina

Table 4.1.   Percent and Number of Foreign-Born Fathers

Immigrant Country of Origin	Percent	Number
Foreign-Born Fathers	100.0	5,174,574
Mexico	36.1	1,867,357
Cuba	2.2	111,589
Central America	6.6	342,743
Dominican Rep	2.0	101,116
Haiti	1.4	70,681
Jamaica	1.5	75,181
Caribbean, English-Speaking	1.7	87,842
South America	4.8	246,812
Japan	1.0	53,627
Korea	1.9	96,859
China	2.7	137,320
Hong Kong	0.6	32,224
Taiwan	1.0	50,220
Philippines	3.6	186,333
Hmong	0.4	18,042
Cambodia	0.6	28,697
Laos	0.6	31,308
Thailand	0.3	13,019
Vietnam	3.4	174,993
Indochina, total	5.1	266,059
India	3.7	193,017
Pakistan/Bangladesh	1.3	64,912
Afghanistan	0.2	8,234
Iran	1.1	55,220
Iraq	0.4	18,295
Israel/Palestine	0.5	24,961
Other West Asia	1.7	87,514
Former USSR	1.9	96,405
Other Europe, Canada	13.2	680,536
Africa, Blacks	1.8	94,219
Africa, Whites	1.2	62,302
Other	1.2	62,966

a"Vietnam" includes Indochina not specified; "Other Europe, Canada" includes Australia and New Zealand; "Africa, Whites" includes Asian Africans.

Source: Calculated from Census 2000 5pct microdata (IPUMS) by Donald J. Hernandez, Nancy A. Denton, and Suzanne E. Macartney, Center for Social and Demographic Analysis, University at Albany, State University of New York, with funding from The William and Flora Hewlett Foundation.

(5.1 percent of all immigrant fathers), including Vietnam (3.4 percent), the Hmong, and others born in Cambodia, Laos, or Thailand. Additional Asian countries accounting for the largest proportions of immigrant fathers are India (3.7 percent), Philippines (3.6 percent), China (2.7 percent), and Korea (1.9 percent), while West Asian countries taken together account for 5.2 percent of foreign-born fathers.

Because immigrant fathers have origins in a very large number of countries, it is not possible to discuss results individually for most countries of origin. Detailed results are presented in the tables, while in the text we focus especially on thirteen country/region origin groups that are especially vulnerable because of their challenging social and economic circumstances. Among men in these thirteen groups, most from Mexico and Central America are Hispanics, most from Haiti are blacks, and most from the Dominican Republic are black Hispanics. We also distinguish blacks from Africa separately. Immigrants from Indochina and the Indian subcontinent typically classify themselves as Asian, while those from Afghanistan, Iraq, and the former Soviet Union mainly classify themselves as white. In the post-9/11 era, it is also important to note that those from Iraq, Afghanistan, Pakistan, and Bangladesh are mainly Muslim.

Most immigrants seek economic opportunities in the United States, but many also are driven from their homeland by war or by persecution because of their race, religion, nationality, or political opinion. The Vietnam War between 1965 and 1975 engulfed much of Indochina. The 1980s brought war to much of Central America. Iraq and Afghanistan also have suffered from wars and their sequelae for more than a quarter century (since 1980), and the dissolution of the Soviet Union in 1991 opened the West to many refugees. Immigrant fathers with these thirteen origins are especially likely to live in poverty.

Men with these thirteen origins account for 57 percent of all immigrant fathers in Census 2000. Because most immigrant fathers are race-ethnic minorities, and in view of the historical and current disadvantages experienced by many race-ethnic minority groups in the United States, results for immigrant fathers with these thirteen countries/regions of origin are placed in context by providing comparisons to native-born fathers in eight race-ethnic groups. These groups include five non-Hispanic race groups: 1) American Indians, including Alaskans; 2) Asians; 3) blacks; 4) native Hawaiian and other Pacific Islanders; and 5) whites, as well as three Hispanic groups who can be distinguished in the census as 1) Mexican; 2) mainland-origin Puerto Rican, that is, Puerto Rican origin and born in one of the fifty states; and 3) island-origin Puerto Rican, that is, born in Puerto Rico.

IMMIGRANT FATHERS ARE
SPREAD ACROSS THE UNITED STATES

It is well known that a few states account for most immigrants, but it also is important to note that the proportion of fathers who are immigrants is substantial in most states. The proportion of fathers who are foreign-born ranges from 20–49 percent in nine states (Arizona, California, Florida,

Hawaii, Illinois, Nevada, New Jersey, New York, and Texas) and the District of Columbia (see table 4.2). Further, the proportion is at least one in ten in ten additional states (Colorado, Connecticut, Georgia, Maryland, Massachusetts, Oregon, Rhode Island, Utah, Virginia, and Washington). In another sixteen states at least one in twenty fathers are immigrants. While one in twenty (5 percent) may not seem large, it is important to remember that the average student/teacher ratio in public primary, middle, and high schools across the United States (excluding Massachusetts and Tennessee) is in the range of 14.8–16.0 (National Center for Education Statistics, 2002). Thus, in places where 5–10 percent of children have an immigrant father, the average classroom will include one of these children. Many of these families have limited economic resources, speak a language other than English at home, and have fathers who are limited English proficient (see below).

Table 4.2.   Foreign-Born and Native-Born Fathers in the United States, Fifty States and the District of Columbia

	Within Each State: Percent of Fathers		Across States: Percent of Fathers	
	Foreign-Born	*Native-Born*	*Foreign-Born*	*Native-Born*
United States	17.8	82.2	100.0	100.0
Alabama	3.9	96.2	0.3	1.8
Alaska	9.0	91.0	0.1	0.3
Arizona	23.0	77.0	2.3	1.7
Arkansas	5.2	94.8	0.3	1.1
California	43.9	56.1	30.4	8.4
Colorado	14.5	85.5	1.3	1.7
Connecticut	15.4	84.6	1.1	1.3
Delaware	9.9	90.2	0.2	0.3
District of Columbia	24.6	75.4	0.1	0.1
Florida	25.3	74.7	7.2	4.6
Georgia	11.3	88.7	1.9	3.2
Hawaii	23.6	76.4	0.6	0.4
Idaho	8.9	91.1	0.3	0.6
Illinois	21.2	78.8	5.3	4.2
Indiana	5.0	95.0	0.6	2.6
Iowa	5.0	95.0	0.3	1.3
Kansas	8.6	91.4	0.5	1.1
Kentucky	3.1	97.0	0.3	1.8
Louisiana	4.9	95.1	0.4	1.8
Maine	4.0	96.0	0.1	0.5
Maryland	15.3	84.7	1.6	1.9
Massachusetts	18.0	82.0	2.2	2.1
Michigan	7.9	92.1	1.6	4.0
Missouri	4.5	95.5	0.5	2.3

	Within Each State: Percent of Fathers		Across States: Percent of Fathers	
	Foreign-Born	Native-Born	Foreign-Born	Native-Born
Montana	3.0	97.0	0.1	0.4
Nebraska	7.0	93.0	0.3	0.7
Nevada	26.8	73.2	1.1	0.6
New Hampshire	6.1	93.9	0.2	0.6
New Jersey	26.7	73.3	4.6	2.7
New Mexico	15.8	84.2	0.6	0.7
New York	29.0	71.0	10.1	5.4
North Carolina	8.7	91.3	1.4	3.1
North Dakota	2.9	97.1	0.0	0.3
Ohio	4.5	95.5	1.0	4.7
Oklahoma	6.9	93.1	0.5	1.4
Oregon	14.4	85.6	1.0	1.3
Pennsylvania	6.2	93.8	1.5	4.8
Rhode Island	18.5	81.5	0.4	0.3
South Carolina	5.2	94.8	0.4	1.6
South Dakota	3.3	96.7	0.1	0.3
Tennessee	4.7	95.3	0.5	2.3
Texas	25.0	75.0	11.2	7.3
Utah	10.5	89.5	0.6	1.0
Vermont	4.6	95.4	0.1	0.3
Virginia	12.9	87.1	1.8	2.7
Washington	16.1	83.9	2.0	2.2
West Virginia	1.9	98.1	0.1	0.8
Wisconsin	5.6	94.4	0.6	2.3
Wyoming	4.6	95.4	0.1	0.2

It also is well known that many immigrants live in the largest metropolitan areas, but it is perhaps less often recognized that many smaller metropolitan areas also have large and growing concentrations of immigrants. Moreover, many immigrants live in the rural portions of most states.

Immigrant fathers are concentrated in large cities. Only about one quarter of native-born fathers live in the ten largest Consolidated Metropolitan Statistical Areas (CMSAs) compared with 54 percent of immigrant fathers. The proportion of immigrant fathers is generally, but not always, higher in central cities than in suburban areas (see table 4.3). In the Los Angeles and San Francisco CMSAs, for example, 65 percent and 47 percent of fathers are immigrants but the proportion is also very high in suburban areas (47 percent and 39 percent, respectively). Many fathers in the central cities of the New York CMSA also are immigrants (54 percent), while the proportion in the suburbs is substantially lower (26 percent). In several of the largest CMSAs (Chicago, Boston, Dallas, and Houston), the levels are lower still, but the pattern of high concentration in central cities continues to hold

Table 4.3. Foreign-Born and Native-Born Fathers in the Ten Largest Consolidated Metropolitan Areas (CMSAs)

	CMSA Total		Percent of Fathers: Central City CMSA		Suburban CMSA	
Consolidated Metropolitan Area	Foreign-Born	Native-Born	Foreign-Born	Native-Born	Foreign-Born	Native-Born
New York, NY-Northeastern NJ/CT/PA	36.8	63.2	54.3	45.7	26.1	74.0
Los Angeles-Orange County, CA	53.0	47.0	64.7	35.3	47.1	52.9
Chicago-Gary-Kenosha, IL/IN/WI	28.1	71.9	42.2	57.9	22.4	77.6
Washington, DC/MD/VA	20.4	79.6	20.1	80.0	20.8	79.2
San Francisco-Oakland, CA	41.9	58.1	47.4	52.6	39.1	60.9
Philadelphia-Wilmington-Atlantic City, PA/NJ	11.1	88.9	16.4	83.6	9.8	90.3
Boston-Worcester-Lawrence, MA/NH/ME/CT	20.1	79.9	35.7	64.3	16.1	83.9
Detroit-Ann Arbor-Flint, MI	11.4	88.7	10.9	89.1	11.4	88.6
Dallas-Fort Worth, TX	26.6	73.4	36.2	63.8	19.7	80.3
Houston-Galveston-Brazoria, TX	33.1	66.9	49.6	50.4	24.7	75.3

true, while in others the proportion of fathers who are immigrants is greater in the suburbs than in the central cities (Washington-Baltimore at 21 percent vs. 20 percent, and Detroit at 11.4 percent vs. 10.9 percent).

Many smaller metropolitan areas also have high percentages of immigrant fathers. Immigrants account for 25 percent or more of all fathers in the non-metropolitan region of California, and in most metropolitan areas, with the exception of Sacramento (24 percent), Santa Rosa–Petaluma (23 percent), Chico (15 percent), San Luis Obispo (17 percent), and Redding (8 percent). The proportion of fathers who are foreign-born also reaches 20 percent or more in Honolulu, Hawaii; in Richland, Seattle, and Yakima, Washington; in Salem, Oregon; in Las Vegas and Reno, Nevada; in Phoenix, Tucson, and Yuma, Arizona; in seven of the twenty smaller metropolitan regions in Texas; in Bridgeport, Danbury, Stamford, and Waterbury, Connecticut; in Providence, Rhode Island; and in Fort Lauderdale, Miami-Hialeah, Naples, and West Palm Beach, Florida. Many additional metropolitan areas have smaller but substantial proportions (10–19 percent) of fathers who are immigrants.

Although rural regions in many states have smaller proportions of immigrant fathers, in twenty-one states 5 percent or more are foreign-born. In these rural regions, the corresponding number of children with an immigrant father is large enough that every other classroom will, on average, include a student who has a foreign-born father, or the average teacher might expect to encounter such a student every second year. This includes the rural regions of states often not thought of as magnets for immigrants, including Connecticut (9 percent), Delaware (8 percent), Georgia (7 percent), Idaho (9 percent), Kansas (8 percent), Nebraska (6 percent), New Hampshire (6 percent), North Carolina (6 percent), Oregon (9 percent), Rhode Island (10 percent), Utah (6 percent), and Vermont (6 percent). In fact, in the rural regions of only five states (Kentucky, Mississippi, Ohio, South Dakota, and West Virginia) do immigrant fathers account for fewer than 2.5 percent of all fathers, and only in these places will the average teacher have a student with an immigrant father in class less often than one year out of every four.

Thus, immigrant fathers (and their children) are highly concentrated in a few states and large metropolitan areas, but they also are spread widely in substantial numbers across many smaller metropolitan areas and the rural portions of most states.

HIGH POVERTY AMONG IMMIGRANT FATHERS

Economic resources are essential to provide for the necessities of life, and the official poverty measure is most commonly used to assess economic deprivation in the United States. The official poverty rate of fathers in Census 2000 was 7.5 percent, but the level of 15 percent for immigrant fathers is more than twice the level of 5.8 percent experienced by native-born fathers (see table 4.4). Poverty rates vary enormously, however, across groups. The official poverty rate for U.S.-born white and Asian fathers is 3–4 percent, while the rate doubles or triples to 8 percent for U.S.-born fathers who are Native Hawaiian and other Pacific Islander, and 12–16 percent for those who are black, Mexican, other Hispanic/Latino, mainland or island origin Puerto Rican, or Native American.

Official poverty rates range from 6–10 percent for immigrant fathers in about a half-dozen country/region of origin groups for which results are presented in table 4.4, but for the thirteen countries/regions of origin official poverty rates are at levels similar to or higher than experienced by most native-born race-ethnic groups, at 12–18 percent for Central America, Haiti, Laos, Vietnam, Pakistan/Bangladesh, the former Soviet Union, and blacks from Africa, and this rises further to the higher levels of 19–22 percent for the Dominican Republic, Cambodia, Afghanistan, and Iraq, 24 percent for Mexico, and 31 percent for the Hmong.

Although the official poverty measure is most often used to assess economic need, this measure has come under increasing criticism because it has been updated since 1965 only for inflation, but not for increases in the real standard of living, and because it does not take into account the local cost of living, which varies greatly across the United States (Citro and Michael, 1995; Hernandez, Denton, and Macartney, 2007a). A new alternative measure, referred to as the "basic budget poverty rate," provides a more complete picture of economic need in the United States by taking into account the local cost of food, housing, transportation for parents to commute to work, childcare/early education, and health care as well as federal taxes and the Earned Income Tax Credit (Bernstein, Brocht, and Spade-Aguilar, 2000; Boushey, Brocht, Gundersen, and Bernstein, 2001; Hernandez et al., 2007a).

Compared to official rates, basic budget poverty rates for white and Asian fathers born in the United States are 11–14 percentage points higher, at 14–18 percent vs. 3–4 percent. The differences are still larger for other native race-ethnic groups in the range of 22–31 percent, with corresponding basic budget poverty levels of 35–40 percent for most groups, and 47 percent for island-origin Puerto Ricans. Difference between the basic budget and official rates are similar at 23–33 percent for many of the thirteen immigrant country of origin groups, but this rises to the much higher level of 35–44 percent for immigrant fathers with the highest poverty rates, that is, fathers who are Hmong or from Mexico, Central America, the Dominican Republic, Haiti, and Afghanistan. Fathers with these six origins have basic budget poverty rates of 53–75 percent, while the rates are lower but quite

Table 4.4. Percentage of Fathers of Children, Ages Zero to Seventeen, in Poverty by Immigrant Country or Race-Ethnic Origin

	Official Poverty[a]	Deep Official Poverty[b]	Near Official Poverty[c]	Basic Budget Poverty[d]	Basic Budget Poverty[e]	Basic Budget Poverty[f]	Basic Budget Poverty[g]	Basic Budget Poverty[h]
Total	**7.5**	**2.6**	**23.9**	**25.8**	**5.4**	**9.4**	**12.2**	**20.6**
Fathers: All Native-Born	*5.8*	*2.1*	*20.2*	*21.3*	*3.9*	*6.7*	*8.9*	*16.4*
White	4.4	1.4	17.1	17.9	2.7	4.9	6.7	13.4
Black	12.3	5.1	33.5	34.6	8.9	14.2	17.9	27.9
Puerto Rican, Mainland origin	12.1	4.7	32.3	39.8	10.3	16.8	20.8	33.5
Puerto Rican, Island origin	16.4	6.9	41.7	47.2	14.5	22.6	27.3	39.6
Mexican	11.9	4.1	36.4	38.8	7.8	14.3	18.7	31.3
Other Hispanic/Latino	11.1	4.1	34.5	36.9	7.5	13.3	17.8	29.6
Asian	3.1	1.3	11.2	14.1	2.8	5.4	6.9	11.6
Hawaiian/Pacific Islander	8.3	2.6	27.4	35.8	8.1	15.5	19.3	29.3
Native American	15.1	5.7	39.8	39.4	9.7	15.9	20.5	31.8
Fathers: All Foreign-Born	*15.1*	*5.1*	*41.0*	*47.0*	*12.6*	*22.1*	*27.4*	*39.9*
Mexico	23.5	7.1	62.1	67.4	17.9	32.0	40.3	58.3
Central America	16.3	4.8	49.8	59.1	14.6	27.3	34.3	50.2
Cuba	10.8	4.0	31.9	35.6	9.3	16.3	20.9	28.3

(continues)

Table 4.4. *(continued)*

	Official Poverty[a]	Deep Official Poverty[b]	Near Official Poverty[c]	Basic Budget Poverty[d]	Basic Budget Poverty[e]	Basic Budget Poverty[f]	Basic Budget Poverty[g]	Basic Budget Poverty[h]
Dominican Republic	19.3	7.3	51.1	63.0	19.6	32.2	39.2	54.5
Haiti	14.8	5.7	43.2	53.3	14.1	25.0	30.6	44.6
Jamaica	7.3	3.3	24.7	33.5	7.4	13.5	17.2	27.2
Caribbean, English-Speaking	8.7	4.2	26.9	37.0	8.7	15.5	19.1	29.4
South America	11.1	4.1	33.6	42.9	10.8	19.4	24.0	35.4
Japan	4.6	2.4	14.0	17.5	4.1	6.6	7.8	13.6
Korea	11.9	6.9	30.9	37.9	12.3	20.2	23.7	32.4
China	11.5	3.4	31.1	37.8	11.6	20.0	24.7	32.3
Hong Kong	6.0	2.2	18.1	23.1	6.4	11.6	13.9	19.8
Taiwan	5.1	2.4	14.5	17.3	5.4	8.5	10.4	13.9
Philippines	3.5	1.2	14.6	20.0	3.3	6.7	8.9	15.5
Hmong	31.2	11.1	69.3	74.5	26.5	37.6	43.3	68.9
Cambodia	20.6	7.4	44.7	49.9	19.2	29.1	32.5	42.3
Laos	18.4	6.3	44.8	48.4	14.1	22.6	27.0	41.2
Thailand	8.7	4.1	27.2	32.8	6.7	14.0	16.4	26.0
Vietnam[i]	13.7	4.4	35.2	41.5	13.0	20.9	25.3	34.4
India	5.5	2.3	16.2	19.6	5.2	8.9	10.9	16.2
Pakistan/Bangladesh	17.4	5.7	41.0	47.0	17.0	26.8	31.6	41.4

	[a]	[b]	[c]	[d]	[e]	[f]	[g]	[h]
Afghanistan	22.3	7.6	47.7	57.4	21.7	33.4	37.5	51.7
Iran	8.0	3.4	19.3	23.6	7.6	12.0	14.6	19.4
Iraq	20.4	8.1	44.0	47.1	17.1	26.1	28.8	39.1
Israel/Palestine	11.7	5.3	24.7	31.6	11.6	16.0	18.7	27.0
Other West Asia	13.6	5.9	32.3	38.8	12.3	19.7	22.8	33.3
Former USSR	16.1	5.7	33.7	39.3	14.7	22.1	25.2	33.8
Other Europe, Canada[i]	5.2	2.3	16.9	20.9	4.5	7.6	9.8	16.4
Africa, Blacks	12.0	5.3	32.1	40.6	11.1	18.1	22.0	34.7
Africa, Whites[j]	7.6	3.5	20.8	25.2	7.1	11.7	13.8	21.3
Other	11.0	5.2	30.9	36.2	10.4	17.7	21.3	30.7

[a] below 100% of threshold
[b] below 50% of threshold
[c] below 200% of threshold
[d] Basic Budget Poverty is based on all costs for a decent standard of living, including food, housing, other necessities, transportation for work, childcare, and health insurance.
[e] based on food & housing
[f] based on food, housing & other necessities
[g] based on food, housing, other necessities & transportation
[h] based on food, housing, other necessities, transportation & childcare
[i] "Other Europe, Canada" includes Australia and New Zealand; "Africa, Whites" includes Asian Africans.
[j] "Vietnam" includes Indochina not specified; "Other Europe, Canada" includes Australia and New Zealand; "Africa, Whites" includes Asian Africans.

Calculated from Census 2000 5% microdata (IPUMS) by Donald J. Hernandez, Nancy A. Denton, and Suzanne E. Macartney, Center for Social and Demographic Analysis, University at Albany, State University of New York, with funding from The William and Flora Hewlett Foundation.

high at 39–50 percent for the remaining seven immigrant origin groups. Fathers with these levels of family income lack resources to fully pay the cost of decent housing, food, clothing, and high quality childcare and early education, as well as for books and other educational resources.

STRONG FAMILIES AMONG IMMIGRANT FATHERS

Families provide not only economic resources but also critical human resources that sustain and nurture entire families, including fathers and children. Thus, family composition, reflected in the presence of a mother, the number of siblings, and the presence and number of other relatives and non-relatives in the home, has important implications for immigrant fathers and their children. In this regard, immigrant families have valuable strengths.

The presence of two parents in the home tends to confer, on average, an advantage in the educational success of children, compared to those with one parent in the home (Cherlin, 1999; McLanahan and Sandefur, 1994). About nineteen of every twenty immigrant fathers (95 percent) live in a two-parent family, similar to the proportion among native-born fathers (94 percent), and there is little variation across groups. The proportion of immigrant fathers living in two-parent families is in the narrow range of 93–98 percent for most groups studied here, and the proportion is slightly less at 90–92 percent only for immigrant fathers from the Dominican Republic, Haiti, Jamaica, and the English-speaking Caribbean, and those who are blacks from Africa (see table 4.5). The range is slightly lower for various race-ethnic groups of native-born fathers (88–95 percent). Thus, immigrant and native-born fathers living with children are similar in their commitment to two-parent family living.

Immigrant fathers are, however, substantially more likely to live in a three-generation family, including a parent (or wife's parent), thereby providing a grandparental presence in the home for his children. Overall, immigrant fathers are about twice as likely as native-born fathers to have such a grandparent in the home (13 percent vs. 6 percent) (see table 4.5). Among native-born fathers the proportion varies from 4 percent for whites to 10–14 percent for most race-ethnic minorities, to a high of 17 percent for native Hawaiian and other Pacific Islanders. The variation is even greater across immigrant groups. Among the thirteen high poverty immigrant groups, the proportion with a grandparent in the home rises from 8 percent for immigrant fathers who are from Afghanistan or are blacks from Africa to 12–15 percent for those from Mexico, Central America, the Dominican Republic, Haiti, Vietnam, Pakistan/Bangladesh, Iraq, and the former Soviet Union, to 21–24 percent for Cambodia, Laos, and the Hmong.

Table 4.5. Family Composition in the Home: Fathers of Children, Ages Zero to Seventeen, by Immigrant Country or Race-Ethnic Origin

	Two-Parent Family	Father-Only Family	4+ Own Children 0–17	2+ Nuclear Families[a]	Grandparent	"Responsible" Grandparent[b]	Child 0–17 Other Than Own Child	Other Adult Relative	Non-Relative
						Percent of Fathers by Presence of Another Parent or Other Household Members:			
Total	**94.1**	**5.9**	**5.9**	**0.5**	**6.9**	**2.0**	**4.5**	**16.7**	**3.5**
Fathers: All Native-Born	*93.9*	*6.1*	*5.3*	*0.3*	*5.7*	*1.8*	*3.5*	*13.8*	*2.7*
White	94.9	5.1	4.9	0.2	4.2	1.1	2.4	12.5	2.3
Black	87.6	12.4	6.8	0.5	11.9	5.6	8.8	19.7	4.1
Puerto Rican, Mainland origin	91.5	8.5	5.7	0.6	11.2	3.8	6.1	15.8	4.1
Puerto Rican, Island origin	93.4	6.6	6.9	0.6	10.3	3.1	8.1	25.5	4.6
Mexican	91.0	9.0	7.2	1.9	13.7	4.4	9.3	20.5	4.8
Other Hispanic/Latino	91.6	8.4	6.6	1.1	11.7	4.1	7.2	17.4	4.0
Asian	94.6	5.4	2.9	0.8	11.7	2.6	3.5	14.3	3.0
Hawaiian/Pacific Islander	88.8	11.2	9.3	1.9	16.7	3.8	8.6	24.2	6.2
Native American	89.3	10.7	8.8	0.8	10.3	4.9	7.9	18.9	4.5
Fathers: All Foreign-Born	*95.0*	*5.0*	*8.6*	*1.3*	*12.8*	*2.7*	*9.2*	*29.7*	*7.4*
Mexico	94.6	5.4	13.5	2.5	13.4	3.5	16.4	39.7	11.3

(continues)

Table 4.5. *(continued)*

	Two-Parent Family	Father-Only Family	4+ Own Children 0–17	2+ Nuclear Families[a]	Grandparent	"Responsible" Grandparent[b]	Child 0–17 Other Than Own Child	Other Adult Relative	Non-Relative
	Percent of Fathers by Presence of Another Parent or Other Household Members:								
Central America	93.3	6.7	7.4	1.4	13.9	3.2	12.3	35.5	14.2
Cuba	95.3	4.7	3.5	0.5	14.2	2.2	4.2	20.2	4.9
Dominican Republic	92.1	7.9	6.2	1.0	15.2	4.0	9.4	32.6	8.1
Haiti	92.0	8.0	10.9	0.7	14.7	2.7	9.4	36.3	7.5
Jamaica	90.2	9.8	5.8	0.5	13.5	4.0	9.1	28.0	4.9
Caribbean, English-Speaking	91.8	8.2	5.0	0.4	13.3	3.1	6.1	27.4	4.6
South America	94.6	5.4	4.0	0.9	11.7	2.2	7.1	27.4	9.1
Japan	95.9	4.1	4.0	0.2	3.7	0.8	1.3	8.8	2.4
Korea	97.0	3.0	0.7	0.1	12.5	1.6	1.6	17.5	1.8
China	96.6	3.4	1.7	0.6	19.7	4.0	3.4	19.0	3.9
Hong Kong	98.1	1.9	2.0	0.1	16.6	2.8	1.0	16.8	1.8
Taiwan	97.2	2.8	1.1	0.1	13.4	1.2	1.5	14.7	2.7
Philippines	95.7	4.3	4.4	1.4	23.4	3.2	7.0	31.6	6.6
Hmong	96.7	3.3	59.1	1.3	23.5	3.2	13.0	38.9	3.1
Cambodia	94.9	5.1	14.7	2.3	23.5	5.3	12.1	42.0	7.4
Laos	92.6	7.4	18.8	2.1	20.9	4.4	12.0	36.3	5.5

Thailand	92.6	7.4	3.9	1.2	12.5	2.1	6.3	26.8	4.1
Vietnam[c]	95.8	4.2	7.8	0.8	15.8	3.0	5.7	33.1	5.7
India	98.0	2.0	1.6	0.5	15.3	1.4	2.4	18.3	1.8
Pakistan/ Bangladesh	96.9	3.1	9.1	0.8	12.5	1.6	4.3	25.7	3.8
Afghanistan	95.8	4.2	12.6	1.2	8.1	0.7	5.1	32.2	3.1
Iran	96.6	3.4	2.8	0.1	10.5	1.1	1.2	20.3	2.0
Iraq	96.8	3.2	13.3	0.7	13.1	3.1	4.4	31.2	1.7
Israel/Palestine	97.7	2.3	12.3	0.4	3.1	0.7	1.9	16.8	2.7
Other West Asia	96.7	3.3	8.6	0.4	10.3	1.5	2.9	19.2	3.0
Former USSR	96.8	3.2	7.1	0.3	12.2	1.9	1.6	19.4	1.7
Other Europe, Canada[c]	96.2	3.8	4.5	0.2	5.7	1.0	1.8	15.9	2.3
Africa, Blacks	91.9	8.1	11.9	0.2	7.6	1.4	5.3	24.8	5.5
Africa, Whites[c]	97.1	2.9	5.1	0.1	7.6	1.1	1.6	17.5	2.3
Other	95.2	4.8	7.4	0.5	12.7	2.4	5.2	23.7	4.3

[a] A nuclear family consists of at least one child and the child's parent(s).

[b] Grandparents who have primary responsibility for the care of their grandchildren.

[c] "Vietnam" includes Indochina not specified; "Other Europe, Canada" includes Australia and New Zealand; "Africa, Whites" includes Asian Africans.

Calculated from Census 2000 5% microdata (IPUMS) by Donald J. Hernandez, Nancy A. Denton, and Suzanne E. Macartney, Center for Social and Demographic Analysis, University at Albany, State University of New York, with funding from The William and Flora Hewlett Foundation.

Grandparents in the home can provide essential childcare, nurturing, and economic resources, and this can be especially important in families with larger numbers of children. The vast majority of both immigrant and native-born fathers, at least 81 percent in various groups, have comparatively small families with one to three children ages zero to seventeen years in the home, with the exception of the Hmong, among whom only 41 percent have such small families (see table 4.5). There is, nevertheless, noteworthy variation across groups in the proportion with larger families with four or more children. Aside from the Hmong, immigrant fathers most likely to have large families (10–19 percent) are from Mexico, Haiti, Cambodia, Laos, Afghanistan, Iraq, Israel/Palestine, and blacks from Africa.

Brothers and sisters can be a liability but also an asset from the perspective of an individual child. Children in larger families must share available resources, such as parents' time and financial resources, with that larger number of siblings, and they tend, on average, to be less successful in their education outcomes, including completing fewer years of school (Blake, 1985, 1989; Hernandez, 1986). But older children also can serve as childcare providers for younger siblings, as companions for siblings of similar age, and as a support network throughout life. Thus, larger families must spread resources more thinly, but they also have greater human resources to share.

Moreover, the three country/regional groups with the highest proportions in large families (Cambodia, Laos, and the Hmong) also are among the four most likely to have a grandparent in the home. Looking more broadly at household composition, five of the nine country/region origin groups most likely to have four or more siblings in the home are also most likely to have at least one additional adult relative in the home, and three of them are among those with high proportions (7–14 percent) with non-relatives in the home. Thus, while immigrant fathers from many of the thirteen country/region of origin groups with high poverty rates tend to have larger families with four or more children zero to seventeen years of age, immigrant fathers with these origins tend to have families with grandparents, other adult relatives, or non-relatives in the home, who are potential sources of additional income for the families and of childcare and nurturing for the dependent children in the home.

IMMIGRANT FATHERS AND FAMILIES IN HIGH POVERTY GROUPS HAVE A STRONG COMMITMENT TO WORK

A large majority of immigrant fathers in the thirteen high poverty immigrant groups work for pay (see table 4.6). The largest group, immigrant fathers from Mexico, have a basic budget poverty rate of 67 percent, despite the very high 92 percent who worked during the past year, a proportion working nearly as high as the 96–97 percent experienced by white and Asian

Table 4.6: Part 1. Employment of Fathers of Children, Ages Zero to Seventeen, by Immigrant Country or Race-Ethnic Origin

	Father Works Full-Time[a]	Father Works Part-Time[a]	Father No Work	Wife Works Full-Time[a]	Wife Works Part-Time[a]	Wife No Work	Other Adult Worker in Home[b]
				Percent of Fathers:			
Total	**78.6**	**15.7**	**5.6**	**38.5**	**35.5**	**26.0**	**15.5**
Fathers: All							
Native-Born	*80.5*	*14.3*	*5.2*	*39.8*	*36.9*	*23.2*	*13.6*
White	83.2	12.9	3.9	38.6	38.0	23.4	13.1
Black	66.6	20.5	12.9	51.8	30.8	17.4	15.2
Puerto Rican, Mainland origin	71.7	18.5	9.8	41.0	31.9	27.1	14.2
Puerto Rican, Island origin	64.8	18.7	16.4	37.3	30.3	32.4	18.7
Mexican	72.4	20.0	7.5	38.6	33.0	28.4	19.4
Other Hispanic/ Latino	72.8	19.7	7.5	38.8	34.4	26.8	16.3
Asian	81.6	14.2	4.3	43.9	32.6	23.5	15.3
Hawaiian/Pacific Islander	68.4	21.6	10.0	45.0	31.0	24.0	24.2
Native American	63.6	24.6	11.7	38.4	36.7	24.9	15.1
Fathers: All							
Foreign-Born	*70.0*	*22.4*	*7.6*	*32.5*	*29.0*	*38.5*	*24.3*
Mexico	64.6	27.4	8.0	23.7	28.4	47.9	32.9

(continues)

Table 4.6: Part 1. *(continued)*

	Father Works Full-Time[a]	Father Works Part-Time[a]	Father No Work	Wife Works Full-Time[a]	Wife Works Part-Time[a]	Wife No Work	Other Adult Worker in Home[b]
				Percent of Fathers:			
Central America	68.3	24.5	7.1	31.9	30.5	37.6	32.5
Cuba	73.7	18.4	7.9	42.4	28.3	29.3	18.0
Dominican Republic	61.0	24.7	14.4	34.3	31.0	34.7	24.6
Haiti	66.9	20.7	12.4	50.2	27.6	22.2	23.4
Jamaica	70.6	19.6	9.8	55.3	28.4	16.3	21.5
Caribbean, English-Speaking	72.6	18.6	8.8	48.9	24.8	26.3	20.4
South America	71.8	21.8	6.3	33.2	31.7	35.1	23.9
Japan	81.1	15.3	3.6	26.8	24.9	48.2	8.8
Korea	67.9	23.3	8.8	31.7	24.2	44.1	10.5
China	71.6	21.7	6.7	44.7	26.9	28.5	16.5
Hong Kong	79.2	16.6	4.2	42.3	27.3	30.3	12.8
Taiwan	80.1	13.9	6.0	41.2	23.9	35.0	9.9
Philippines	74.9	18.4	6.6	59.0	25.3	15.6	29.0
Hmong	56.9	19.7	23.4	33.9	27.1	39.0	22.4
Cambodia	61.0	18.4	20.6	43.0	21.2	35.9	26.8
Laos	64.2	19.2	16.5	46.5	22.4	31.1	27.4
Thailand	74.8	17.1	8.1	45.0	29.2	25.8	19.0

Vietnam[c]	70.3	19.8	9.9	41.6	26.8	31.6	26.0
India	80.1	15.7	4.1	35.9	25.1	39.0	14.4
Pakistan/ Bangladesh	71.1	23.7	5.2	17.8	22.7	59.5	17.4
Afghanistan	60.2	27.8	12.0	20.7	27.7	51.5	19.6
Iran	77.8	15.7	6.5	29.4	33.2	37.3	12.6
Iraq	65.6	19.9	14.5	23.1	27.3	49.6	21.4
Israel/Palestine	78.5	15.8	5.7	23.1	31.8	45.1	10.0
Other West Asia	72.9	18.9	8.2	22.7	26.4	50.9	12.4
Former USSR	65.2	23.9	10.9	37.3	29.7	33.0	14.7
Other Europe, Canada[c]	79.3	15.9	4.7	34.3	34.3	31.4	14.3
Africa, Blacks	68.1	24.6	7.3	42.7	32.6	24.7	16.2
Africa, Whites[c]	77.4	17.8	4.8	31.2	31.8	37.0	11.9
Other	70.9	20.5	8.6	38.7	29.4	31.8	16.1

[a]Full-time indicates the person works 35 hours per week or more, 48 weeks a year or more; part-time indicates less than full-time.
[b]Adult workers are age 18 or more, earning $2500 per year or more.
[c]"Vietnam" includes Indochina not specified; "Other Europe, Canada" includes Australia and New Zealand; "Africa, Whites" includes Asian Africans.

Calculated from Census 2000 5% microdata (IPUMS) by Donald J. Hernandez, Nancy A. Denton, and Suzanne E. Macartney, Center for Social and Demographic Analysis, University at Albany, State University of New York, with funding from The William and Flora Hewlett Foundation.

Table 4.6: Part 2. Employment of Fathers of Children, Ages Zero to Seventeen, by Immigrant Country or Race-Ethnic Origin

	Percent of Married Fathers with:							
	Father Full-Time, Wife Full-Time[a]	Father Full-Time, Wife Part-Time[a]	Father Full-Time, Wife Not Working[a]	Father Part-Time, Wife Full-Time[a]	Father Part-Time, Wife Part-Time[a]	Father Part-Time, Wife Not Working[a]	Father Not Working, Wife Working	Neither Spouse Working
Total	**32.0**	**27.8**	**19.9**	**4.8**	**6.4**	**4.2**	**3.1**	**2.0**
Fathers: All Native-Born	*33.3*	*29.7*	*18.5*	*4.8*	*6.0*	*3.1*	*3.0*	*1.6*
White	32.9	31.5	19.5	4.3	5.5	2.8	2.4	1.2
Black	39.5	19.4	10.4	8.1	8.3	3.5	7.3	3.5
Puerto Rican, Mainland origin	32.9	22.2	18.6	5.5	7.3	5.0	5.0	3.5
Puerto Rican, Island origin	28.5	19.1	18.5	5.2	7.5	5.8	7.3	8.2
Mexican	31.1	23.4	19.6	5.5	8.0	5.9	3.6	2.9
Other Hispanic/Latino	31.3	24.4	18.8	5.6	8.4	5.2	3.6	2.8
Asian	37.2	26.4	18.9	5.3	5.2	3.3	2.5	1.2
Hawaiian/Pacific Islander	33.4	20.3	16.9	7.9	8.7	4.4	5.8	2.7
Native American	27.8	22.9	14.8	7.3	10.7	5.9	6.4	4.1
Fathers: All Foreign-Born	*25.7*	*19.1*	*25.8*	*4.9*	*8.3*	*9.0*	*3.5*	*3.7*
Mexico	18.2	16.7	30.3	4.1	9.9	13.2	3.2	4.3

Central America	24.5	19.4	25.0	5.5	9.6	9.3	3.5	3.2
Cuba	35.0	19.4	20.1	5.2	7.3	5.8	3.8	3.4
Dominican Republic	23.7	17.4	20.9	7.0	9.8	7.6	7.4	6.2
Haiti	36.9	16.4	14.0	8.2	8.6	4.1	7.6	4.1
Jamaica	42.2	18.8	10.7	9.3	6.9	2.8	6.5	2.7
Caribbean, English-Speaking	37.9	17.2	18.8	7.1	5.9	4.9	5.6	2.6
South America	26.6	21.3	24.4	5.1	9.0	7.5	2.8	3.3
Japan	23.2	20.2	37.9	2.6	3.9	8.8	1.9	1.6
Korea	25.9	15.3	26.8	4.0	7.7	11.5	3.0	5.8
China	35.6	16.8	19.5	6.5	8.5	6.4	4.1	2.5
Hong Kong	35.7	20.7	23.1	5.3	6.0	5.2	2.0	2.1
Taiwan	36.0	18.1	26.3	3.3	4.8	5.7	2.9	3.0
Philippines	47.3	16.8	11.3	8.3	7.2	2.8	4.9	1.6
Hmong	27.0	15.5	14.8	4.9	7.8	6.7	5.8	17.6
Cambodia	35.7	12.0	14.0	5.2	6.8	6.3	4.5	15.6
Laos	37.5	13.7	14.0	6.2	6.3	6.5	5.2	10.7
Thailand	36.8	20.6	18.5	5.4	6.8	4.7	4.6	2.5
Vietnam[b]	34.3	16.2	20.1	4.9	8.4	6.4	4.6	5.1
India	30.4	19.3	30.6	4.1	5.1	6.5	2.1	1.9
Pakistan/Bangladesh	14.5	15.5	41.4	2.5	6.4	14.5	1.6	3.6
Afghanistan	14.5	17.7	29.3	2.9	9.3	14.9	4.0	7.3
Iran	23.7	26.5	28.2	4.2	5.3	5.8	3.0	3.4
Iraq	17.2	18.9	29.9	3.8	6.8	9.1	3.7	10.6
Israel/Palestine	19.4	24.7	34.7	2.6	5.9	7.1	2.3	3.2

(continues)

Table 4.6: Part 2. *(continued)*

	Percent of Married Fathers with:							
	Father Full-Time, Wife Full-Time[a]	Father Full-Time, Wife Part-Time[a]	Father Full-Time, Wife Not Working[a]	Father Part-Time, Wife Full-Time[a]	Father Part-Time, Wife Part-Time[a]	Father Part-Time, Wife Not Working[a]	Father Not Working, Wife Working	Neither Spouse Working
Other West Asia	18.3	19.8	35.4	3.2	5.0	10.5	2.9	4.9
Former USSR	29.3	18.3	17.9	6.1	8.8	9.0	4.6	6.0
Other Europe, Canada[b]	28.2	26.7	24.9	4.6	6.5	4.6	2.7	1.9
Africa, Blacks	32.3	20.7	15.9	8.0	10.4	6.0	3.9	2.8
Africa, Whites[b]	25.0	24.7	27.8	4.3	6.4	7.2	2.6	2.1
Other	30.4	19.9	21.1	6.2	7.5	6.9	4.1	3.9

[a]Full-time indicates the person works 35 hours per week or more, 48 weeks a year or more; part-time indicates less than full-time.
[b]"Vietnam" includes Indochina not specified; "Other Europe, Canada" includes Australia and New Zealand; "Africa, Whites" includes Asian Africans.

Calculated from Census 2000 5% microdata (IPUMS) by Donald J. Hernandez, Nancy A. Denton, and Suzanne E. Macartney, Center for Social and Demographic Analysis, University at Albany, State University of New York, with funding from The William and Flora Hewlett Foundation.

Table 4.6: Part 3. Employment of Fathers of Children, Ages Zero to Seventeen, by Immigrant Country or Race-Ethnic Origin

	Percent of Single Fathers:				Percent of All Fathers:		
	Father Works More Than Full-Time[a]	Father Works Full-Time or More[b]	Father Works Part-Time[b]	Father Does Not Work	Father Works More Than Full-Time[a]	Wife Works More Than Full-Time[a]	Both Spouses Work More Than Full-Time[a]
Total	**17.3**	**63.0**	**22.3**	**14.8**	**28.1**	**5.0**	**2.2**
Fathers: All Native-Born	*17.9*	*63.7*	*21.5*	*14.8*	*29.8*	*5.2*	*2.3*
White	21.6	70.8	19.4	9.8	32.5	5.4	2.5
Black	9.3	46.8	25.1	28.1	16.5	4.5	1.6
Puerto Rican, Mainland origin	8.8	49.7	26.5	23.8	19.4	3.4	1.3
Puerto Rican, Island origin	10.4	47.6	22.8	29.6	15.5	3.2	1.1
Mexican	11.9	55.8	26.6	17.6	19.7	3.6	1.4
Other Hispanic/Latino	12.4	54.6	25.8	19.6	21.9	4.1	1.7
Asian	16.0	64.7	20.9	14.4	26.7	6.2	2.7
Hawaiian/Pacific Islander	8.1	51.2	26.8	22.0	17.7	6.0	1.9
Native American	12.4	47.4	31.1	21.5	20.0	4.3	1.7
Fathers: All Foreign-Born	*13.7*	*58.8*	*26.5*	*14.8*	*20.3*	*4.0*	*1.8*
Mexico	10.8	53.5	30.1	16.4	14.2	2.1	0.8

(continues)

Table 4.6: Part 3. *(continued)*

	Percent of Single Fathers:				Percent of All Fathers:		
	Father Works More Than Full-Time[a]	Father Works Full-Time or More[b]	Father Works Part-Time[b]	Father Does Not Work	Father Works More Than Full-Time[a]	Wife Works More Than Full-Time[a]	Both Spouses Work More Than Full-Time[a]
Central America	10.9	60.7	26.1	13.1	15.5	2.9	1.1
Cuba	12.8	58.8	19.8	21.4	24.8	5.2	2.4
Dominican Republic	10.4	48.3	28.1	23.6	14.6	3.2	1.0
Haiti	8.6	62.6	17.7	19.7	12.1	3.3	0.7
Jamaica	11.0	60.9	24.9	14.2	17.1	5.6	1.7
Caribbean, English-Speaking	9.9	57.3	26.8	15.9	16.8	4.7	1.7
South America	15.1	63.4	25.4	11.2	23.9	4.0	1.9
Japan	25.3	77.9	15.2	6.9	35.1	4.2	1.7
Korea	24.6	64.6	24.5	10.9	32.2	8.7	6.0
China	20.3	64.6	27.1	8.3	20.1	7.4	4.1
Hong Kong	13.2	63.3	27.5	9.2	24.9	6.8	3.1
Taiwan	12.9	70.8	18.1	11.1	24.7	6.6	3.9
Philippines	9.8	65.6	23.2	11.2	12.2	5.4	1.3
Hmong	2.5	46.7	29.1	24.2	5.7	2.3	1.2
Cambodia	10.7	49.3	20.4	30.3	12.1	5.1	3.0
Laos	9.2	52.8	22.9	24.3	10.2	4.8	2.0
Thailand	11.9	60.9	19.2	19.9	21.1	6.0	2.4
Vietnam[c]	14.1	63.5	21.9	14.6	17.3	6.5	3.4

India	21.4	67.3	22.2	10.4	26.7	5.4	3.3
Pakistan/ Bangladesh	25.1	59.4	34.3	6.3	26.4	2.5	1.6
Afghanistan	5.3	31.3	42.7	26.0	19.3	4.1	0.9
Iran	22.6	61.2	28.6	10.3	37.3	5.3	3.2
Iraq	5.5	51.2	26.7	22.1	22.4	3.8	2.0
Israel/Palestine	17.2	64.9	21.9	13.2	39.9	4.1	2.6
Other West Asia	21.0	59.3	23.2	17.5	30.9	4.0	2.0
Former USSR	14.4	53.8	25.9	20.4	19.7	4.6	2.1
Other Europe, Canada[c]	24.8	69.3	22.2	8.5	33.9	5.6	2.9
Africa, Blacks	15.2	59.1	27.3	13.5	17.9	4.5	2.0
Africa, Whites[c]	28.1	75.1	17.1	7.8	33.5	5.7	2.9
Other	14.4	58.7	21.1	20.3	24.6	7.0	4.0

[a] More than full-time indicates the person works 50 hours per week or more, 48 weeks per year or more.
[b] Full-time indicates the person works 35 hours per week or more, 48 weeks per year or more; part-time indicates less than full-time.
[c] "Vietnam" includes Indochina not specified; "Other Europe, Canada" includes Australia and New Zealand; "Africa, Whites" includes Asian Africans.

Calculated from Census 2000 5% microdata (IPUMS) by Donald J. Hernandez, Nancy A. Denton, and Suzanne E. Macartney, Center for Social and Demographic Analysis, University at Albany, State University of New York, with funding from The William and Flora Hewlett Foundation.

Table 4.6: Part 4. Employment of Fathers of Children, Ages Zero to Seventeen, by Immigrant Country or Race-Ethnic Origin

	Percent of Fathers Employed Full-Time[a]				Percent of Wives Employed Full-Time[a]			
	Father H.S. Grad	Father Not H.S. Grad	Father English Fluent	Father Limited English Proficient (LEP)	Wife H.S. Grad	Wife Not H.S. Grad	Wife English Fluent	Wife Limited English Proficient (LEP)
Total	**82.2**	**60.5**	**80.4**	**63.8**	**40.8**	**24.8**	**40.0**	**27.0**
Fathers: All Native Born	*83.2*	*60.1*	*80.7*	*63.9*	*41.2*	*26.4*	*40.0*	*31.2*
White	85.2	65.1	83.3	75.8	39.6	26.4	38.6	33.7
Black	71.5	45.4	66.6	63.8	55.0	31.4	51.9	43.0
Puerto Rican, Mainland origin	77.1	53.7	72.5	64.5	44.8	23.7	42.4	32.4
Puerto Rican, Island origin	72.7	51.5	70.5	56.1	42.4	25.4	42.0	29.4
Mexican	77.9	58.1	74.0	61.5	44.0	22.6	41.0	25.9
Other Hispanic/Latino	77.9	56.1	73.9	62.9	42.5	23.8	40.1	28.9
Asian	83.2	50.3	82.4	60.6	44.8	26.9	44.9	33.2
Hawaiian/Pacific Islander	71.2	49.7	68.8	—	46.0	33.2	44.6	—
Native American	68.5	45.7	64.6	43.0	41.7	21.8	38.8	30.0
Fathers: All Foreign Born	*75.7*	*61.2*	*76.8*	*63.8*	*38.1*	*23.0*	*39.2*	*26.2*
Mexico	71.6	61.7	69.7	62.8	31.5	19.8	31.9	20.0

Central America	74.6	63.3	73.3	65.7	37.9	26.8	39.1	28.1
Cuba	79.1	59.6	83.7	62.6	46.6	28.4	49.3	33.1
Dominican Republic	68.5	52.3	67.7	57.9	39.4	26.4	42.0	29.9
Haiti	70.0	60.4	69.9	63.8	54.4	42.0	53.6	46.7
Jamaica	74.0	60.6	70.7	—	57.6	44.2	55.6	—
Caribbean, English-Speaking	75.8	61.0	72.9	62.0	53.2	29.3	49.3	38.4
South America	73.9	63.8	78.7	65.9	35.5	24.6	39.5	28.1
Japan	81.8	63.2	84.2	74.4	26.4	39.0	37.8	9.3
Korea	68.5	55.6	75.8	64.0	31.6	33.7	37.6	29.7
China	75.7	58.7	80.8	66.3	46.8	37.9	54.7	40.2
Hong Kong	82.7	58.3	85.5	71.0	44.2	33.0	45.8	38.8
Taiwan	80.9	—	85.7	75.3	41.5	—	48.8	36.2
Philippines	76.2	58.5	77.5	68.5	60.2	40.3	60.8	53.8
Hmong	72.2	37.0	68.4	52.9	43.6	27.8	39.2	32.0
Cambodia	72.1	48.7	70.6	57.6	55.2	33.8	51.4	40.4
Laos	72.1	54.8	70.9	61.6	54.0	39.3	46.6	46.4
Thailand	77.2	—	79.7	69.7	45.9	40.7	44.6	45.4
Vietnamᵇ	76.2	58.2	80.2	66.3	47.3	33.6	46.9	39.7
India	81.4	63.1	82.4	71.6	37.0	26.1	38.2	30.6
Pakistan/Bangladesh	72.8	59.0	75.0	63.2	20.2	8.8	23.9	11.3
Afghanistan	62.6	—	74.9	45.9	26.0	5.4	33.3	11.6
Iran	79.3	51.8	83.3	63.7	30.3	17.4	33.6	21.1
Iraq	72.1	52.8	76.3	54.0	27.9	14.6	30.2	16.8

(continues)

Table 4.6: Part 4. Employment of Fathers of Children, Ages Zero to Seventeen, by Immigrant Country or Race-Ethnic Origin

	Percent of Fathers Employed Full-Time[a]				Percent of Wives Employed Full-Time[a]			
	Father H.S. Grad	Father Not H.S. Grad	Father English Fluent	Father Limited English Proficient (LEP)	Wife H.S. Grad	Wife Not H.S. Grad	Wife English Fluent	Wife Limited English Proficient (LEP)
Israel/Palestine	80.8	64.0	81.9	66.2	24.3	13.2	25.9	12.4
Other West Asia	75.7	57.7	76.8	63.5	25.1	11.0	26.2	15.8
Former USSR	67.1	46.4	77.4	58.5	39.3	15.6	48.9	30.8
Other Europe, Canada[b]	81.3	66.2	82.1	67.8	35.2	27.3	35.3	30.1
Africa, Blacks	69.4	51.5	70.2	58.1	45.6	23.7	47.3	27.7
Africa, Whites[b]	77.7	70.7	80.4	64.4	31.5	26.8	34.2	21.4
Other	73.0	59.5	76.5	62.3	38.9	38.1	41.7	34.7

Note: "—" indicates sample size is too small to produce statistically reliable results.

[a] Full-time indicates the person works 35 hours per week or more, 48 weeks a year or more.

[b] "Vietnam" includes Indochina not specified; "Other Europe, Canada" includes Australia and New Zealand; "Africa, Whites" includes Asian Africans.

Calculated from Census 2000 5% microdata (IPUMS) by Donald J. Hernandez, Nancy A. Denton, and Suzanne E. Macartney, Center for Social and Demographic Analysis, University at Albany, State University of New York with funding from The William and Flora Hewlett Foundation.

native-born fathers. The proportions working are similarly high at 89–95 percent for immigrant fathers from Central America, Vietnam, Pakistan/ Bangladesh, and the former Soviet Union, and for blacks from Africa, and nearly as high at 83–88 percent for immigrant fathers from the Dominican Republic, Haiti, Laos, Afghanistan, and Iraq. Among the two remaining immigrant origins with lower proportions working, the proportions are still high, at about four out of five, for Cambodia (79 percent) and the Hmong (77 percent). Corresponding proportions working among native-born fathers in race-ethnic groups other than white and Asian are in a similar range of 84–93 percent. Across the board, then, immigrant and native-born fathers living with children have a strong commitment to work.

The same is true for the wives of immigrant fathers (see table 4.6). Among the thirteen high poverty groups, the proportion with wives working last year falls to 50 percent or less only for Pakistan/Bangladesh (41 percent), Afghanistan (49 percent), and Iraq (50 percent), but this rises to a majority for Mexico (52 percent) and to the range of 61–78 percent for the remaining eight immigrant origins. These proportions tend to be somewhat lower than the range of 72–77 percent for most native-born groups, but many immigrant fathers also have at least one additional worker in the home.

The proportion with another worker in the home rises from a low of 15 percent for the former Soviet Union, 16 percent for blacks from Africa, and 17 percent for Pakistan/Bangladesh to one fifth or one-fourth (20–27 percent) for most other immigrant groups, and then further still to 33 percent for Mexico and Central America (see table 4.6). Most of these proportions are somewhat higher than for native-born fathers, among whom 15–19 percent have another worker in the home, with the exception of native Hawaiian and other Pacific Islanders (24 percent).

It is especially noteworthy that the comparatively lower proportion of immigrant fathers from Mexico with a working wife tends to be counterbalanced by the comparatively high proportion of these fathers with another worker in the home. Overall, then, the commitment to work in immigrant families is strong. More than three-fourths, and typically close to 90 percent, of immigrant fathers with high-poverty immigrant origins worked during the past year. More than half of immigrant fathers in most of these groups lived with a wife who worked, and many, typically one-fifth to one-third, also lived with another working person.

NOT WORKING FULL-TIME AMONG IMMIGRANT FATHERS

The high level of commitment among immigrant fathers to working for pay is not matched by the availability of full-time year-round jobs. The proportion not working full-time year-round rises from 17–18 percent for white and Asian fathers, to 27–36 percent for other native-born race-ethnic groups. The proportion not working full-time year-round for immigrant fathers in most of the high poverty groups (29–36 percent) is similar to most native-born groups, although it is somewhat higher for the Dominican Republic, Afghanistan, and Cambodia (39–40 percent), and especially the Hmong (43 percent).

LOW EDUCATION AMONG IMMIGRANT FATHERS

Father's educational attainments are often limited among immigrant groups with high poverty rates (see table 4.7). The proportion not graduating from high school is lowest among immigrant fathers from Pakistan/ Bangladesh, Afghanistan, former Soviet Union, and blacks from Africa, and these proportions are similar to native-born fathers who are white, Asian, or native Hawaiian or other Pacific Islander (5–15 percent). For most other native-born groups about one in five or one in four (19–28 percent) did not graduate from high school, but this jumps to about one-third (32–34 percent) for immigrant fathers from Haiti, Vietnam, and Iraq, to more than four in ten (43–47 percent) for the Hmong and those from Cambodia, Laos, and the Dominican Republic, 56 percent for Central America, and 71 percent for Mexico.

For some groups, the proportion of immigrant fathers who have not entered, let alone graduated from, high school is quite high. The proportion who have completed only up to eight years of school among immigrant fathers from Pakistan/Bangladesh, Afghanistan, former Soviet Union, and blacks from Africa is, again, similar to most native-born groups (1–5 percent). Between 10–15 percent have completed no more than eight years of school among immigrant fathers from Haiti, Vietnam, and Iraq, and native-born fathers who are island-origin Puerto Ricans. This jumps to 21–30 percent for immigrant fathers with origins in the Dominican Republic, Cambodia, and Laos, and then to 31 percent for Central America, 35 percent for the Hmong, and 46 percent for Mexico.

Fathers (and mothers) who have completed fewer years of school tend to have children who also complete fewer years of school and who have lower paying jobs during adulthood (Blau and Duncan, 1967; Featherman and Hauser, 1978; Sewell and Hauser, 1975; Sewell, Hauser, and Wolf, 1980). Fathers who have completed no more than elementary school may be especially limited in the knowledge required to help their children succeed in school. The educational aspirations of immigrant parents for their children often are high (Hernandez and Charney, 1998; Kao, 1999), but their knowledge about the U.S. education system may be quite limited, especially immigrant parents who have completed only a few years of school. Parents with such limited

Table 4.7. Education of Fathers of Children, Ages Zero to Seventeen, by Immigrant Country or Race-Ethnic Origin

	Percent of fathers:									
	Father 0–4 Years of School	Father 0–8 Years of School	Father Not H.S. Grad	Father H.S. Grad or Some College	Father College Grad	Wife 0–4 Years of School	Wife 0–8 Years of School	Wife Not H.S. Grad	Wife H.S. Grad or Some College	Wife College Grad
Total	**1.7**	**5.5**	**16.7**	**55.8**	**27.5**	**1.5**	**4.8**	**14.3**	**59.5**	**26.3**
Fathers: All Native-Born	*0.3*	*1.8*	*11.8*	*60.1*	*28.1*	*0.2*	*1.3*	*9.2*	*63.6*	*27.2*
White	0.2	1.4	9.6	59.1	31.3	0.1	1.0	7.5	63.0	29.5
Black	0.8	2.3	18.9	67.4	13.7	0.3	1.2	13.7	68.8	17.5
Puerto Rican, Mainland origin	0.7	3.2	23.4	65.2	11.4	0.6	2.6	18.0	67.5	14.5
Puerto Rican, Island origin	4.0	13.1	37.2	51.0	11.9	2.2	9.1	30.2	56.5	13.4
Mexican	1.6	6.0	27.6	61.5	10.9	2.0	7.2	25.3	63.3	11.5
Other Hispanic/ Latino	1.4	4.7	23.4	62.3	14.3	1.1	4.4	19.7	66.0	14.3
Asian	0.2	0.9	5.0	41.8	53.2	0.6	1.3	4.8	46.9	48.2
Hawaiian/Pacific Islander	0.1	0.6	12.7	70.0	17.3	0.1	0.8	7.7	74.9	17.4
Native American	0.6	3.5	21.4	65.9	12.7	0.4	2.4	16.5	69.3	14.2
Fathers: All Foreign-Born	*8.1*	*22.4*	*39.1*	*35.9*	*25.0*	*7.3*	*20.6*	*37.4*	*40.7*	*21.9*
Mexico	16.2	45.8	70.7	25.5	3.8	13.4	40.9	66.6	29.8	3.6

(continues)

Table 4.7. *(continued)*

				Percent of fathers:					
	Father 0–4 Years of School	Father 0–8 Years of School	Father Not H.S. Grad	Father H.S. Grad or Some College	Father College Grad	Wife 0–4 Years of School	Wife 0–8 Years of School	Wife Not H.S. Grad	Wife H.S. Grad or Some College	Wife College Grad
Central America	11.6	31.4	55.5	36.6	7.9	11.2	29.9	53.7	38.3	8.0
Cuba	1.8	7.5	27.7	47.4	24.9	1.3	5.4	23.0	54.2	22.8
Dominican Republic	6.2	20.7	46.7	42.1	11.2	4.4	16.3	38.8	50.3	10.9
Haiti	3.9	9.8	32.5	51.6	15.9	4.9	11.2	34.1	53.4	12.5
Jamaica	1.5	5.4	25.4	57.9	16.8	0.6	2.3	17.0	62.4	20.6
Caribbean, English-Speaking	2.0	6.4	21.8	59.5	18.7	1.6	5.0	17.9	63.0	19.1
South America	1.9	8.2	20.9	52.1	26.9	2.1	7.8	21.0	55.6	23.5
Japan	0.3	0.4	3.6	38.9	57.5	0.1	0.5	3.8	56.6	39.6
Korea	0.5	1.5	4.8	39.9	55.3	0.6	1.8	5.9	49.7	44.4
China	4.8	13.3	24.1	23.3	52.7	5.2	13.1	23.7	31.8	44.5
Hong Kong	1.8	5.3	14.6	32.0	53.4	2.0	6.3	16.7	40.7	42.6
Taiwan	0.4	1.3	3.3	19.4	77.3	0.2	1.2	3.3	31.6	65.1
Philippines	0.8	2.5	7.0	48.5	44.5	0.6	2.4	5.9	40.0	54.0
Hmong	32.2	35.2	43.4	48.1	8.5	45.8	48.4	61.6	34.0	4.4
Cambodia	22.5	29.6	47.3	43.5	9.2	29.2	38.6	57.3	37.9	4.8
Laos	21.3	27.2	45.4	47.8	6.7	25.9	34.2	51.5	42.2	6.3

Thailand	3.4	5.2	12.8	46.5	40.7	4.2	8.3	18.2	46.0	35.8
Vietnam[a]	7.3	13.3	32.6	45.5	21.9	9.6	19.1	41.7	43.6	14.7
India	0.7	1.5	7.2	16.8	76.0	0.9	2.3	10.1	24.1	65.8
Pakistan/ Bangladesh	1.1	3.4	12.4	28.2	59.4	2.9	6.6	20.8	35.8	43.4
Afghanistan	2.9	3.8	14.6	54.6	30.8	6.1	10.7	25.7	53.6	20.7
Iran	0.5	1.6	5.3	28.7	66.0	0.7	1.7	6.9	48.7	44.5
Iraq	6.5	15.0	33.8	41.3	24.9	9.9	19.9	36.2	45.5	18.4
Israel/Palestine	0.7	2.9	13.9	41.4	44.7	0.8	2.0	10.5	46.6	42.9
Other West Asia	1.8	6.3	15.3	37.6	47.1	2.3	6.2	16.9	49.9	33.2
Former USSR	0.9	2.3	9.6	39.7	50.7	0.9	1.8	8.5	43.5	48.0
Other Europe, Canada[a]	1.3	4.6	13.1	49.0	38.0	1.1	3.7	10.7	55.2	34.1
Africa, Blacks	1.6	2.9	7.5	37.0	55.5	3.1	5.9	13.3	53.8	32.8
Africa, Whites[a]	0.5	1.3	4.8	33.0	62.2	0.6	1.6	7.0	44.1	48.9
Other	2.0	5.7	16.1	46.0	37.9	1.6	5.2	16.7	51.2	32.1

[a]"Vietnam" includes Indochina not specified; "Other Europe, Canada" includes Australia and New Zealand; "Africa, Whites" includes Asian Africans.

Calculated from Census 2000 5% microdata (IPUMS) by Donald J. Hernandez, Nancy A. Denton, and Suzanne E. Macartney, Center for Social and Demographic Analysis, University at Albany, State University of New York, with funding from The William and Flora Hewlett Foundation.

educational attainments may, therefore, be less comfortable with the education system, less able to help their children with schoolwork, and less able to negotiate with teachers and school officials.

These conclusions suggest both the value and the need for special efforts by educators to reach out to immigrant parents, as well as to assure opportunities for immigrant parents to increase their own educational accomplishments. Programs aimed at fostering increased education attainments among immigrant parents might have the double benefit of increasing the occupational prospects and income of these parents, as well as enhancing the capacity of these parents to foster the educational success of their children.

ENGLISH PROFICIENCY AMONG IMMIGRANT FATHERS

Immigrant groups with large proportions of limited-English-proficient fathers also often are ones with fathers who have limited educational attainments. Moreover, immigrant fathers with limited English skills are less likely than English-fluent fathers to find well-paid, full-time, year-round work, and they may be less able to help their children with school subjects taught in English. Because many education, health, and social service organizations do not provide outreach in the native language of immigrant fathers, these fathers may be cut off from programs important to their well being and that of their children and families.

Among the thirteen high poverty groups discussed here, the proportion of immigrant fathers who are limited in their English proficiency is as low as one-fifth (18 percent) among blacks from Africa, and as low as one-third among those from Pakistan/Bangladesh (see table 4.8). About half (48–51 percent) are limited English proficient among immigrant fathers from Haiti, Afghanistan, and Iraq. Two-thirds to three-fourths (65–74 percent) are limited English proficient among immigrant fathers from Mexico, Central America, the Dominican Republic, the former Soviet Union, Cambodia, Laos, Vietnam, and the Hmong. Thus, about half or more are limited in their proficiency with English among immigrant fathers from twelve of the thirteen countries/regions who experience very high poverty rates in the United States. It is likely, then, that increased educational opportunities for immigrant fathers from these countries that provided access to English-language training might substantially improve their ability to find well-paid jobs that would help to lift their families out of poverty.

IMMIGRANT FATHERS IN
LINGUISTICALLY ISOLATED HOUSEHOLDS

The U.S. Census Bureau defines a linguistically isolated household as one in which no person over age thirteen speaks English exclusively or very well.

Table 4.8. Limited English Proficiency of Fathers of Children, Ages Zero to Seventeen, by Immigrant Country or Race-Ethnic Origin

Percent of fathers with:

	Bilingual	Limited English Proficiency									
	Child English Fluent and Speaks Other Language at Home[a]	Child Limited English Proficient (LEP)[a]	Father and Child LEP[a]	Wife and Child LEP[a]	Father LEP	Wife LEP	Father or Wife LEP	Both Father and Wife LEP	Linguistically Isolated Household[b]	Father in U.S. <10 Years and LEP	Father in U.S. ≥10 Years and LEP
Total	**12.3**	**5.9**	**3.0**	**3.1**	**10.6**	**11.1**	**13.3**	**8.2**	**5.3**	**13.9**	**31.9**
Fathers: All Native Born	*4.4*	*1.9*	*0.3*	*0.4*	*1.5*	*2.2*	*2.9*	*0.7*	*0.5*	*0.2*	*0.9*
White	2.6	1.2	0.1	0.2	0.5	1.1	1.4	0.1	0.1	—	—
Black	2.8	1.6	0.1	0.2	0.7	1.3	1.7	0.1	0.1	—	—
Puerto Rican, Mainland origin	31.4	12.1	2.6	2.7	10.1	13.6	18.5	4.4	3.7	—	—
Puerto Rican, Island origin	52.7	19.6	9.4	9.2	39.7	37.5	52.2	24.1	14.3	8.3	31.2
Mexican	25.6	11.1	3.2	4.0	12.2	16.1	20.4	7.1	4.8	—	—
Other Hispanic/ Latino	24.4	9.1	2.2	2.7	9.7	11.7	15.7	5.1	3.5	—	—
Asian	9.1	3.2	0.9	1.1	3.8	8.0	9.3	2.2	1.5	—	—
Hawaiian/Pacific Islander	6.4	3.3	1.2	1.4	2.5	3.6	4.9	0.9	0.6	—	—
Native American	8.7	3.7	1.2	1.4	4.5	4.7	6.7	2.2	1.3	—	—

(continues)

Table 4.8. Limited English Proficiency of Fathers of Children, Ages Zero to Seventeen, by Immigrant Country or Race-Ethnic Origin

Percent of fathers with:

	Bilingual		Limited English Proficiency								
	Child English Fluent and Speaks Other Language at Home[a]	*Child Limited English Proficient (LEP)*[a]	*Father and Child LEP*[a]	*Wife and Child LEP*[a]	*Father LEP*	*Wife LEP*	*Father or Wife LEP*	*Both Father and Wife LEP*	*Linguistically Isolated Household*[b]	*Father in U.S. <10 Years and LEP*	*Father in U.S. ≥10 Years and LEP*
Fathers: All Foreign Born	*49.3*	*24.6*	*15.4*	*15.3*	*52.5*	*51.6*	*61.3*	*42.4*	*27.7*	*16.4*	*37.6*
Mexico	55.6	36.2	24.1	23.4	73.8	68.6	82.0	59.9	39.6	18.6	55.0
Central America	58.2	28.3	17.4	17.5	65.4	65.1	75.6	54.2	36.4	15.9	50.2
Cuba	60.8	20.2	11.7	11.0	47.2	42.3	55.0	34.2	23.2	24.1	23.3
Dominican Republic	64.1	28.3	18.1	16.9	69.1	63.1	78.9	52.5	32.6	19.5	49.6
Haiti	52.7	18.4	10.4	10.9	49.6	49.6	60.1	38.3	22.1	13.8	35.7
Jamaica	4.8	1.4	0.3	0.3	1.9	2.3	3.4	0.6	0.4	0.7	1.2
Caribbean, English-Speaking	6.3	2.2	0.6	0.6	3.2	3.4	5.1	1.3	0.9	1.1	2.2
South America	61.6	21.2	12.9	13.2	53.7	55.4	66.0	42.4	28.1	21.0	33.0
Japan	21.2	21.6	12.9	15.6	31.5	38.5	41.0	28.5	23.6	33.1	16.4
Korea	58.8	29.2	19.0	19.9	66.6	74.3	79.7	60.8	41.3	25.0	41.9
China	57.5	32.1	20.6	21.1	63.1	69.2	74.9	56.9	41.2	23.9	39.0

Hong Kong	53.9	23.1	14.0	14.1	43.8	49.8	56.3	37.1	24.9	12.1	31.9
Taiwan	65.5	19.2	11.3	11.5	53.3	60.6	67.0	46.6	31.0	12.9	41.8
Philippines	32.0	10.4	4.8	4.8	28.8	25.9	35.7	18.7	10.0	8.2	21.3
Hmong	53.7	42.3	31.7	31.4	74.1	73.5	81.1	66.3	33.5	17.8	56.4
Cambodia	56.6	29.1	21.1	20.6	74.0	76.6	83.6	66.5	28.8	5.2	68.9
Laos	58.8	28.1	18.9	18.6	71.5	70.3	78.7	62.5	30.8	8.1	63.5
Thailand	45.9	14.6	9.2	9.8	49.3	47.9	56.8	39.8	24.6	9.5	45.7
Vietnam[c]	50.4	37.2	24.9	25.4	70.8	74.0	80.1	64.3	42.5	21.7	49.4
India	58.2	13.3	4.5	5.4	21.1	30.2	34.3	16.8	10.6	8.5	12.4
Pakistan/Bangladesh	62.6	19.7	9.2	11.2	33.2	48.1	53.2	27.4	18.8	14.4	18.7
Afghanistan	70.7	17.3	8.0	9.2	50.6	57.9	65.7	42.2	22.0	11.6	38.0
Iran	55.7	12.3	5.0	5.8	28.1	33.6	39.3	22.0	11.7	8.7	19.5
Iraq	56.2	20.9	11.9	13.1	47.9	53.6	62.8	38.3	22.4	27.6	20.0
Israel/Palestine	49.0	10.6	4.5	4.1	21.6	20.6	29.9	12.0	7.6	8.2	13.7
Other West Asia	52.5	15.0	6.2	6.7	28.8	33.2	42.1	19.6	13.3	10.3	18.9
Former USSR	67.2	24.4	17.1	17.2	65.0	64.0	73.5	55.3	34.5	48.0	16.5
Other Europe, Canada[c]	27.9	7.3	3.6	3.7	19.5	18.5	24.2	13.6	7.9	10.3	13.0
Africa, Blacks	28.4	13.5	4.7	5.7	17.8	23.7	27.8	12.7	10.4	9.8	7.6
Africa, Whites[c]	38.8	9.9	3.8	4.4	18.8	23.7	29.0	13.2	8.9	9.9	10.1
Other	47.7	17.7	9.9	10.5	39.7	42.4	49.2	32.5	19.9	12.7	28.9

Note: "—" indicates sample size is too small to produce statistically reliable results or category does not apply to the native group.

[a] Among fathers with a child ages 5–17 years.

[b] Households in which no one over the age of 13 speaks English exclusively or very well.

[c] "Vietnam" includes Indochina not specified; "Other Europe, Canada" includes Australia and New Zealand; "Africa, Whites" includes Asian Africans.

Calculated from Census 2000 5% microdata (IPUMS) by Donald J. Hernandez, Nancy A. Denton, and Suzanne E. Macartney, Center for Social and Demographic Analysis, University at Albany, State University of New York with funding from The William and Flora Hewlett Foundation.

Although a substantial majority of fathers in many high poverty immigrant groups are themselves limited English proficient, the proportions living in linguistically isolated households are generally two-fifths to three-fifths smaller (see table 4.8). For example, at the lowest levels of English fluency, 73 percent of immigrant fathers from Mexico are limited in their English proficiency, while a little more than one-half as many (40 percent) live in linguistically isolated households. Similarly, at high levels of English fluency, 18 percent of immigrant fathers who are blacks from Africa are limited English proficient, while a little more than half as many (10 percent) live in linguistically isolated households.

Who are the other persons in the households of these immigrant fathers who are more fluent in English? Some are the wives of immigrant fathers. Among five of thirteen immigrant groups studied here, at least 10 percent of immigrant fathers live with a U.S.-born spouse or partner, at 14 percent for Central America and Iraq, and 17–19 percent for Mexico, the Dominican Republic, and blacks from Africa. Thus, among these latter three immigrant groups between one in six and one in five immigrant fathers is married to or cohabiting with a U.S.-born American citizen. Additional English-fluent members of the household no doubt often are the adolescent children in the home who are older than age thirteen. In fact, many of the children of immigrant fathers were born in the United States and are, therefore, U.S. citizens.

Insofar as the wives and partners of immigrant fathers are born in the United States and are fluent in English, they are comparatively well positioned to work effectively with teachers, school administrators, health care providers, and various officials in health and social service agencies on behalf of their children and husbands/partners. Insofar as it is only the adolescent children in the home who are fluent in English, the parents are not in a position to help with school work and so on, but these children may act as the primary intermediary between the family and educational, health, social service, justice, and other institutions.

This role may be critical in helping immigrant fathers negotiate and integrate into the unfamiliar terrain of American society, but it can also lead to conflicts by undermining traditional father-child roles and parental authority (Park, 2001, 2002; Portes and Rumbaut, 2001; Sung, 1987; Valenzuela, 1999; Zhou and Bankston, 1998). Also, although adolescents may be fluent in everyday English, they may not have the technical vocabulary necessary either in English or in the father's origin-country language for effective contacts with health, social service, or legal organizations/agencies. Moreover, English-language skills of children and wives/partners will be of limited or no use in helping immigrant fathers to obtain or to work effectively in higher-paying jobs requiring English skills.

IMMIGRANT FATHERS WORKING IN VARIOUS INDUSTRIES

One or more of the thirteen high poverty groups discussed here are concentrated in sixteen industries that touch most aspects of the lives of all Americans: the food they eat (agriculture; food processing; restaurants), the places they live, work, and play (construction; janitorial services; hotels), and the clothing they wear (fiber, thread, textile mills; knitting, cutting, and apparel sewing), the vehicles they drive (motor vehicle and motor vehicle equipment manufacturing; retail parts/accessories; repair/maintenance; car washing), the personal services they use (domestic labor; dry cleaning and laundry; and beauty/nails), and basic economic functioning of the nation (electronics; plastics; trucking and warehouse; recycling and waste; selected processing, fabrication, and manufacturing with wood, minerals, and metals; and wholesaling for selected wood, mineral, and metal products).

As the largest immigrant population, immigrant fathers from Mexico are concentrated in thirteen of these sixteen industries, with employment rates 1.2 to 8.5 times greater in these industries than fathers as a whole (see table 4.9). The smaller immigrant groups have high concentrations in a smaller number of these industries, but among all except two of these immigrant groups the concentration ratios for at least five of these industries range from 1.2 to 31.9 times greater than for fathers as a whole. By comparison the ratios for white fathers in native-born families are less than 1.0 in twelve of these sixteen industries, and only 1.02–1.08 in the remaining four industries. Thus, particular industries within the economy rely especially on immigrant fathers to provide needed workers.

These industries typically pay less well than other industries. For example, the average yearly earnings for white fathers in native-born families in the other industries are $44,000, compared to a range of $18,000–$40,000 in fifteen of the sixteen industries reported here. Equally important, the earnings of immigrant fathers from the thirteen countries studied here in the industries in which they are concentrated are less than for native-born whites fathers with only three exceptions, those who are blacks from Africa working in the restaurant industry, and those from Pakistan/Bangladesh and the former Soviet Union working in electronics.

The differences between the immigrant and the white fathers in these sixteen industries are often quite large, typically $5,000–$15,000 per year. Insofar as the official poverty thresholds in Census 2000 were in the range of $17,000–$22,000 for families with two parents and two to four children, the lower annual earnings of immigrant fathers compared to native-born white fathers in these industries can be seen as accounting for substantial poverty among the immigrants.

Table 4.9: Part 1. Concentration in Specified Industries of Fathers of Children, Ages Zero to Seventeen, by Immigrant Country or Race/Ethnic Origin

					Concentration of fathers in industry for specific group, compared to all fathers[1]					
	Agriculture	Food Processing	Restaurant	Construction	Janitorial Services	Landscaping	Hotel	Garment	Motor Vehicle	Domestic Labor
Total Percent[2]	**1.92**	**2.50**	**2.64**	**13.30**	**0.68**	**1.06**	**0.67**	**0.67**	**4.29**	**0.05**
Fathers: All Native-Born	*0.87*	*0.91*	*0.70*	*1.00*	*0.85*	*0.77*	*0.70*	*0.81*	*1.02*	*0.60*
White	0.94	0.86	0.59	1.03	0.72	0.75	0.57	0.72	1.03	0.40
Black	0.33	1.15	1.28	0.62	1.63	0.74	1.27	1.67	1.00	1.40
Puerto Rican, Mainland origin	0.22	0.94	1.26	0.67	1.90	0.79	1.96	0.79	0.83	0.80
Puerto Rican, Island origin	0.52	1.28	1.28	0.66	2.31	1.61	2.81	1.78	1.04	0.60
Mexican	1.03	1.42	1.09	1.13	1.07	1.21	0.94	0.66	1.11	1.60
Other Hispanic/Latino	0.78	1.00	1.11	1.08	1.24	0.95	1.09	0.58	1.02	1.20
Asian	0.40	0.70	0.99	0.40	0.54	0.45	2.84	0.45	0.34	0.40
Hawaiian/Pacific Islander	0.88	1.05	1.11	1.16	1.06	1.50	5.52	0.39	0.50	2.00
Native American	1.00	0.89	0.79	1.39	0.84	1.07	0.97	0.67	1.00	1.60
Fathers: All Foreign-Born	*1.63*	*1.43*	*2.39*	*1.02*	*1.71*	*2.05*	*2.34*	*1.91*	*0.91*	*2.80*
Mexico	4.03	2.42	2.81	1.59	2.03	4.27	2.01	2.36	1.07	3.40

Central America	0.51	1.64	2.58	1.40	3.65	3.08	3.28	2.67	1.17	5.20
Cuba	0.27	1.38	1.01	1.00	1.49	1.04	1.96	1.16	0.99	0.60
Dominican Republic	0.19	1.11	2.15	0.60	3.79	0.72	2.88	3.61	1.07	2.20
Haiti	0.36	0.99	2.49	0.53	1.87	1.25	7.36	1.15	0.55	3.60
Jamaica	0.24	0.65	1.10	0.97	1.57	0.75	2.49	0.64	0.94	2.00
Caribbean, English-Speaking	0.09	0.57	0.91	0.93	1.04	0.44	2.07	1.58	0.97	3.40
South America	0.22	0.88	2.38	0.88	3.71	0.98	3.15	1.99	0.86	7.80
Japan	0.14	0.77	1.90	0.49	0.38	0.48	0.82	0.45	1.25	0.00
Korea	0.14	0.43	2.63	0.47	1.75	0.41	1.09	3.73	0.62	0.60
China	0.12	0.68	7.74	0.31	0.35	0.11	1.34	3.58	0.35	1.40
Hong Kong	0.08	0.63	4.98	0.22	0.31	0.04	3.25	2.27	0.34	0.00
Taiwan	0.07	0.45	2.42	0.21	0.06	0.29	1.60	1.22	0.35	1.00
Philippines	0.42	0.78	0.91	0.31	0.82	0.29	5.01	0.81	0.47	2.60
Hmong	0.36	2.13	1.03	0.18	1.78	0.28	0.22	7.55	1.14	1.40
Cambodia	0.29	2.10	4.15	0.31	0.51	0.28	1.22	3.96	0.68	5.00
Laos	0.87	2.50	1.86	0.25	1.93	0.40	1.54	2.85	1.44	0.80
Thailand	0.00	0.85	4.60	0.40	2.79	0.12	4.27	0.93	0.82	0.00
Vietnam+	0.16	1.02	2.67	0.31	0.63	1.11	1.79	2.99	0.99	1.40
India	0.23	0.34	1.09	0.15	0.10	0.06	4.01	0.55	0.41	1.00
Pakistan/Bangladesh	0.14	0.46	2.84	0.31	0.15	0.14	4.15	0.54	0.55	0.00

(continues)

Table 4.9: Part 1. (continued)

		Concentration of fathers in industry for specific group, compared to all fathers[1]								
	Agriculture	Food Processing	Restaurant	Construction	Janitorial Services	Landscaping	Hotel	Garment	Motor Vehicle	Domestic Labor
Afghanistan	0.00	0.70	4.48	0.31	1.91	0.54	0.48	0.49	0.90	0.00
Iran	0.08	0.36	2.20	0.55	0.21	0.07	1.40	1.03	0.98	0.60
Iraq	0.00	1.00	1.77	0.56	0.16	0.39	3.13	0.61	1.54	1.60
Israel/Palestine	0.14	0.60	1.22	0.51	0.71	0.49	1.15	1.18	0.58	0.20
Other West Asia	0.15	0.62	2.56	0.44	0.56	0.30	1.28	1.22	1.12	0.80
Former USSR	0.07	0.59	0.69	0.75	1.12	0.25	0.66	0.96	0.93	5.20
Other Europe, Canada+	0.38	0.80	1.59	1.01	1.16	0.56	1.52	1.01	0.87	1.00
Africa, Blacks	0.03	0.49	1.03	0.21	1.43	0.14	3.94	0.48	0.42	2.40
Africa, Whites+	0.23	0.54	2.49	0.42	0.75	0.22	3.46	1.10	0.51	0.60
Other	0.30	0.83	2.41	0.53	2.16	1.14	2.37	1.58	0.63	0.00

[1] Estimates are only for working fathers, and are calculated as the ratio of two proportions: (1) proportion in specified group of fathers working in specified industry, and (2) proportion of overall fathers working in specified industry. A ratio of 1.00 indicates that fathers in this group are as likely as fathers overall to be working in the specified industry. A ratio of 2.00 indicates that fathers in this group are twice as likely as fathers overall to be working in the specified industry. A ratio of .50 indicates that fathers in this group are one-half as likely as fathers overall to be working in the specified industry.

[2] Numbers in "Total Percent" row indicate the percent of all working fathers in the specified industry. Thus, this row of estimates is calculated differently than all other estimates in the table.

"__" indicates value is less than 0.01 and is not statistically reliable.

+ "Vietnam" includes Indochina not specified; "Other Europe, Canada" includes Australia and New Zealand; "Africa, Whites" includes Asian Africans.

Calculated from Census 2000 5% microdata (IPUMS) by Donald J. Hernandez, Nancy A. Denton, and Suzanne E. Macartney, Center for Social and Demographic Analysis, University at Albany, State University of New York, with funding from The William and Flora Hewlett Foundation.

Table 4.9: Part 2. Concentration in Specified Industries of Fathers of Children, Ages Zero to Seventeen, by Immigrant Country or Race/Ethnic Origin

	Dry Cleaning, Laundry	Beauty/ Nails	Electronics	Plastics	Trucking/ Warehouse	Recycling/ Waste	Selected Manufacturing	Wholesaling, Selected	Other Industries
	Concentration of fathers in industry for specific group, compared to all fathers[1]								
Total Percent[2]	**0.20**	**0.11**	**2.37**	**1.20**	**2.66**	**0.66**	**6.31**	**0.54**	**58.15**
Fathers: All Native-Born	*0.70*	*0.73*	*0.92*	*1.01*	*1.05*	*1.00*	*1.04*	*0.96*	*1.03*
White	0.60	0.64	0.97	1.02	0.98	0.91	1.08	0.98	1.03
Black	1.10	1.18	0.63	1.11	1.54	1.65	0.91	0.83	1.07
Puerto Rican, Mainland origin	1.45	1.09	0.63	0.76	0.94	1.35	0.68	0.85	1.14
Puerto Rican, Island origin	2.00	1.82	0.82	1.46	1.17	1.26	1.09	1.52	0.98
Mexican	0.80	1.18	0.81	0.86	1.30	1.18	0.81	1.13	0.95
Other Hispanic/ Latino	0.70	1.27	0.79	0.67	1.13	1.20	0.67	0.81	1.03
Asian	1.65	1.55	1.76	0.39	0.35	0.55	0.33	0.33	1.31
Hawaiian/Pacific Islander	0.95	2.00	0.65	0.48	0.82	1.30	0.49	0.48	1.03
Native American	0.75	1.09	0.50	0.64	1.09	1.41	0.91	0.81	0.96
Fathers: All Foreign-Born	*2.40*	*2.27*	*1.39*	*0.95*	*0.77*	*0.98*	*0.82*	*1.24*	*0.85*
Mexico	1.90	0.45	0.61	1.23	0.98	1.55	1.07	1.43	0.51

(continues)

Table 4.9: Part 2. *(continued)*

	Dry Cleaning, Laundry	Beauty/ Nails	Electronics	Plastics	Trucking/ Warehouse	Recycling/ Waste	Selected Manufacturing	Wholesaling, Selected	Other Industries
	Concentration of fathers in industry for specific group, compared to all fathers[1]								
Central America	2.65	1.00	0.73	0.99	1.26	1.68	0.75	1.52	0.70
Cuba	1.30	0.91	0.60	0.48	1.53	0.73	0.51	1.50	1.04
Dominican Republic	4.65	1.82	0.58	0.96	0.85	0.74	0.75	2.46	1.00
Haiti	4.15	0.55	0.52	0.81	0.60	1.47	0.38	0.78	1.10
Jamaica	2.40	1.73	0.65	0.49	0.88	1.38	0.37	0.52	1.12
Caribbean, English-Speaking	1.55	0.36	0.64	0.68	0.64	0.98	0.40	1.09	1.16
South America	2.35	1.09	0.95	0.79	0.91	0.88	0.63	1.41	0.98
Japan	1.65	1.73	2.73	0.69	0.44	0.26	0.59	1.24	1.13
Korea	27.60	6.73	1.57	0.29	0.26	0.32	0.27	3.11	1.09
China	2.60	2.27	2.97	0.43	0.13	0.18	0.27	0.70	0.99
Hong Kong	2.55	5.45	3.28	0.12	0.06	0.14	0.38	1.78	1.10
Taiwan	2.25	1.73	5.40	1.05	0.19	0.27	0.22	0.98	1.18
Philippines	0.70	1.45	2.58	0.71	0.38	0.36	0.54	0.50	1.23
Hmong	0.80	0.91	3.32	2.00	0.36	0.12	2.44	0.33	0.86
Cambodia	2.35	1.64	4.09	1.37	0.60	0.67	1.57	0.81	0.82
Laos	2.00	3.27	4.00	2.48	0.24	0.55	2.15	1.39	0.76
Thailand	1.35	0.00	2.82	1.93	0.21	0.32	0.72	0.28	0.97
Vietnam+	2.65	31.91	5.04	0.95	0.24	0.24	1.30	0.59	0.87
India	1.70	0.36	3.26	0.79	0.39	0.03	0.39	0.98	1.30

Pakistan/ Bangladesh	4.10	0.73	1.60	0.65	0.20	0.09	0.28	1.06	1.25
Afghanistan	0.00	3.09	1.34	0.21	0.20	0.68	0.17	1.22	1.19
Iran	3.75	1.73	2.30	0.34	0.48	0.73	0.33	1.72	1.17
Iraq	1.05	3.45	1.89	1.76	0.52	0.12	0.86	0.94	1.05
Israel/Palestine	2.95	3.55	1.31	0.18	0.65	0.52	0.33	1.91	1.27
Other West Asia	1.50	5.27	1.53	0.57	0.38	0.47	0.51	1.04	1.17
Former USSR	2.05	2.18	1.78	0.53	1.04	0.39	0.86	0.50	1.13
Other Europe, Canada+	0.60	2.00	1.42	0.96	0.71	0.67	0.96	0.93	1.01
Africa, Blacks	0.80	0.91	1.24	0.41	0.59	0.48	0.40	0.43	1.36
Africa, Whites+	2.45	2.45	1.30	0.55	0.35	0.17	0.36	0.31	1.24
Other	6.60	1.64	1.81	0.73	0.53	0.42	0.57	2.20	1.08

[1] Estimates are only for working fathers, and are calculated as the ratio of two proportions: (1) proportion in specified group of fathers working in specified industry, and (2) proportion of overall fathers working in specified industry. A ratio of 1.00 indicates that fathers in this group are as likely as fathers overall to be working in the specified industry. A ratio of 2.00 indicates that fathers in this group are twice as likely as fathers overall to be working in the specified industry. A ratio of .50 indicates that fathers in this group are one-half as likely as fathers overall to be working in the specified industry.

[2] Numbers in "Total Percent" row indicate the percent of all working fathers in the specified industry. Thus, this row of estimates is calculated differently than all other estimates in the table.

"—" indicates value is less than 0.01 and is not statistically reliable.

+ "Vietnam" includes Indochina not specified; "Other Europe, Canada" includes Australia and New Zealand; "Africa, Whites" includes Asian Africans.

Calculated from Census 2000 5% microdata (IPUMS) by Donald J. Hernandez, Nancy A. Denton, and Suzanne E. Macartney, Center for Social and Demographic Analysis, University at Albany, State University of New York, with funding from The William and Flora Hewlett Foundation.

IMMIGRANT FATHERS IN MIXED-CITIZEN-STATUS FAMILIES

The 1996 welfare reform drew a sharp distinction, for the first time, between noncitizen immigrants and citizens regarding eligibility requirements for important public benefits and services. As a result, many noncitizen fathers who are ineligible for specific public benefits may not be aware that their citizen (U.S.-born) children are eligible, or they may hesitate to contact government authorities on behalf of their children (Capps, Kenney, and Fix, 2003; Fix and Passell, 1999; Fix and Zimmerman, 1995; Hernandez and Charney, 1998; Zimmerman and Tumlin, 1999).

All together, 50 percent of immigrant fathers live in mixed-citizenship-status nuclear families (see table 4.10). The highest proportions among the thirteen countries of origin studied here are found for immigrant fathers from Mexico and Central America (64 percent), followed by the Dominican Republic (58 percent), Haiti, Cambodia, Laos, and blacks from Africa (51–54 percent). Even among the countries of origin where immigrant fathers are least likely to live in mixed-citizenship-status nuclear families—Vietnam, Afghanistan, Iraq, former Soviet Union—about one-third (28–37 percent) live in such families. Insofar as immigrant fathers with these origins experience especially high poverty rates, their children may be especially likely to need and be eligible for, but not have access to, critical public benefits and services.

EARLY EDUCATION FOR YOUNG CHILDREN OF MANY IMMIGRANT FATHERS

Negative consequences for educational success of children, which can flow from fathers' limited education, high poverty, and other circumstances in fathers' families, can begin early in the educational career of young children of immigrant fathers. Participation in early education programs can promote school readiness and education success in elementary school and beyond (Gormley, Gayer, Phillips, and Dawson, 2005; Haskins and Rouse, 2005; Lynch, 2004), and children with low family incomes and limited English proficiency may be especially likely to benefit from early education programs (Gormley and Gayer, 2005; Takanishi, 2004).

Among white fathers in native-born families the proportions with young children who are enrolled in pre-K/nursery school are 39 percent at three years of age and 63 percent at four years of age. Pre-K/nursery school enrollment rates reach or exceed these levels for only two of the thirteen high poverty immigrant groups, Haiti at 41 percent and 60 percent for children ages three and four years of age, respectively, and blacks from Africa at 47 percent and 64 percent, respectively. At three years of age, only between

Table 4.10. Fathers' Mobility and Immigrant Situation: Fathers of Children, Ages Zero to Seventeen, by Immigrant Country or Race-Ethnic Origin

	Percent of Fathers:			
	Father in U.S. <10 Years	Father Moved within U.S. in Past 5 Years[a]	In Family with One Immigrant Spouse, and One Non-Immigrant Spouse	Mixed-Status Nuclear Family[b]
Total	**4.6**	**44.1**	**6.1**	**10.4**
Fathers: All Native-Born	*0.5*	*42.3*	*3.5*	*1.8*
White	—	40.9	2.6	1.4
Black	—	48.8	2.9	1.4
Puerto Rican, Mainland origin	—	53.7	9.1	4.6
Puerto Rican, Island origin	16.3	52.5	12.5	7.5
Mexican	—	48.5	15.8	9.7
Other Hispanic/ Latino	—	47.4	10.5	5.6
Asian	—	33.7	22.3	7.2
Hawaiian/Pacific Islander	—	45.3	5.7	2.1
Native American	—	47.2	2.4	1.2
Fathers: All Foreign-Born	*25.1*	*52.6*	*18.0*	*49.9*
Mexico	22.8	53.7	16.5	63.5
Central America	20.2	54.7	13.5	64.4
Cuba	28.9	53.0	25.9	36.2
Dominican Republic	24.5	51.1	19.2	58.3
Haiti	21.5	48.3	8.2	54.4
Jamaica	20.4	47.8	24.6	50.5
Caribbean, English-Speaking	19.8	44.8	22.5	45.8
South America	29.3	58.3	19.6	46.3
Japan	32.0	57.6	15.8	24.5
Korea	30.0	63.3	4.4	41.4
China	36.0	53.2	2.9	38.2
Hong Kong	17.5	38.4	13.2	23.1
Taiwan	16.9	42.9	5.0	29.0

(*continues*)

Table 4.10. *(continued)*

	Father in U.S. <10 Years	Father Moved within U.S. in Past 5 Years[a]	In Family with One Immigrant Spouse, and One Non-Immigrant Spouse	Mixed-Status Nuclear Family[b]
			Percent of Fathers:	
Philippines	20.9	45.9	12.4	35.2
Hmong	20.1	50.8	2.9	46.1
Cambodia	7.3	39.7	2.3	47.4
Laos	9.8	47.1	6.0	51.0
Thailand	12.5	43.6	17.3	46.1
Vietnam[c]	24.9	49.7	5.3	33.2
India	35.3	55.0	5.2	46.3
Pakistan/ Bangladesh	33.4	64.0	7.5	44.4
Afghanistan	19.0	53.7	8.3	37.3
Iran	12.9	48.4	24.6	32.5
Iraq	37.9	55.2	14.0	33.3
Israel/Palestine	22.2	41.8	38.2	30.8
Other West Asia	23.4	49.6	24.1	36.0
Former USSR	64.0	67.1	4.0	27.7
Other Europe, Canada[c]	24.4	48.1	39.0	35.3
Africa, Blacks	35.4	59.4	19.0	52.0
Africa, Whites[c]	28.9	51.9	26.7	34.1
Other	22.5	52.4	19.1	44.3

Note: "—" indicates sample size is too small to produce statistically reliable results or category does not apply to the native group.

[a] Among fathers with a child ages 5–17 years.
[b] Father, spouse, or at least one child is not a U.S. citizen, and father, spouse, or at least one child is a U.S. citizen.
[c] "Vietnam" includes Indochina not specified; "Other Europe, Canada" includes Australia and New Zealand; "Africa, Whites" includes Asian Africans.

Calculated from Census 2000 5% microdata (IPUMS) by Donald J. Hernandez, Nancy A. Denton, and Suzanne E. Macartney, Center for Social and Demographic Analysis, University at Albany, State University of New York, with funding from The William and Flora Hewlett Foundation.

one-fifth and one-third (23–32 percent) are enrolled for fathers from seven of the thirteen high poverty countries, and this falls further to only 17 percent for Mexico and 15 percent for Cambodia. Similarly, among fathers with a child of age four, the proportion with the child enrolled in pre-K/nursery school varies from about one-half (46–54 percent) for the Dominican Republic, Vietnam, Pakistan/Bangladesh, Iraq, former Soviet Union, to 43 percent for Central America, 37 percent for Mexico, 35 percent for Laos, and 22 percent for Cambodia, much below the 63 percent for native-born white fathers.

Why are enrollment rates low for some groups? Familistic cultural values are sometimes cited as a possible reason, particularly for Hispanic immigrants, reflecting the idea that these familistic values may lead parents to prefer that children be cared for at home rather than in formal educational settings by nonrelatives (Liang, Fuller, and Singer, 2000). But socioeconomic or structural factors offer an alternative explanation (Hernandez et al., at press; Takanishi, 2004). The high cost of early education can pose an insurmountable barrier for poor families, and most low-income families eligible for childcare assistance do not receive such assistance because of limited funding (Mezey, Greenberg, and Schumacher, 2002). Parents with limited education may not be aware that early education programs are potentially important and that most highly educated parents enroll their children in such programs to foster children's educational success. In immigrant neighborhoods with many non-English speakers, openings in early education programs may be too few to accommodate the demand (Hill-Scott, 2005), and programs with available space may not reach out to immigrant parents in their home language (Matthews and Ewen, 2006). Similarly, if teachers are not able to communicate with children in their home language, parents may hesitate to enroll their children.

Recent research indicates that socioeconomic or structural influences, as reflected in family poverty, mother's education, and parental occupation, can in fact account for most or all of the enrollment gap for children in immigrant families from Mexico, Central America, and Indochina (Hernandez et al., at press). Although these results may be surprising, especially for Hispanics, they are consistent with the strong commitment in Mexico to early education, where universal enrollment at three years of age will become obligatory in 2008–2009 (OECD Directorate for Education, 2006). In fact, in Mexico where preschool is free, 81 percent of children aged four were enrolled in 2005, compared to only 71 percent among whites in U.S. native-born families in 2004, and 55 percent for children in immigrant families in the United States in 2004 who were from Mexico (Yoshikawa, et al., 2007; Hernandez, Denton, and Macartney, 2007b). Thus, public policies to assist immigrant fathers in providing early education for their young children, especially for high poverty groups, could prove both effective and beneficial to these fathers and their children.

HOUSING COST BURDEN AMONG IMMIGRANT FATHERS

Immigrant fathers with low incomes may have to spend very high proportions of their incomes on housing. Moderate housing cost burden is defined as spending at least 30 percent but less than 50 percent of household income for housing (including utilities), and severe housing cost burden is defined as paying 50 percent or more for housing (U.S. Bureau of the

Census, 1994; Millennial Housing Commission, 2002). Fewer than one in five (18 percent) of white native-born fathers experience moderate or severe housing cost burden, but the proportion is nearly double to triple this level for the thirteen high poverty immigrant groups, rising from 30–33 percent for fathers from Cambodia, Laos, Vietnam, the Hmong, and blacks from Africa to 36–38 percent for Mexico, Central America, and the former Soviet Union, 41–45 percent for the Dominican Republic, Haiti, Pakistan/ Bangladesh, and Iraq, and 55 percent for Afghanistan. Fathers who must pay a large proportion of their income to provide a home for their families have fewer resources available, than do other fathers at the same income level, to pay for food, clothing, and other necessities.

HOME OWNERSHIP AMONG IMMIGRANT FATHERS

Immigrant fathers, including fathers from most high poverty groups, often are buying their own homes, putting down deep roots in their local communities. Only among immigrant fathers from the Dominican Republic, who often live in the extremely high-cost New York metropolitan region, is the proportion living in owned as opposed to rented homes as low as 29 percent. This indicator of commitment to the local community rises from 41 percent for Central America to 44–45 percent for Pakistan/Bangladesh, and blacks from Africa, to about one-half (47–54 percent) for Mexico, Haiti, the Hmong, Afghanistan, and the former Soviet Union. Substantially larger proportions (57–64 percent) are homeowners among immigrant fathers from Cambodia, Laos, Vietnam, and Iraq. Given the high poverty rates among immigrant fathers from these countries, these high rates of home-ownership and investment in the local community are especially striking.

OVERCROWDED HOUSING AMONG IMMIGRANT FATHERS

Reflecting the high cost of housing, many immigrant fathers live in over-crowded housing with more than one person per room. Only one in twenty (5 percent) native-born white fathers and one in ten (12 percent) Asian native-born fathers live in overcrowded housing. This climbs to 21–27 percent for native-born Hispanic groups and 34 percent for native Hawaiian and other Pacific Islanders. Among fathers in high poverty immigrant groups, the proportion in overcrowded housing is in the some-what higher range of 35–37 percent for fathers from Afghanistan, Iraq, and the former Soviet Union, and this jumps further to 41–53 percent for Dominican Republic, Haiti, Cambodia, Laos, Vietnam, and Pakistan/ Bangladesh, and then much higher to 58 percent for Central America, 64 percent for Mexico, and 75 percent for the Hmong. The large numbers of persons in these homes may help fathers by contributing to the family income, childcare, emotional support, and other needs, but this crowding may also contribute to the stresses of daily life.

OVERALL SUMMARY

This is the first national study to present a demographic portrait of immigrant fathers by detailed country/region of origin. The results show that immigrant fathers are drawn widely from around the world, but particularly from Latin America and Asia, and that, although they are highly concentrated in a few states and large metropolitan areas, they also are widely spread across many smaller metropolitan areas and the rural regions of most states.

This chapter focuses especially on immigrant fathers with thirteen countries of origin who experience high poverty in the United States, and who often immigrated in search of economic opportunities, but who also often left war-torn countries or to escape persecution. These immigrant fathers have a strong commitment to work, with very high employment rates, although many do not find full-time year-round jobs. Immigrant fathers in these high poverty groups are concentrated in industries which touch the lives of all Americans and which are important to the national economy. But these industries typically are comparatively low paid, and fathers earn less than the average within these industries.

Despite the high levels of poverty that they experience in the United States, these immigrant fathers have strong families; most live in two-parent families, often with additional adult relatives or non-relatives in the home. Thus, these large families include persons, beyond the parents and dependent children, who might earn incomes to help support the family or provide additional emotional support or nurturance, and childcare, but their presence also often leads to overcrowded housing. Housing cost burdens are high for many of these immigrant fathers; they spend a large portion of their income on housing. But high levels of home ownership demonstrate the strong commitment of immigrant fathers to their adopted communities.

Many immigrant fathers in these high poverty groups have low educational attainments and limited English proficiency, although many have at least one family member who is English fluent, either a U.S.-born wife or adolescent child. With a wife or child who is a U.S. citizen, immigrant fathers often live in mixed-citizenship-status families, with children who are eligible for government benefits because they were born in the United States, but whose parental immigrant circumstances may act to limit their access to the needed benefits and services for which they are eligible as U.S. citizens.

Although the young children of immigrant fathers are especially likely to benefit from enrollment in early education programs, they often have less access to these programs than do children of native-born white fathers, largely because of socioeconomic or structural barriers. Public policies to improve the access of immigrant fathers to English-language programs and of their children to early education programs could prove quite beneficial to the economic and social circumstances of these immigrant fathers and their children.

Insofar as the children of immigrant fathers in these high poverty groups are mainly race-ethnic minorities who are leading the demographic transformation of America to a society in which no single race-ethnic group holds the majority, and insofar as these children will play an important role in providing economic support for the predominately white baby-boom generation during retirement, the well-being and future prospects of these fathers and children is important to all Americans.

ACKNOWLEDGMENTS

The authors wish to thank Hui-Shien Tsao for programming assistance and Jessica F. Singer for research assistance. The authors also acknowledge and appreciate support from the William and Flora Hewlett Foundation, the Foundation for Child Development, the National Institute of Child Health and Human Development (5 R03 HD 043827-02), and the Center for Social and Demographic Analysis at the University at Albany (5 R24—HD 04494301A1). The authors alone are responsible for the content and any errors of fact or interpretation. The Census 2000 data file used in this research was prepared by Ruggles, Sobek, Alexander, Fitch, Goeken, Hall, King, and Ronnande (2004).

REFERENCES

Bernstein, J., Brocht, C., and Spade-Aguilar, M. (2000). *How much is enough? Basic family budgets for working families.* Washington, DC: Economic Policy Institute.

Blake, J. (1985). Number of siblings and educational mobility. *American Sociological Review, 50,* 84–94.

———. (1989). *Family size and achievement.* Berkeley, CA: University of California Press.

Blau, P. M., and Duncan, O. D. (1967). *The American occupational structure.* New York: Wiley.

Boushey, H., Brocht, C., Gundersen, B., and Bernstein, Y. J. (2001). *Hardships in America: The real story of working families.* Washington, DC: Economic Policy Institute.

Capps, R., Kenney, G., and Fix, M. (2003). *Health insurance coverage of children in mixed-status immigrant families. Snapshots of America's children, No. 12.* Washington, DC: The Urban Institute.

Cherlin, A. J. (1999). Going to extremes: Family structure, children's well-being, and Social Sciences. *Demography, 36*, 421–28.

Citro, D. F., and Michael, R. T. (1995). *Measuring poverty: A new approach.* Washington, DC: National Academy Press.

Featherman, D. L., and Hauser, R. M. (1978). *Opportunity and change.* New York: Academic Press.

Fix, M., and Passel, J. (1999). *Trends in noncitizens' and citizens' use of public benefits following welfare reform: 1994–97.* Washington, DC: The Urban Institute.

Fix, M., and Zimmerman, W. (1995). When should immigrants receive benefits? In I. V. Sawhill (Ed.), *Welfare reform: An analysis of the issues* (69–72). Washington, DC: The Urban Institute.

Gormley, W. T., and Gayer, T. (2005). Promoting school readiness in Oklahoma: An evaluation of Tulsa's pre-K program. *Journal of Human Resources, 40*, 533–58.

Gormley, W. T., Gayer, T., Phillips, D., and Dawson, B. (2005). The effects of universal pre-K on cognitive development. *Developmental Psychology, 41*, 872–84.

Haskins, R., and Rouse, C. (2005). Closing achievement gaps. *The Future of Children, Policy Brief, Spring 2005.* Princeton, NJ: Princeton-Brookings.

Hernandez, D. J. (1986). Childhood in sociodemographic perspective. In R. H. Turner and J. F. Short, Jr. (Eds.), *Annual review of Sociology, Volume 12* (159–80). Palo Alto, CA: Annual Reviews.

Hernandez, D. J., and Brandon P. D. (2002). Who are the fathers of today? In C. S. Tamis-LeMonda and N. Cabrera (Eds.), *Handbook of father involvement: Multidisciplinary perspectives* (33–62). Mahwah, NJ: Erlbaum.

Hernandez, D. J., and Charney, E. (Eds.). (1998). *From generation to generation: The health and well-being of children in immigrant families.* Washington, DC: National Academy Press.

Hernandez, D. J., and Darke, K. (1999). Socioeconomic and demographic risk factors and resources among children in immigrant and native-born families: 1910, 1960, and 1990. In D. J. Hernandez (Ed.), *Children of immigrants: Health, adjustment, and public assistance* (19–125). Washington, DC: National Academy Press.

Hernandez, D. J., Denton, N. A., and Macartney, S. E. (2007a). Child poverty in the U.S.: A new family budget approach with comparison to European countries. In H. Wintersberger, L. Alanen, T. Olk, and J. Qvortrup (Eds.), *Children's economic and social welfare.* Odense: University Press of Southern Denmark.

———. (2007b). *Children in immigrant families—The U.S. and 50 states: National origins, language, and early education.* Publication #2007-11 Children in America's Newcomer Families. Washington, DC/Albany, NY: Child Trends and Center for Social and Demographic Analysis at University at Albany. Retrieved May 1, 2007, from www.albany.edu/csda/children, research brief 1.

———. (at press). Early childhood education programs: Accounting for low enrollment in newcomer and native families. In M. Waters and R. Alba (Eds.), *The next generation: Immigrant youth and families in comparative perspective.* Ithaca, NY: Cornell University Press.

102   *Donald J. Hernandez, Nancy A. Denton, and Suzanne E. Macartney*

Park, L. (2001). Between adulthood and childhood: The boundary work of immigrant entrepreneurial children. *Berkeley Journal of Sociology, 45,* 114–35.

——. (2002). Asian immigrant entrepreneurial children. In L. T. Vo and R. Bonus (Eds.), *Contemporary Asian American communities* (161–74). Philadelphia: Temple University Press.

Portes, A., and Rumbaut, R. G. (2001). *Legacies: The story of the immigrant second generation.* Berkeley: University of California Press.

Ruggles, S., Sobek, M., Alexander, T., Fitch, C. A., Goeken, R., Hall, P. K., et al. (2004). *Integrated public use microdata series: Version 3.0* [Machine-readable database]. Minneapolis: Minnesota Population Center [producer and distributor]. Retrieved January 2006 from www.ipums.org.

Sewell, W. H., and Hauser, R. M. (1975). *Education, occupation and earnings.* New York: Academic Press.

Sewell, W. H., Hauser, R. M., and Wolf, W. C. (1980). Sex, schooling, and occupational status. *American Journal of Sociology, 83,* 551–83.

Sung, B. L. (1987). *The adjustment experience of Chinese immigrant children in New York City.* New York: The Center for Migration Studies.

Takanishi, R. (2004). Leveling the playing field: Supporting immigrant children from birth to eight. *The future of Children, Special issue on Children of Immigrants, 14*, 61–79.

U.S. Census Bureau. (1994). *Housing for lower-income households* (Statistical Brief, SB/94/18). Retrieved January 9, 2006, from http://www.census.gov/aspd/www/statbrief/sb94_18.pdf.

———. (2004). *Interim projections consistent with Census 2000 (for 2000–2005) released by the Census Bureau on March 18 2004.* Retrieved October 23, 2006, from http://www.census.gov/population/www/projections/popproj.hgml.

Valenzuela, A., Jr. (1999). Gender role and settlement activities among children and their immigrant families. *American Behavioral Scientist, 42*, 720–42.

Yoshikawa, H., McCartney, K., Myers, R., Bub, K., Lugo-Gil, J., Knaul, F., and Ramos, M. (2007). *Preschool education in Mexico: Expansion, Quality Improvement, and Curricular Reform.* Florence, Italy: UNICEF Innocenti Research Centre Working Paper. Available at http://www.unicef-irc.org/publications/pdf/iwp_2007_03.pdf.

Zhou, M., and Bankston, C. L. (1998). *Growing up American: How Vietnamese children adapt to life in the United States.* New York: Sage.

Zimmermann, W., and Tumlin, K. (1999). *Patchwork policies: State assistance for immigrants under welfare reform.* Washington, DC: The Urban Institute, Occasional Paper No. 24.

5

Immigrant Fathers' Labor Market Activity and Its Consequences for the Family

Roberto M. De Anda and James D. Bachmeier

The immigrant population in the United States grew rapidly in the past couple of decades. According to the 2000 decennial census, there were thirty-one million immigrants living in the country, representing 11 percent of the total U.S. population. Today, one in five children is the child of an immigrant (Van Hook and Fix, 2000). It is important to examine the economic activity of immigrant fathers because, in large measure, the well being of their families depends on it. In this chapter, we compare the labor market activity of immigrant fathers from Latin America, Asia, Africa, and other parts of the world to white and black fathers born in the United States. Succinctly stated, labor market activity refers to a person's behavior in the world of work—that is, whether a person is working or not working; if working, the time spent at work and the type of job held. An important outcome of this labor market activity is earnings. We also discuss the consequences of immigrant fathers' labor market behavior on their families.

The study of labor market behavior of immigrant fathers is warranted for the following reasons. First, the time that fathers spend at work is going to affect the amount of time that they will have available to devote to their families (Hofferth, Stueve, Pleck, Bianchi, and Sayer, 2002). Second, if fathers experience employment instability such as joblessness or part-time work, then their earnings will be negatively affected. This is important because most of household income is derived from employment. Consequently, the earnings of fathers will have a strong influence on the structure of opportunities faced by their children. For example, fathers' earnings will affect the type of community where the family will live, which in turn will determine the quality of the schools the children attend and their general well-being (Cabrera et al., 2000; Hernandez, 1999; Van

Hook et al., 2004). Children living in poverty, for instance, will be more likely to have low academic achievement, and will have a higher risk for delinquency and crime (Duncan and Brooks-Gunn, 1997). This will most likely have intergenerational repercussions since schooling is a key variable for social mobility.

Three questions guide our research. First, are there differences between immigrant fathers and U.S.-born white fathers in their labor market activity? Second, does the labor market activity among immigrant groups differ? Third, what are the consequences of labor market outcomes for the family? To address the first two questions, we use data from the 2000 Integrated Public Use Microdata Series (IPUMS), which is a 5 percent sample of the decennial census. We provide descriptive measures of employment status, hours and weeks of work, occupational distribution, and annual earnings. Additionally, we disaggregate selected components of the analysis by immigrant-related variables—English-language ability, length of U.S. residence, and citizenship status. Finally, we discuss the implications of labor market behavior on fatherhood and suggest directions for future research.

LABOR MARKET INCORPORATION OF IMMIGRANTS

The literature on the economic activity of immigrants in the United States offers a picture of their labor market incorporation. Generally speaking, immigrants are expected to go through a period of adjustment in the labor market following their arrival in the country. For example, immigrants may not be familiar with the way the labor market operates; they may have to learn how to go about looking for a job or the location of available employment. More importantly, the types of jobs that immigrants take will hinge on the skills that they bring with them. For instance, immigrants with low levels of education are more likely to accept lower status jobs located at the bottom of the occupational hierarchy. Such jobs tend to be low-wage and unstable (high risk of unemployment). But even when employed, poorly educated immigrants might not be working as many hours as immigrants with higher levels of schooling. On the other hand, immigrants with high levels of education are more likely to accept better jobs, which are characterized by their stability and good pay (Massey, Arango, Hugo, Kouaouci, Pellegrino, and Taylor, 1998; Piore, 1979; Waldinger, 2001).

In addition to schooling, studies have identified two other individual-level factors that influence immigrants' labor market outcomes: the ability to speak English, and the length of residence in the United States. Research shows that there is a positive association between English-language proficiency and employment outcomes. For example, the ability to speak English well is strongly associated with a higher likelihood of employment and better earnings (Chiswick, 1991; Dávila and Mora, 2001; DeFreitas, 1991). We expect to find that immigrants with limited English ability will not fare as well in the labor market as those who are proficient in English.

The relationship between length of residence and labor market performance is well documented. In general, empirical studies invariably show that immigrants experience more unfavorable labor market outcomes than native workers. Immigrants, for example, have lower earnings than U.S.-born white workers. But, as immigrants gain experience in the labor market, their earnings improve (Borjas, 1990). As with earnings, the longer the immigrant resides in the United States, the more favorable other labor market outcomes will be—that is, if they are employed or not employed, and, if employed, the number of hours of work. For example, Chiswick (1978) found that in their initial years of residence in the United States, Mexican immigrants changed employment often, learning more about various jobs. Piore (1979) also found that recent immigrants experience higher rates of job turnover and are likely to end up in unstable, low-skilled jobs that are common in secondary labor markets. Recent immigrants have also been found to be more prone to experience involuntary part-time work than those who have lived in the country longer or who are native workers (De Anda, 1992). Therefore, poorer labor market outcomes (fewer hours of work, bad jobs, and lower earnings) are expected among recent immigrants compared to earlier immigrants or native-born white workers.

Besides English-language ability and length of residence, we also include in our analysis citizenship status, an often-neglected dimension of immigrant economic incorporation. Although there is scant research on the economic incentives to becoming a U.S. citizen, we speculate that, in addition to wanting to participate in the political system, immigrants decide to become U.S. citizens to improve their labor market mobility. Immigrants who become naturalized might want to send prospective employers a signal that they have a stronger attachment to the job market than those who are not U.S. citizens. For example, they might want to signal that they are better candidates for on-the-job training than those who decide against naturalization. Additionally, U.S. citizenship will open doors to jobs in the public sector, since those who lack U.S. citizenship are ineligible for employment. We expect to find that naturalized immigrants will experience better employment outcomes relative to those who are not U.S. citizens.

Moreover, how well immigrants do in the labor market is also determined by the type of job held—that is, by class of worker and occupation. There are three categories of class of worker: the self-employed and workers in the private or public sector. Regardless of nativity status, most workers tend to be employed in the private sector. However, self-employment has been found to improve immigrants' labor market fortunes (Portes and Zhou, 1996). In broad strokes, immigrants with low levels of human capital, including limited English proficiency, are likely to pursue self-employment as a means of circumventing labor market discrimination in hiring or promotion (Dávila and Mora, 2004). But even immigrants with high levels of human capital are likely to be self-employed, for example, physicians (Bates and Dunham, 1992). Lastly, public sector jobs are desirable to immigrants because such jobs are stable and offer good wages and fringe benefits.

Occupational position is another important indicator of a person's level of education, skill, and autonomy in the labor process. These occupational characteristics may provide the incumbent with power at the workplace (Kalleberg and Berg, 1987), which in turn might influence employment outcomes such as on-the-job training and career ladders. Additionally, high-status occupations allow workers to negotiate favorable employment terms such as wages and layoffs. In general, the risk of poor employment outcomes will be higher in occupations that require little skill and education, but the risk will be lower in occupations that require higher levels of skill and education. For example, workers in low-status occupations (operatives and laborers) are more likely to be unstably employed—that is, experience intermittent spells of joblessness (DeFreitas, 1991), work part-time (De Anda, 1992; Tilly, 1996), and receive low pay (Catanzarite, 2000). Hence, we anticipate finding that immigrants with low levels of human capital will be more often concentrated in low-status occupations.

In sum, we expect to find that low-skilled immigrant fathers (Mexicans and other Latin Americans) will have poorer labor force outcomes relative to high-skilled immigrants (Africans and Europeans) and native-born white fathers. More specifically, immigrants from Mexico and other Latin American countries will have lower labor force participation rates, higher rates of joblessness, fewer hours of work, and lower earnings, and will be overrepresented in low-skilled occupations. These employment patterns will likely intensify for recent immigrants.

DATA AND MEASURES

To better understand the labor market activity of immigrant fathers, we examine descriptive statistics using data from the 5 percent sample of the 2000 decennial census obtained from the Integrated Public Use Microdata Series (IPUMS) at the University of Minnesota (Ruggles et al., 2004). Our analytic sample is limited to resident fathers, aged sixteen years and above, in the civilian non-institutionalized population. In certain analyses, it is necessary to impose further sample restrictions, such as examining only foreign-born fathers (i.e., excluding native-born) and/or focusing on the activities of those fathers actually participating in the U.S. labor market or those who worked during 1999. All analyses are appropriately weighted.

Operationalization of Variables

Fathers are defined as those men who reported having their own, non-adult children (biological or adopted) living in the same household. This definition is admittedly limited, as it excludes those fathers whose children live in another household. However, we argue that there is analytic value in this perceived drawback, as importantly, the operational definition of "father" used in this study excludes those immigrant fathers residing in the United States whose families have stayed behind in the country of origin. This allows a more precise comparison of immigrant fathers to those born in the United States, as it approximates what one might loosely refer to as the "traditional" family arrangement.

We compare labor market activity for several groups based on fathers' nativity and racial/ethnic identification. First, we compare employment outcomes between native-born fathers (those born on U.S. soil or those born overseas to U.S. citizen parents) and foreign-born fathers. Second, we examine differences across seven racial/ethnic and nativity groups. We focus on two groups of native-born fathers: whites and blacks. Respondents classified as white indicated that they were born in the United States and do not claim a Latino/Hispanic background. Respondents classified as native-born blacks identified racially as black or African American and also do not identify as Latino. These two groups—whites and blacks—traditionally stand as opposite poles in terms of U.S. labor market outcomes, and scholars of the "new" immigrant incorporation generally have used these two groups as benchmarks against which to measure the economic progress of contemporary immigrants—an ethnically and racially diverse population (Alba and Nee, 2003; Bean and Stevens, 2003).

Five groups of immigrant fathers are compared to these two native-born groups. Because immigrants from Mexico comprise fully one-third of all authorized immigrants to the United States, and over half of all unauthorized immigrants, Mexican-born fathers are examined separately from a second group of immigrant fathers consisting of those originating in all other Latin American nations. Asian-born fathers are those hailing from countries in East and Southeast Asia as well as those originating in the Pacific Islands. Fathers in the "Africa/Caribbean" group are those born in sub-Saharan Africa and in non-Spanish-speaking countries in the Caribbean. Finally, fathers in the "Other Foreign-Born" group originate in a number of nations including European countries and nations whose majority populations are of European origin, specifically Australia, New Zealand, and Canada. Also included in this "other" group are fathers originating in nations in Southwestern Asia, the Middle East, and Northern Africa.

Focusing on the immigrant sample, within- and between-group variation is analyzed for three "immigrant-related" variables: length of U.S. residence (whether the length of residence is fewer than ten years, or ten years or greater), English-language proficiency (whereby limited-English-proficient fathers are those reporting no ability to speak English or limited ability where English is spoken "not well," while English-proficient fathers speak only English or report speaking English well or very well), and citizenship (simply delineates between those immigrant fathers who have become naturalized U.S. citizens and those who have not).

Comparisons among these five immigrant groups described above are made for five outcome variables pertaining to fathers' labor market activity: 1) employment status, 2) employment stability, 3) class of worker, 4) occupation, and 5) earnings.

Fathers' *employment status* refers to three categories of labor force behavior: employed, unemployed, or not in the labor force. *Employment stability* is measured using two indicators: usual hours worked per week and the number of weeks worked during the previous year. Comparisons using this variable are restricted only to those fathers who worked at least one week during 1999. Group comparisons for these variables are made using mean comparisons and through analyses of group distributions across several categories. For hours worked per week, fathers fall into one of four categories: fewer than thirty-five hours per week, thirty-five to forty hours, forty-one to forty-eight hours, and more than forty-eight hours per week. For weeks per year, fathers are grouped into one of four categories: one to twenty-six weeks, twenty-seven to thirty-nine weeks, forty to forty-nine weeks, and fifty to fifty-two weeks.

Class of worker is made up of three categories: self-employed, employed in the private sector (includes both for-profit and not-for-profit employees), and public sector employees working for the federal, state, or local government. Class of worker analyses are based on the fathers' most recent occupation and are limited to those fathers who worked within the previous five-year period, 1995–1999. *Occupational differences* are examined across seven groups of occupations: managerial and professional, clerical and sales, craft and repair, operative, services, farm laborer, and laborer. Similar to class of worker analyses, occupation comparisons are based on the fathers' most recent occupation and are limited to those employed between 1995 and 1999.

Finally, within- and between-group comparisons are made according to the *average earned income* reported by working fathers during 1999. An additional perspective is provided by examining group distributions across five quintiles based on the earnings of all fathers nationwide. Fathers in the top earnings quintile are those who earned at least $64,000 in 1999; those in the second quintile earned between $43,000 and $63,999; the third quintile ranges from $31,000 to $42,999; the fourth quintile ranges from $20,000 to $30,999; and the lowest 20 percent of income earning fathers are those who earned less than $20,000 of individual earned income during 1999.

RESULTS OF ANALYSIS

Employment Status

The results presented in figure 5.1 show the employment status—employed, unemployed, and out of the labor force—of fathers by nativity status. Native-born fathers were more often employed (89.3 percent) than foreign-born fathers (77.0 percent). As anticipated, unemployment rates were lower for the native-born (2.5 percent) in contrast to their foreign-born counterparts (3.6 percent). It must be kept in mind that the jobless figures are low by historic standards, as 2000 represents the tail end of an economic expansion characterized by lower-than-average levels of joblessness. Even so, the share of immigrant fathers not actively participating in the labor force was more than twice as high relative to native-born fathers (19.4 percent and 8.2 percent, respectively). In short, immigrant fathers have a weaker attachment to the labor force relative to their U.S.-born counterparts.

Figure 5.2 presents results that compare employment status between U.S.-born non-Latino white fathers (hereafter referred to as white), U.S.-born blacks, and major racial/ethnic immigrant groups. Compared to all immigrant groups (and U.S.-born blacks), white fathers born in the United

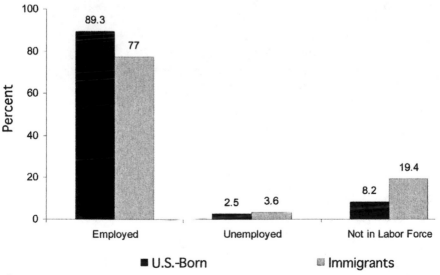

Figure 5.1.

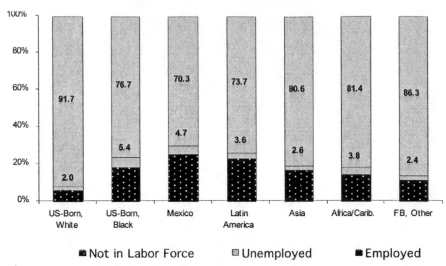

● Not in Labor Force   ▣ Unemployed   ● Employed

Figure 5.2.

States had the most successful employment outcomes. Of all the immigrant groups, on the other hand, Mexican immigrant fathers had the least
successful employment outcomes: they had the lowest employment (70.3
percent), the most joblessness (4.7 percent), and the highest out-of-the-
labor-force levels (25.0 percent). There are two interrelated reasons that
might help explain why fully one-fourth of Mexican immigrants are out of
the labor force, that is, they are not working or looking for work. It is possible that undocumented migrants who are working are reluctant to supply
this information to the Bureau of the Census, a federal government agency,
given that, since the passage of the Immigration Reform and Control Act
(IRCA) in 1986, it is illegal to work in this country without authorization.
Relatedly, legal immigrants who are active in the informal labor market
might not consider their activity "real" work, and hence might not be willing to supply this information.

Overall, Latin American migrants (other than Mexicans) fared more
poorly than Asians, Africans/Caribbeans, and the Other Immigrant group.
Fathers in these three groups are characterized more favorably than U.S.-
born black fathers, in that they report lower rates of joblessness and non-
participation in the labor force. In sum, Mexican immigrant fathers are
the most disadvantaged of all immigrant groups due to their high levels
of unemployment and more importantly their non-participation in the
labor force.

Table 5.1 displays data on unemployment for selected groups of foreign-
born fathers by characteristics related to immigration—English-language

Table 5.1.   Percent of Fathers Unemployed, by Immigrant-Related Characteristics among Selected Immigrant Groups

	English Language Proficiency		Length of U.S. Residence		Citizenship Status	
	Limited	*Proficient*	*<10 Years*	*10+ Years*	*Non-Citizen*	*Naturalized*
Mexico	4.3	4.0	4.7	4.7	5.0	3.9
Other Latin America	3.7	2.7	4.1	3.4	4.2	2.7
Asia/Pacific Islands	2.9	1.8	2.5	2.6	2.9	2.5
Africa/ Caribbean	4.6	2.7	5.0	3.4	4.7	3.1
Other	4.2	1.7	2.9	2.1	2.7	2.1

proficiency, length of U.S. residence, and citizenship status. From the perspective of human capital theory (Becker, 1993), migrants who have invested in learning English should expect better labor market outcomes than those who are limited English proficient or LEP. Consistently, LEP migrants were more often jobless than their English-proficient counterparts. Migrants from Africa and the Caribbean who were unable to speak English well were the most likely to be jobless (4.6 percent) of all LEP immigrants. They were closely followed by LEP Mexican immigrants (4.3 percent). Of the major immigrant groups, Asians and Pacific Islanders who were limited English proficient were the least likely to experience joblessness.

The length of residence of migrants in the United States can be used as a very crude measure of labor market experience. According to human capital theory, the longer an immigrant lives in the country, the more knowledge he accumulates about how the labor market operates. For example, those who have lived in the country longer can expect better opportunities to be employed rather than jobless. Recent immigrants—those with less than ten years of U.S. residence—from Africa and the Caribbean were more likely to be unemployed (5 percent) than any other immigrant group. But, after having lived in the United States for ten years or more, their jobless rate dropped to 3.4 percent. For Mexican immigrants, on the other hand, the likelihood of unemployment did not vary by length of residence. Also, whether an immigrant becomes a U.S. citizen or not seems to influence unemployment. Mexican immigrants who were not U.S. citizens were unemployed more often than any of the other immigrant groups. But even when Mexicans become naturalized citizens, they are more likely to be jobless than other migrants. Nonetheless, for all immigrant groups, becoming a U.S. citizen attenuates joblessness.

To summarize, the results indicate that limited-English-speaking immigrant fathers were more likely to be unemployed than their peers who were fluent in English, but the difference was not significantly large (the exception was the Other Immigrant group). This suggests that limited English proficiency does not seem to hinder immigrants from getting jobs. But it should be pointed out that this does not imply that the jobs held by LEP fathers are good jobs—that is, jobs that offer good pay and opportunities for advancement. Similarly, the longer immigrants live in the United States, the lower their level of unemployment. The exception was Mexicans, for whom the length of residence did not seem to matter: the level of unemployment remained the same regardless of length of residence. Lastly, the results suggest that the decision to naturalize reduces the likelihood of unemployment for all immigrant groups.

Employment Stability

Table 5.2 shows the average hours of work per week and average weeks of work per year for native- and foreign-born fathers. The standard workweek in the United States is thirty-five to forty hours per week. In fact, the Bureau of the Census classifies a person as a full-time worker if he works thirty-five or more hours per week. Fathers born in the United States worked an average of 45.7 hours per week, while foreign-born fathers worked 43.9 hours. It should be pointed out that both groups of fathers worked more hours than the standard workweek. A more detailed look at several racial/ethnic groups of immigrants shows that most groups had a very similar workweek: they worked, on average, about forty-four hours per week. The exception

Table 5.2.   Average Hours Worked Per Week and Weeks Worked Per Year by Fathers of Selected Racial/Ethnic and Nativity Groups

	Mean Hours Worked Per Week	Mean Weeks Worked Per Year
U.S.-Born Total	*45.7*	*49.1*
Non-Latino White	46.2	49.5
Non-Latino Black	43.0	47.1
Immigrant Total	*43.9*	*46.9*
Mexico	43.0	45.7
Other Latin America	43.5	46.9
Asia/Pacific Islands	43.8	47.5
Africa/Caribbean	43.3	47.6
Other	45.9	48.2

was the Other Immigrant group, which averaged around forty-six hours. A similar pattern is observed for the mean weeks worked per year. Fathers born in the United States worked 49.1 weeks per year, whereas most immigrant groups worked between 45.7 and 48.2 weeks (averaging 46.9 weeks). However, none of the immigrant groups exceeded the average number of weeks worked throughout the year by native-born white fathers.

Figure 5.3 displays the percentage distribution of part- and full-time work for U.S.-born and immigrant fathers. Data are presented for part-time work (one to thirty-four hours) and three categories of full-time work: thirty-five to forty hours (a standard workweek), forty-one to forty-eight hours (more than a standard workweek), and more than forty-eight hours (overwork). More than half of immigrant fathers (57.9 percent) worked a standard workweek, while a little less than half (46.9 percent) of native-born fathers did so. More native-born fathers worked forty-one to forty-eight hours per week than their foreign-born counterparts (14.5 percent and 10.3 percent, respectively). The gap is even wider for native- and foreign-born fathers working more than forty-eight hours per week: a little over one-third (34.5 percent) of native-born fathers, compared with about one-fourth (25.6 percent) of immigrant fathers, worked these hours.

In broad terms, the results show that immigrant fathers work a standard workweek more often than their native-born counterparts. But fathers born in the United States tend to overwork more often than those who are

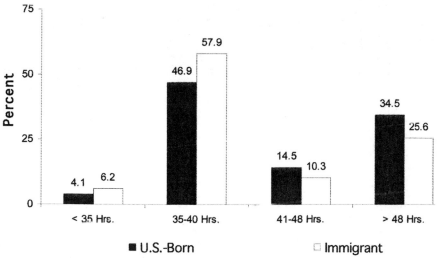

Figure 5.3.

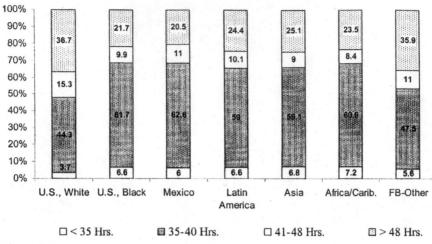

□ < 35 Hrs.   ▨ 35-40 Hrs.   □ 41-48 Hrs.   ▥ > 48 Hrs.

Figure 5.4.

foreign-born. In general, this finding suggests that immigrant fathers have more time available to spend with their families than native-born fathers.

Figure 5.4 presents a more detailed picture of the percentage distribution of part- and full-time work for fathers; it provides information for U.S.-born whites and the racial/ethnic groups of interest. Part-time work represents employment hardship, as most of these workers would prefer to work full-time (Tilly, 1996). Of all racial/ethnic immigrant groups (and native-born whites and blacks), Mexican fathers work a standard workweek (62.6 percent) most often, while native-born whites have the lowest proportion of standard work hours of all groups (43.3 percent). The most salient difference between native-born white and immigrant fathers is at the top end of the distribution of hours worked per week. While more than one-third (36.7 percent) of native-born white fathers worked more than forty-eight hours per week, only one-fifth (20.5 percent) of Mexican immigrant fathers worked as many hours. For Latin Americans, Asians, and African/Caribbean fathers, their share of overwork was about the same—25 percent. The exception was the Other Immigrant group, of which more than one-third (35.9 percent) overworked.

With the exception of the Other Immigrant group, immigrant fathers are more likely to work a standard workweek than native-born whites. Native-born white fathers are more often overworked relative to immigrant fathers (again, the exception is the Other category). This strongly suggests that immigrant fathers will have more time at their disposal than their native-born counterparts to get involved in family activities.

Class of Worker

In addition to hours worked per week, the labor market fortunes of workers are also influenced by the type of jobs they have. A useful typology is the Bureau of the Census's class of worker classification: the self-employed, those in the private sector, and public sector employees. Table 5.3 presents the percentage distribution of class of worker for native- and foreign-born fathers. Native-born fathers were distributed as follows: 13.1 percent were self-employed, 73.2 percent were employed in the private sector, and 13.6 percent were in the public sector. Foreign-born fathers were self-employed about as often as native-born fathers (13.1 percent and 12.7 percent, respectively). In general, immigrant fathers were more often employed in the private sector, but were underrepresented in the public sector relative to native-born white and black fathers.

Differences within migrant father groups are more salient than between native- and foreign-born fathers. For example, Mexicans were less often self-employed relative to all other immigrant fathers, but more likely to be employed in the private sector. The most significant difference was Mexicans' underrepresentation in the public sector, which includes jobs that typically require U.S. citizenship. The low percentage of Mexicans employed in the public sector is probably due to the low rates of naturalization of Mexican immigrants relative to other immigrant groups. Fathers in the Other Immigrant group were well represented among the self-employed (18.6 percent), as well as Asians and Pacific Islanders (14.9 percent). It should be pointed out that African and Caribbean fathers were the most likely to be employed in the public sector, along with Asians and Pacific Islanders.

Table 5.3. Distribution of Immigrant and Non-Immigrant Fathers across Class of Worker Categories by Selected Racial/Ethnic Groups (Percent)

	Self-Employed	Private, For-Profit	Private, Non-Profit	Public Sector
U.S. Born	13.1	69.2	4.0	13.6
Non-Latino, White	14.4	68.9	4.0	12.5
Non-Latino, Black	5.8	69.6	4.2	20.2
Immigrant	12.7	76.2	3.5	7.3
Mexico	8.7	85.1	2.0	3.9
Other Latin America	12.5	77.2	3.6	6.4
Asia/Pcific Islands	14.9	69.7	4.5	10.5
Africa/Caribbean	11.2	69.7	6.0	14.5
Other	18.6	68.1	4.4	8.7

Table 5.4.   Percent of Immigrant Fathers Self-Employed by Immigrant-Related Characteristics

	English Language Proficiency		Length of U.S. Residence		Citizenship Status	
	Limited	Proficient	<10 Years	10+ Years	Non-Citizen	Naturalized
Mexico	8.1	9	6.3	9.4	8.2	9.9
Other Latin America	11.7	12.8	9.9	13.4	11.6	14
Asia/Pacific Islands	19.1	13.9	9	16.9	13.5	15.8
Africa/ Caribbean	9.7	11.2	8.7	12	9.6	12.5
Other	14.4	18.9	10.8	22.3	14.5	22.7

Table 5.4 shows the percentage distribution of self-employed immigrant fathers by migrant-related characteristics—language proficiency, length of U.S. residence, and citizenship status. Immigrants might seek self-employment as a way to avoid being discriminated against in the labor market. It is worth noting that LEP Asians and Pacific Islanders had the highest percentage (19.1 percent) of self-employment, while LEP Mexicans were the least often self-employed (8.1 percent). In terms of length of residence in the United States, the most often self-employed recent immigrants were the Other Immigrant group (10.8 percent), closely followed by the Other Latin Americans (9.9 percent). Fathers in the Other Immigrant group who were not U.S. citizens were well represented among the self-employed (14.5 percent), whereas Mexicans were the least likely non-citizens to be self-employed (8.2 percent).

Occupation

The occupational distribution of immigrant and non-immigrant fathers is presented in table 5.5. Of all the immigrant groups, Mexicans' occupational distribution differs the most from that of native-born whites. While Mexicans were severely underrepresented in high-status occupations (managerial/professional and clerical/sales), they were disproportionately concentrated in low-status occupations. For example, for every Mexican employed in managerial or professional occupations, there were roughly four whites similarly employed (11.2 percent vs. 44.1 percent).

At the opposite end of the occupational distribution, Mexicans fared very poorly. They were more than three times as often employed as laborers relative to whites—15.8 percent and 4.5 percent, respectively. On the other hand, Asians and Pacific Islanders and those in the Other Immigrant

Table 5.5. Distribution of Immigrant and Non-Immigrant Fathers across Occupational Categories by Racial/Ethnic Group (Percent)

	Manager/Professional	Clerical/Sales	Craft/Repair	Operative	Services	Farm Laborer	Laborer
U.S.-Born	*41.2*	*11.9*	*19.9*	*14.3*	*7.0*	*0.5*	*5.1*
Non-Latino, White	44.1	11.7	20.3	13.1	5.8	0.4	4.5
Non-Latino, Black	25.1	13.3	15.5	22.6	14.6	0.4	8.6
Immigrant Total	*31.2*	*9.5*	*17.9*	*19.0*	*11.1*	*2.6*	*8.7*
Mexico	11.2	5.9	22.5	26.1	12.1	6.5	15.8
Other Latin America	24.7	11.2	20.5	21.3	13.7	0.5	8.1
Asia/Pacific Islands	47.1	12.5	12.0	13.3	12.1	0.2	2.9
Africa/Caribbean	39.0	13.1	14.3	14.3	13.7	0.2	4.4
Other	55.0	11.0	13.7	10.9	6.1	0.2	3.0

group were overrepresented in high-status occupations and underrepresented in the least skilled occupations (farm workers and laborers) relative to native-born whites. For instance, 47.1 percent of Asians and Pacific Islanders were employed in managerial and professional occupations, while the corresponding figure for whites was 44.1 percent. Similarly, only 2.9 percent of Asians and Pacific Islanders were laborers, but 4.5 percent of whites were so employed.

The data show striking differences in the occupational distribution of immigrant fathers. In large measure, this is a result of the level of education among immigrants. Groups with high levels of human capital (Asians and Pacific Islanders) have a higher percentage of managers and professionals than whites, whereas immigrants that bring low levels of schooling (Mexicans) are severely underrepresented among those occupational groups. Not only is occupational position a source of status and prestige, it is also closely linked to earnings.

Earnings

Figure 5.5 presents the distribution of annual earnings divided into quintiles (five equal parts) for native- and foreign-born fathers in 1999. Overall, more than half (57.5 percent) of immigrant fathers were concentrated in the two lowest quintiles earning less than $31,000, compared with 35.9 percent of U.S.-born fathers. The differences are even more pronounced for those in the bottom quintile: more than twice as many immigrant fathers earned less than $20,000 per year relative to U.S.-born fathers (32.1 percent

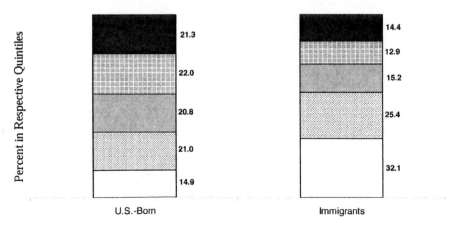

□ < $20k (Bottom 20%)   ▤ $20k-31k   ▨ $31k-43k   ▦ $43k-64k   ■ > $64k (Top 20%)

Figure 5.5.

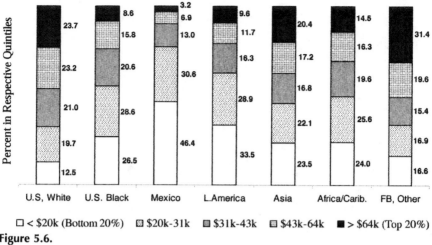

□ < $20k (Bottom 20%)   ▩ $20k-31k   ▨ $31k-43k   ▨ $43k-64k   ■ > $64k (Top 20%)

Figure 5.6.

vs. 14.9 percent). At the top of the earnings distribution, immigrant fathers were underrepresented in the highest quintile, which includes those earning $64,000 or more, compared with their native-born counterparts: 14.4 percent and 21.3 percent, respectively. In general, then, immigrant fathers seem to be underrepresented in the top quintile and overrepresented in the bottom quintile.

As figure 5.6 shows, the differences in earnings shares are salient both when comparing immigrant groups with U.S.-born fathers and across immigrant groups. Mexican fathers were the most disadvantaged immigrant group. A little over three-fourths (77.0 percent) of Mexican fathers were in the two lowest quintiles—that is, they earned less than $31,000 in 1999. A closer look reveals that nearly one-half (46.4 percent) of them were in the bottom quintile with earnings of less than $20,000. Only 3.2 percent of Mexicans were in the top quintile, earning $64,000 or more. The differences are striking compared with white fathers: 12.5 percent were in the bottom quintile, whereas 23.7 percent were in the top quintile. After Mexicans, the second most disadvantaged were the Other Latin Americans, of whom more than half (62.4 percent) were concentrated in the two lowest quintiles, and less than 10 percent in the top quintile. It is worth noting that a larger percentage of the Other Immigrant group (Europeans and others) was in the top quintile, compared with native-born white fathers (31.4 percent and 23.7 percent, respectively).

Once again, these results strongly suggest that high levels of education will produce favorable earnings returns in the labor market. Education channels individuals into high-status, high-paying occupations. For immigrants with

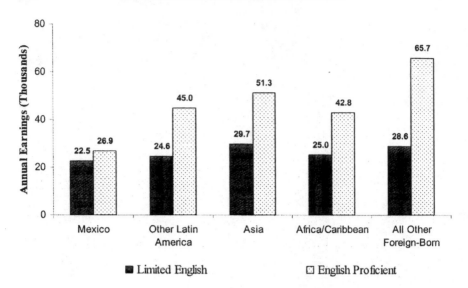

Figure 5.7.

low levels of schooling, the opposite holds: they are locked into dead-end, low-paying occupations.

Figure 5.7 displays average annual earnings of immigrant fathers by English-language proficiency. For each immigrant group, the inability to speak English well exerts an earnings penalty. But the earnings penalty varies substantially among the different groups of migrants. Although the earnings gap between English-speaking and non-English-speaking Mexicans is the smallest of all immigrant groups ($26,895 vs. $22,521), it is due in great measure to their very low earnings relative to other immigrant groups. The Other Immigrant group has the largest earnings differential: while English-proficient fathers earned $65,693, LEP fathers only earned $28,557. English-speaking ability, then, is another important form of human capital that affects immigrant fathers' labor market outcomes.

Figure 5.8 shows the average annual earnings of immigrant fathers by length of residence in the United States. Looking at earnings by length of residence is a good way to examine the degree of labor market incorporation of immigrants. The assumption is that the longer their stay, the higher their earnings will be. With the exception of the Other Immigrant group, the earnings gains for those with up to ten years of living in the United States are pretty flat. Contrary to expectations, Asian immigrants experience a precipitous decline in annual earnings instead of an increase. All immigrant groups, however, gained ground after having lived more than

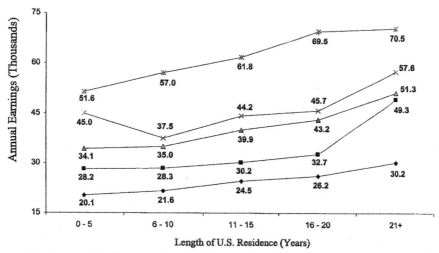

Figure 5.8.

ten years in the United States. Of all immigrant groups, Mexicans made the smallest overall gains in earnings from the first five years of U.S. residence to twenty or more years—from an average of $20,148 to $30,164. This is in stark contrast to the Other Immigrant group, which started at $51,560 and climbed to an average of $70,466.

Although we did not control for other variables, this crude measure of labor market incorporation clearly shows the divergent paths among immigrants. These findings suggest that immigrant groups who start at the bottom due to low levels of human capital will be handicapped in their struggle to move up the economic ladder.

Figure 5.9 displays data on the average annual earnings of foreign-born fathers by citizenship status. In terms of labor market outcomes, citizenship status provides an opportunity to measure the economic benefits of naturalization. Although we do not take other variables into consideration, naturalization increased the earnings of all immigrant groups. In absolute terms, the largest gain accrued to Other Latin Americans and the smallest to the Other Immigrant group. Becoming a U.S. citizen increased the earnings of Other Latin Americans by 36 percent, going from $28,805 to $44,978. The second largest gain accrued to Mexicans, for whom earnings increased by 25.7 percent. Although naturalization provided the smallest gain, only 12 percent, to the Other Immigrant group, it should be kept in mind that their average annual earnings were by far the highest of any immigrant group.

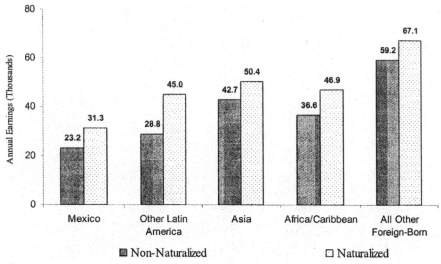

Figure 5.9.

DISCUSSION

Our results show that all immigrant groups of fathers, with the exception of the Other Immigrant group, performed less favorably in the labor market relative to native-born white fathers. In general, immigrant fathers had lower levels of employment, and higher levels of joblessness and non-participation in the labor force, compared with U.S.-born white fathers. Overall, Mexicans were the most disadvantaged immigrant group. They experienced the highest levels of marginal employment as measured by the prevalence of joblessness, part-time work, and non-participation in the labor force. Mexican immigrant fathers were also concentrated in the lowest rungs of the occupational hierarchy and had the lowest earnings of any immigrant group.

In terms of worktime, our results revealed striking differences between immigrant fathers and their native-born white counterparts. Although most fathers—independently of nativity—worked a standard workweek, the biggest difference was at both ends of the distribution of work hours. At the high end, more than one-third of white fathers worked more than forty-eight hours, whereas only one-fifth of Mexicans worked as many hours. The other immigrant groups fell somewhere in between with about one-fourth of them working excessive hours. The exception was the Other Immigrant group whose propensity to overwork was about the same as that of native white fathers. Because most groups of immigrant fathers worked fewer hours than their native-born counterparts, the former will be more accessible to their children—that is, they will be available for interaction whether it actually occurs or not (Pleck and Masciadrelli, 2004). In short, long hours of work limit the amount of time potentially available to interact with family members and might hinder the quality of the interaction (Crouter, Bumpus, Head, and McHale, 2001). But even if fathers have more time available to spend with their families, as is the case for Mexicans, the quality of their interactions might leave a lot to be desired if they are under severe stress due to a lack of economic resources. Future studies should pay close attention to the quality of father-child interactions, particularly for fathers who experience economic hardship.

In the case of Mexican immigrant fathers, one-fourth were not active in the formal labor force—that is, they were not working or looking for work. There is scant information about how Mexican fathers who are out of the labor force manage to make ends meet. Further research should examine the extent to which they are involved in the informal labor market. If they are active in the informal labor market, then they might be working intermittently and/or working very long hours to earn enough money to support their families. In either case, they are likely to face time constraints and economic distress. Researchers should also investigate whether immigrants' strategy to live in extended or multiple family arrangements serves to buffer the deleterious consequences of employment hardship.

In general, immigrant-related characteristics were associated with labor market outcomes. For example, a lack of English-language proficiency negatively affected earnings. The results for length of U.S. residence showed that for most immigrant groups, the first ten years of living in the country entailed a process of adjustment in the labor market. The data showed that more than ten years are needed for earnings to increase. Lastly, immigrants who became U.S. citizens saw their labor market outcomes improve. It seems, however, that the biggest challenge is intergenerational mobility. That is, given the socioeconomic characteristics of the least economically favored immigrant fathers, what are their children's prospects for social mobility?

Another consideration in terms of employment outcomes is immigrant fathers' legal status. Those working under precarious undocumented status, for instance, may face levels of workplace exploitation not experienced by authorized workers (Cranford, 2005; Waldinger and Lichter, 2003), and their uncertain legal status may inhibit their ability to redress grievances or search for better employment circumstances. Research on how fathers' legal status affects the lives of their foreign- and U.S.-born children is greatly needed.

An important activity of fathering is breadwinning, which is closely linked to fathers' labor market participation (Pleck and Masciadrelli, 2004). For recent immigrants from less developed countries (e.g., Latin

America and Mexico), their self-perception as breadwinner might be initially enhanced because they are likely to be working more and earning more than they would have in their country of origin. This is likely to happen even if they are employed in low-status jobs at low wages relative to U.S. standards. But the longer they live in the United States and begin to compare themselves to native-born fathers, the more likely they are to take notice of their relative inability to provide financially for their families and consequently to come to see themselves as inadequate breadwinners. This is more likely to occur if their labor market situation has not improved in a significant way since their arrival in the United States. Consequently, lack of labor market mobility is bound to be corrosive on their identity as breadwinner.

Another consequence for immigrant fathers who have experienced limited job mobility is that their spouses and children may come to see them as inadequate breadwinners, particularly as their children become acculturated and adapt U.S. values and norms. As children acculturate, they may adopt the views that native-born white children have of their fathers as family providers. As a result, the gap between immigrant fathers' traditional cultural perceptions of breadwinning and that of their acculturated children might widen. We are presenting this as a testable hypothesis. In all likelihood this will diminish fathers' positive self-perception as breadwinner. Accordingly, social scientists interested in studying immigrant fathers' relations with their families should pay close attention to the interplay between limited economic mobility and cultural change over time.

Overall, the findings presented in this chapter simultaneously serve as a source for both optimism and concern with regard to the future economic mobility and incorporation of immigrant fathers and their families. For several economic indicators, some immigrant groups—specifically those from Asia and those in the Other Immigrant group, comprised largely of well-educated persons originating in Europe, the Middle East, and India—appear to be reaching a level of labor market parity with native-born white fathers. On the other hand, Mexican-born fathers appear to be lagging behind these groups, and, on several indicators, report labor market outcomes similar to those of U.S.-born black fathers, traditionally the most marginalized in the U.S. workforce. These findings for immigrant fathers support the perspectives of scholars of contemporary U.S. immigrant incorporation, who have identified Mexican immigrants for a delayed pattern of intergenerational economic mobility relative to other immigrant groups (Bean and Stevens, 2003) or, worse, for a downward mobility pattern into the socioeconomic ranks of the urban underclass (Portes and Rumbaut, 2001). Above all, our findings reinforce that the future of immigrant families is not a monolithic trend, but rather that immigrant economic outcomes are forming diverse patterns based on national origin.

REFERENCES

Alba, R., and Nee, V. (2003). *Remaking the American mainstream: Assimilation and contemporary immigration.* Cambridge, MA: Harvard University Press.

Bates, T., and Dunham, C. R. (1992). Facilitating upward mobility through small business ownership. In G. E. Peterson and W. Vroman (Eds.), *Urban labor markets and job opportunity.* Washington, DC: Urban Institute Press.

Bean, F., and Stevens, G. (2003). *America's newcomers and the dynamics of diversity.* New York: Sage.

Becker, G. S. (1993). *Human capital.* Third edition. Chicago: University of Chicago Press.

Borjas, G. (1990). *Friends or strangers: The impact of immigrants on the U.S. economy.* New York: Basic Books.

Cabrera, N. J., Tamis-LeMonda, C. S., Bradley, R. H., Hofferth, S., and Lamb, M. E. (2000). Fatherhood in the twenty-first century. *Child Development, 71,* 127–36.

Catanzarite, L. (2000). Brown-collar jobs: Occupational segregation and earnings of recent immigrant Latinos. *Sociological Perspectives, 43,* 45–75.

Chiswick, B. R. (1978). The effects of Americanization on the earnings of foreign-born men. *Journal of Political Economy, 86,* 897–921.

———. (1991). Speaking, reading, and writing among low-skilled immigrants. *Journal of Labor Economics, 9,* 149–70.

Cranford, C. J. (2005). Networks and exploitation: Immigrant labor and the restructuring of the Los Angeles janitorial industry. *Social Problems, 52,* 379–97.

Crouter, A. C., Bumpus, M. F., Head, M. R., and McHale, S. M. (2001). Implications of overwork and overload for the quality of men's family relationships. *Journal of Marriage and the Family, 63,* 404–16.

Dávila, A., and Mora, M. T. (2001). Hispanic ethnicity, English skill investments, and earnings. *Industrial Relations, 40,* 383–88.

———. (2004). English-language skills and the earnings of self-employed immigrants in the U.S.: A note. *Industrial Relations, 43,* 386–91.

De Anda, R. M. (1992). Involuntary part-time work among Chicanos: Its causes and consequences. In T. Mindiola and E. Zamora (Eds.), *Chicano discourse* (69–87). Houston: Mexican American Studies Program, University of Houston.

DeFreitas, G. (1991). *Inequality at work: Hispanics in the U.S. labor force.* New York: Oxford University Press.

Duncan, G., and Brooks-Gunn, J. (Eds.). (1997). *Consequences of growing up poor.* New York: Sage.

Hernandez, D. J. (Ed.). (1999). *Children of immigrants: Health, adjustments, and public assistance.* Washington, DC: National Academy Press.

Hofferth, S. L., Stueve, J. L., Pleck, J., Bianchi, S., and Sayer, L. (2002). The demography of fathers: What fathers do. In C. S. Tamis-LeMonda and N. Cabrera (Eds.), *Handbook on father involvement: Multidisciplinary perspectives* (63–90). Mahwah, NJ: Erlbaum.

Kalleberg, A. L., and Berg, I. (1987). *Work and industry: Structures, markets, and processes.* New York: Plenum.

Massey, D. S., Arango, J., Hugo, G., Kouaouci, A., Pellegrino, A., and Taylor, J. E. (1998). *World in motion: Understanding international migration at the end of the millennium.* Oxford: Oxford University Press.

Piore, M. J. (1979). *Birds of passage: Migrant labor in industrial societies.* London: Cambridge University Press.

Pleck, J. H., and Masciadrelli, B. P. (2004). Paternal involvement by U.S. residential fathers: Levels, sources, and consequences. In M. E. Lamb (Ed.), *The role of the father in child development* (222–71). Hoboken, NJ: Wiley.

Portes, A., and Rumbaut, R. G. (2001). *Legacies: The story of the immigrant second generation.* Berkeley: University of California Press.

Portes, A., and Zhou, M. (1996). Self-employment and the earnings of immigrants. *American Sociological Review, 61,* 219–30.

Ruggles, S., Sobek, M., Alejander, T., Fitch, C. A., Goeken, R., Hall, P. K., King, M., and Ronnander, C. (2004). *Integrated public use microdata series: Version 3.0.* Minneapolis: Minnesota Population Center.

Tilly, C. (1996). *Half a job: Bad and good part-time jobs in a changing labor market.* Philadelphia: Temple University Press.

Van Hook, J., Brown, S. L., and Kwenda, M. N. (2004). A decomposition of trends in poverty among children of immigrants. *Demography, 41,* 649–70.

Van Hook, J., and Fix, M. (2000). A profile of the immigrant student population. In J. R. De Velasco, M. Fix, and T. Clowell (Eds.), *Overlooked and underserved: Immigrant children in U.S. secondary schools* (9–33). Washington, DC: Urban Institute Press.

Waldinger, R. (2001). *Strangers at the gates: New immigrants in urban America.* Berkeley: University of California Press.

Waldinger, R., and Lichter, M. I. (2003). *How the other half works: Immigration and the social organization of labor.* Berkeley: University of California Press.

6

Transcending Confucian Teachings on Fathering: A Sign of the Times or Acculturation?

Susan S. Chuang and Yanjie Su

In the past several decades, the roles that fathers play in their children's lives have gained a great deal of attention (Lamb, 2004). Researchers have reported that children form significant and important relationships with their fathers and that positive father involvement has beneficial effects on their children's development (for review, see Lamb, Chuang, and Cabrera, 2003; Parke, 2002; J. H. Pleck and Masciadrelli, 2004). With the tremendous immigrant growth of Asians in Canada and the United States, it becomes imperative to study fatherhood in Chinese families. Unfortunately, our current knowledge of fathering is primarily based on middle-class Euro-American families with limited understanding of fathering in non-Euro-American families (for overview, see Lamb and Lewis, 2004).

Asian families are the fastest growing immigrant group in Canada. Between 2001 and 2006, for example, 1.1 million immigrants arrived in Canada, of which 58.3 percent were born in Asian countries, including the Middle East. Immigrants from the People's Republic of China accounted for 14 percent of the recent immigrant population (Statistics Canada, 2006).

CURRENT VIEWS ON FATHERING ROLES

While fathers' overt behavior, termed as "father involvement," has gained the greatest attention (for methodological overview, see Pleck and Masciadrelli, 2004), some researchers have investigated conceptions of fathering roles. As pointed out by Bronte-Tinkew, Carrano, and Guzman (2006), the focus on conceptions of fathering is only recent. However, how fathers conceptualize and organize their views on their roles as parents will affect their levels of involvement with their children, which, in turn, affects children's psychological and socioemotional development (Parke, 2002). Tamis-LeMonda (2004) argued that fathers assume multiple roles beyond that of economic provider, such as teacher, protector, and role model. Dienhart (2001) noted a shift toward a more egalitarian parental partnership. Such shift in conceptions of fathering has influenced researchers' views that fathers are now more "invested" in family relationships and childcare (see Lamb, 2004; Tamis-LeMonda and Cabrera, 2002).

Others have framed fathering within role identity theory, which emphasizes the duality of societal expectations and the subjective personal interpretations that one attributes to these societal expectations (e.g., Bronte-Tinkew, Carrano, and Guzman, 2006; Pleck and Stueve, 2004). In Bronte-Tinkew et al.'s (2006) study on four ethnic groups (non-Hispanic white, non-Hispanic black, Hispanic, and other race), fathers' reports on their personal perceptions of their roles in the family were based on their own unique experiences and contextual factors (differing by race, ethnicity, income, and educational levels). For example, economically disadvantaged fathers, less educated fathers, fathers of other races, and Hispanic fathers were less likely to believe that their roles as caregiver, playmate, or emotional supporter would positively impact their children's lives. However, researchers have collapsed these fathering roles into one construct, which limits our knowledge of how fathers' perceptions of each role may impact their levels of behavior. Perhaps fathers believe that playing with their children rather than expressing emotions to them is more important to child development. Unfortunately, other research on father identity also faces similar methodological limitations. For example, Henley and Pasley (2005) conceptualized "father identity" along two dimensions: identity satisfaction and identity investment, while Sanderson and Thompson (2002) queried fathers' view of self-identity along five global statements (e.g., "being a father is important to me," "being a father is important in my family"). Such global measures of fathering do not lend themselves to parsing out the various conceptions of fatherhood that may be qualitatively distinct from each other (e.g., breadwinner, playmate, caregiver).

To date, the literature on conceptions of fathering roles lacks a coherent framework, with the general tendency of researchers to use global assessments of father roles or identities. Such predetermined measures confine the boundaries of paternal identities rather than tapping into potential nuances, which may differ by various factors such as ethnicity, education, employment, or country of origin. As fathers conceptualize various roles, researchers need to delineate and examine each role. As we delve more explicitly into conceptions of fathering, we will gain a better understanding of how fathers' beliefs may inform their paternal involvement (behaviors).

To date, how Chinese fathers conceptualize their roles in their families and whether these roles may change due to sociocultural circumstances such as immigrating to a new country is unclear. Rather, our current knowledge is based on Chinese traditions, adages, and Confucianism, which may have less influence on contemporary Chinese families.

CONFUCIAN CONCEPTIONS OF FATHERING

To place Chinese fathers into context, fathers need to be understood historically, with the focus on Confucianism, which was a major socializing agent through much of Chinese history. According to Confucius, the father's role is defined as *yi jia zhi zhu* (一家之主), translated as "master of the family." The father possesses a more powerful position in the family than the mother, controlling the financial resources and making the important decisions about the family and the children. Gender roles were also clearly defined: men should not speak about issues *inside* the home, while women should not speak about issues *outside* the home. Thus fathers are to be aloof and distant in the family setting (Ho, 1987; Shek, 2001). These traditional roles of mothers and fathers were assumed to guide families in dividing the family obligations and responsibilities and maintaining social order within the family unit.

The father-child relationship was structured around the ideology of filial piety, the cornerstone of Confucianism. Filial piety is defined as bringing honor and not disgrace to the family name. Children are expected to be obedient, respectful, and loyal to their father (de Groot, 1882–1910; Freeman, 1965). The existing research on Asian fathering has drawn heavily from Confucianism and the traditional Chinese adage, "strict father, kind mother" (Wilson, 1974). In such a relationship, fathers assumed the role of a stern disciplinarian and were not encouraged to engage in emotional indulgence with their children (Fei, 1935; Ho, 1987; Wilson, 1974; Wolf, 1970).

As we delve into the limited research on Chinese fathering, few have questioned the relevance of traditional Chinese notions of fathering. Researchers have not critically examined whether the existing conceptualizations of Chinese fathering are reflective of immigrant fathers of today.

CONTEMPORARY VIEWS ON CHINESE FATHERING

Over the years, China has undergone many historical and social changes. For example, the communist revolution, increasing numbers of women entering the workforce, the Marriage Law in 1950 that established the equality of the sexes, and laws that protected the interests of women and children undoubtedly altered the roles of fathers (Abbott, Ming, and Meredith, 1992). Moreover, family size (e.g., the one-child policy, instituted in 1992) has changed the nature of the father-child relationship, so fathers tend to "spoil" their children (for review, see Shwalb, Nakazawa, Yamamoto, and Hyun, 2004). As some researchers have reported, the one-child policy may have created a "Westernized" parenting approach—becoming more "child-centered," especially among the well-educated population (Chang, Schwartz, Dodge, and McBride-Chang, 2003). With these profound social and cultural changes the degree to which Confucianism influences fathering remains unclear.

Although the literature on Chinese fathers is sparse, the research on parenting styles and practices provides us with some insight into how fathering is perceived. Focusing on perceptions of parenting styles, some researchers see the traditional parenting roles of "strict father, warm mother." For example, Chinese adults perceived their mothers as being more warm and less restrictive than their fathers, although mothers also placed higher demands on their children (Berndt, Cheung, Lau, Hau, and Lew, 1993; Lau, Lew, Hau, Cheung, and Berndt, 1990). Similarly, Shek reported that, compared to mothers, adolescents perceived their fathers as less positive, more harsh, and less concerned with them (Shek, 1998).

However, when assessing self-reports on parenting styles, some researchers challenged the Chinese traditional roles of parenting. Chao and Kim (2000) were the first to examine parenting differences among immigrant Taiwanese American mothers and fathers of elementary school-aged children. The findings revealed that mothers and fathers did not significantly differ from each other in terms of how they rated their parenting styles as well as their views on how parents should train their children (e.g., "Parents must train children to work very hard and be disciplined") (Chao and Kim, 2000).

Assessing the influence of Confucianism on fathering, Ho and Kang's (1984) intergenerational study explored Hong Kong fathers and their fathers (grandfathers). Findings revealed that the current generation of fathers was less supportive of the ideologies of filial piety and of traditional ideas about child training than their own fathers. As compared to their fathers, the current generation of fathers subscribed less to the idea of children respecting their elders and more to children's expression of opinions, independence, self-mastery, creativity, self-respect, and all-round development (Ho and Kang, 1984). Likewise, Lin and Fu (1990) reported that although Taiwanese and Taiwanese American fathers had higher ratings on parental control than did Euro-American fathers, they also had higher ratings on encouraging their children's independence (Lin and Fu, 1990). These findings suggest that the influence of Confucianism on parenting may be less pervasive than previously thought.

With the increasing rise of Chinese families immigrating to other countries such as Canada and the United States, some researchers have examined the acculturation influence on parenting beliefs and practices. Although researchers have not explored acculturation influences on fathering per se, some researchers have examined parenting practices and found some cultural differences due to acculturation. Specifically, Lin and Fu (1990) found that for both mothers and fathers of six- to seven-year-old children, immigrant-Chinese parents were less controlling than Chinese parents. Chiu's (1987) study of Chinese and immigrant-Chinese mothers of three-year-old children also revealed similar results. Thus, researchers contend that through acculturation, parents are adapting and adjusting their parenting practices and beliefs accordingly.

While these studies provide some insight into the dynamics of Chinese family functioning, the majority of these studies are based on global measures (e.g., typologies of parenting styles), which may not capture the sociocultural nuances of family interactions and functioning. Chao's (1994) qualitative work on Taiwanese American mothers' views on childrearing practices stressed the importance of how meanings that are attached to constructs may vary between ethnic groups. For example, Taiwanese American mothers defined their children's independence as self-reliance whereas Euro-American mothers viewed independence as self-expression (Chao, 1994). In a previous study, I (Chuang, 2006) explicitly examined parenting in everyday situations and assessed the degree to which Confucian teachings were still relevant among contemporary families. First-generation Taiwanese mothers of six- to eight-year-old children were queried about their concepts of independence and individuality in relation to their children's everyday life events. Contradicting Confucian teachings of filial piety and absolute parental authority over children, the findings revealed that Chinese mothers were similar to Euro-American (e.g., see Nucci and Smetana, 1996) and Japanese (Yamada, 2004) mothers in that they believed that children should have "a voice" to express themselves and make their own decisions for some parts of their lives (e.g., choosing their clothes). This evidence may be indicative of a general cultural change in Asian societies such that Confucianism may not be as influential on today's Asian families.

CHINESE FATHERS' LEVELS OF FATHER INVOLVEMENT

As researchers place greater attention on fatherhood, the primary focus has been on fathers' actual behaviors, which have been coined as "father involvement." One of the most prominent and widely adopted models of father involvement was conceptualized by Lamb, Pleck, Charnov, and Levine (1987). These scholars conceptually distinguished three types of father involvement: 1) engagement, which refers to direct interaction with the child, including caretaking and play; 2) accessibility or availability to the child, in which the father is within earshot distance of the child; and 3) the assumption of responsibility for the child by ensuring that the child is appropriately cared for and reared (see Lamb, 2004).

Recently, there has been some evidence that contemporary Chinese fathers are not aligning themselves with the traditional parenting roles as defined by Confucian teachings. According to the Chinese National Bureau of Statistics (2001), 77 percent of the men believed that men should do half of the domestic work. Only half of the men and women believed that men and women should maintain the traditional parent-role differentiation, in which men would primarily be responsible for activities in society while women would primarily be responsible for activities in the home. Chinese fathers were also reporting higher levels of familial responsibilities and involvement in their children's lives (Chinese National Bureau of Statistics, 2001). These census data indicate that contemporary fathers are conceptualizing a more egalitarian parenting approach, making less family role distinctions between men and women.

While few researchers have explored issues of parental responsibilities among Chinese families, the evidence on the "shift" away from traditional roles in fathers' behaviors is inconsistent. For example, some studies did not support this "shift" in fathers' behaviors. Jankowiak's (1992) observational study of urban Chinese families in their homes found that fathers spent very little time caring for young children, especially infants. One woman stated that if "a man held an infant, he might become confused and drop it" (349). Similarly, Sun and Roopnarine's (1996) sixty-minute home observations of Chinese families of one-year-old children in Taiwan revealed that paternal involvement in childcare duties was minimal. Moreover, the types of division of household labor were gendered: mothers reported that they engaged in more food preparation, cleaning, and child-related work whereas fathers were more responsible for household repairs (Sun and Roopnarine, 1996).

However, Abbott, Ming, and Meredith (1992) examined fathers (children ranging in age from infancy to seventeen years of age) from mainland China and reported that fathers were equally responsible for helping their child with school work, taking him/her to and from school, disciplining, and taking the child on social activities. Moreover, compared to mothers, fathers stated that they were more likely to comfort their child when the child was fussy or upset, helped the child to solve problems, and taught the child values (Abbott, Ming, and Meredith, 1992).

In terms of play, Sun and Roopnarine (1996) reported that Taiwanese fathers engaged in limited play with their one-year-old children (2.18 minutes over a sixty-minute observation). However, the observations were conducted during mealtime, providing a methodological constraint. Su (1968) stated that although Chinese fathers reported their involvement in their middle-school-aged children's play or recreational activities, it was the question of how often fathers played with their children that needed attention. Overall, only 12 percent of fathers spent time with their children in social activities every day while 40 percent of the fathers' social engagements were on the weekends (Su, 1968).

Along these dimensions of father involvement (engagement, responsibility, accessibility), some researchers have explored the determinants of paternal involvement, such as levels of education and income. Based on the National Survey of Families and Households (NHFH), Marsiglio (1991) reported that fathers with higher levels of education generally spent more time with their children in specific activities that were related to education such as homework and reading activities but not in other activities such as leisure play (Marsiglio, 1991). However, based on the 1997 Child Development Supplement to the Panel Study of Income Dynamics (Hofferth, Davis-Kean, Davis, and Finkelstein, 1998), Yeung, Sandberg, Davis-Kean, and Hofferth (2001) reported that fathers' higher levels of education were associated with higher levels of engagement with their children (ranging in ages from infancy to twelve years of age). On the other hand, fathers' earnings had significant negative effects on their levels of interactions with their children during workdays, although the magnitude of the amount of time was relatively small. That is, for every $10,000 increase, fathers spent 3.5 minutes less in their total involvement with their children (Yeung, Sandberg, Davis-Kean, and Hofferth, 2001; also see NICHD Early Child Care Research Network, 2000).

While levels of education are linked to fathering, researchers tend to examine educational differences between two primary educational groups—high school and less, some college and above. However, there may be implications of parenting based on higher levels of education (between undergraduate and graduate levels). In 1992, the Canadian government explicitly altered the immigrant selection procedures for more highly educated immigrants. The immigrant landscape dramatically changed in 1992, and the educational attainment of a degree (of immigrants aged fifteen years or older) rose from 17 percent to 45 percent in 2004 (Statistics Canada, 2006). Thus, the influences of education on fathering and father-child interactions need to be further explored.

With the sociocultural changes in China and the acculturation process of adjusting into a new culture, along with a general increase in levels of education, the conceptions of Chinese fathering are complex. In past research, acculturation differences were found among parents' parenting styles (e.g., Chiu, 1987; Lin and Fu, 1990), while other studies challenged the influence of Confucianism on contemporary families (e.g., Chuang, 2006). Due to the scarce and contradictory findings on Chinese fathers, a comparative study of fathers *in* China and *from* China would provide a more accurate portrait of fathers, allowing researchers to examine potential acculturative influences (differences between the two groups). Moreover, since fathers are rarely the informants (see Pleck, this volume, for discussion), this study specifically recruited fathers. This exploratory study will address the following questions: 1) What are the conceptions of fathering among native Chinese and first-generation immigrant-Chinese fathers and are there acculturative differences?; 2) What are the levels of father involvement and do these levels differ by country?; and 3) What are the potential links between paternal beliefs and practices?

METHOD

Participants

Initially, the present study included sixty-eight intact first-generation immigrant Chinese Canadian (born in mainland China) and fifty-nine Chinese fathers of one-year-old children from Beijing, China. Due to the small sample of fathers with high school education or less (three Chinese Canadian and five Chinese fathers) and the evidence that parenting conceptions and beliefs do differ by levels of education (e.g., Yeung et al., 2001), these fathers were not included in the study. As a result, participants were sixty-five Chinese Canadian and fifty-four Chinese fathers of one-year-old children (twenty-five and twenty-seven fathers of sons, respectively) (Ms = 1.15, 1.06 years of age, SDs = .20, .36, respectively). Chinese Canadian and Chinese fathers' mean years of age were 36.78 and 33.08 years of age, respectively (SDs = 4.23, 3.90 years, respectively). The fathers' levels of education were generally high across the two countries and were divided into two educational groups: 1) university-educated (UE), and 2) graduate-educated (GE), including professional degrees such as M.D., Ph.D., and L.L.B. There were thirty-four (twenty girls) Chinese Canadian and thirty-five (seventeen girls) Chinese fathers in the university group, and thirty-two (nineteen girls) Chinese Canadian and sixteen (nine girls) native Chinese fathers in the graduate group. A preliminary ANOVA revealed that Chinese Canadian fathers were significantly more educated than their native counterparts (F (1, 117) = 4.60, p < .05, Ms = 1.51, 1.31, SDs = .50, .47, respectively).

For immigrant fathers, the years of residency in Canada and the United States ranged from six months to seven years (M years = 3.78, SD = 1.39). In terms of employment, most of the Chinese Canadian and Chinese fathers were employed full-time, except for seven immigrant-Chinese fathers who were unemployed. The mean household yearly income was $40,000–$60,000/year for the immigrant-Chinese families and $72,000–$96,000 YN for the families in China.

Procedure

Families first completed Background Information Questionnaires that were then given to a trained bilingual Chinese research assistant on the day of the interview. All interviews were conducted in the families' home. The interview consisted of questions that focused on the fathers' views on their parental roles in the family. Fathers also filled out a detailed report of their daily activities over two types of days (workday, non-workday), focusing on their social interactions with their children. The interview and detailed report of their days took approximately thirty minutes to complete. For the fathers in Canada, most of the interviews were conducted in Mandarin, the preferred language (eight fathers preferred English). Interviews were audio-taped and later transcribed verbatim into Chinese. Two bilingual Chinese students, fluent in both Mandarin and English, translated the interviews into English. To attain accuracy in the translation process, the students first translated 20 percent of the interviews and any discrepancies were discussed and agreed upon. The interviews were then transcribed accordingly.

Conceptions of Fathering Interview

A semi-structured interview was developed to tap into fathers' conceptions of parenting roles and responsibilities. Parental roles and duties were categorized into mutually exclusive categories: Breadwinner, caregiver (i.e., taking care of the child's emotional and physical needs), disciplinarian, educator/trainer, household duties (e.g., cleaning dishes, vacuuming), playmate for the child, and other. The Parental Role coding system was developed by examining 20 percent of the interview responses. Then, two coders coded 25 percent of the interviews and interrater reliability was high (Kappa − .84). Up to three responses were coded. All role responses were based on proportions, and arcsine transformations were used to correct for non-normality (Winer, Brown, and Michels, 1991). For ease of presentation, the means in table 6.1 are untransformed. Only categories that included 10 percent or more of the responses were included in the analyses.

Measures of Father Involvement

To assess the fathers' levels of involvement with their children, a detailed time diary recall method (Robinson, 1977) was used. Fathers were asked to fill out a chart on the details of their last workday (weekday) and their last non-workday (weekend day) in a period of twenty-four hours, with the focus on activities with their children. The chart included categories of: actual time, what they were doing and with whom, room location, and if they were doing anything else. For example, a father would report that from 5:30 to 6:15 p.m., he changed his child's diapers in the bedroom by himself and was also playing with her.

The fathers' reports of their weekday and weekend day activities were computed by the number of minutes that fathers spent with their children. Based on the Lamb model (Lamb et al., 1987), each segment of time was categorized into two dimensions of father involvement: 1) Engagement—with specific coding for two subdivisions: Care and Play, and 2) Accessibility (within earshot distance of the child)—with specific coding for two subdivisions: a) general accessibility when the father is awake; and b) doing household chores such as laundry, cooking meals. The third dimension, Sole Responsibility (the only adult being responsible for the child), was not included since this dimension was rarely found among this sample.

RESULTS

Preliminary Analyses

Since our current knowledge on determinants of father involvement indicates that both the fathers' levels of education and income levels may influence fathering, we first examined the association between these two factors. The correlation was nonsignificant, and thus two sets of analyses were conducted on fathers' beliefs about their roles and their levels of involvement. A series of regression analyses for household income revealed no significant main or interaction effects, so this factor was dropped from the analyses. Fathers' levels of education, however, revealed significant results that are discussed below.

Conceptions of Fathering Interview

To examine conceptions of fathering, Chinese Canadian and Chinese fathers were asked to define their parental roles and duties in their families. Upon reflection, they described their role as multidimensional, including: economic provider, playmate, caregiver, doing household chores, and educator. To examine whether fathering conceptions differed by country and fathers' educational levels, a 2 (Child's Gender) × 2 (Country: Canada, China) × 2 (Father's Education: undergraduate, graduate) × 5 (Role: economic provider, playmate, caregiver, doing household chores, educator) repeated-measures ANOVA analysis, with "role" treated as the repeated mea-

Table 6.1. Mean Proportions of Immigrant-Chinese-Canadian and Chinese Fathers' Views of Paternal Roles in the Family by Fathers' Level of Education

Type of Role	Educational Group		Total
	University	Graduate	
Breadwinner	.26 (.35)	.15 (.25)	.21 (.31)
Caregiver	.31 (.35)	.28 (.30)	.30 (.33)
Playmate	.12 (.23)	.10 (.18)	.11 (.21)
Household Chores	.13 (.27)	.10 (.21)	.12 (.25)
Educator/Trainer	.09 (.20)	.19 (.28)	.13 (.24)
Emotional Support	.01 (.07)	.06 (.18)	.03 (.13)
Disciplinarian	0	.01 (.07)	0 (.05)
Other	.07 (.26)	.12 (.33)	.09 (.29)

Note. Standard deviations are in parentheses.

sure, was conducted. The analysis revealed only a significant main effect for role, $F(4, 106) = 5.20$, $p < .001$. A series of Bonferroni t-tests revealed that fathers were generally more likely to view themselves as economic providers than as playmates ($p < .001$). Moreover, fathers viewed themselves as caregivers more often than educators, playmates, or responsible for household chores ($ps < .0001$) (see table 6.1).

Relationships between Roles

The next question was to examine whether fathers' conceptions of the various roles were perceived as mutually independent of each other or intertwined. Thus, a series of correlational analyses were conducted on the five roles with the specific focus on the interplay of culture and education on these role conceptions. Thus, the analyses were conducted for each educational group (UE, GE) by country.

Canada

For Chinese Canadian fathers, both UE and GE fathers who viewed their roles as economic providers were less likely to view themselves as caregivers ($rs = -.38$, $ps < .05$). Moreover, GE fathers who were more likely to mention the role of an educator were less likely to include caregiver as their role ($r = -.39$, $p < .01$)

China

Similar to their Chinese Canadian counterparts, UE fathers in China negatively associated economic provider with caregiver ($r = -.37$, $p < .05$), but GE Chinese fathers did not.

Fathers' Levels of Involvement

To explore the level of father involvement in children's lives and the extent to which levels of education may influence fathers' behaviors, two 2 (Child's Gender) × 2 (Country: Canada, China) × 2 (Father's Education: undergraduate, graduate) × 4 (Father Involvement: accessibility, household chores, play, care) repeated-measures ANOVAs, with "father involvement" treated as the repeated measures, were conducted for the two types of days, a workday and non-workday.

Workday

For the workday, the analysis revealed significant main effects for country, $F (1, 111) = 7.28$, $p < .01$, and father involvement, $F (3, 109) = 101.41$, $p < .001$, and significant interactions for father involvement × child's gender, $F (3, 109) = 2.79$, $p < .05$, and country × father's education, $F (1, 111) = 5.80$, $p < .05$.

Comparing both countries, fathers in Canada spent significantly more time with their children than did fathers in China (Ms = 6:34, 4:32, SDs = 3:39, 2:42, respectively). Focusing on fathers' time with their families, not surprisingly, post-hoc Bonferroni t-tests revealed that fathers, regardless of nationality, were significantly more accessible to their children rather than engaging in other activities such as household chores, caring for, and playing with their children. Fathers also spent more time playing with and caring for their children than engaged in household chores ($ps < .001$) (see table 6.2). Focusing on play, a series of post-hoc ANOVAs revealed that fathers generally spent more time playing with their daughters than sons (Ms = 1:20, :53, SDs = 1:21, 1:03, respectively).

For fathers in China but not Canada, further post-hoc ANOVA analyses revealed that GE fathers were significantly more accessible to their daughters than were UE fathers (Ms = 4:58, 2:21, SDs = 2:20, 1:27, respectively). Moreover, for UE fathers, fathers were more accessible to sons than to daughters (Ms = 3:12, 2:21, SDs = 1:41, 1:27, respectively).

Table 6.2. Immigrant-Chinese-Canadian and Chinese Fathers' Absolute Levels of Father Involvement by Type of Day (Hours and Minutes)

| | Type of Day/Country | | | | | |
| | Workday | | | Non-Workday | | |
Father Involvement	Canada	China	Total	Canada	China	Total
Accessibility	3:54	3:07	3:04	6:26	5:06	5:52
Household Chores	:24	:06	:16	1:30	:38	1:11
Care	1:01	:27	:45	1:22	:50	1:06
Play	1:15	:59	1:06	2:31	2:18	2:27
Total	6:24	4:39	5:40	11:49	8:52	10:35

Non-Workday

Similar to the analyses for workday, the repeated-measures ANOVA revealed significant main effects for father involvement, F (3, 109) = 126.63, p < .001, and country, F (1, 111) = 14.67, p < .001. As presented in table 6.2, a series of post-hoc Bonferroni t-tests found that Chinese Canadian fathers were generally more involved with their children than their native Chinese counterparts. Also, fathers were generally more accessible to their children rather than engaged in household chores, caring for, and playing with their children. They also spent greater amounts of time playing with their children than caring for them or doing household chores (ps < .001).

Links between Conceptions of Fathering Roles and Levels of Father Involvement

The next step was to explore the possible links between fathers' conceptions of fathering roles and their fathering behaviors in everyday events during the workdays and non-workdays. A series of correlational analyses were conducted among conceptions of fathering roles and the four categories of father involvement (care, play, general accessibility, and household duties), for each group of fathers by their levels of education and country (see table 6.3 for overview).

Table 6.3. Associations among Immigrant-Chinese-Canadian and Chinese Fathers' Conceptions of Fathering Roles and Absolute Levels of Father Involvement by Fathers' Educational Level and Type of Day

Father Role	Country	Educational Level	Type of Day	Father Involvement	r
Economic Provider	Canada	university	workday	care	−.40*
Educator	Canada	university	workday	chores	.41**
		graduate	non-workday	accessibility	−.42*
	China	university	non-workday	care	−.33*
Household Chores	China	graduate	workday	play	.56**
		graduate	non-workday	chores	.69**
		graduate	non-workday	care	.95***
Playmate	Canada	university	workday	play	.49**
		graduate	non-workday	play	.45**
	China	university	workday	chores	.43**
		graduate	workday	play	.62**
Caregiver	Canada	university	workday	care	.41*
		graduate	non-workday	accessibility	.38*
	China	graduate	workday	care	.85***

Note. * < .05; ** < .01; *** < .001.

Economic Provider

Only UE Canadian fathers' conceptions of an economic provider were linked to their levels of involvement. Specifically, these fathers who were more likely to view themselves as an economic provider spent less time in taking care of their children during the workdays ($r = -.40, p < .05$).

Educator

Immigrant UE fathers who viewed themselves as an educator were more likely to spend more time on household chores during the workdays ($r = .43, p < .05$). However, immigrant GE fathers were less likely to be accessible on the weekends if they believed that their role was as an educator ($r = -.42, p < .05$). For UE fathers in China, the educator role was negatively associated with their levels of care of their infants on the weekends ($r = -.33, p < .05$).

Household Chores

Only for GE fathers in China, fathers who believed that they were responsible for household chores were also more likely to play with their children during the workdays, and more likely to do more household chores and care for their children during the weekends ($rs = .56, .69, .95, ps < .01, .01, .001$, respectively).

Playmate

For most fathers, except for UE fathers in China, believing that their fathering role included playmate had a significant impact on how they spent their time with their families. Specifically, UE immigrant fathers were more likely to spend more time playing with their children during the workdays while GE immigrant fathers found greater play time during the weekends ($rs = .53, .45, ps < .01$, respectively). During the workdays in China, GE fathers were found to play with their children for longer periods of time while UE fathers spent more time doing household chores ($rs = .62, .43, ps < .01$, respectively).

Caregiver

Chinese Canadian UE and Chinese GE fathers who mentioned caregiver as one of their roles also engaged in more caregiving activities during the workdays ($rs = .41, .85, ps < .05, .001$, respectively). For GE fathers, Chinese Canadian fathers were more accessible to their children during the weekends if they viewed their role as caregiver ($r = .38, p < .05$).

DISCUSSION

The present study extends our current understanding of Chinese fathers within differing sociocultural contexts. Directing our attention to two cultural contexts, Canada and China, as well as the use of interviews on fathering roles and time diary accounts of fathers' levels of involvement with their children, provided greater clarity into the realm of fathering among Chinese families. The attempt to delineate between two influential factors, culture and acculturation, as well as paternal educational levels, provided more insight into the dynamics and relationships within Chinese families in everyday life. Specifically, since our knowledge on Chinese fathering is scarce and contradictory, it was important to use a comparative sample to examine how Chinese fathering has changed, as compared to past findings and historical accounts (no differences between Chinese Canadian and Chinese fathering) and potential acculturation influences (differences between the two groups).

Conceptual Framework for Chinese Fathering

As researchers examine fatherhood, many have concluded that fathers' views of fathering go beyond that of "breadwinners" (for overview, see Lamb and Tamis-LeMonda, 2004; Pleck and Masciadrelli, 2004). Portrayals or roles of fathering have undergone various historical and social changes (for review, see E. H. Pleck, 2004). Rather than relying on questionnaires with preconceived notions of fathering, which have been used in the past (for overview, see Pleck and Masciadrelli, 2004), this investigation provided fathers with the opportunity to define their paternal roles in their families. The results revealed that although fathers' role as breadwinner has remained steady, fathers viewed their roles in the families as multidimensional.

Contrary to Chinese tradition, fathers also conceptualized their roles as caregivers and as being responsible for household chores. These perceptions, like the roles of economic provider and playmate, did not differ by country of residence or gender of the child. Rather, the fluidity and shift from men's traditional gender role as economic provider to "feminine" roles such as caregiver and doing household chores is parallel to the general growing societal expectations that fathers need to be more actively involved in their children's daily activities (Lamb, 2004). Moreover, as found in this study, the role of economic provider was second to the role of caregiver. One possibility for this finding may be that these fathers did not emphasize the economic provider role since it may have been an "assumed role." It is nevertheless interesting that caregiver played such a significant role in their conceptions of fatherhood.

Both Chinese and Chinese Canadian fathers clearly delineated a different approach to fatherhood that moved beyond Confucian views of fathers as "master(s) of the family," in which it was thought that Chinese fathers should remain aloof and distant. Rather, as found in terms of engagement, regardless of their child's gender, fathers viewed themselves as their children's playmates. Although not supportive of past studies on Chinese families (e.g., Jankowiak, 1992; Sun and Roopnarine, 1996), these findings are in line with fathers' levels of play in other ethnic groups (e.g., see Jain, Belskey, and Crnic, 1996; Lamb, Chuang, and Hwang, 2004; Tamis-LeMonda, 2004; Yeung, Sandberg, Davis-Kean, and Hofferth, 2001). Thus, the historical view that Chinese fathers should stay "outside" of the family (not engaging in everyday childcare) may be less influential on today's Chinese societies.

Supportive of Confucian teachings was Chinese and Chinese Canadian fathers' view of educator or trainer as a part of their parental role. As stated in the *Three-Character Classic*, a book written in the thirteenth century and memorized by millions of Chinese children, "Rearing without education is the fault of the father" (see Ho, 1987). This emphasis on training/educating is also within Confucian teachings, where the notion of educator/trainer is an integral role in fathering, and in parenting in general. This training emphasis has been found in contemporary maternal parenting (e.g., see Chao, 1994; Chen and Luster, 2002; Chuang, 2006; Kelley and Tseng, 1992), and more recently, among Chinese fathers (Chao and Kim, 2000). This understanding of how parents may educate their children in everyday life may provide greater insight into their views of child socialization and child outcomes such as academic achievement. This finding illustrates the complexities of the changing beliefs about fathering: in some instances, Confucian teachings are visible in fathers' beliefs about their roles (e.g., being an educator and trainer), while in other instances fathers are actively engaged in various aspects of childcare and household duties.

Contrary to the traditional gender roles defined by Confucius, however, fathers did not define themselves as disciplinarians. Through ethnographic observations of Chinese families in their homes, Wolf (1970) and Jankowiak (1992) concluded that fathers assumed these roles. One possibility for this inconsistency may be due to the age of these fathers' children (one-year-olds). Perhaps the disciplinarian role would be more evident when the children are older and discipline becomes more relevant. Thus, fathering roles need to be further explored at various stages of development.

As we examine the interrelationships between the various roles, a pattern emerges for the role of caregiver. In particular, immigrant-Chinese and Chinese fathers with a university degree were less likely to perceive themselves as caregivers if they viewed themselves as economic providers.

Also, immigrant-Chinese fathers with graduate degrees negatively associated caregiving with their roles as educators. Interestingly, only Chinese fathers with graduate degrees viewed the various fathering roles as distinct from each other. While associations among various roles differ by levels of education as well as immigrant status, there is no clear explanation for these associations. What can be emphasized here, however, is that Chinese fathers' conceptions of fathering are not unidimensional but rather, complex and dynamic.

FATHERS' LEVELS OF INVOLVEMENT

Past research on fathering has primarily conceptualized and operationalized father involvement as a temporal and readily observable phenomenon (Hawkins and Palkovitz, 1999; Lamb, 2004; Pleck, 2004). Since little is known about the family dynamics and interactions in Chinese-Canadian and Chinese families, we used the time diary approach as an avenue to get a glimpse into these families.

In general, while fathers in mainland China as well as Canada are actively involved in their infants' lives in various daily activities, the Chinese Canadian fathers are more likely to be engaged with their infants during weekdays. This finding may reflect fathers' acculturative adjustment into a new country, being more removed from the social pressures of following Chinese traditions.

Although few studies have used similar time diary methodologies with fathers of young children and coding systems may have differed among studies, it is interesting to reveal that Chinese fathers' levels of involvement are comparable to Swedish fathers' (Lamb, Chuang, and Hwang, 2004) and higher than American fathers' (Yeung et al., 2001). Thus, Chinese fathers' levels of involvement are on par with those of other fathers from around the world.

Accessibility

For both weekdays and weekend days, Chinese and Chinese Canadian fathers spent greater amounts of time being accessible to their children than engaging in care, play, or household chores. Further exploration revealed that in China during the workdays, fathers' levels of education influenced their availability to their children, with higher educated fathers being more accessible. For university level fathers, they were generally more accessible to their sons than to their daughters. This dynamic influence of education and culture in relation to fathers' levels of accessibility needs further investigation, especially since studies have revealed that children, as they grow older, value their fathers' "being there" (for review, see Pleck and Masciadrelli, 2004).

Care

In both countries, Chinese fathers were actively engaged in childcare duties from feeding to bathing to putting the infant to sleep, which contradicts past work on Chinese fathers from urban China (Jankowiak, 1992) and Taiwan (Sun and Roopnarine, 1996). These results are on par with those for other cultural groups. For example, Chinese Canadian and Chinese fathers spent an average of forty-five minutes during the workdays taking care of their children; Swedish fathers spent an average of fifty-six minutes (Lamb, Chuang, and Hwang, 2004). According to Yeung et al. (2001), American fathers generally spent thirty-two minutes with their young children. While these results need to be interpreted with caution, the bottom line is that Chinese fathers are involved in their children's lives. With the sociocultural changes in China, the boundaries of "women's work" and "men's work" are not as rigid and traditional.

Play

As seen in table 6.2, both immigrant and native Chinese fathers played with their children throughout the week, engaging in more time playing with their children than doing household chores. In contrast to Sun and Roopnarine's (1996) conclusions that Chinese fathers do not engage in "rough" play, the present fathers reported more involvement in active play with their children than any other forms of play (e.g., watching a video, going shopping). Moreover, some researchers have recognized that parental involvement with children differed by the gender of the child, and this study also revealed gender differences. In general, these fathers, regardless of country, spent more time playing with their daughters than their sons. This finding does not evidence preferential treatment toward sons compared to daughters, as one would expect (see Ho, 1987, for review). This differential treatment by the child's gender may be the consequence of the one-child policy as well as the importance of women in today's society (e.g., employment).

Fathering Roles and Levels of Father Involvement

In a more qualitative approach, a closer examination at the correspondence between the interviews and time diary accounts provided greater insight into the functioning of fathering practices and beliefs. The translation from beliefs to practices is complex since factors such as levels of education and acculturation influence these conceptions and practices. As found in the present study, for example, the caregiving role was linked with levels of care for Chinese Canadian fathers and graduate-educated fathers in China. The fathers' role as playmate was also linked with their actual levels of play but like the role of caregiver, the link was not significant for university-level fathers in China. For some fathers, the role of educator had a negative influence on their levels of involvement (see table 6.3). While these associations between the educator role and levels of involvement are puzzling, it raises the importance of further exploring the rationale or meaning behind these role conceptions. That is, researchers need to go beyond the labeling of roles to exploring how fathers may operationalize these roles and the goals and purposes that are attached to each role.

Some limitations of the studies, however, need to be taken into consideration. First, the present study is an exploratory study that examined a small sample of fathers in two major metropolitan cities in Canada and China. Thus, the results may not be generalizable or reflective of other Asian groups. Caution is also needed when interpreting the present findings of fathers' levels of involvement in comparison to past findings since there may be some discrepancies in terms of how the researchers coded the fathers' time. However, these findings do evidence that immigrant-Chinese fathers are not "traditional" fathers as defined by Confucius or Chinese traditions.

This shift to a more "contemporary" parenting paradigm for fathers in Chinese families appears to be in line with the general realization that fathers play an important role in their children's lives (for review, see Lamb, Chuang, and Cabrera, 2003; Lamb and Lewis, 2004). With the increased employment of women in the workforce and the political climate of promoting father involvement (e.g., paternity leaves, parenting programs dedicated to fathers, custody issues), fathers have generally increased their levels of involvement over time (Lamb, 2004; Tamis-LeMonda and Cabrera, 2002).

Moreover, with the increasing focus on the dynamics of ethnic change due to migration and adaptation, researchers have noted the influence of cultural change in a wide range of attitudes and behaviors (e.g., see Berry, 1990; Rosenthal and Feldman, 1992). However, as illustrated here, fathers' conceptual framework of fatherhood transcends the traditional notions of Chinese fathering, incorporating roles that were traditionally viewed as "women's work." This comparative study allowed us to recognize that these perceptions of fathering roles are an indication of a general cultural shift in societal mindsets of Asians, rather than an influence from a more "Westernized" culture. Further exploration of frameworks of fatherhood in different ethnic and socioeconomic groups would be a meaningful way of advancing the scholarship on fathering.

REFERENCES

Abbott, D. A., Ming, Z. F., and Meredith, W. H. (1992). An evolving redefinition of the fatherhood role in the People's Republic of China. *International Journal of Sociology of the Family, 22,* 45–54.

Berndt, T. J., Cheung, P. C., Lau, S., Hau, K., and Lew, W. J. F. (1993). Perceptions of parenting in Mainland China, Taiwan, and Hong Kong: Sex differences and societal differences. *Developmental Psychology, 29,* 156–64.

Berry, J. W. (1990). Psychology of acculturation. In J. Berman (Ed.), *Cross-cultural perspectives: Nebraska symposium on motivation* (201–34). Lincoln: University of Nebraska Press.

Bronte-Tinkew, J., Carrano, J., and Guzman, L. (2006). Resident fathers' perceptions of their roles and links to involvement with infants. *Fathering, 4,* 254–85.

Chang, L., Schwartz, S., Dodge, K. A., and McBride-Chang, C. (2003). Harsh parenting in relation to child emotion regulation and aggression. *Journal of Family Psychology, 17,* 598–606.

Chao, R. (1994). Beyond parental control and authoritarian parenting style: Understanding Chinese parenting through the cultural notion of training. *Child Development, 65,* 1111–19.

Chao, R., and Kim, K. (2000). Parenting differences among immigrant Chinese fathers and mothers in the United States. *Journal of Psychology in Chinese Societies, 1,* 71–91.

Chen, F-. M., and Luster, T. (2002). Factories related to Parenting Practices in Taiwan. *Early Child Development and Care, 172,* 413–30.

Chinese National Bureau of Statistics. (2001). Fifth Bulletin of national population census (no. 1). Retrieved on March 31, 2003, from http://stats.gov.cn/tjgb/rkpcgb/qgrkpcgb/200203310083.htm.

Chiu, L. H. (1987). Child-rearing attitudes of Chinese, Chinese-American, and Anglo-American mothers. *International Journal of Psychology, 22,* 409–19.

Chuang, S. S. (2006). Taiwanese-Canadian mothers' beliefs about personal freedom for their young children. *Social Development, 15,* 520–36.

De Groot, J. (1882—1910). *The religious system of China, 6 Vols.* Leiden: Brill.

Dienhart, A. (2001). Make room for daddy: The pragmatic potentials of a tag-team structure for sharing parenting. *Journal of Family Issues, 22,* 973–99.

Fei, X. (1935). *Peasant life in rural China.* Shanghai: Shanghai Press.

Freeman, M. (1965). *Lineage in southern China.* London: University of London Press.

Hawkins, A. J., and Palkovitz, R. (1999). Beyond ticks and clicks: The need for more diverse and broader conceptualizations and measures of father involvement. *Journal of Men's Studies, 8,* 11–32.

Henley, K., and Pasley, K. (2005). Conditions affecting the association between father identity and father involvement. *Fathering, 3,* 59–80.

Ho, D. Y. F. (1987). Fatherhood in Chinese culture. In M. E. Lamb (Ed.), *The father's role: Cross-cultural perspectives* (227–45). Hillsdale, NJ: Erlbaum.

Ho, D. Y. F., and Kang, T. K. (1984). Intergenerational comparisons of childrearing attitudes and practices in Hong Kong. *Developmental Psychology, 20,* 1004–16.

Hofferth, S. L., Davis-Kean, P., Davis, J., and Finkelstein, J. (1998). *Child development supplement to the Panel Study of Income Dynamics, 1997* (user's guide). Ann Arbor:

Institute for Social Research, University of Michigan. Retrieved on September 17, 2000, from http://www/isr.umich.edu/src/child-development/home.html.

Jain, A., Belsky, J., and Crnic, K. (1996). Beyond fathering behaviors: Types of dads. *Journal of Family Psychology, 10,* 431–42.

Jankowiak, W. (1992). Father-child relations in urban China. In B. S. Hewlett (Ed.), *Father-child relations: Cultural and biosocial contexts* (345–63). New York: De Gruyter.

Kelley, M. L., and Tseng, H. M. (1992). Cultural differences in child-rearing: A comparison of immigrant Chinese and Caucasian American mothers. *Journal of Cross-Cultural Psychology, 23,* 444–55.

Lamb, M. E. (2004). *The role of the father in child development* (fourth ed.). Hoboken, NJ: Wiley.

Lamb, M. E., Chuang, S. S., and Cabrera, N. (2003). Promoting child adjustment by fostering positive paternal involvement. In R. M. Lerner, F. Jacobs, and D. Wertlieb (Eds.), *Handbook of applied developmental science, Vol. 1* (211–32). Thousand Oaks, CA: Sage.

Lamb, M. E., Chuang, S. S., and Hwang, C. P. (2004). Internal reliability, temporal stability, and correlates of individual differences in paternal involvement: A 15-year longitudinal study in Sweden. In R. Day and M. E. Lamb (Eds.), *Conceptualizing and measuring father involvement* (129–48). Mahwah, NJ: Erlbaum.

Lamb, M. E., and Lewis, C. (2004). The development and significance of father-child relationships in two-parent families. In M. E. Lamb (Ed.), *The role of fathers in children's development* (272–306). Mahwah, NJ: Erlbaum.

Lamb, M. E., Pleck, J. H., Charnov, E. L., and Levine, J. A. (1987). A biosocial perspective on paternal behavior and involvement. In J. B. Lancaster, J. Altman, A. S. Rossi, and L. R. Shorroa (Eds.), *Parenting across the lifespan: Biosocial dimensions* (111–42). New York: Aldine de Gruyter.

Lamb, M. E., and Tamis-LeMonda, C. S. (2004). The role of fathers in children's development. In M. E. Lamb (Ed.), *The role of fathers in children's development* (1–31). Mahwah, NJ: Erlbaum.

Lau, S., Lew, W. J. F., Hau, K.-T., Cheung, P. C., and Berndt, T. J. (1990). Relations among perceived parental control, warmth, indulgence, and family harmony of Chinese in Mainland China. *Developmental Psychology, 26,* 674–77.

Lin, C. Y., and Fu, V. R. (1990). A comparison of child-rearing practices among Chinese, immigrant Chinese, and Caucasian-American parents. *Child Development, 61,* 429–33.

Marsiglio, W. (1991). Paternal engagement activities with minor children. *Journal of Marriage and the Family, 53,* 973–86.

NICHD Early Child Care Research Network. (2000). Factors associated with fathers' caregiving activities and sensitivity with young children. *Journal of Family Psychology, 14,* 220–19.

Nucci, L., and Smetana, J. G. (1996). Mothers' concepts of young children's arenas of personal freedom. *Child Development, 67,* 1870–86.

Parke, R. D. (2002). Fathers and families. In M. H. Bornstein (Ed.), *Handbook of parenting.* Second ed. Vol. 3: *Being and becoming a parent* (27–73). Mahwah, NJ: Erlbaum.

Pleck, E. H. (2004). Two dimensions of fatherhood: A history of the good dad–bad dad complex. In M. E. Lamb (Ed.), *The role of the father in child development* (fourth ed., 32–57). New York: Wiley.

Pleck, J. H., and Masciadrelli, B. P. (2004). Paternal involvement in U.S. residential fathers: Levels, sources, and consequences. In M. E. Lamb (Ed.), *The role of the father in child development* (fourth ed., 222–71). New York: Wiley.

Pleck, J. H., and Stueve, J. (2004). A narrative approach to paternal identity: The importance of parental identity "conjointness." In R. R. Day and M. E. Lamb (Eds.), *Conceptualizing and measuring paternal involvement* (83–107). Mahwah, NJ: Erlbaum.

Robinson, J. P. (1977). *How Americans use time: A socio-psychological analysis.* New York: Praeger.

Rosenthal, D. A., and Feldman, S. S. (1992). The relationship between parenting behavior and ethnic identity in Chinese-American and Chinese-Australian adolescents. *International Journal of Psychology, 27,* 19–31.

Sanderson, S., and Thompson, V. L. S. (2002). Factors associated with perceived paternal involvement in childrearing. *Sex Roles, 46,* 99–111.

Shek, D. T. L. (1998). Adolescents' perceptions of paternal and maternal parenting styles in a Chinese context. *Journal of Psychology, 132,* 527–37.

———. (2001). Paternal and maternal influences on family functioning among Hong Kong Chinese families. *The Journal of Genetic Psychology, 162,* 56–74.

Shwalb, D. W., Nakazawa, J., Yamamoto, T., and Hyun, J.-H. (2004). Fathering in Japanese, Chinese, and Korean cultures: A review of the research literature. In M. E. Lamb (Ed.), *The role of the father in child development* (fourth ed., 146–81). New York: Wiley.

Statistics Canada. (2006). The Daily: 2006 Census: Immigration, citizenship, language, mobility and migration. Retrieved January 14, 2008, from http://www.statcan.ca/Daily/English/071204/d071204a.htm.

Su, C. W. (1968). [The child's perception of parent's role]. *Psychology and Education, 2,* 87–109. (Published in Chinese, with an English abstract).

Sun, L. C., and Roopnarine, J. L. (1996). Mother-infant, father-infant interaction and involvement in child care responsiveness in new and expectant fathers. *Evolution and Human Behavior, 21,* 79–95.

Tamis-LeMonda, C. S. (2004). Conceptualizing fathers' roles: Playmates and more. *Human Development, 47,* 220–27.

Tamis-LeMonda, C., and Cabrera, N. (Eds.). (2002). *Handbook of father involvement: Multidisciplinary perspectives.* Mahwah, NJ: Erlbaum.

Wilson, R. W. (1974). *The moral state: A study of the political socialization of Chinese and American children.* New York: The Free Press.

Winer, B. T., Brown, D. R., and Michels, K. M. (1991). *Statistical principles in experimental design.* New York: McGraw-Hill.

Wolf, M. (1970). Child training and the Chinese family. In M. Freedman (Ed.), *Family and kinship in Chinese societies* (221–46). Palo Alto, CA: Stanford University Press.

Yamada, H. (2004). Japanese mothers' views of young children's areas of personal discretion. *Child Development, 75,* 164–79.

Yeung, W. J., Sandberg, J. F., Davis-Kean, P. E., and Hofferth, S. L. (2001). Children's time with fathers in intact families. *Journal of Marriage and the Family, 64,* 780–92.

7

Asian Immigrant Fathers as Primary Caregivers of Adolescents

Akira Kanatsu and Ruth K. Chao

The image of Asian fathers has often been constructed on East Asian cultures (i.e., Chinese, Korean, and Japanese) because of their shared traditions and historical values. Both Korean and Japanese cultures are deeply influenced by Chinese culture. As a result, these cultures hold similar heritage, largely based on Confucianism, in their religion, philosophy, politics, science, language, and literature (Chao and Tseng, 2002; Shwalb, Nakazawa, Yamamoto, and Hyun, 2004). Such similarity also appears in the division of traditional parenting roles between fathers and mothers. For example, these cultures have shared a common slogan—"strict father, kind mother" (e.g., Chao and Tseng, 2002; Ho, 1987; Shwalb et al., 2004). This slogan characterizes the traditional father's role in East Asian families as undisputed leader and disciplinarian (Kitano, 1969; Sung, 1967; Wolf, 1970), in contrast to the mother's protective caregiver role. Providing financial and emotional support to mothers, but not taking care of children, has also been an important aspect of the paternal role in East Asian cultures (Shwalb et al., 2004). Asian fathers, due to their strong breadwinner role, were often reported to have markedly lower levels of parental involvement compared with fathers of other ethnic groups (Ishii-Kuntz, 2000; Jankowiak, 1992; Parke et al., 2005; Sun and Roopnarine, 1996). Thus, images or generalizations of Asian fathers, especially those from East Asian countries, tend to emphasize their role as breadwinner, while negating their role as caregivers of their children.

Generalization of the image of aloof, stern, and uninvolved Asian fathers to other Asian cultures, or even to recent East Asian fathers, however, requires further examination. Among Filipinos, for example, patriarchal authority has not been emphasized as much as it has been in East Asian cultures. Filipino parents have often shared family decisionmaking and responsibilities (Javillonar, 1979). Furthermore, many East Asian countries have experienced dramatic changes in the last decade from modernization, economic growth, and globalization that some claim have resulted in similar, but distinctive parental roles for mothers and fathers (Shwalb et al., 2004). In the review of research on East Asian fathers in Asia, Shwalb et al. (2004) found that Chinese fathers, although their primary role was still the breadwinner and their role as caregiver was secondary to mothers, appeared to be more involved in household responsibilities than Korean and Japanese fathers. It was suggested that this variation might be caused by the higher and more established maternal employment status in China than in other East Asian countries. In fact, family income and employment status of parents, especially those of mothers, are reported as strong determinants of paternal involvement in childcare (Fagan, 1998; Parke, 1996, 2002; Russell, 1999).

Changes in the economic situation and employment status are most relevant to Asian immigrant families. Recent urbanization and economic restructuring in Asian countries (Chao and Tseng, 2002; Han, 1997; Ho and Kang, 1984; Ishii-Kuntz, 2000), as well as downward socioeconomic changes in the process of migration (Chao and Tseng, 2002), have led to increases in maternal participation in the labor force. These shifts, therefore, could increase Asian immigrant fathers' involvement in parenting. Research, however, has rarely been conducted on Asian fathers who are involved in parenting. Thus, descriptive studies of Asian immigrant fathers who are more involved in caregiving and how their parental practices change through the process of immigration will increase our understanding of current Asian fathers in the United States. In order to examine fathers who are involved in caregiving, this study first looks at Asian immigrant fathers and mothers, in two-parent families, who were identified as primary caregivers on adolescents' reports. This study will, then, test differences in the mean levels of caregiving, and also associations of their parental practices with adolescent adjustment outcomes for first- (foreign-born) and second-generation (American-born with parents that are foreign-born) Asian immigrant youth.

DETERMINANTS OF PATERNAL INVOLVEMENT FOR ASIAN IMMIGRANTS

Economic and structural changes in China seem to have increased parental involvement as well as positive attitudes toward parenting among Chinese fathers. In Hong Kong, substantially higher levels of paternal involvement were found relative to the previous generation (Ho and Kang, 1984). Also, due to the urbanization in China, Jankowiak (1992) found that college-educated Chinese men indicated greater importance for demonstrating care and affection toward their children rather than the traditional style of aloofness. Furthermore, Chinese fathers were found to use less disciplinary and coercive practices than Chinese mothers (Shek, 2005; Tang, 1998). Shek (2005) suggested that the traditional adage of Asian parents has become more akin to "strict *mother*, kind father" in contemporary Chinese society.

Migration to the United States has also often led to downward occupational mobility among many Asian immigrant families as their education and training in their country of origin is not recognized in the United States (Chao and Tseng, 2002). Such disruptions in occupational potential among Asian immigrants are also associated with increases in maternal participation in the labor force and higher paternal responsibilities in parenting (Kim and Kim, 1998). In addition, Asian parents who migrate to Western cultures often have to negotiate between the parenting roles, beliefs, and practices of their ethnic cultures and those of the dominant culture in order for them and their children to adapt to a new society. According to Parke (1996), cultural attitudes concerning the roles of males and females might be the most important factor in accounting for the levels of parental involvement in caregiving behaviors. In other words, fathers who held more positive attitudes toward paternal caregiving were more likely to be involved in parenting. In fact, both factors of increased maternal employment and acculturative changes in cultural views have led to increases in parental involvement among Asian immigrant fathers, compared with their counterparts in their countries of origin (Ishii-Kuntz, 2000). These results suggest that Asian immigrant fathers are more involved in caregiving than fathers in Asia, but not much is known about their parental practices.

THE SHIFT FROM "CAREGIVING" TO "PARENTING"

Studies that have examined father involvement have typically focused on infant and childhood caregiving. The ways primary caregivers were identified depended on the amount of time the parents were engaged with children, their availability, caretaking tasks they performed, and resources they provided (Lamb, Pleck, Charnov, and Levine, 1985). In some studies, primary caregiving fathers were identified in terms of the time they spent taking care of their children relative to mothers or to other more traditional fathers. When compared with mothers, fathers who spent more time were often stay-at-home fathers with wives who were employed full-time. This arrangement was most common when children were very young and needed constant care (e.g., during infancy). When compared with more traditional fathers, however, fathers who were more involved in parenting were not necessarily stay-at-home fathers. These fathers were involved because they were available and motivated. In other research, involved fathers were also identified as those who were primary caregivers during certain time periods (e.g., while mothers were at work), but mothers were considered the primary caregivers when they were available (Radin, 1994). In these cases, fathers usually worked outside the home and shared the responsibilities of caregiving with mothers.

These studies of primary caregiving fathers tended to involve infants or very young children, but as children get older, the nature of "caregiving" changes, shifting more to "parenting." Parenting includes the establishment of a relationship between parents and children that may influence, and also be a reflection of, their parenting. Parenting thus cannot be separated from the relationship between parents and their children, particularly for adolescents. In other words, adolescents may identify their fathers as their primary caregivers not necessarily because they provide more care than mothers, but because they have better communication and relationship quality with their fathers. Thus, qualities of the parent-child relationship, such as adolescents' communication with and respect for parents, may become more critical in determining whom adolescents regard as their primary caregiver.

Moreover, we know little about the parenting of fathers as primary caregivers of adolescents. When adolescents identify their fathers as the primary caregiver, how do adolescents perceive fathers' parenting, and what consequences do fathers' parenting practices have for adolescents' adjustment?

PARENTAL PRACTICES

A two-factor model of parenting, involving control and responsiveness, has long been recognized as representing the core dimensions of parenting for explaining child and adolescent outcomes. As children enter adolescence, parents must be able to balance the control or regulation of adolescents with their increasing need for autonomy. Such balancing requires a different type of control, described below, in terms of supervision and monitoring (Patterson, Reid, and Dishion, 1992).

Parental Control

Parental control has been categorized into psychological and behavioral control (Baumrind, 1967; Schaefer, 1965). At the heart of the distinction is the notion that psychological forms of control adversely affect adolescent development by impeding the development of autonomy and self-direction, whereas behavioral regulation serves a positive socializing function by providing youth with needed guidance and supervision (Steinberg, 1990).

That is, psychological control refers to control attempts that inhibit or interfere with children's development of independence and self-direction by keeping the child emotionally dependent on the parent. Guilt induction and withdrawal of affection are often used to measure parental psychological control. Guilt induction constitutes parents' attempts to restrict children's autonomy by bringing up past mistakes or changing subjects in conversation. Withdrawal of affection often involves conveying disapproval by not looking at or talking to the children. Behavioral regulation, on the other hand, concerns the regulation, supervision, and management of behaviors (Barber, 1996). Parental monitoring (i.e., awareness and supervision) of children's whereabouts, activities, and companions has been found to be a fundamental component of effective behavioral regulation, especially in middle childhood and adolescence (Brown, Mounts, Lamborn, and Steinberg, 1993; Patterson et al., 1992).

Among studies conducted in Asia, lower levels of psychological control (Barber and Harmon, 2002), but higher levels of behavioral control or strictness (Berndt, Cheung, Lau, Hau, and Lew, 1993; Shek, 1998) have been found for fathers compared to mothers. This pattern for strictness, however, was not supported among Asian parents who have immigrated to the United States. Among Asian immigrants from China, Korea, and Vietnam, fathers and mothers were similar in their levels of strictness (Chao and Kim, 2000; Kim, 1996). Further studies are needed to determine whether these results reflect a decrease in paternal strictness or an increase in maternal strictness, due to the process of migration. Additionally, there is some initial research suggesting that strictness or behavioral control may have beneficial consequences or effects for Asians, as it does for Euro-Americans. Similar to the research on Euro-Americans (Barber, Olsen, and Shagle, 1994; Mason, Cauce, and Gonzales, 1997; Steinberg, Elmen, and Mounts, 1989), studies of Asians and Asian Americans have found that monitoring was negatively associated with delinquent behaviors (e.g., alcohol use) and positively associated with academic outcomes (McNeal, 1999; Sui-Chu and Willms, 1996).

Research has also suggested a strong connection between parental control and warmth among Asian/Asian American families. Although the authoritarian parenting style was found to be detrimental to Euro-American adolescents' adjustments, Asian American adolescents, who reported the highest authoritarian parenting style, were found to maintain the highest grades across ethnic groups (Dornbusch, Ritter, Leiderman, Roberts, and Fraleigh, 1987; Steinberg, Lamborn, Dornbusch, and Darling, 1992). This result suggested the possibility of a different meaning and consequence of parental control for Asian adolescents. Chao (1994) explained the difference by introducing *guan*, the more culturally relevant term of parental control for Asian parents. When translated, *guan* means "to govern" as well as "to care for" or "to love." Thus, parental control and strictness can have more positive effects on Asian adolescents' adjustment if interpreted as parental care or warmth.

Parental Warmth

Parental warmth has been defined as a quality of the parent-child relationship characterized by affection and responsiveness that was believed to be universally beneficial for children (Rohner, 1975). When compared with Euro-American parents, first-generation Chinese immigrant parents indicated similar levels of warmth (Jose, Huntsinger, Huntsinger, and Liaw, 2000). In a two-year longitudinal study in China, paternal warmth predicted twelve-year-olds' school achievement, whereas maternal warmth predicted their emotional adjustment (Chen, Liu, and Li, 2000). Studies of Chinese and Chinese Americans also indicated that a lack of parental warmth often had serious consequences for children and adolescents, including increased depression, anxiety, aggression, emotional instability, and decreased life satisfaction (Chen et al., 2000; Lin, 2002; Rohner, 1975; Rohner, Khaleque, and Cournoyer, 2005; Stewart et al., 1998). However, further studies are needed that specifically focus on Asian immigrant fathers and their parenting, especially in families in which they are considered the primary caregivers.

The purpose of this study, therefore, is to examine in Asian immigrant families the factors related to adolescents' identification of their fathers as the primary caregivers, and the consequences of these fathers' parental practices for adolescents' adjustment in first- and second-generation immigrant adolescents. Unlike most research on primary caregiving fathers, this study includes a large sample of Asian immigrant families comprising three sub-ethnic groups (Chinese, Korean, and Filipino) and both first- and second-generation immigrant adolescents. Based on the reports by Asian/Asian American adolescents, this study will first examine the characteristics that are associated with the identification of fathers as primary caregivers by comparing demographic characteristics of father primary caregiving families to those of mother primary caregiving families. Then the levels of parental practices and their associations with adolescents' adjustment outcomes (i.e., psychological, behavioral, and academic adjustments) will be compared between first- and second-generation adolescents. This analysis should provide an initial understanding of whether there are different consequences of parenting by primary caregiving fathers across generations that may be due to the process of migration and possible cultural differences. Youth who are recent immigrants may experience a greater cultural clash with their fathers' parenting in that their caregiving is not consistent with traditional roles for fathers. Thus, fathers' parenting may have stronger consequences for these youth than for youth who are born in the United States to immigrant parents.

For the determinants associated with the identification of primary caregivers, as reported in other research, parents' employment status is expected to differ between father and mother primary caregiver groups. That is, there will be lower paternal and higher maternal participation in the labor force, among families in which fathers are the primary caregivers. Regarding the parent-child relationship factors, adolescents who identify their fathers as primary caregivers will report higher communication and respect for fathers than for mothers. No differences are expected in the levels of parental practices between the generations of adolescents. With regard to the associations between these fathers' parental practices and adolescent outcomes, the effects of fathers' parenting on adolescents' adjustment should be stronger for first- than for second-generation youth.

METHOD

Participants

A total of 1,353 first- (those born abroad) and second- (those born in the United States to at least one immigrant parent) generation Asian/Asian American ninth graders from intact (i.e., two-parent) families were drawn from eight high schools in the Los Angeles area between the 2002 and 2004 academic years. The sample consisted of 387 (28.6 percent) first-generation and 966 (71.4 percent) second-generation immigrants. Of those first-generation adolescents, years in the United States ranged from 0 to 14.92 years with the mean and standard deviation of 6.72 and 4.11 years respectively. Of the entire sample, 668 (49.4 percent) were female and 680 (50.3 percent) were male adolescents, with a mean age of 14.2 years. Of those adolescents, 167 (12.3 percent) identified their fathers as the primary caregivers, whereas 1,186 (87.7 percent) identified their mothers. Sub-ethnic groups included 447 Chinese (33.0 percent), 415 Koreans (30.7 percent), and 221 Filipinos (16.3 percent). For this study, adolescents who specified their ethnicity as Taiwanese or Chinese from Hong Kong were also included in the Chinese sub-ethnic group. Because of the small sample sizes, other sub-ethnic groups (e.g., Southeast Asian, South Asian, and Vietnamese) were combined and identified as "Other Asians." This group consisted of 270 youths (20 percent).

Procedures

A passive consent procedure was used with parents, asking that they respond to or send back consent forms only if they did *not* wish their children to participate. All parents received copies of the consent letter in English, Spanish, Chinese, and Korean along with a postage paid, pre-addressed envelope for returning the forms. The participation rate was high (80.6 percent). Of all adolescents eligible to participate, fewer than 9.3 percent either refused to participate or did not have parental consent; another 10.1 percent either were absent on the day of the study or did not receive their parental consent forms.

Adolescents were given fifty minutes (the whole class period) to complete the surveys that included the following items/measures in English.

MEASURES

Demographic Characteristics

Primary Caregiver (PCG)

Adolescents were asked to identify the person who takes care of them *most* of the time followed by the responses, "mother," "father," "stepmother," "stepfather," or "other: please specify." Only those adolescents who identified their father or mother as the primary caregiver were the focus of this study.

Mothers' and Fathers' Employment Status

For each parent, adolescents reported their employment status by selecting the most appropriate response from "Employed full-time," "Employed part-time," "Homemaker," "Student," and "Not currently working." If adolescents indicated that their parents were either homemakers, students, or not employed, parents were considered to be non-working.

Homeownership

Because of the large proportion of missing reports for household income, homeownership was included as a measure of families' socioeconomic status. Adolescents reported whether their parents owned their homes.

Mothers' and Fathers' Education

For each parent, adolescents reported the highest level of education completed, from the following eight options: 1 = no formal schooling, 2 = some elementary school, 3 = finished elementary school, 4 = finished middle school, 5 = finished high school, 6 = some vocational or college training, 7 = finished four-year college degree, and 8 = finished graduate degree.

Table 7.1. Demographic Characteristics by Primary Caregiver

	Mother PCG	Father PCG
	Frequency (Proportion %)	
Sub-Ethnicity		
Chinese	392 (33.1%)	55 (32.9%)
Korean	380 (32.0%)	35 (21.0%)
Filipino	183 (15.4%)	38 (22.8%)
Other	231 (19.5%)	39 (23.4%)
Generation		
First	337 (28.4%)	50 (29.9%)
Second	849 (71.6%)	117 (70.1%)
Gender of Adolescents		
Female	598 (50.6%)	70 (42.2%)
Male	584 (49.4%)	96 (57.8%)
Mother's Employment Status		
Working Full-Time	637 (54.9%)	137 (83.0%)
Working Part-Time	165 (14.2%)	12 (7.3%)
Not Working	358 (30.9%)	16 (9.7%)
Father's Employment Status		
Working Full-Time	1023 (88.6%)	115 (83.3%)
Working Part-Time	70 (6.1%)	20 (12.3%)
Not Working	62 (5.4%)	27 (16.7%)
Homeownership		
Homeowner	903 (78.2%)	135 (82.8%)
Not Homeowner	252 (21.8%)	28 (17.2%)
	Mean (Standard Deviation)	
Mother's Education	6.46 (1.31)	6.52 (1.40)
Father's Education	6.74 (1.30)	6.74 (1.37)

Note: * $p < .05$; ** $p < .01$.

Frequencies/proportions and means/standard deviations for the above demographic characteristics are presented in table 7.1 for each PCG group.

Parent-Child Relations

Communication with Father and Mother

Adolescents' perception of their communication with each parent was assessed using eight items from the communication scale (Barnes and Olson, 1985; Boutakidis and Lisman, 2001). This measure captured the notion of "open communication" (e.g., "I find it easy to discuss problems with my parent") and quality of communication, influenced by cultural/linguistic differences between parents and adolescents (e.g., "I feel that my parent cannot express her/himself to me"). Responses were coded on a five-point scale ranging from 1 = *strongly disagree* to 5 = *strongly agree*. Exploratory factor analyses with a varimax rotation indicated one-factor structures for both parents. Thus, separate scale scores were created for both fathers and mothers by averaging the eight items for each parent. The alphas for the communication with father were .82 for father PCG and .85 for mother PCG groups. The alphas for the communication with mother were .86 for father PCG and .85 for mother PCG groups.

Respect for Father and Mother

Respect was assessed using eight items that were created by Chao (2001) based on the Parental Identification measure derived by Bowerman and Bahr (1973). This measure not only captured adolescents' identification with parents (e.g., "I have a high regard for my parent"), but also their respect for and obedience to fathers and mothers (e.g., "I respect my parent's opinions about important things in my life"). Responses were coded on a five-point scale ranging from 1 = *strongly disagree* to 5 = *strongly agree*. Again, exploratory factor analyses with a varimax rotation indicated one-factor structures for both parents. Therefore, separate scale scores were created for both fathers and mothers by averaging the eight items for each parent. These scales possessed strong internal consistency with alphas of .88 and .89 for respect for mother (for father and mother PCG groups, respectively) and .85 and .90 for respect for father (for father and mother PCG groups, respectively).

Adolescents' Adjustment Outcomes

Behavioral Adjustment

Adolescents' behavioral adjustment was assessed by the internalizing and externalizing scales of the youth self-report form (YSR) of the child behavioral checklist (CBCL) (Achenbach, 1991). The *internalizing scale* consisted of subscales for depression-anxiety, somatic complaints, and withdrawal. The depression-anxiety subscale contained fifteen items such as "I cry a lot," and "I feel that no one loves me." The somatic complaints subscale consisted of ten items such as "I feel dizzy or lightheaded," and "I feel overtired without good reason." Another seven items such as "I am too shy or timid," and "I keep from getting involved with others," comprised the withdrawal subscale. The *externalizing scale* consisted of two subscales, aggression and delinquency. Seventeen items such as "I am mean to others," and "I try to get a lot of attention," comprised the aggression subscale. The delinquency subscale contained fourteen items such as "I lie or cheat." Responses for all the items of the internalizing and externalizing scales were coded on a three-point scale ranging from 0 = *not true* to 2 = *very true or often true*. Because exploratory factor analyses indicated one-factor structures for both internalizing and externalizing scales, the scales were created by averaging all the items comprising each scale. The two scales possessed good internal consistency for both PCG groups. The alphas for the internalizing scale were .89 for both father and mother PCG groups. The alphas for the externalizing scale were .86 and .87 for father and mother PCG groups, respectively.

Standardized Test Scores

Adolescents' standardized test scores were obtained directly from school records. Between the 2002 and 2003 academic years, the schools changed their standardized tests from the Stanford Achievement Test, Ninth Edition (Stanford 9) to the California Achievement Test, Sixth Edition Survey (CAT/6 Survey). In order to make these test scores comparable, the scores were converted into national percentile rankings, which were normally distributed and had a range of 1 to 99 and a mean score of 50. The z-scores of the national percentile ranks for each test were then converted into the normal curve equivalent (NCE) scores using the formula below.

$$NCE = 50 + 21.06 * \text{z-score of the national percentile rank}$$

The NCE scores had a mean of 50 and a standard deviation of 21.06 in the norming population. The mean of language, math, and reading test scores from the eighth and ninth grades were calculated to create a total achievement score.

Grade Point Average (GPA)

Adolescents' report cards were also obtained directly from school records. The grade point averages (GPA) were calculated from the ninth grade fall and spring report cards.

Parental Practices

Adolescents reported the levels of the following parental practices only for the parent whom they identified as the primary caregiver.

Psychological Control

Adolescents' perceptions of parents' psychological control were assessed by eight items based on Barber's (1996) subscale of psychological control derived from the Children's Report on Parent Behavior Inventory (CRPBI) (Schludermann and Schludermann, 1988). The responses for the psychological control items were on a five-point scale ranging from 1 = *not at all like* to 5 = *a lot like*. An exploratory factor analysis with a varimax rotation indicated that a two-factor structure (with all items loading at .40 and above) best fit the data. The first factor, labeled *intrusiveness/guilt induction*, consisted of items such as "My parent is a person who brings up past mistakes when s/he criticizes me," and "My parent is a person who changes the subject whenever I have something to say." The second factor, labeled *withdrawal of affection*, consisted of items such as "My parent is a person who will avoid looking at me when I disappointed her/him," and "My parent is a person who, if I have hurt her/his feelings, stops talking to me until I please her/him." Separate scale scores were created by computing the mean of all items in each factor. The internal consistencies were somewhat low for intrusiveness/guilt induction (5 items, α = .69 and .67 for father and mother PCG groups, respectively) and withdrawal of affection (2 items, r = .55 and .60 for father and mother PCG groups, respectively). One item ("My parent is a person who is less friendly with me if I do not see things her/his way") was dropped because it loaded on both factors.

Monitoring

Adolescents' perceptions of parental monitoring were assessed by five items from the monitoring/behavioral control scale by Steinberg et al. (1992). The items on this scale asked adolescents how much their primary caregivers tried to monitor their social interactions with their friends, locations, and activities (e.g., "How much does your parent try to know where you are most afternoons after school?" and "How much does your parent try to know who your friends are?"). The items were on a three-point scale ranging from 1 = *doesn't try* to 3 = *tries a lot*. An exploratory factor analysis with a varimax rotation indicated a one-factor structure. The scale possessed good internal consistency with alphas of .78 and .74 for father and mother PCG groups, respectively.

Warmth

Adolescents' perceptions of parental warmth were assessed by ten items from the acceptance-rejection subscale of the CRPBI (Schludermann and Schludermann, 1988). The responses were on a five-point scale ranging from 1 = *not at all like* to 5 = *a lot like*. This measure included items such as "My parent is a person who believes in showing her/his love for me," and "My parent is a person who is able to make me feel better when I am upset." Again, an exploratory factor analysis with a varimax rotation indicated a one-factor structure. The internal consistencies of this scale were excellent, with alphas of .91 for both father and mother PCG groups.

RESULTS

Analyses of Characteristics Associated with Father as Primary Caregiver

In order to examine the characteristics most associated with fathers being the PCG, logistic regression analyses were conducted with the demographic characteristics (Step 1), parent-child relations (Step 2), and adolescents' adjustment (Step 3) as the predictors, and the dichotomous variable, fathers as PCG (coded as 1, with mothers as PCG coded as 0), as the outcome. The unstandardized coefficients and standard errors are presented in table 7.2. For the demographic characteristics, Asian immigrant fathers were more likely to be identified as the PCG when mothers were working full-time and when fathers were not working full-time. Although in initial analyses adolescents' gender (being male) was related to whether they reported the

Table 7.2.   Unstandardized Coefficients (B) and Standard Errors for Logistic Regression Analyses of Primary Caregiver (Father)

	1	2	3
Constant	−2.59** (.68)	−3.33** (.91)	−3.58** (1.11)
Demographic			
Korean	−.48† (.25)	−.55* (.26)	−.58* (.27)
Filipino	.07 (.26)	−.26 (.28)	−.32 (.29)
Other Asian	.22 (.25)	.13 (.27)	.14 (.28)
Second-Generation	−.24 (.21)	−.30 (.22)	−.32 (.23)
Male	.24 (.18)	.12 (.19)	.12 (.20)
Mother Working Full-Time	1.58** (.29)	1.84** (.31)	1.84** (.31)
Mother Working Part-Time	.41 (.42)	.41 (.45)	.38 (.45)
Father Working Full-Time	−1.39** (.28)	−1.52** (.31)	−1.53** (.31)
Father Working Part-Time	−.37 (.39)	−.33 (.41)	−.36 (.42)
Homeowner	.36 (.26)	.30 (.28)	.31 (.28)
Mother's Education	−.04 (.08)	−.08 (.08)	−.07 (.08)
Father's Education	.11 (.09)	.13 (.09)	.13 (.09)
Parent-Child Relations			
Communication with Mother		−1.26** (.22)	−1.20** (.22)
Communication with Father		1.06** (.22)	1.09** (.22)
Respect for Mother		−.73* (.34)	−.73* (.34)
Respect for Father		1.18** (.36)	1.17** (.36)
Adolescents' Adjustment			
Internalizing			.45 (.42)
Externalizing			−.02 (.54)
Standardized Test Scores			.00 (.01)
GPA			−.07 (.18)
χ^2	$\chi^2(12) = 89.736$**	$\chi^2(4) = 79.365$**	$\chi^2(4) = 1.589$

Note: Above ethnic groups are compared to Chinese (omitted group); mother/father working full-time and part-time are each compared to non-working (omitted group); $\dagger p < .10$; $*p < .05$; $**p < .01$

father as the PCG, once other demographic factors were examined together, it was not significantly associated with the identification of their fathers as the PCG. In the second step, when the parent-child relationship variables were added to the model, Korean fathers were less likely to be identified as the PCG than Chinese fathers, although this association was marginal in the first step. In examining adolescents' communication and respect for both mother and father, adolescents who reported higher levels of communication with and respect for fathers, and *lower* levels for mothers, were more likely to identify their fathers as primary caregivers. Finally, as indicated in the third step, there was no significant association between adolescents' adjustment outcomes and the identification of fathers as the primary caregivers. Thus, when fathers were identified as the primary caregiver, youths also tended to report that: 1) their mothers were more likely, and fathers less likely, to be engaged in full-time employment, 2) they were more likely to be of Chinese than Korean descent, and 3) they have better relationships with fathers and poorer relationships with mothers.

Generational Analyses of the Parental Practices of PCG Fathers

In order to examine the effect of immigration on Asian fathers' parental practices, the following analyses were conducted to compare the mean levels of parental practices between first- and second-generation adolescents of the father primary caregiver group. These analyses included 167 adolescents who identified their fathers as the primary caregivers. The covariates in these analyses included the demographic characteristics of sub-ethnicity, adolescents' gender, fathers' education, and mother-father employment status (fathers are not working and mothers are working were coded as 1, whereas all other father-mother employment possibilities were coded as 0). In comparisons between the first- and second-generation youth on these sample characteristics, a higher proportion of second-generation youth reported their mothers were working full-time while fathers were not employed full-time, and also that their parents owned their homes. In order to test for generational differences in the mean levels of parenting practices of PCG fathers, a multivariate analysis of covariance was conducted. No significant difference was found for the overall test between first- and second-generation youth, F (4, 151) = .158, $p = .96$. Because of the small sample size, univariate analyses of variance were also examined separately for each parenting variable. However, the results still showed no significant differences across generations in the levels of parenting practices.

Then, regression analyses were conducted for each outcome to test for generational differences in the *associations* between fathers' parental practices and adolescent adjustment outcomes. These generational differences

Table 7.3.   Unstandardized Coefficients (B) and Standard Errors for Regression Analyses of Generational Comparison

	Internalizing	Externalizing	Standard Test Score	GPA
Second-Generation (1)	−.04 (.05)	.03 (.04)	3.40 (2.29)	−.12 (.11)
Intrusiveness/Guilt Induction (2)	*.17** (.06)*	.05 (.05)	−4.39 (2.72)	.03 (.13)
Withdrawal of Affection (3)	.04 (.05)	−.03 (.04)	−1.87 (2.15)	−.00 (.10)
Monitoring (4)	.04 (.12)	−.14 (.09)	*10.98* (5.23)*	*.58* (.25)*
Warmth (5)	−.02 (.06)	.09† (.04)	−4.82† (2.71)	−.06 (.12)
(1) x (2)	*−.17* (.07)*	−.01 (.05)	5.80† (3.32)	.09 (.15)
(1) x (3)	−.04 (.06)	.05 (.04)	1.90 (2.57)	.01 (.12)
(1) x (4)	−.13 (.14)	−.01 (.10)	−10.64† (6.11)	−.40 (.29)
(1) x (5)	−.05 (.07)	−.07 (.05)	*9.36** (3.30)*	−.21 (.16)
	$F(15, 145)$ $= 2.087^*$	$F(15, 146)$ $= 2.581^{**}$	$F(15, 145)$ $= 2.927^{**}$	$F(15, 148)$ $= 2.731^{**}$

Note. All analyses included the following covariates: Sub-ethnicity, Adolescent's Gender, Parents' Employment Status, and Fathers' Education. †$p < .10$; *$p < .05$; **$p < .01$

were tested by estimating two-way interactions between second-generation (with first-generation as the omitted group) and each parental practice variable (with the parental practices centered on the mean of the sample). The unstandardized regression coefficients and standard errors for the co-efficients of PCG, parenting scales, and the two-way interaction terms are presented in table 7.3.

Generational differences were found in the association between intrusiveness/guilt induction and internalizing symptoms. The interaction was interpreted using the following steps. First, the interaction was graphically represented such that each point in the graph showed the predicted level of adolescents' internalizing symptoms for intrusiveness/guilt induction at low levels (1 standard deviation below the mean), at the mean, and at high levels (1 standard deviation above the mean). This graph is displayed in figure 7.1. Next, after graphing the interactions, we then tested whether each slope was significantly different from zero, based on Cohen, Cohen, West, and Aiken's test of simple slopes (2003). As displayed in figure 7.1, intrusiveness/guilt induction was associated with higher internalizing symptoms among first-generation adolescents, $t(145) = 2.85$, $p < .01$, whereas the association was almost zero among second-generation adolescents.

Another significant difference between the generations of youths was found in the association between parental warmth and standardized test scores. The interaction was interpreted using the same process. As displayed in figure 7.2, parental warmth had a more positive association with standardized test scores among second-generation than first-generation youth.

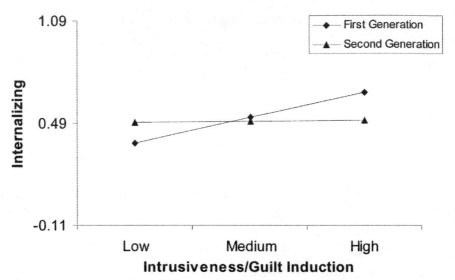

Figure 7.1.

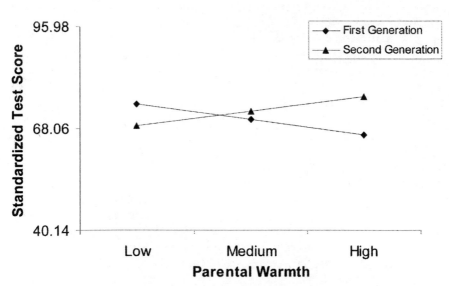

Figure 7.2.

The test of simple slopes indicated a somewhat negative association among the first-generation, t (148) $= -1.78$, $p = .08$, but no association among the second-generation.

Only one generational difference in the association involving parental monitoring of PCG fathers was found, and this was marginal. That is, fathers' monitoring was somewhat more positively related to the standardized test scores of first- than second-generation youth. Based on the test of simple slopes, there was no association between parental monitoring and standardized test scores for second-generation youth. Thus, when generational differences were found in the associations between fathers' parenting and adolescents' adjustment, they tended to be stronger for first- than second-generation youth.

DISCUSSION

The purpose of this study was to investigate among a larger, more representative sample of Asian immigrants the characteristics most associated with adolescents' identification of their fathers as primary caregivers, and to examine primary caregiving fathers' parental practices for possible generational differences in their effects. This was the first study to examine the characteristics and the parenting practices of Asian immigrant fathers who were primary caregivers in two-parent households. As this study found, over 12 percent of youth in the sample identified their fathers as the primary caregivers. Despite the much smaller proportion of adolescents identifying their fathers as primary caregivers relative to mothers, the sample was large enough to enable us to conduct analyses within these families to determine possible generational differences in the effects of parenting. Generational differences in Asian immigrant families were found such that caregiving by fathers had greater consequences for youth who were immigrants than youth born in the United States to immigrant parents, even after controlling for the demographic characteristics mentioned above. That is, immigrant youth may be impacted more from such non-traditional roles for fathers as caregivers than youth born in the United States, because such roles are less normative or culturally consistent with the values of immigrant youth than youth born in the United States.

As hypothesized, being a primary caregiver was associated with not working full-time, and with a better quality relationship with the adolescent. When mothers were employed full-time and fathers were *not* employed full-time, adolescents were more likely to identify their father as the primary caregiver. This finding supports previous studies, which indicated the parents' employment status was one of the strongest determinants of fathers' involvement in parenting. Also, results for the importance of parent-child relationships during adolescence revealed that greater parent-child communication and respect were associated with being identified as the primary caregiver. Adolescents who indicated higher levels of communication with and respect for fathers, *and* lower levels of communication with and respect for mothers were more likely to identify their fathers as the primary caregiver.

Although it was not hypothesized, Korean adolescents were less likely than Chinese adolescents to identify their fathers as the primary caregivers after controlling for other demographic differences. This result might reflect the influence of the stronger breadwinner role in Korean families than in Chinese families, due to the more established maternal participation in the labor force in China (Shwalb et al., 2004). According to the cultural attitudes argument (Parke, 1996), Chinese fathers may hold more positive attitudes toward parenting due to their shared roles with their wives, and thus become more involved in parenting than Korean fathers. Further testing, however, is necessary to support this argument.

No significant differences were found in the mean levels of parental practices between first- and second-generation adolescents. That is, the first-generation adolescents of Asian immigrant fathers, who were identified as primary caregivers, perceived similar levels of parenting as the second-generation adolescents.

A few differences in the *effects* of parental practices, however, were found between the generations. These differences seem to suggest that the effects of these fathers' parental practices were usually stronger for first- than for second-generation youth. That is, whereas intrusiveness/ guilt induction, monitoring, and warmth were related to adolescents' adjustment outcomes among first-generation adolescents, these parental practices were not related to adjustment outcomes among second-generation adolescents. Also, with some domains of parenting, the effects for first-generation youth were not always consistent with what has been found for youth from European American families. That is, although for first-generation youth, parental *monitoring* was positively related to standardized test scores, warmth was somewhat negatively related to this school performance outcome. However, because this study did not examine longitudinal changes in such associations, the direction of the effects cannot be determined. For example, it is unclear whether these fathers of first-generation youth were responding to the youths' lower school performance with parental warmth or whether these youth responded to such warmth from fathers by being less serious about school and their performance in school.

Another explanation, though, could be that increases in fathers' warmth may reflect the higher level of acculturation for both the father and adolescent, which may not be conducive to higher school performance. That is, some studies have reported declines in school performance for Asian American youth born in the United States compared to their immigrant or foreign-born counterparts (Tseng, Chao, and Padmawidjaja, 2007).

Additionally, there were limitations to the study in that the survey was in English only, and there may be important differences among the first-generation youth as to whether they understood the survey items and/or were able to complete the items. Thus, the findings for first-generation youth may be overrepresented by those that are more fluent in English, and perhaps also more acculturated compared to the general population of Asian immigrant youth. Moreover, additional differences between the first- and second-generation youth may have been found than those reported above, if the sample of first-generation youth had included those that were less fluent in English. The majority (64 percent) of the first-generation youth in the study had immigrated to the United States before they were ten years of age so they had at least four years of schooling in the United States. However, these numbers represent only those who completed items for whether they were born in the United States, and if not, what their age was at immigration. Another limitation was the small sample size that did not allow for tests of sub-ethnic group differences in these generational patterns. However, when testing for possible sub-ethnic group differences in the sample overall, there were no differences in mean levels of parenting practices among the sub-ethnic groups. Nevertheless, further study with a larger sample is needed to examine the possible sub-ethnic $\times$ generation variation in the levels and consequences of paternal parenting practices among Asian immigrant families.

Unlike previous studies, this study found that another important criterion related to adolescents' selection of fathers over mothers as their primary caregivers had to do with the quality of their relationships with each parent, net of all other factors examined. That is, Asian immigrant parents were perceived as the primary caregivers by adolescents based on the greater communication and respect adolescents held for them. These results suggest that, during adolescence, the quality of parent-child relations may be stronger determinants of adolescents' identification of the primary caregiving parent than their levels of parenting. However, further studies are needed that include adolescents' reports of parenting practices and parent-child relations for both primary and non-primary caregiving parents.

Ultimately, this study was also able to examine the consequences of parenting by Asian immigrant fathers who were primary caregivers, and to determine important differences among them due to immigration. The fact that the parenting of primary caregiving fathers had a greater impact on first- than second-generation immigrants may indicate that this parenting is experienced differently by these youth. Thus, potential differences between the family socialization experiences of first- and second-generation youth would have been masked or lost, if they were examined together as "children of immigrants."

AUTHOR NOTE

This research was supported by National Institute of Health grant RO1 HD38949-02 awarded to Ruth K. Chao. Inquiries may be addressed to Ruth K. Chao, 1137 Olmsted Hall, Department of Psychology, University of California at Riverside, Riverside, CA 92521. Phone: 951-827-7334, Fax #: 951-827-3897.

REFERENCES

Achenbach, T. M. (1991). *Integrative guide for the 1991 CBCL/4–18 YRS and TRF profiles.* Burlington: University of Vermont, Department of Psychiatry.

Barber, B. K. (1996). Parental psychological control: Revisiting a neglected construct. *Child Development, 67*, 3296–3319.

Barber, B. K., and Harmon, E. L. (2002). Violating the self: Parental psychological control of children and adolescents. In B. K. Barber (Ed.), *Intrusive parenting* (15–52). Washington, DC: American Psychological Association.

Barber, B. K, Olsen, J. E., and Shagle, S. C. (1994). Associations between parental psychological and behavioral control and youth internalized and externalized behaviors. *Child Development, 65*, 1120–36.

Barnes, H. L., and Olson, D. H. (1985). Parent-adolescent communication and the Circumplex model. *Child Development, 56*, 438–47.

Baumrind, D. (1967). Child care practices anteceding three patterns of preschool behavior. *Genetic Psychology Monographs, 75*, 43–88.

Berndt, T. J., Cheung, P. C., Lau, S., Hau, K., and Lew, W. J. F. (1993). Perceptions of parenting in Mainland China, Taiwan, and Hong Kong: Sex differences and societal differences. *Developmental Psychology, 29*, 156–64.

Boutakidis, I., and Lisman, C. (2001). *Parent-child communication scale.* Unpublished assessment instrument, University of California, Riverside.

Bowerman, C. E., and Bahr, S. J. (1973). Conjugal power and adolescent identification with parents. *Sociometry, 36*, 366–77.

Brown, B. B., Mounts, N., Lamborn, S. D., and Steinberg, L. (1993). Parenting practices and peer group affiliation in adolescence. *Child Development, 64*, 467–82.

Chao, R. (1994). Beyond parental control and authoritarian parenting style: Understanding Chinese parenting through the cultural notion of training. *Child Development, 65*, 1111–19.

———. (2001). *Parental respect scale.* Unpublished assessment instrument, University of California, Riverside.

Chao, R., and Kim, K. (2000). Parenting differences among immigrant Chinese fathers and mothers in the United States. *Journal of Psychology in Chinese Societies, 1*, 71–91.

Chao, R., and Tseng, V. (2002). Parenting of Asians. In M. H. Bornstein (Series Ed.), *Handbook of parenting.* Vol. 4: *Social conditions and applied parenting* (second ed., 59–93). Mahwah, NJ: Erlbaum.

Chen, X., Liu, M., and Li, D. (2000). Parental warmth, control, and indulgence and their relations to adjustment in Chinese children: A longitudinal study. *Journal of Family Psychology, 14,* 401–9.

Cohen, J., Cohen, P., West, S., and Aiken, L. (2003). *Applied multiple regression/ correlation analysis for the behavioral sciences* (third ed.). Mahwah, NJ: Erlbaum.

Dornbusch, S., Ritter, P., Leiderman, P., Roberts, D., and Fraleigh, M. (1987). The relation of parenting style to adolescent school performance. *Child Development, 58,* 1244–57.

Fagan, J. (1998). Correlates of low-income African American and Puerto Rican fathers' involvement with their children. *Journal of Black Psychology, 24,* 351–67.

Han, K. H. (1997). Changes in images of fathers. *Sociocultural Research Center Reports, 8,* 33–52.

Ho, D. Y. F. (1987). Fatherhood in Chinese culture. In M. E. Lamb (Ed.), *The father's role: Cross-cultural perspectives* (227–45). Hillsdale, NJ: Erlbaum.

Ho, D. Y. F., and Kang, T. K. (1984). Intergenerational comparisons of childrearing attitudes and practices in Hong Kong. *Developmental Psychology, 20,* 1004–16.

Ishii-Kuntz, M. (2000). Diversity within Asian American families. In D. H. Demo, K. R. Allen, and M. A. Fine (Eds.), *Handbook of family diversity* (274–92). New York: Oxford University Press.

Jankowiak, W. (1992). Father-child relations in urban China. In B. S. Hewlett (Ed.), *Father-child relations: Cultural and biosocial contexts* (345–63). New York: De Gruyter.

Javillonar, G. V. (1979). The Filipino family. In M. S. Das and P. D. Bardis (Eds.), *The family in Asia* (344–80). London: Allen and Unwin.

Jose, P., Huntsinger, C., Huntsinger, P., and Liaw, F.-R. (2000). Parental values and practices relevant to young children's social development in Taiwan and the United States. *Journal of Cross-Cultural Psychology, 31,* 677–702.

Kim, C. K., and Kim. S. (1998). Family and work roles of Korean immigrants in the United States. In H. I. MocCubbin, E. A. Thompson, A. I. Thompson, and J. E. Fromer (Eds.), *Resiliency in Native American and immigrant families* (225–74). Thousand Oaks, CA: Sage.

Kim, S. (1996). The effects of parenting style, cultural conflict, and peer relations on academic achievement and psychosocial adjustment among Korean immigrant adolescents. *Dissertation Abstracts International, 57,* 578.

Kitano, H. L. (1969). *Japanese Americans: The evolution of a subculture.* Englewood Cliffs, NJ: Prentice Hall.

Lamb, M. E., Pleck, J. H., Charnov, E. L., and Levine, J. A. (1985). Paternal behavior in humans. *American Zoologist, 25,* 883–94

Lin, E. K. (2001). A cross-cultural examination of the link between parenting and adolescent depression and misconduct (United States, Taiwan, China). Ellen Kuei-Ning Lin, Ph.D., Southern Illinois University at Carbondale. Dissertation, May.

Mason, C. A., Cauce, A. M., and Gonzales, N. (1997). Parents and peers in the lives of adolescents: An interactive approach to the study of human behavior. In R. W.

Taylor and M. C. Wang (Eds.), *Social and emotional adjustment and family relations in ethnic minority families* (85–98). Mahwah, NJ: Erlbaum.

McNeal, R. B., Jr. (1999). Parental involvement as social capital: Differential effectiveness on science achievement, truancy, and dropping out. *Social Force, 78,* 117–45.

Parke, R. D. (1996). *Fatherhood.* Cambridge, MA: Harvard University Press.

———. (2002). Fathers and families. In M. H. Bornstein (Ed.), *Handbook of parenting.* Vol. 3: *Status and social conditions of parenting* (second ed., 27–73). Mahwah, NJ: Erlbaum.

Parke, R. D., Dennis, J., Flyr, M. J., Morris, K. L., Leidy, M. S., and Schofield, T. J. (2005). *Fathers: Cultural and ecological perspectives.* In T. Luster and L. Okagaki (Eds.), *Parenting: An ecological perspective* (103–44). Mahwah, NJ: Erlbaum.

Patterson, G. R., Reid, J. B., and Dishion, T. J. (1992). *A social interactional approach.* Vol. 4: *Antisocial boys.* Eugene, OR: Castalia Publishing Company.

Radin, N. (1994). Primary-caregiver fathers in intact families. In A. E. Gottfried and A. W. Gottfried (Eds.), *Redefining families: Implications for children's development* (55–97). New York: Plenum.

Rohner, R. P. (1975). *They love me, they love me not.* New Haven, CT: Human Relations Area Files.

Rohner, R. P., Khaleque, A., and Cournoyer, D. E. (2005). Parental acceptance-rejection: Theory, methods, cross-cultural evidence, and implications. *Ethos, 33,* 299–334.

Russell, G. (1999). Primary caregiving fathers. In M. E. Lamb (Ed.), *Parenting and child development in "nontraditional" families* (57–82). Mahwah, NJ: Erlbaum.

Schaefer, E. S. (1965). A configurational analysis of children's reports of parent behavior. *Journal of Consulting Psychology, 29,* 552–57.

Schludermann, E. H., and Schludermann, S. M. (1988). *Children's Report on Parent Behavior (CRPBI-108, CRPBI-30) for children and older adolescents.* Technical Report. Winnipeg, MB, Canada: University of Manitoba.

Shek, D. T. L. (1998). Adolescents' perceptions of paternal and maternal parenting styles in a Chinese context. *Journal of Psychology, 132,* 527–37.

———. (2005). Perceived parental control and parent-child relational qualities in Chinese adolescents in Hong Kong. *Sex Roles, 53,* 635–46.

Shwalb, D. W., Nakazawa, J., Yamamoto, T., and Hyun, J.-H. (2004). Fathering in Japanese, Chinese, and Korean cultures: A review of the research literature. In M. E. Lamb (Ed.), *The role of the father in child development* (fourth ed., 146–81). New York: Wiley.

Steinberg, L. (1990). Interdependence in the family: Autonomy, conflict, and harmony in the parent-adolescent relationship. In S. S. Feldman and G. R. Elliott (Eds.), *At the threshold: The developing adolescent* (255–76). Cambridge, MA: Harvard University Press.

Steinberg, L., Elmen, J. D., and Mounts, N. S. (1989). Authoritative parenting, psychosocial maturity, and academic success among adolescents. *Child Development, 60,* 1424–36.

Steinberg, L., Lamborn, S. D., Dornbusch, S. M., and Darling, N. (1992). Impact of parenting practices on adolescent achievement: Authoritative parenting, school involvement, and encouragement to succeed. *Child Development, 63,* 1266–81.

Stewart, S. M., Rao, N., Bond, M. H., McBride-Chang, C., Fielding, R., and Kennard, B. D. (1998). Chinese dimensions of parenting: Broadening Western predictors and outcomes. *International Journal of Psychology, 33*, 345–58.

Sui-Chu, E. H., and Willms, J. D. (1996). Effects of parental involvement on eighth-grade achievement. *Sociology of Education, 69*, 126–41.

Sun, L. C., and Roopnarine, J. L. (1996). Mother-infant, father-infant interaction and involvement in child care responsiveness in new and expectant fathers. *Evolution and Human Behavior, 21*, 79–95.

Sung, B. L. (1967). *The story of the Chinese in America.* New York: Collier Books.

Tang, C. S.-K. (1998). Frequency of parental violence against children in Chinese families: Impact of age and gender. *Journal of Family and Violence, 13*, 113–30.

Tseng, V., Chao, R. K., and Padmawidjaja, I. (2007). *Asian Americans' educational experiences.* In F. Leong, A. Inman, A. Ebreo, L. Yang, L. Kinoshita, and M. Fu (Eds.), *Handbook of Asian American psychology* (second ed., 102–23). Racial and Ethnic Minority Psychology (REMP) series. Thousand Oaks, CA: Sage Publications.

Wolf, M. (1970). Child training and the Chinese family. In M. Freedman (Ed.), *Family and kinship in Chinese societies* (221–46). Palo Alto, CA: Stanford University Press.

8

Korean Immigrant Fathering: Dealing with Two Cultures

Eunjung Kim

The population of foreign-born and first-generation Asian immigrants in the United States has grown rapidly during the last few decades. Following Chinese and Indian immigrants, Koreans are the third largest Asian-born population in the United States (U.S. Census Bureau, 2000). Like other Asian settlers, first-generation Korean immigrants need to deal with two cultures. Korean culture is based on collectivism and Confucianism (Hofstede, 1980). With immigration, Koreans become surrounded by middle-class Euro-American culture, which focuses on individualism (Hofstede, 1980). These changes in social context present special challenges to Korean immigrant parents. They not only need to adapt to the migrant situation but also need to fulfill their roles as parents. However, not much is known about Korean immigrant parenting, especially fathering. The purpose of this chapter is to review the literature related to Korean immigrant fathers. It includes: 1) Korean immigrants' demographic characteristics; 2) the cultures of Koreans, Euro-Americans, and Korean immigrants; 3) empirical studies in Korean immigrant fathering and children's development, concluding with 4) suggestions for Korean immigrant fathers and community leaders as well as practitioners and researchers who work with Korean immigrants.

KOREAN IMMIGRANTS' DEMOGRAPHIC CHARACTERISTICS

Korean immigration to the United States began in 1903 (I. Kim, 2004). For several decades, the Korean immigrant population was very small. However, after the U.S. government eased its restrictions on Asian immigration in

1965, the Korean immigrant population increased from fewer than seven hundred thousand in 1970 to more than 1.5 million by 2002 (I. Kim, 2004). In general, Koreans who entered into the United States after 1965 were young, married, and college-educated professionals. They migrated voluntarily, hoping for more political and social security and better opportunities for their children's education (K. Shin and Shin, 1999). Korean immigrants are concentrated in large cities such as Los Angeles (24 percent), New York (16 percent), Washington, DC (7 percent), San Francisco (5 percent), Chicago (4 percent), and Seattle (4 percent) (I. Kim, 2004).

According to the 2000 census, almost one half (49.2 percent) of Korean immigrants came to the United States with a baccalaureate, or higher, degree and formerly worked as professionals in Korea (I. Kim, 2004). However, their education in Korea was often not recognized in the United States. Their lack of English proficiency further hindered full utilization of their knowledge and skills. Only 16 percent of Korean immigrant males and 11 percent of females hold professional occupations in the United States. Many other Korean immigrants had to make the difficult decision to change their careers and start family businesses. Korean immigrants dominate certain types of small businesses, such as green groceries, dry cleaners, liquor stores, and nail salons in metropolitan cities such as Los Angeles, New York, Washington, DC, and Chicago (I. Kim, 2004). The downward movements from professional careers to occupations that do not utilize their education have some ramifications for family configurations and parenting such as absence of parents at home due to long working hours.

CULTURES OF KOREANS, EURO-AMERICANS, AND KOREAN IMMIGRANTS

To truly understand the changes in Korean fathers' experiences in the United States, it is important to understand the differences in cultures, especially cultural values, family systems, and communication styles, among Koreans, Korean immigrants, and Euro-Americans.

Korean Cultural Values, Family Systems, and Communication

Collectivism and Confucianism

Korean culture is based on collectivism (Hofstede, 1980) and Confucianism (Abelmann, 1997; Oak and Martin, 2000). In a collectivistic society, individuals emphasize the implications of their own behavior for others, value harmony, share resources, share both positive and negative outcomes, are controlled by shame, and feel that they are a part of their group members' lives (Hui and Triandis, 1986). With collectivism, Koreans tend to develop a strong in-group (e.g., family) identity and view the in-group as an extension of the self (Triandis, 1994). Individuals within the group have strong and cohesive ties and expect to be interdependent (Hofstede, 1980).

This collectivistic tendency is reflected in Confucianism, which stresses the importance of family. The fundamental philosophy of Confucianism includes clear hierarchical relationships and obedience to authority. This philosophy is deeply embedded in Korean values, customs, morals, social structures, family systems, communications styles, and etiquette (Oak and Martin, 2000). Some traditional family values established under Confucianism are authority of fathers, wives' obedience to husbands, children's obedience to parents, filial piety, submission of self to family, and high expectation in education. Recently a Korean scholar suggested that Koreans observe Confucian values more than the Chinese, who went though Mao Tse-tung's Chinese revolution, and the Japanese, who went though Meiji restoration (K. Kim, 2002).

Family Systems

Korean traditional cultural norms strictly define roles and hierarchy for each family member. Korean fathers function as the head of the family. Fathers are expected to be the principal breadwinners, leaders, and decisionmakers, and have authority over the wives/mothers and children (Oak and Martin, 2000). However, current Korean male culture has some characteristics that cause fathers to lose their authority within the family (U.S. Dooranno Father School, 2005). Many Korean fathers tend to put a higher priority on work than on their families. After work, many Korean fathers socialize with their colleagues. This after-work male culture disconnects fathers from home. Because fathers are absent, mothers and children get closely united. In this face-saving culture, Korean fathers tend to belittle their wives and children in front of others, not to insult them, but because this is considered as humbleness. Praising wives and children in front of others is considered foolish. Some fathers may occasionally use verbal and physical violence toward wives and children. This violence may be repeated by the next generation (U.S. Dooranno Father School, 2005). Generally, Korean fathers' relationships with their children are formal and distant, and fathers rarely express their love through words or physical expressions of affection (Oak and Martin, 2000).

Korean mothers are considered the primary caregivers of children in discipline, education, and emotional support (K. Kim and Kim, 1995; Rohner and Pettengill, 1985). Within the Korean culture, mothers should obey their husbands, dutifully serve their husbands and their husbands' family members, and carry on the husbands' families' lineage by producing children, especially sons. These traditional paternal and maternal roles are well expressed in a popular Korean phrase, *om bu ja mo*, "strict father, benevolent mother" (Rohner and Pettengill, 1985; Shwalb, Nakazawa, Yamamoto, and Hyun, 2004).

In childrearing, Korean parents believe that a child's behavior reflects parental standards. Therefore, they assume full responsibility for their children's behaviors and outcomes. As a result, parents, especially fathers, tend to be authoritarian, extensively involving themselves in their children's decisionmaking processes (Lehrer, 1996). Korean fathers consider their strict control and extensive involvement with their children's daily lives as a demonstration of their love and interest in their offspring's well being. Korean adolescents, in turn, tend to perceive high parental control as a sign of parental love and interest in them (Rohner and Pettengill, 1985). Children are expected to be passive, obedient, and self-disciplined (W. Kim, Kim, and Rue, 1997). They should respect and obey their parents, be loyal to the family, and fulfill their obligation of filial piety to their parents when their parents get older (L. Lee, 1995). Because the first son inherits the family name and takes over his father's role, he is more appreciated than any daughter, who becomes a member of another family upon marriage. Children do not usually go directly to their father when they want something, but rather to their mother, who acts as a mediator (Oak and Martin, 2000).

Communication

The patriarchal and hierarchal systems embedded within Korean families are well reflected in unique ways of communicating. The relationships of the individuals to one another determine Koreans' choice of words (Oak and Martin, 2000). An example of this formality is as follows: the English word "good-bye" can be translated two ways in Korean. The words *chal-kat-ta-wa* and *chal-kat-ta-o-se-yo* both can be literally translated as "go and come back well." However, when a husband is speaking to a wife or a parent to a child, the word used is *chal-kat-ta-wa*. When a wife says "good-bye" to her husband, she has to use the polite verb ending, *o-se-yo* (Oak and Martin, 2000). In addition, hierarchical Korean culture promotes the use of unidirectional communication, flowing from parents to children without allowing children's response. Korean communication patterns are reactive and rely more on nonverbal body language than verbal language. Koreans make little eye contact when they communicate. If children look their parents directly in the eye, it is considered rude. When Koreans use nonverbal language, miscommunication can easily occur because they usually use subtle and indirect nonverbal expressions and do not freely clarify their feelings with words (W. Kim et al., 1997; Oak and Martin, 2000). When

Korean families migrate to the United States, these cultural values are often in direct contrast with what they will experience in this country.

Euro-American Cultural Values, Family Systems, and Communication

Individualism

In contrast to Korean collectivistic culture, many Euro-Americans practice individualism (Hofstede, 1980). In an individualistic society, individuals share resources only with their immediate nuclear family, are less willing to subordinate their personal goals to those of a group, are willing to confront others, feel personally responsible for their successes and failures, and experience some degree of separation and distance from others (Hui and Triandis, 1986). American society typically supports the autonomy, self-reliance, and independence of each person (Hofstede, 1980). Compared to Korean culture, Euro-American culture does not put as much emphasis on social class, occupational status, birth order, or gender (Storm, S. Park, and Daniels, 1987; Oak and Martin, 2000). In American society, class distinction exists to some extent, but it is subtler. Everyone is considered to be a special, unique person who has equal rights. Social protocol and etiquette are considered as polite conveniences, as opposed to the Korean way of submission to others. Individuals are expected to develop their own opinions, set their own goals, make their own choices, and solve their own problems (Storm et al., 1987).

Family Systems

The value of individualism is reflected in Euro-American family systems. Compared to Korean families, Euro-American families display more horizontal, democratic, egalitarian relationships among family members (Storm et al., 1987). In childrearing, there is a social trend toward greater equality of the mothers' and fathers' roles (Phinney, Ong, and Madden, 2000). Euro-American fathers are more involved with their children compared to Korean fathers (Shwalb et al., 2004). Although Euro-American children have obligations to their families and parents, they also have greater equality with their parents and more independence with less emphasis on obedience than do Korean children.

The cultural norm of Euro-Americans is to raise children to be autonomous, independent, and self-reliant (Holmbeck, Paikoff, and Brooks-Gunn, 1995). The parents try to nurture their children to regulate their behaviors and to practice socially appropriate behaviors without explicit parental control (Pettengill and Rohner, 1985). Because the Euro-American norm is to raise children to be autonomous, in the United States strict parental control can be seen as an intrusion and inhibition of adolescents' growing autonomy (Grolnick and Farkas, 2002).

Communication

In terms of communication styles, Euro-American families typically practice equality in language; they emphasize the use of direct and explicit verbal language. They communicate their feelings freely and maintain eye contact as well as physical contact. Parents express their warmth liberally by using verbal and nonverbal means. Euro-Americans emphasize self-promoting and assertive communication patterns (W. Kim et al., 1997). These communication styles are more effective than the one-way Korean style of communication in teaching children to function successfully in mainstream society.

All of these differences show that, in stark contrast to Euro-American culture, which encourages children's independence and autonomy, Korean culture is hierarchical and more controlling. Because they live in two cultures, Korean immigrant fathers must effectively bridge these two cultures to establish good relationships with their families.

Korean Immigrant Cultural Values, Family Systems, and Communication

Two Cultures

Most first-generation Korean immigrant families maintain their cultural heritage and their Korean language while adopting some aspects of American culture (e.g., food) and learning English. In a study with ninety-eight Korean immigrant fathers who live in the Midwest, approximately 75 percent of fathers thought that it was important not only to maintain Korean values and customs but also to adopt American values and customs (E. Kim and Wolpin, at press). However, their level of American cultural adoption was low. For example, approximately 93 percent of Korean immigrant fathers usually ate Korean food. 64 percent of Korean immigrant fathers continued to read Korean newspapers while only 37 percent subscribed to and read American newspapers. While 46 percent of Korean immigrant fathers frequently socialized with other Korean immigrant friends, only 9 percent made friends outside their own ethnic community (E. Kim and Wolpin, at press).

Korean Churches

One significant factor in maintaining traditional Korean culture is the involvement of Korean immigrants with their ethnic churches. Korean churches have been a major source of social networking for Korean immigrants since the early 1900s (Choe, 2004; Kwon, 2004). Between 70 and 78 percent of Korean immigrants attend Korean churches (W. Hurh and Kim, 1990; W. Hurh, Kim, and Kim, 1979; O. Kim, 1999; Kwon, 2004), which allow Korean immigrants to embrace their religious search for meaning, belonging, and psychological ease in the way they feel comfortable. The church environment also supports maintaining personal relationships based on hierarchical interactions. Church members celebrate major Korean traditional holidays as part of church events. Many churches offer Korean-language schools for children on weekends. Language schools also promote traditional Korean arts such as music, dance, crafts, and calligraphy. In addition, Korean churches function as informational and referral centers (Choi, 1997; Phipps, True, and Murray, 2003). Consequently, involvement with Korean churches can isolate Korean immigrant fathers from mainstream American culture.

Family Systems

Another influence of Confucianism among first-generation immigrants is that they maintain traditional roles with fathers as breadwinners, mothers as caregivers, and children as obedient offspring (K. Kim and Kim, 1995). In contrast, second- and third-generation Korean American youths may want to change these expectations in order to pursue their individual happiness. Because of this difference, many first-generation Korean immigrant parents fear that their offspring are losing their Korean ethnic identities and traditional cultural values. This makes them worry that their children will become individualistic, which they consider to be a negative characteristic (Nah, 1993). Disagreements and conflicts can be particularly difficult between Korean immigrant fathers and children because fathers, as the traditional heads of the household, expect to practice their authority by choosing colleges (and determining the course of study), professions, and spouses for their children, even though living in the United States (Lehrer, 1996).

Challenges

Practicing Confucianism in America, where Euro-American cultural values support individualism, egalitarianism, and diversity, puts Korean immigrant parent-child relationships in a unique and challenging position. B. Lee (2004) suggests that Korean immigrant parents and children experience a lack of personal connection in three ways. First, stressing the importance of hierarchy within the family places a division between parents and children. This generational division makes communication difficult.

Second, filial piety, the idea that children must respect their parents, leads to the perception that the parents' primary role is to provide for their children, while the children's primary role is to serve and respect their parents. Third, most Korean immigrant parents sacrifice time and money for their children's education. However, parents see education for the second generation as a status symbol, with more emphasis placed on college name recognition than on the knowledge gained or any self-improvement on the part of the child. This lack of personal connection leads to a lack of intimacy between parents and children. Korean immigrant children rarely share details of their personal lives with their parents, joke and laugh with their parents, or watch movies and go to concerts together (B. Lee, 2004).

E. Kim and Hong (2007) found that in some cases Korean immigrant fathers recognize that they do not express affection because they are influenced by strict Confucian values. Although first-generation Korean immigrant fathers are warm and accepting, they are not trained to express their warmth to their children through either verbal or nonverbal behaviors. These fathers rather believe that they show love by fulfilling their parental responsibilities such as providing housing, food, and education to their offspring (E. Kim and Cain, 2008). As Korean immigrant fathers adapt to American culture, however, they try to increase their expressiveness (E. Kim and Hong, 2007).

Communication

Communication between Korean immigrant fathers and their children presents another difficulty. There are two reasons for this. First, as mentioned earlier, hierarchical Korean culture often uses unidirectional communication, flowing from parents to children without allowing children's response. Many first-generation Korean immigrant fathers continue to use this traditional communication style. Second, Korean immigrant fathers have serious difficulty speaking fluent English, despite their high education level. While almost all (99 percent) fathers reported that they were fluent in speaking Korean, only 40 percent reported that they speak English well (E. Kim and Wolpin, at press).

In contrast, their children, who attend American schools, speak English as their language of choice. For example, in Kim and Wolpin's (at press) study, approximately 95 percent of adolescents (75 percent of whom were born in United States and 25 percent of whom were born in Korea) were fluent in English, and 63 percent spoke Korean well. Therefore, many immigrant Korean families experience communication problems between fathers who are not fluent in English and their children, who are. To counteract this, Korean parents try to teach children Korean by talking to them in Korean at home, by sending them to Korean-language schools, and by sending them to Korea during summer break (E. Kim and Hong, 2007). Unfortunately, simply teaching the Korean language to the children does not alleviate communication problems. Park (1995) found that 80 percent of adolescents wished that their parents spoke English more fluently. As the disparity between which language is spoken by each generation grows more pronounced, establishing meaningful communication between fathers and children is an obvious challenge (E. Kim and Hong, 2007).

In summary, there is a profound cultural difference between Korea and the United States, in part characterized by societal differences in individualism and collectivism, respectively (Hofstede, 1980). These differences impact many aspects of Korean immigrants' success in parenting. However, there is a paucity of studies that examine Korean immigrant father-child relationships.

EMPIRICAL STUDIES IN KOREAN IMMIGRANT FATHERING AND CHILDREN'S DEVELOPMENT

Scholars suggest that two main aspects of parenting are parental warmth and parental control (Maccoby and Martin, 1983). Using these dimensions, two approaches to studying the effects of parenting on children's developmental outcomes have emerged. The dimensional tradition studies the influences of parenting itself, described in terms of parental warmth and control (Maccoby and Martin, 1983). The typological tradition examines the interaction effects of parental warmth and parental control, yielding four parenting styles: authoritative, authoritarian, permissive, and neglecting. In the very limited previous research on Korean immigrant parenting, both research traditions were applied.

Dimensional Approach

Parental Warmth and Parental Control

In the dimensional approach, parental warmth is defined as the quality of affectionate ties between parents and their children and of the behaviors that parents express toward their children. According to the parental acceptance-rejection theory (Rohner, Khaleque, and Cournoyer, 2007), the dimension of parental warmth ranges from acceptance to rejection. Parental acceptance refers to the warmth and affection that parents feel and express toward their children. Parental rejection refers to the absence of these feelings and behaviors, as well as the presence of behaviors and affects such as hostility and aggression, indifference and neglect, and undifferentiated rejection. Rohner (1991) has claimed that this characterization of parenting and its effects upon children's overall psychological adjustment could be applied reliably regardless of differences in family culture or language.

The theory also examines parental behavioral control, which ranges from permissive to strict (Rohner, 2007). Permissive parents exercise minimum control and allow adolescents to do things their own way. Moderately controlling parents establish a few clear limits and then allow adolescents to regulate their own activities within these limits. Firm parents guide the adolescent's behaviors by a firm schedule and parental intervention. Restrictive parents enforce many rules on the adolescents' behaviors and limit the adolescents' autonomy (Rohner, 2007).

Empirical Studies

Eight studies examined Korean immigrant fathers using the parental acceptance-rejection theory (E. Kim, 2001; E. Kim, 2005; E. Kim, at press; E. Kim and Cain, 2008; E. Kim, Cain, McCubbin, 2006; K. Kim and Rohner, 2002; Pettengill and Rohner, 1985; Rohner and Pettengill, 1985). In these studies, Korean immigrant fathers perceived themselves as warm and moderately controlling (Pettengill and Rohner, 1985). Korean immigrant adolescents also perceived their fathers as warm and moderately controlling (E. Kim, 2001, 2005; E. Kim and Cain, 2008; K. Kim and Rohner, 2002).

However, in E. Kim's (2001) study, although both fathers and adolescents think that Korean immigrant fathers are warm, 94 percent of fathers perceive themselves as warm, whereas only 76 percent of adolescents perceive their fathers as being warm. This discrepancy may be related to general perception differences between fathers and adolescents, as adolescents may remember more of the small hurtful incidents that their fathers may not recognize or remember (Rohner, personal communication, October 16, 2000). Or it may be the result of fathers answering the questionnaire in a way that is socially desirable while their adolescents report what they really perceive.

This discrepancy may also reflect the perception differences regarding parental warmth. While Korean American fathers usually do not explicitly express their love, their adolescents, who are growing up in the United States, may expect it from their fathers as they observe what their American friends' fathers do. If Korean American fathers communicate this cultural difference to their adolescents, the adolescents may understand. However, without this communication, adolescents, who might not be aware of these cultural differences, may not perceive their fathers to be as warm as their fathers believe themselves to be (E. Kim, 2001). Wu and Chao (2005) found that while both Euro-American and Chinese immigrant adolescents reported similar levels of ideal parental warmth, Chinese immigrant adolescents reported lower levels of warmth than their counterparts. This discrepancy between ideal and perceived warmth was related to Chinese immigrant adolescents' adjustment problems.

Korean immigrant adolescents' perception of paternal warmth was positively related to their academic achievement (K. Kim and Rohner, 2002), psychological adjustment (E. Kim, at press), and degree of depressive symptoms (E. Kim and Cain, 2008). When adolescents perceived their fathers as less warm and more rejecting, they also perceived that these fathers were less involved in their schooling (K. Kim and Rohner, 2002).

Three studies captured the changing nature of Korean immigrant fathering by examining the relationship between paternal control and warmth for Korean adolescents, Korean immigrant adolescents, and Korean immigrant fathers. First, Rohner and Pettengill (1985) found that Korean adolescents who lived in Korea perceived strict paternal control as a sign of paternal warmth and affection, and as more attention and involvement. This finding is in sharp contrast to Pettengill and Rohner's (1985) finding that Korean immigrant adolescents perceived strict paternal control as a sign of hostility and aggression. Also, the higher the paternal control, the more father-adolescent conflict Korean immigrant adolescents experienced (Pettengill and Rohner, 1985).

Expanding on the results of these studies, E. Kim (2005) found that Korean immigrant fathers' report of higher paternal behavioral control was positively correlated with their report of higher warmth and affection. This finding is consistent with the traditional view of Korean fathers, who perceive themselves as the main authority of the household. Korean fathers practice their authority through extensive involvement in adolescents' decisionmaking and by controlling adolescents' behaviors (Lehrer, 1996; Rohner and Pettengill, 1985). Therefore, Korean immigrant fathers might still express their parental acceptance and interest in their children through higher levels of behavioral control, resulting in a positive correlation between fathers' report of parental behavioral control and parental warmth and affection. In other words, Korean immigrant fathers maintained traditional Korean parenting attitudes (E. Kim, 2005).

However, in the same study, E. Kim (2005) found that adolescents of these Korean immigrant fathers perceived their fathers' higher behavioral control as more hostile and aggressive, and as undifferentiated rejection. This adolescent perception is probably related to the cultural value placed on autonomy and independence in the United States. Especially as children enter middle school, they are given more freedom and are expected to be more self-reliant than they were in elementary school. Consequently, adolescents struggle to increase their autonomy and independence. These young adolescents may perceive their parents' greater behavioral control as an indication that the parents don't understand their children's lives and their need for more autonomy. These adolescents may experience more conflicts with their parents and may argue with them about parental be-havioral control, resulting in increased perceptions of parental hostility and lowered warmth/affection (E. Kim 2005).

In another study, E. Kim and Cain (2008) found that adolescents' per-ceived low paternal warmth and higher intergenerational acculturation conflicts with fathers were positively correlated with adolescent depres-sive symptoms. However, intergenerational acculturation conflicts were the only predictor for adolescent depression. Adolescents who perceived high intergenerational acculturation conflicts (i.e., more than sometimes) experienced elevated depressive symptoms compared to adolescents who perceived low conflicts. This was especially true for those adolescents who perceived conflicts in academic expectations, sacrificing one's interests, ways of expressing love, saving face, expressing opinions, and showing respect to the elderly. These findings are congruent with existing anecdotal literature on how Korean immigrant parents and children might experience conflicts due to maintaining Confucian culture in American society (Lehrer, 1996). This study also extended the literature by examining the influence of conflicts on adolescents' mental health.

Typological Approach

Parenting Styles

In contrast to the dimensional approach, which studies parental warmth and control as an independent variable, the typological tradition studies the influence of the parenting styles, including authoritarian, authorita-tive, permissive, and neglecting, on offspring's development (K. Kim and Rohner, 2002). Parenting styles are a function of two dimensions, which are labeled parental warmth and parental control (Baumrind, 1991; Mac-coby and Martin, 1983). Authoritarian parents were found to be less warm but valued high control and children's obedience. In contrast, permissive parents were warm but not controlling and did not set limits. Authoritative parents were both warm and effectively controlling in their requirement for mature behavior from their children. Finally, neglecting parents were nei-ther warm nor controlling (Baumrind, 1991; Maccoby and Martin, 1983).

Empirical Studies

Two studies used the typological approach in examining Korean immi-grant fathering. Both studies found that this approach may not appropri-ately capture Korean immigrant fathering because it was developed from a Western cultural context (K. Kim and Rohner, 2002; Shrake, 1996). Shrake (1996) found that Korean immigrant adolescents perceived their fathers as warm despite their perception of high authoritarian control. Adolescents' perception of parental authoritarian control was negatively related to behavioral problems and positively related to emotional problems. Adolescents' perceived paternal warmth was related to fewer emotional and behavioral problems. This finding did not quite fit with the description of authoritarian parenting, which is usually conceptualized as fathers who are low in warmth but high in control. Shrake (1996) explained that this "authoritarian yet warm" fathering style might be related to culturally specific characteristics of Korean immigrant parenting, where authoritarian control is often parallel with great sacrifice by the parents for their children. Further, in K. Kim and Rohner's (2002) study with Korean immigrant adolescents, approximately 73 percent of adolescents' perceived paternal parenting style did not fit into Baumrind's parenting style scheme. Adolescents raised by authoritative or permissive fathers performed better academically than adolescents who were raised by authoritarian fathers. No difference was found between adolescents who were raised by authoritative or permissive fathers (K. Kim and Rohner, 2002).

These findings for Korean immigrant fathers are similar to studies on Chinese immigrant parenting. Gorman (1998) also had difficulty in characterizing Chinese immigrant parenting behaviors as either authoritative or authoritarian because Chinese immigrant parenting stems from cultural attitudes and beliefs very different from those of Euro-Americans. Studies of Chinese immigrants suggest that the concepts of authoritative and authoritarian may be somewhat ethnocentric, as they do not capture the important feature of Chinese immigrant parenting behaviors: training (Chao, 1994; Chao and Tseng, 2002). The concept of "training" for the Chinese parents of preschool age children includes high involvement, caring, and physical closeness that the authoritarian style does not include, but is incorporated into the authoritative style. The authoritative parenting style had more positive effects on school grades and school effort for Euro-American youth than for first-generation Chinese youth (Chao, 2001). For Chinese youth, the authoritative parenting style was no better than the authoritarian style for predicting school performance.

In summary, depending on which parenting theory was used, Korean immigrant fathers are described as either "authoritarian yet warm" or "accepting and moderately controlling." Paternal warmth was positively related to adolescents' academic performance, psychological adjustment, fewer problem behaviors, and lower depressive symptoms (E. Kim and Cain, 2008; E. Kim et al., 2006; K. Kim and Rohner, 2002; Shrake, 1996). In addition, intergenerational acculturation conflicts with fathers were related to their adolescent's elevated levels of depressive symptoms. These findings suggest that first-generation Korean immigrant fathers may need to learn how to increase their warmth and how to decrease or solve intergenerational acculturation conflicts with their children.

SUGGESTIONS TO FATHERS, COMMUNITY LEADERS, PRACTITIONERS, AND RESEARCHERS

To help Korean immigrant fathers' adjustment and to support optimal developmental outcomes in their children, the family, community, and professionals must work together. Based on the literature reviewed, suggestions are provided for Korean immigrant fathers, Korean community leaders, researchers who work with the population, and other practitioners.

Suggestions for Korean Immigrant Fathers

Korean immigrant fathers need to develop in three areas: understanding the differences between Korean and American culture, learning how to express their warmth, and learning ways to decrease conflicts with children.

Understanding the Differences between Korean and American Culture

In the United States, Korean immigrant fathers live in an individualistic society where values contradict their heritage, which is based on collectivistic Confucian values. Knowing the differences between Korean culture and American culture is a critical factor in understanding their life situation as a migrant. By learning how their heritage and culture shaped them, Korean immigrant fathers will more clearly see how this influences their fathering behaviors. At the same time, they need to know about individualistic American values that their children are learning outside the home. Without this understanding, it would be difficult for Korean immigrant fathers to fully comprehend their children's behaviors. Once they learn the differences between the two cultures, they will be able to recognize why they parent in the way they do. They also will be able to make necessary changes in their parenting based on what they learned.

Ways to Show Paternal Warmth

Parental warmth continues to be shown in study after study to be a primary ingredient of effective parenting. In the United States, parental warmth is conveyed through verbal and nonverbal expressions such as hugs, praise, encouragement, and telling children they are loved (Rohner, Khaleque, and Cournoyer, 2007). However, Korean immigrant fathers typically do not express their affection using verbal and nonverbal cues. Rather, these fathers believe that they show love by fulfilling their parental responsibilities such as providing housing, food, and education to their offspring (E. Kim and Cain, 2008). These fathers could benefit by understanding their children's point of view. Korean immigrant adolescents wish their fathers would show more physical and verbal signs of affection. When this discrepancy is significant, this conflict is related to adolescents' elevated depressive symptoms (E. Kim and Cain, 2008). Hong (2003) also found that Korean immigrant adolescents wanted their fathers to explicitly express their love (Hong, 2003).

It is exciting to see some Korean immigrant fathers acknowledging the need for expressing their warmth and actually trying to increase their expressiveness (E. Kim and Hong, 2007). Studies show that paternal warmth is related to adolescents' psychological adjustment and better mental health (E. Kim, at press; E. Kim and Cain, 2008). Korean fathers may feel uncomfortable in expressing their affection at first, but as they practice these behaviors, this discomfort could be reduced. They also need to learn that it is acceptable to praise and compliment their children, even in public. In Korea, praising children in front of other people is considered inappropriate (U.S. Dooranno Father School, 2005). By praising, fathers can shape desired behaviors in children (Webster-Stratton, 2001). Expressing affection and praising children can be effectively practiced when fathers spend consistent, short amounts of time (e.g., ten to fifteen minutes) with their children (Webster-Stratton, 2001). This special time can be any joint activity that the children choose, such as playing or reading a book. When focused attention is given to children in this way, they feel loved.

Ways to Decrease Intergenerational Acculturation Conflicts

Intergenerational acculturation conflicts come from living in two different cultures. Therefore, mutual understanding of both cultures is essential for both fathers and children. That way, Korean immigrant fathers can come closer to understanding the American culture in which they now live, and the children can better understand the Korean culture their fathers grew up in. One way of overcoming these differences is good communication.

However, establishing good communication is challenging due to the lack of a common language. Having a common language is possible when both fathers and children are fluent either in English or in Korean. However, as shown in E. Kim and Wolpin's (at press) study, only 40 percent of Korean immigrant fathers speak fluent English, while 63 percent of children are fluent in Korean. Many Korean immigrant fathers work long hours running small businesses where the need to speak English is reduced to specific responses to customers' requests (I. Kim 2004). This limits their need for fluency in English and consumes the time needed to learn the language. Even when they attend ESL classes, learning to speak English fluently is not easy for these fathers who migrated to the United States as adults (Buttaro, 2004).

It is not realistic to suggest that immigrant Korean fathers cease speaking their native language as the answer to increasing their fluency in English. So to facilitate better communication in the home, many Korean immigrant parents send their children to Korean-language schools and to Korea for the summer so that their children can speak the Korean language (E. Kim and Hong, 2007). Since no study has been conducted to examine how effective this strategy is in keeping parent-child communication open, and no research is available as to how fathers who primarily speak Korean communicate with children who primarily speak English, there are no research-based solutions offered for this challenging problem.

Korean families need to learn two-way communication and conflict resolution skills. For example, twelve conflict resolution skills are provided for free on the Internet (The Conflict Resolution Network, 2007). Two of these specific skills that are most relevant for the situation are: 1) learning empathy to listen for understanding and to build rapport, and 2) learning the win-win approach to respect all parties' needs. Since English proficiency is limited for many Korean immigrant fathers, this education needs to be done in Korean through Korean community organizations, such as Korean churches or Korean community centers. This observation leads to a very important contribution that can be made by Korean immigrant community leaders.

Suggestions for Korean Immigrant Community Leaders

Community leadership functions among first-generation Korean immigrants usually involve Korean association leaders, mainstream professionals, and ministers of Korean churches. Ministers, especially, have a critical leadership role because three out of four Korean immigrants attend Korean ethnic churches (W. Hurh and Kim, 1990; W. Hurh et al., 1979; O. Kim, 1999; Kwon, 2004). Korean immigrants rely on their ministers for psychosocial, emotional, and spiritual guidance. Many times, troubled first-generation Korean immigrant parents seek advice from their ministers, who themselves are often first-generation Korean immigrants, for their personal family matters, including mental health issues (J. Shin, 2002). Some Korean immigrant youths may also utilize religious practices and religious counseling in dealing with personal issues (Yeh and Inose, 2002).

To help these families, ministers need to understand the complex cultural issues that affect family interactions. They also need to hold support workshops on the topic of positive fathering. For example, the fathers' school movement, which was developed in Korea, has been introduced in Korean immigrant churches (U.S. Dooranno Father School, 2005). In this program, Korean immigrant fathers learn the meaning of fatherhood, the impact of

Korean traditional culture on fathering, how to move away from the traditional hierarchical parenting practices, and the importance of maintaining good relationships with their wives and children.

Suggestions for Practitioners

Practitioners who are bilingual and bicultural have an optimal position for helping both Korean immigrant fathers and children. Overall, first-generation Korean immigrants are not comfortable discussing family matters (e.g., teen behavioral problems) with outside professionals (J. Shin, 2002). They consider family a private entity and they try to save face, based on their Confucian cultural background. Therefore, it is important to make fathers understand that it is acceptable to seek professional help if necessary and that this help is confidential. This kind of information will help fathers seek the support they need. Practitioners with non-Korean ethnic backgrounds need to understand the Korean cultural background and challenges facing Korean immigrants living in the United States. Without this understanding, these practitioners may misinterpret family conflict situations and will not be able to offer the culturally competent interventions that will be most helpful for these families.

Suggestions for Researchers

Little empirical evidence exists on immigrant Korean fathers. What exists has identified the relationship between lack of paternal warmth and adolescents' poor academic success, poor psychological adjustment, and increased problem behaviors. The evidence also indicates that intergenerational cultural conflicts between fathers and adolescents are related to depression in adolescent children. This research is a good beginning. More research is needed in: 1) understanding the relationship between sending children to Korean-language schools and having common language and communication levels; 2) examining the relationship between parents' attending ESL programs and their adjustment in the United States; 3) exploring the Korean immigrant father's perception of his relationship with his children using a qualitative study; and 4) determining the impact of using traditional communication styles on conflicts. Part of this research will include an evaluation of the effects of the father school on paternal parenting practices. This evaluation needs be conducted as a community-academic partnership. The desired outcome of this line of research is to develop a program that teaches cultural awareness as well as parenting skills that include positive aspects of both Korean and American parenting styles.

SUMMARY

The goal of this chapter was to review issues related to Korean immigrant fatherhood. Korean immigrant fathers continue to practice collectivistic Confucian culture in the United States. This brings special challenges and conflicts in Korean immigrant families. Few empirical studies capture these challenges and their influence on children and adolescent developmental outcomes. To facilitate competent Korean immigrant fathering, not only individual fathers but also community leaders, professionals, and researchers need to work together to address these challenges.

REFERENCES

Abelmann, N. (1997). Traditional culture and society. In J. Koo and A. Nahm (Eds.), *An introduction to Korean culture.* Elizabeth, NJ: Hollym.

Baumrind, D. (1991). The influence of parenting style on adolescent competence and substance use. *Journal of Early Adolescence, 11,* 56–95.

Buttaro, L. (2004). Second-language acquisition, culture shock, and language stress of adult female Latina students in New York. *Journal of Hispanic Higher Education, 3,* 21–49.

Chao, R. (1994). Beyond parental control and authoritarian parenting style: Understanding Chinese parenting through the cultural notion of training. *Child Development, 65,* 1111–19.

———. (2001). Extending research on the consequences of parenting style for Chinese Americans and European Americans. *Child Development, 72,* 1832–43.

Chao, R., and Tseng, V. (2002). Parenting of Asians. In M. H. Bornstein (Ed.), *Handbook of parenting* (vol. 4, 59–94). Mahwah, NJ: Erlbaum.

Choe, Y. (2004). History of the Korean church: A case study of Christ United Methodist Church, 1903–2003. In I. J. Kim (Ed.), *Korean-Americans: Past, present, and future* (38–62). Elizabeth, NJ: Hollym.

Choi, G. (1997). Acculturative stress, social support, and depression in Korean American families. *Journal of Family Social Work, 2,* 81–97.

The Conflict Resolution Network. (2007). *12 skills summary: Conflict resolution skills.* Retrieved May 3, 2007, from http://www.crnhq.org/twelveskills.html.

Gorman, J. (1998). Parenting attitudes and practices of immigrant Chinese mothers of adolescents. *Family Relations, 47,* 73–80.

Grolnick, W. S., and Farkas, M. (2002). Parenting and the development of children's self-regulation. In M. H. Bornstein (Ed.), *Handbook of parenting* (vol. 5, 88–110). Mahwah, NJ: Erlbaum.

Hofstede, G. (1980). *Culture's consequences: International differences in work-oriented values.* Beverly Hills, CA: Sage.

Holmbeck, G., Paikoff, R., and Brooks-Gunn, J. (1995). Parenting adolescents. In M. H. Bornstein (Ed.), *Handbook of parenting* (vol. 1, 91–118). Mahwah, NJ: Erlbaum.

Hong, S. (2003). *The identity profiles of the 2nd generation Korean Americans in Washington state.* Unpublished manuscript, 100 Korean Immigration Celebration Conference, Seattle, Washington.

Hui, C. H., and Triandis, H. C. (1986). Individualism-collectivism: A study of cross-cultural researchers. *Journal of Cross-Cultural Psychology, 17,* 225–48.

Hurh, W. M., Kim, H. C., and Kim, K. C. (1979). *Assimilation patterns of Korean immigrants in the United States: A case study of Korean immigrants in the Chicago area.* Lanham, MD: University Press of America.

Hurh, W., and Kim, K. C. (1990). Correlates of Korean immigrants' mental health. *Journal of Nervous and Mental Disease, 178,* 703–11.

Kim, E. (2001). *Korean American parent-child relationships, parental acculturation, and young adolescents' psychosocial functioning.* Unpublished doctoral dissertation, University of Wisconsin, Madison.

———. (2005). Korean American parental control: Acceptance or rejection? *Ethos: Journal of the Society for Psychological Anthropology, 33,* 347–66.

———. (at press). Parental warmth and psychological adjustment in young Korean American adolescents. *Journal of Child and Adolescent Psychiatric Nursing.*

Kim, E., and Cain, K. (2008). Korean American adolescent depression and parenting. *Journal of Child and Adolescent Psychiatric Nursing, 21,* 105–15.

Kim, E., Cain, K., and McCubbin, M. (2006). Maternal and paternal parenting, acculturation, and young adolescents' psychological adjustment in Korean American families. *Journal of Child and Adolescent Psychiatric Nursing, 19,* 112–29.

Kim, E., and Hong, S. (2007). First-generation Korean American parents' perceptions on discipline. *Journal of Professional Nursing, 23,* 60 68.

Kim, E., and Wolpin, S. (at press). Acculturation and characteristics of Korean American families. *The Journal of Cultural Diversity: An Interdisciplinary Journal.*

Kim, I. (2004). A century of Korean immigration to the United States: 1903–2003. In I. J. Kim (Ed.), *Korean-Americans: Past, present, and future* (13–37). Elizabeth, NJ: Hollym.

Kim, K. (2002). *When Confucius dies then the nation lives.* Seoul, Korea: Bada Books.

Kim, K. C., and Kim, S. (1995). Family and work roles of Korean immigrants in the United States. In E. T. H. McCubbin, A. Thompson, and J. Fromer (Eds.), *Resiliency in ethnic minority families. Vol. 1: Native and immigrant American families* (225–42). Madison: University of Wisconsin.

Kim, K., and Rohner, R. P. (2002). Parental warmth, control, and involvement in schooling: Predicting academic achievement among Korean American adolescents. *Journal of Cross-Cultural Psychology, 33,* 127–40.

Kim, O. (1999). Mediation effect of social support between ethnic attachment and loneliness in older Korean immigrants. *Research in Nursing & Health, 22,* 169–75.

Kim, W., Kim, L., and Rue, D. (1997). Korean American children. In G. Johnson-Powell, J. Yamanoto, W. Wyatt, and W. Arroyo (Eds.), *Transcultural child development: Psychological assessment and treatment* (183–207). Hoboken, NJ: John Wiley & Sons.

Kwon, O. (2004). The role of Korean churches in formation and incorporation of the Korean community in the Washington, D.C. area. In I. J. Kim (Ed.), *Korean-Americans: Past, present, and future* (239–70). Elizabeth, NJ: Hollym.

Lee, B. (2004). Confucian ideals and American values. In I. J. Kim (Ed.), *Korean-Americans: Past, present, and future* (273–77). Elizabeth, NJ: Hollym.

Lee, L. (1995). *Korean Americans.* New York: Marshall Cavendish Corporation.

Lehrer, B. (1996). *The Korean American.* New York: Chelsea House Publishers.

Maccoby, E., and Martin, J. (1983). *Socialization in the context of the family: Parent-child interaction.* Hoboken, NJ: Wiley.

Nah, K. (1993). Perceived problems and service delivery for Korean immigrants. *Social Work, 38,* 289–96.

Oak, S., and Martin, V. (2000). *American/Korean contrast: Patterns and expectations in the U.S. and Korea.* Elizabeth, NJ: Hollym.

Park, E. (1995). Voices of Korean-American students. *Adolescence, 30,* 945–53.

Pettengill, S. M., and Rohner, R. (1985). Korean-American adolescents' perceptions of parental control, parental rejection and parent-adolescent conflict. In I. R. Lagunes and Y. H. Poortinga (Eds.), *From a different perspective: Studies of behavior across cultures* (240–49). Lisse: Swets & Zeitinger.

Phinney, J. S., Ong, A., and Madden, T. (2000). Cultural values and intergenerational value discrepancies in immigrant and non-immigrant families. *Child Development, 71,* 528–39.

Phipps, E. J., True, G., and Murray, G. F. (2003). Community perspectives on advance care planning: Report from the community ethics program. *Journal of Cultural Diversity, 10,* 118–23.

Rohner, R. (1991). *Handbook for the study of parental acceptance and rejection.* Storrs: University of Connecticut.

———. (2007). *Glossary of significant concepts in parental acceptance-rejection theory (PARTheory).* Retrieved April 1, 2007, from http://vm.uconn.edu/~rohner/.

Rohner, R., Khaleque, A., and Cournoyer, D. E. (2007). *Parental acceptance-rejection theory, methods, evidence, and implications.* Retrieved February 2, 2007, from http://vm.uconn.edu/~rohner.

Rohner, R., and Pettengill, S. M. (1985). Perceived parental rejection and parental control among Korean adolescents. *Child Development, 36,* 524–28.

Shin, J. (2002). Help-seeking behaviors by Korean immigrants for depression. *Issues in Mental Health Nursing, 23,* 461–76.

Shin, K., and Shin, C. (1999). The lived experience of Korean immigrant women acculturating into the United States. *Health Care for Women International, 20,* 603–17.

Shrake, E. (1996). *Perceived parenting style, ethnic identity, and associated problem behaviors among Korean American adolescents.* Unpublished dissertation, University of California–Los Angeles.

Shwalb, D., Nakazawa, J., Yamamoto, T., and Hyun, J. (2004). Fathering in Japanese, Chinese, and Korean cultures. In M. E. Lamb (Ed.), *The role of the father in child development* (146–81). Hoboken, NJ: Wiley.

Storm, R., Park, S. H., and Daniels, S. (1987). Child rearing dilemmas of Korean immigrants to the United States. *International Journal of Experimental Research in Education, 24,* 91–102.

Triandis, H. C. (1994). *Culture and social behavior.* New York: McGraw-Hill.

U.S. Census Bureau. (2000). *General population characteristics.* Retrieved September 8, 2006, from http://www.census.gov/.

U.S. Dooranno Father School. (2005). *Father School Leader Training*. Los Angeles: Dooranno.

Webster-Stratton, C. (2001). *The parents and children series: A comprehensive course. Leader's guide*. Seattle, WA: The Incredible Years.

Wu, C., and Chao, R. K. (2005). Intergenerational cultural conflicts in norms of parental warmth among Chinese American immigrants. *International Journal of Behavioral Development, 29*, 516–23.

Yeh, C., and Inose, M. (2002). Difficulties and coping strategies of Chinese, Japanese, and Korean immigrant students. *Adolescence, 37*, 69–82.

9

Acculturation via Creolization: Constructing Latino American Fathering Identities

Carl F. Auerbach, Louise Bordeaux Silverstein,
Carrie Zlotnick-Woldenberg, Aris Peguero,
and Sara Tacher-Rosse

This chapter reports the experiences of three samples of immigrant Latino fathers (one Puerto Rican American, one Dominican American, and one Mexican American) who were redefining their fathering identities as part of the developmental process of immigration. The fathers reported how they were transforming their traditional Latino fathering identities as they encountered contrasting U.S. cultural norms. This cultural change process is usually referred to as "acculturation." However, we think that the concept of acculturation does not capture the complexities of this process.

We will argue, in contrast, that cultural change is more accurately understood as a process that we call "creolization." The term creolization has been used in linguistics to refer to a process of language development, that is, the creative development of a new language that occurs when two cultural groups speaking different languages come into contact. We think that this process of creating a third cultural variant is an accurate description of the changes in fathering identities in the immigrant fathers we have studied.

We believe that these fathers are not simply giving up their Latino fathering identities and gradually taking on U.S. fathering identities. Rather, they are creating entirely new Latino American fathering identities that are a creative melange of traditional Latino values and U.S. cultural norms. We begin with a brief overview of the concept of acculturation, followed by a definition of our concept of creolization. We then present research data that illustrate how these Latino fathers were creating creolized Latino American fathering identities. We conclude with a discussion of how the concept of creolization can provide a helpful theoretical framework for understanding change in non-immigrant families as well.

197

THEORETICAL FRAMEWORK

Acculturation

The work of J. W. Berry (1980) has become the standard in the discourse on acculturation. Berry defined acculturation as cultural change caused by the association of two or more cultures. Berry proposed four types of acculturation based on two binary distinctions stated in the form of questions. First, does the person from the non-dominant culture retain her/his original cultural identity? Second, does the person from the non-dominant culture develop a positive relationship with the dominant culture? For purposes of his typology, these questions are answered as "yes" or "no."

The combination of answers to these questions yields four varieties of acculturation. *Assimilation*, the melting pot concept, occurs when the immigrant's cultural identity is lost, and there is a positive relation to the dominant culture. *Integration*, or biculturalism, takes place when an immigrant's cultural identity is retained and there is a positive relation to the dominant culture. *Rejection*, the unmeltability idea, describes the situation in which cultural identity is retained, but the person remains isolated from the dominant culture. Finally, *deculturation* occurs when cultural identity is lost, and there is isolation from the dominant culture.

Berry's typology sees the dominant culture replacing or coexisting with an immigrant's culture of origin. However, he does not allow the possibility that a third cultural variant spontaneously emerges. In the case of biculturalism, immigrants maintain their original cultural identity, while simultaneously developing an identity that is congruent with the host culture. However, these identities remain separate and the individual continues to migrate between the two cultures.

Others have built on Berry's model. Leyendecker and Lamb (1999) expanded Berry's concept of biculturalism, defining it as a process that is both additive and transformational, assuming less passivity on the part of the immigrant group. LaFromboise, Coleman, and Gerton (1998) have suggested that biculturalism reflects a positive relationship with both cultures without the immigrant having to choose between them. Birman (1998) proposed that biculturalism conferred the immigrant who has a strong sense of self with the ability to negotiate both cultures and function adaptively in each. However, all of these researchers stop short of arguing that acculturation resulted in a synthesis of the immigrant and the dominant culture, thereby generating a viable new culture.

Creolization and Related Concepts

We originally became aware of the term, creolization, from the work of Hannerz (1987), a cultural anthropologist. We were drawn to this concept of creolization because one of us (Silverstein) was raised in New Orleans where creole culture is the dominant culture. In the nineteenth century, Louisiana whites of French and Spanish descent referred to themselves as Creoles as a way of differentiating themselves from the Anglo-Americans who moved to the province after the Louisiana Purchase in 1803 (Thernstrom, 1980). In the twentieth century, Creole came to refer primarily to people of color born in Louisiana, mainly in New Orleans, who had both African and French ancestry. Hall (1995) defined Creole more inclusively, as any person of non-American parents who was born in the Americas.

The concept of creolization has historically been associated with two meanings: a negative one that we want to disavow, and a positive one that we want to articulate. The negative connotation stems from the fact that a creole is a person of mixed descent, a mix of the dominant colonizing group and the non-dominant indigenous population. The colonizing group used the term pejoratively because of racist attitudes that assumed the inferiority of a mixed race creole compared to the "pure race" European conquerors. From the colonized population's perspective, the creole population was associated with the trauma of conquest and domination.

In contrast, our bias toward the process of creolization is a positive one. Our thinking about this term has been strongly influenced by New Orleans culture where creole refers to a vibrant French-Spanish-African cultural context that extends to people, food, music, and language. We assume that the blending of genes, languages, and cultural norms strengthens human development.

In addition to cultural anthropology, the term creolization is used in linguistics. It describes the process by which a new language develops when two separate cultures, each speaking their own language, come into contact and need to communicate with each other (Thomason, 2006). Initially, representatives of the two cultures develop a simplified code called a *pidgin*. The pidgin consists of words for common objects and actions, drawn from both languages. It has no grammar, so that meaning is conveyed by context alone. Often, the next generation after the initial cultural contact will develop the pidgin into a full-fledged language called a *creole*. The grammar and vocabulary of the creole are a blend of the two original languages, with some features of its own. Once formed, the creole can stand in many relations to the original languages from which it is derived—replacing them, becoming a dialect of them, modifying them, and so forth, depending upon local conditions in complex ways.

The Yiddish language is an example of the creolization process. It arose around 1100 as a combination of several German dialects in the ghettos of Central Europe. Although its vocabulary is basically German, it includes words from Hebrew, Romance languages, and English. In the twelfth century, Jewish minstrels began to expand the language into a broader cultural variant that ultimately developed into Yiddish literature and theater (Yiddish Homepage).

Although many U.S. citizens view monolingualism as the norm, most of the world is multilingual, and cultures and languages regularly come into contact. Thus, linguists view creolization as one of the important mechanisms of language evolution. Our work extends the creolization concept to processes of cultural evolution.

We propose using creolization as a descriptive metaphor for the cultural change that occurs when two cultures come into contact. Creolization goes beyond the idea that cultural change is primarily an accommodation to the dominant culture. It recognizes the creative contribution of immigrant cultures. Such a synthesis is easily recognizable in jazz, which can be seen as a musical creolization, a complex synthesis of West African rhythms and structures with Euro-American instruments and melodies. In the case of jazz, the dominant culture absorbed something from another culture, resulting in a new and different musical phenomenon that was neither European nor African, but distinctly American (originally African American), and that has clearly enhanced American culture.

In the field of family studies, Inclan and Hernandez (1992) and Comas-Diaz (2001) have all used the term "transculturation" in a manner that is similar to our use of creolization. Inclan and Hernandez (1992) presented four possible outcomes of cultural contact, three of them marked by passivity on the part of the immigrant group. "Mediation," in contrast, represented a synthesis of both cultures. Comas-Diaz (2001) pointed out that many Latino Americans "live in the hyphen, creating a space whereby transculturation changes both the Latino and mainstream cultures" (119). These concepts of transculturation share the assumption that a distinct third culture emerges from the dynamic encounter of conflicting cultural values.

Despite the conceptual similarity of "creolization" and "transculturation," we chose to use the term creolization to describe cultural contact for two reasons. First, to explicitly draw the parallel between linguistic change and cultural change, and thus begin to formulate a general theory that encompasses them both. Second, because of the linguistic parallels, the concept of creolization allows us to present specific mechanisms by which elements of different cultures combine.

In the following sections, we will describe the evolution of fathering identities among the Latino fathers that we studied. We begin by describing the cultural clash that these men experienced between traditional Latino values and U.S. cultural ideology about gender and parenting.

Entre Dos Mundos: Immigration as a Catalyst for Cultural Change

The term "Latino" has generally been used to describe people of Indo-Hispanic background who live in the Caribbean and the Americas (Bernal and Knight, 1997). We recognize that there is no single Latino population, but rather many different languages, cultures, and ethnic identities. Researchers who group Latinos together in an effort to identify patterns of shared experiences run the risk of overlooking or discounting the distinctiveness of the individual groups. In particular, variables such as social class, education, immigration history, and political experience, to name just a few, significantly differentiate "Latino" groups. For example, an educated, professional, bilingual Mexican couple who emigrated to the United States for greater professional opportunities may well have more in common with an Anglo professional couple than they have with a Mexican couple from Puebla who emigrated to the United States in search of work.

Moreover, making generalizations about cultural norms risks generating, rather than deconstructing, stereotypes. Each family develops a unique version of traditional and non-traditional values. With these limitations in mind, we will outline some shared experiences that were reported by the Puerto Rican, Dominican, and Mexican fathers in our study, particularly as they relate to three central cultural values that are embedded in the fathering role: *familismo*, *machismo*, and *respeto*.

Traditional Latino family values define the father's role as the breadwinner and protector of the family (*familismo*). Cultural expectations assume that the father maintains the dominant position in the traditional gender and generational hierarchy (*machismo*). As such, he demands *respeto* (respect) and deference from all other family members. The cultural value of *machismo* generates and sustains both the exalted cultural image of the authoritarian, remote, and emotionally distant father and the complementary image of his passive and subservient wife (Mirandé, 1997). Having said this, it is important to note that power relations in even the most traditional Latino households are often more complex than the cultural expectations would suggest. As one example, some Latino couples will engage in extensive power sharing in private, while maintaining the appearance of tradition in public.

However, immigration is a catalyst for cultural changes of all kinds. Often Latinas experience unique problems when their familiar, fixed roles as caretakers and nurturers become more fluid in the United States. Some women adhere rigidly to traditional gender roles in an effort to defend against pressure to assimilate. Others, often driven by economic necessity, accept and adopt practices closer to the U.S. model.

Often there is a gap between practice and ideology as couples enact their family roles. In a working-class household, for example, a woman might find herself contributing to the family income and having decision making power for the first time. Her husband, because she is out of the house at work, may begin helping with household chores. However, as Inclan (2003) has noted, these practices often precede changes in the couple's ideology about men and women's roles. The husband may attempt to preserve an explicit ideology of traditional gender roles, even as the actual gender roles become less polarized. Inclan pointed out that in a middle-class household, the opposite pattern often occurs, in which the couple espouses a more egalitarian ideology, but their behavior continues to reflect the more traditional gendered division of labor.

Montalvo and Gutierrez (1990) have described how cultural pressure takes place at different rates among different family members. Children usually come into contact with the new culture at a faster rate than their parents because of the number of hours they spend in school, and because they are exposed to U.S. peer culture. These contrasting rates of immersion in the new culture inevitably generate stress in the parent-child relationship, because of the new values the children learn. They may, for example, learn more egalitarian values from their teachers and classmates, which may cause them to be less deferential to authority in the home and thus threaten the traditional family values of *machismo* and *respeto*.

Another challenge to these values occurs when the culture of origin and the host culture have different expectations about child development (Inclan and Heron, 1998). This happens, for example, when adolescents, who were expected to stay close to home in their culture of origin, are pushed to greater and earlier independence in the United States and thus are more likely to challenge parental authority. Parental authority is also threatened when a father, who is used to the considerable power over his children that *machismo* and *respeto* confer, finds that power circumscribed by the new legal rights of his children. For example, using corporal punishment as a form of discipline may be commonplace in the country of origin, while U.S. law considers severe corporal punishment to be "child abuse." Indeed, many immigrant parents shy away from contact with social service agencies because they are afraid that social workers will label their disciplinary practices as abusive and take legal action against them.

These cultural clashes between the culture of origin and the new culture generate pressure to change behaviors, attitudes, and identities. The ways in which the men in our study have responded to this pressure to change their fathering behavior is the topic of this article. After a brief description of our research methodology, we present the men's descriptions of their subjective experiences of the change process.

METHODOLOGY

The data were collected as part of the Yeshiva University Fatherhood Project, which investigates the social evolution of fatherhood in a variety of U.S. subcultures. The method used was a qualitative research paradigm in which focus group interviews of fathers were conducted, and the typed transcripts from the focus groups were analyzed using a grounded theory methodology (see Auerbach and Silverstein, 2003).

These data are preliminary because the immigration process was not the focus of our study. However, the qualitative nature of the research allowed the participants to initiate the discussion of these issues, and the concept of creolization emerged as we listened to their stories. Like all qualitative studies, this project has generated hypotheses that must be explored further with subsequent research samples.

Participants

The participants were originally recruited as four separate samples. Although the research was done under the Yeshiva Fatherhood Project as an umbrella research project headed by Auerbach and Silverstein as primary investigators, each sample represented the Psy.D. research project of one of the secondary investigators. The Mexican sample included nineteen fathers, the Dominican twenty-one, and there were two samples of primarily Puerto Rican fathers, one with eighteen fathers and the other with twenty fathers, all living in New York City. For purposes of exposition the data from the two samples of Puerto Rican fathers were combined.

All of the participants were part of convenience samples recruited through a snowball sampling technique. Each of the student researchers had a personal or professional contact within the community they chose to investigate. The student recruited community members willing to serve in the study, and these initial recruits in turn recruited others. The Puerto Rican samples were recruited from a school district and several Catholic churches in New York City. The Mexican sample was also recruited from Catholic churches in New York City. The Dominican sample was recruited from a Pentacostal church in Brooklyn. Because each sample was recruited from a particular community, some of the focus groups included men who knew each other, and some of the men also knew their group's moderator.

The majority of the fathers were in their thirties and forties, with a small number somewhat older. The majority of the men were employed (85 percent) with a mean overall income of $24,000, and a range from $1,000 to $140,000. The majority of the fathers across all samples were married. However, about one-third of the fathers in the Puerto Rican sample were divorced or separated. See table 9.1 for a detailed description of the demographics of the participants.

The amount of time in the United States varied, with the Mexican fathers here from three to twenty-five years; the Dominicans, from five to thirty-five years; and the Puerto Rican sample, from six to forty-eight years. Length of residence was not available for some of the Puerto Rican group because it was the first group of Latino fathers studied, and the

Table 9.1. Demographic Information for the Three Samples of Latino Fathers

	Country of Origin		
Variable	Mexico	Dominican Republic	Puerto Rico
Number in Sample	19	21	38
Mean Age	37	47	44
Age Range	25–56	28–71	20–49
Number of Children: Range	1–7	2–5	1–5
Number Employed	19	16	31
Mean Income	$22,274	$25,000	$24,211
Income Range	$10,000–$38,000	$10,000–$140,000	$1,000–$50,000
Years of Residence in U.S.	3–25	5–35	17–48 (Some not available)
Marital Status	17 married 2 divorced	16 married 5 divorced	27 married 8 divorced 3 separated

researchers had not yet realized the importance of length of residence on the adaptation process.

Interview Process

Four separate interviewers interviewed these samples in focus groups of two to five men. Each interview took one and a half to two hours, and was conducted in Spanish. A Cuban American woman interviewed nineteen of the Puerto Rican participants, and a white Euro-American woman who was certified as a bilingual school psychologist interviewed the remaining twenty-one. The Mexican and Dominican samples were interviewed by a native of the respective country. The three Latino interviewers had immigrated to the United States as teenagers.

The focus group interviews involved several open-ended questions that took the fathers through a narrative account of their fathering experience. The interviewer began by asking the participants when they first decided to become a father and what they thought it would be like. Subsequent questions dealt with the participant's role models, their relationship with their own fathers, how being a father changed them and their family system, and what they were most proud of and most regretted. A final question asked whether anything was left out that the participants wanted to bring up.

Throughout, the interviewer noted and explored issues that the participants' answers had in common. As a result, topics of discussion emerged that the researchers could not have foreseen, but which were important in understanding the fathers and their culture.

Data Analysis

Data from each of the samples were originally analyzed separately. The focus group interviews were audiotaped and then transcribed verbatim. Using a grounded theory technique (Auerbach and Silverstein, 2003), three levels of analysis were generated. Four raters (the two principal investigators and two secondary student investigators) read some or all of the transcripts, independently identified excerpts of relevant text, and grouped the relevant text into "repeating ideas." Repeating ideas are ideas that are used by at least two participants. For example, a repeating idea might be "when the father speaks the son has no say." The two primary investigators and the secondary student investigator then met and agreed upon a single list of repeating ideas (usually between twenty and thirty-five). The repeating ideas were then grouped into a second, more abstract level of themes (usually between seven and fifteen). Themes represent more general concepts implicit in the repeating ideas. For example, the previous repeating idea might be part of the theme of *respeto*.

The themes were then organized into theoretical constructs that provide a theoretical link between the participants' ideas and broader psychological theory. For example, the theme of *respeto* might be one of the elements of cultural conflict between Latino and U.S. culture. Finally, the theoretical constructs were organized into a theoretical narrative that told the story of the men's fathering experiences.

For the purposes of this discussion, the repeating ideas from all of the samples were combined and reorganized by the first and second authors into a new set of themes that highlighted the creolization process. We present a new theoretical narrative, the creolization narrative, based on this new analysis of the data in the discussion section.

RESULTS

Our development of the concept of creolization is very much in process. We are presenting our understanding to date, but this understanding will undoubtedly become more nuanced as we examine more immigrant fathers with this theoretical framework in mind. We begin with a presentation of the creolization of specific values, because that is the way that the men talked about their subjective experiences. However, our interpretation of creolization is in terms of a more generalized adaptation process that we describe in the creolization narrative. We illustrate our presentation with representative statements made by the fathers during the narrative interview. Because the interview was open-ended, the context in which these statements were made was quite variable: they sometimes occurred in response to specific questions, and sometimes emerged from group discussions.

Transforming *Familismo*, *Respeto*, and *Machismo*

The men came to the United States as a way of enacting the traditional Latino value of *familismo*. *Familismo* demands that the individual put the welfare of the family first. Individuals work to improve life conditions for the family as a whole, even if that means sacrificing individual goals. (Leyendecker and Lamb, 1999). Virtually all of the men told us that they came to this country to "better the family." They were seeking improved economic opportunities for themselves and their children.

I wanted them to be something in life better than I had been able to do. (Puerto Rican)

My mom came looking for better economic opportunities in the fifties like other Puerto Ricans. (Puerto Rican)

It [emigrating to the United States] helped me because my children were able to have their own life here. (Puerto Rican)

As the men came into contact with U.S. culture, they were not able to enjoy the same degree of *respeto* that they, or their fathers, had enjoyed prior to immigration. Traditionally, the Latino father is entitled to *respeto* (i.e., honor and status) solely by virtue of his position as male head of household. His authority is rarely questioned. The following are some excerpts from the Mexican and Dominican groups that illustrate the loss of *respeto* relative to the traditional Latino fathering role. First, the men described the amount of *respeto* their father had enjoyed.

I had nothing to say because he was my father and I must respect him. . . . One way or another, he was my father and I had to obey what he said. You had to submit to his way of being. (Mexican)

Always the father had the say, the son had no say. (Mexican)

In Santo Domingo, when the father speaks, everyone listens. (Dominican)

After coming to the United States, these fathers realized that they could no longer enjoy the traditional version of *respeto*. The U.S. father does not have an absolute right to be honored based simply on his position as patriarch. Although U.S. fathers are still authority figures to be respected, the power relationship between U.S. fathers and their children is less absolute than the traditional Latino father-child relationship. U.S. fathers do not have complete dominion over their children, including the right to use physical punishment. U.S. fathers are expected to have a less hierarchical relationship with their children, to play with them, to be more like friends. Many of the Latino fathers began to recognize these cultural differences and the need to change their thinking and behavior. The following quotes reflect this recognition:

> One has to change one's ideas about raising kids in this country. This country makes my role model appear old-fashioned for the life-standard here. (Dominican)

> You cannot maintain the same system of authority that you had before. It is either the culture or the law which keeps you from establishing what you had before. (Dominican)

> Here, the father moves to a secondary place. (Dominican)

However, the fathers did not completely relinquish their demand for *respeto*. Rather, they created a creolized version of *respeto*. In this new version, the father was not automatically entitled to *respeto* by virtue of being the head of the family. *Respeto* had to be earned or negotiated between the father and his children. In the new version of *respeto*, fathers were fallible and could be held accountable. The Mexican fathers clearly expressed this point of view.

> Perhaps I haven't earned my daughter's trust. . . . One has to treat children with respect. (Mexican)

> I am very strict, then I come to my senses and say, if I made a mistake, I tell them, "Forgive me, I made a mistake." (Mexican)

> Perhaps I am not a model father or a person who is totally responsible, but I am trying and doing the most I can in order to fulfill my obligation as a father. (Mexican)

Thus the fathers did not relinquish their desire for *respeto*. Rather, they maintained the value by giving it a slightly more democratic flavor.

Another aspect of *respeto* that changed was the degree of emotional distance some of the fathers maintained between themselves and their children. The traditional Latino father was described as a stern disciplinarian.

> We fathers were only there to discipline our children. (Puerto Rican, describing fatherhood as it used to be)

> I made him eat the cigarette. Next time you will see him spitting blood. (Puerto Rican, quoting his own father)

> In my country, I would not have to concern myself with taking the children out to the park on Sunday, my wife would do that. (Mexican)

The U.S. fathering role, in contrast, prescribed more emotional closeness between fathers and their children, a father who was more like a friend than a stern authority figure. Some of the fathers embraced the value of becoming emotionally close to their children. However, the dominance of the father was preserved.

> A father has to be a friend to his children, not a policeman or an overseer. (Mexican)

> The moment I arrive, I say, "Dennis, take off my shoes." I say, "Jocelyn, put my jacket over there, my little daughter." They run to put things in order. (Mexican)

We also saw evidence for the transformation of *machismo*. Male dominance, sexual prowess, respect from others, and an ability to maintain one's dignity are all aspects of *machismo*. In the context of the family, one mainstay of traditional *machismo* was the fact that fathers fulfilled the sole provider role. Economic power solidified social dominance. In their countries of origin, their mothers and wives did not work because the economies usually did not provide work for women.

> In Puerto Rico, women never worked. It was the man who worked. (Puerto Rico)

In the United States virtually all of the two-parent Latino families in our study had both a father and mother engaged in paid employment. This economic shift caused marital conflict in many couples.

> My wife was supposed to do what I said . . . because when she is married, she belongs to the family that she formed with her husband. (Dominican)

In response to this conflict, some fathers talked about giving up rigid gender roles and forming more of a partnership with their wives.

When a woman has to work, you unite more. (Puerto Rican)

We try to work together. It's a partnership. (Puerto Rican)

These Latino fathers did not embrace U.S. cultural values of gender equality and role-sharing. Rather, the creolized version of *machismo* was used to maintain the traditional value of *familismo*. They saw working wives as a way of providing more economic stability for the family.

It is important that both the husband and wife are working, because you have to get a house, a car. (Puerto Rican)

You always want them [the children] to live better. (Puerto Rican)

Some men reinterpreted the creolized version of *machismo* as enhancing their power and status, both within the marriage, and within the broader society. These fathers saw working wives as an extension of their own provider role. They felt enhanced by the increased opportunities two working parents could provide the children.

[Because my wife is working] I felt more of a person. I feel big and important. I feel proud. (Puerto Rican)

I always aspired to having a high position in society. (Dominican)

We are better off than when we arrived. We have always had jobs here. (Dominican)

One of the fathers reported how he used the U.S. cultural expectation that fathers should play with their children as a way of enhancing his status vis a vis his wife.

Kids always lean to mami's side . . . what I do is that when I get home, I start playing with them and spend time with them so that me and my wife will have fifty-fifty in terms of affection from them. (Dominican)

Thus, in a paradoxical way, the creolization process revised some aspects of traditional masculinity and the traditional fathering role, while serving to preserve other aspects of it. The cultural exchange process caused the men to see the benefits of sharing the provider role, and of assuming a less authoritarian stance with their children, even as they continued to strive to maintain male dominance and privilege.

Not all of the men adjusted as well to these changes in family roles. Some fathers reported feeling competitive with their wives.

She's the one who wears the pants in the family. (Puerto Rican)

My son feared his mother more than he feared me. (Puerto Rican)

They thought the love she is giving them is better than mine. (Puerto Rican)

My wife had to work, and I gave her too much freedom. That's why my marriage failed. (Puerto Rican)

Some fathers felt embittered that they could not maintain the old cultural norms intact.

You can't count on a woman for anything. (Puerto Rican)

These fathers had a high degree of conflict in their marriages, and often were separated from their wives.

However, for those who achieved a positive adjustment to the creolized version of *machismo*, sharing the provider role and relinquishing some power over their children improved, rather than detracted, from a father's status in the family.

The Creolization Narrative

We turn now to a broader narrative of this adaptation process. We conceptualize the first phase of creolization as immigration, which the men described as the enactment of the Latino value of *familismo*. The men immigrated to the United States, motivated by the desire to create a better life for their families. They arrived in this country with their traditional values intact. (It is possible that the process began earlier, perhaps with gathering information and developing expectations about the United States. However, we have no interview data on this point, and thus leave it for further research investigation.)

In the second phase, the men began to realize that the economic and social realities of U.S. culture made it impossible for them to continue their traditional behaviors. For example, economic opportunities made it possible for their wives to work. Similarly, they encountered U.S. youth culture that had a powerful influence on their adolescent children, often in a way that conflicted with their family values. Finally, they found their parental prerogatives circumscribed by institutions such as schools and the social welfare system. These cultural encounters changed the balance of power between husbands and wives and between fathers and children, making it impossible for them to maintain their customary ways of enacting the traditional values of *machismo* and *respeto*.

In the third phase of the creolization process, most of the fathers successfully reorganized, reprioritized, or redefined the traditional values of *machismo* and *respeto*. These men created a new and distinct cultural adaptation of Latino American fathering. This creolized version allowed them to continue to fulfill the traditional Latino value of *familismo*, keeping the family together and making a better life. Those men, in contrast, who could not develop creolized versions of *machismo* and *respeto* ended up estranged from their wives, disappointed by or alienated from their children, and feeling embittered by life in general.

In summary, we have proposed the concept of creolization as the creative synthesis of two cultural ideologies, resulting in a new cultural variant with features of both. Creolization gives us a way to appreciate the creative contribution of immigrants in the process of cultural change. This theoretical framework is an alternative to seeing immigrants as passively accepting the dominant culture, or holding onto two cultures simultaneously. Creolization refers not simply to a mixture of cultures, but to the process of adaptation to a new environment. In the current historical context of globalization, creolization provides a framework for understanding both the subjective experiences of immigrant individuals and families, as well as the broader processes of transnational communities.

DISCUSSION AND IMPLICATIONS

We have found that the concept of creolization is a helpful theoretical framework for understanding change for non-immigrant families as well. Although we developed the creolization narrative in terms of immigration, the theoretical framework applies to any situation in which two cultural systems come into contact and must be integrated. For example, we have begun to rethink our understanding of the evolution of fathering identities in white, European, heterosexual, married fathers in the context of the creolization narrative. We theorize that these fathers integrate the progressive and the traditional fathering role into a creolized "involved fathering" role.

A large body of research has suggested that U.S. fathers are evolving from the traditional fathering role of sole provider and emotionally distant disciplinarian, to the role of nurturing father who is emotionally close to his children and who shares the responsibility for providing with a working wife (Lamb, 1999). Our interpretation of the data from the Yeshiva Fatherhood Project suggests that the creolization metaphor more accurately reflects this evolutionary change process than a unidirectional flow from the traditional to the progressive. U.S. fathers, like the Latino fathers in this study, are retaining some aspects of a traditional fathering identity, and at the same time, adopting some characteristics of a more progressive fathering role.

We have interviewed one hundred white, middle-class couples who entered into marriage and parenthood with an ideology of gender equality and fairness. In the beginning of their marriage, the husbands and wives had more or less the same educational level, and both spouses were in entry-level jobs. In the early years, there was relatively little difference in their income, and a relatively high level of gender equality in terms of shared household responsibility.

In terms of the creolization narrative, this progressive fathering role was then challenged and ultimately creolized as the couple's life unfolded. The birth of the first child pressured most families to revert to a version of family life more typical of the traditional patriarchal family. Because the majority of the wives earned less than their husbands did, and because of pressure in the last decade on mothers to breastfeed, it seemed only "natural" for the wife, rather than the husband, to curtail her participation in paid employment. In these five samples of white, middle-class, suburban, dual-earner couples, the majority of wives took some form of maternity leave, and then returned to work part-time, or changed to a less stressful job that also paid less. In terms of the creolization narrative, these couples felt pressure to adopt the traditional fathering role that granted men power and privilege because of their earning capacity. This conflicts with the progressive fathering role with which they began their married life.

However, the families did not resolve this conflict by reverting to the traditional model of the husband as *sole* provider, and the wife as *sole* caregiver. Rather, because the wives dramatically decreased their financial contribution after the advent of children, the fathers became the *primary* provider. Primary provider status represented a shift from the early years of the marriage when the husband and wife earned more or less the same income. With this shift in status came increased male power and privilege, so that the balance of childcare and housework, even for those wives who worked full-time, shifted away from the role-sharing of the early years to become more of the wife's responsibility.

Despite this regression to more male privilege and power, not one of the fathers in our study reverted to the traditional patriarchal father (i.e., the uninvolved, emotionally remote disciplinarian). Rather, they were much more involved with their children and more emotionally connected to them than their own fathers had been. Many of these men routinely took the children to school, helped them with their homework, and so on. Almost all of the fathers of infants enjoyed giving them their baths at night.

Yet in virtually every family, fathers identified specific childcare responsibilities that they simply refused to do. Some refused to diaper the babies. Others were willing to pick the children up so that their wife could work late occasionally, but would not make dinner. Still others would drive the children to school, but would not get them dressed and fed in the morning. The men provided rationalizations for their refusal (e.g., "I'm not a morning person," "She's just better at it than I am [putting the kids to bed, comforting them when hurt, etc.]"). However, we see these unilateral refusals as an exercise in male privilege. Not one of the wives enumerated a childcare or household task that she simply refused to do.

Thus, these fathers did not fit either the traditional model of patriarchal, remote disciplinarian, or the progressive model of egalitarian, role-sharing parent. Rather, their attitudes toward power and paternal involvement represented a creolized version of fatherhood that incorporated aspects of both the traditional and progressive roles. We call this creolized fathering role "involved fatherhood," blending elements of the traditional and progressive roles. What involved fatherhood keeps of the traditional role is granting men power and privilege as a result of their economic power. What it keeps of the progressive role is (some) involvement with housework and childcare. Perhaps, too, men's need to justify their unequal involvement in childcare, rather than claim it as a right, also shows the influence of the progressive role.

Understanding the importance of creolized versions of identity provides an explanatory framework for the inconsistent and contradictory behaviors we often observe within the same individual. The creolization framework helps clinicians to complicate their understanding of the multiple facets of a client's identity, enhancing their clinical effectiveness.

Applying the concept of creolization to both immigrant Latino fathers and white middle-class fathers is an example of how multiculturalism has transformed the research landscape. Prior to multiculturalism, research was typically done on dominant groups, and then generalized to minority groups, who were too often seen as deficient because they did not fit the dominant model. A commitment to studying multiple subcultures illustrates how information about non-dominant groups can contribute to knowledge about dominant groups as well.

Limitations of the Research

The study suffers from many common research limitations such as small samples, self-selected samples, and self-report data. However, we want to focus on a particular limitation that resulted from the process of multicultural insensitivity or *naivete*. From its inception in 1993, the Yeshiva Fatherhood Project was committed to multiculturalism. However, in truth, the white, middle-class, Jewish, middle-aged primary investigators (Auerbach and Silverstein) had a very primitive understanding of what that meant. They knew enough to reject the idea that there was a monolithic version of U.S. fathering. They understood that fathering would vary by ethnic group and class, and thus planned to study multiple subcultures of fathers.

However, they did not understand that fathering did not simply *vary* by culture, but rather, that culture *constructed* fathering. In the early years of the project, they were also not yet totally comfortable with the qualitative paradigm, and so were concerned with "standardization" of the interview questions across all groups. These two factors, a superficial understanding of multiculturalism, and the lingering influence of the quantitative paradigm, resulted in a failure to include interview questions specifically relevant to some of the diverse groups they were studying (e.g., gay fathers and immigrant fathers).

It is also important to note that this failure to include questions about the immigrant experience occurred despite the fact that three of the four student interviewers were Latino immigrants. Their failure to challenge the professors who were the primary investigators on this point reflects the importance of power relations within research teams.

Fortunately, because the fathers were interviewed in small groups, the interaction between the participants addressed issues relevant to their subjective experiences, even though the authors had not directly asked about these experiences. In the case of Latino fathers, the interview did not ask specifically about how the immigration experience affected their fathering. Yet the stories that the fathers told enabled the researchers to generate hypotheses about the centrality of immigration in the evolution of their fathering identities. Still, the information would undoubtedly be richer had the interview focused on immigration specifically.

This must be considered a major limitation of the study. In subsequent groups, we have begun to include culturally relevant questions. For example, we now ask all immigrant fathers to tell us about their immigration experiences, we ask African American fathers to talk about how institutionalized racism has affected their fathering, and we ask gay fathers about the impact of cultural homophobia and heterocentrism. We call attention to this limitation as a way of acknowledging how complex it is to achieve multicultural sensitivity and competence, even with the best of intentions.

REFERENCES

Auerbach, C. F., and Silverstein, L. B. (2003). *An introduction to coding and analyzing data in qualitative research.* New York: New York University Press.

Bernal, M. E., and Knight, G. P. (1997). Ethnic identity of Latino children. In J. G. Garcia and M. C. Zea (Eds.), *Psychological interventions and research with Latino populations* (15–20). Needham Heights, MA: Allyn & Bacon.

Berry, J. W. (1980). Acculturation as varieties of adaptation. In A. M. Padillo (Ed.), *Acculturation: Theories, models, and some new findings* (9–25). Boulder, CO: Westview Press.

Birman, D. (1998). Biculturalism and perceived competence of Latino immigrant adolescents. *American Journal of Community Psychology, 26*, 335–54.

Comas-Diaz, L. (2001). Hispanics, Latinos, or Americanos: The evolution of identity. *Cultural Diversity and Ethnic Minority Psychology, 7*, 115–20.

Hall, G. M. (1995). *Africans in colonial Louisiana: The development of Afro-Creole culture in the eighteenth century.* Baton Rouge: Louisiana State University Press.

Hannerz, U. (1987). The world in creolization. *Africa, 57,* 546–49.

Inclan, J. (2003). Class, culture, and gender in immigrant families. In L. B. Silverstein and T. J. Goodrich (Eds.), *Feminist family therapy: Empowerment and social location* (333–49). Washington, DC: American Psychological Association Books.

Inclan, J., and Hernandez, M. (1992). Cross cultural perspectives and co-dependence: The case of poor Hispanics. *Journal of Orthopsychiatry, 62,* 245–54.

Inclan, J., and Heron, D. G. (1998). Puerto-Rican adolescents. In J. T. Gibbs, L. N. Huang, and associates (Eds.), *Children of color: Psychological interventions with culturally diverse youth* (240–63). San Francisco: Jossey-Bass Publishers.

LaFromboise, T., Coleman, H. L. K., and Gerton, J. (1998). Psychological impact of biculturalism: Evidence and theory. In N. R. Goldberger and J. B. Veroff (Eds.), *The culture and psychology reader* (489–535). New York: New York University Press.

Lamb, M. E. (Ed.). (1999). *Parenting and child development in "non-traditional" families.* Mahwah, NJ: Erlbaum.

Leyendecker, B., and Lamb, M. E. (1999). Latino families. In M. E. Lamb (Ed.), *Parenting and child development in "non-traditional" families* (257–62). Mahwah, NJ: Erlbaum.

Mirandé, A. (1997). *Hombres y machos: Masculinity and Latino culture.* Boulder, CO: Westview Press.

Montalvo, B., and Gutierrez, M. J. (1990). Nine assumptions for working with ethnic and minority families. In G. W. Saba, B. M. Karrer, and K. V. Hardy (Eds.), *Minorities and family therapy* (35–52). Binghamton, NY: Haworth Press, Inc.

Thernstrom, S. (Ed.). (1980). *Harvard encyclopedia of American ethnic groups.* Cambridge, MA: Belknap Press of Harvard University.

Thomason, S. G. (2006). *Language contact: An introduction.* Washington, DC: Georgetown University Press.

Yiddish Homepage in the *Academy for the Advancement of Science and Technology.* Retrieved June 11, 2003, from http://www.bergen.org/AAST/Projects/Yiddish/English.

10

Immigration and Latino Fatherhood: A Preliminary Look at Latino Immigrant and Non-Immigrant Fathers

Alfredo Mirandé

> When my father died last year, a piece of my heart died with him. My father, that supreme sentimental fool, loved my brothers and me to excess in a kind of over-the-top, rococo fever, all arabesque and sugar spirals, as sappy and charming as the romantic Mexican boleros he loved to sing. *Dame un poquito de tu amor siquiera, dame un poquito de tu amor nomas . . .* Music from my time, father would say proudly, and I could almost smell the gardenias and *Tres Flores* hair oil.
>
> Before my father died, it was simple cordiality that prompted me to say, "I'm sorry," when comforting the bereaved. But with my father's death, I am initiated into the family of humanity, I am connected to all deaths and to their survivors "*Lo siento,*" which translates as both "I am sorry" and "I feel it" all at once. *Lo siento.* Since his death, I feel life more intensely. (Cisneros, 1998)

The above quote is a poetic and moving tribute by writer Sandra Cisneros to her father and calls into question a prevailing view of Latino men as cold, distant, unemotional, and uninvolved with their children. In recent years there has been growing interest and research not only on Latino men, machismo, and masculinity, but also on Latino fathers, particularly immigrant Latino fathers. Latino cultures in general, and Mexican culture in particular, have been described as macho-centric entities where men are ostensibly driven by an excessive phallic obsession and an insatiable need to prove their manhood. It was not until the late 1980s that research focused on Latinos began to describe men as having and producing gender (Viveros Vigoya, 2003).

Although there is growing interest and concern with gender oppression and excessive displays of masculinity or machismo in Latino cultures, there is a dearth of research focusing specifically on how masculinity, appropriate male behavior, and conceptions of fatherhood are constructed among Latinos, as well as the impact of immigration on masculinity and fatherhood. It is only recently that researchers have begun to focus on the role of Latino fathers in the family and participation in parenting and to note the great diversity that is found among Latino fathers. However, few studies have looked at the impact of immigration on Latino fathers or sought to assess differences in the way that immigrant and non-immigrant Latino men define, negotiate, and perform masculinity and fatherhood. The focus of this chapter is to gain a better understanding of Latino men and the relation between immigration and conceptions of masculinity and fatherhood.

IMMIGRATION AND LATINO FATHERS

Despite increased concern with fatherhood and the importance of father involvement in the family, as well as the demographic trends showing that Latinos are the fastest growing and largest racial/ethnic group in the United States, we know surprisingly little about Latino fathers, especially immigrant fathers (Cabrera and Garcia-Coll, 2004). This is unfortunate given early characterizations of the Latino family, particularly the Mexican family, as a male-dominated unit where the father is the unquestioned "Lord and Master" of the household and is relatively uninvolved or absent from the family or with childrearing. Early authors described Latino fathers as "being like fighting roosters, drunks, and irresponsible" (Behnke and Taylor, 2005). This view stemmed from a limited and stereotypical understanding of Latino masculinity and *machismo*.

Fortunately, recent research has provided us with a clearer picture of Latino fathers and their involvement in the family. Despite earlier characterizations, scholars have shown that Latino families are relatively egalitarian with respect to decision making and the distribution of household chores, and that fathers are more actively involved in the family and with children than was previously believed. For example, Coltrane (2001) found that over half of the couples in his study could be described as co-providers in those husbands and wives who had more equal earnings and placed a higher value on the wife's employment. Of particular note, among husbands and wives who shared household labor, working-class couples shared more as compared to their upper-middle-class professional Latino counterparts (Coltrane, 2001).

More recent research has also brought into question the stereotypical macho image of Latino males with respect to their parenting role. Latino fathers, for example, have been shown to be actively involved in childrearing. In fact, some found that Latino fathers exhibited less control and more responsibility for childrearing when compared to non-Hispanic white fathers (Coltrane, Parke, and Adams, 2004; Hofferth, 2003). Looking closely at Latino fathers, Behnke and Taylor's qualitative research (2005) "gives voice" to Latino men's perceptions of their roles and values as fathers. Utilizing a symbolic interactionist approach, they revealed the social construction of fatherhood and how cultural and intergenerational influences shape the formation of fatherhood. Their work found that most Latino men were influenced in their parenting styles by the relationship that they had with their fathers, and their own fathers' model of parenting. Whether positive or negative, their father's parenting style greatly influenced how men defined their own role (Behnke and Taylor, 2005).

In addition, Taylor and Behnke observed that "the process of immigration greatly influences family life and affects parenting styles." When Mexican fathers immigrated to the United States, many transformed their parenting style. Behnke and Taylor identified these two adaptations in parenting styles as "sociocultural change" and "sociocultural continuity" (2005), and in the cases where sociocultural change took place, men altered their parenting styles to accommodate the new cultural expectations. This was particularly important in areas of discipline. Although many viewed physical punishment as an appropriate form of discipline in their native country, these fathers were also aware of popular opinion against the use of physical punishment in the United States. One father, for example, said, "Well, to be in a foreign country, we need to respect the laws so we don't have problems with anybody" (7). Other men, however, reported that living in the United States did not change their parenting style. These fathers felt that parenting, whether in the United States or Mexico, did not differ significantly.

MASCULINITY AND FATHERHOOD

In my own work, I examined Latino men's perceptions of masculinity and fatherhood. For the purpose of this discussion, I will reexamine some of the results from an earlier study of Latino men and masculinity (for details, see Mirandé, 1997). The criteria for inclusion in the sample were that the person was a Latino man, living in an intact two-parent family with at least one school-aged child living at home. In addition to the qualitative open-ended questions, I administered two structured masculinity scales, the Bem Sex Role Inventory (BSRI) and the Mirandé Sex Role Inventory (MSRI), a more nuanced and culturally specific measure. I also collected background and demographic information.

The 105 participants lived in one of three regions in the southwestern United States—southern California (i.e., Riverside, Upland, Ontario), northern California (i.e., San José, Redwood City, East Menlo Park,

San Francisco), or San Antonio, Texas. About one-third opted to be interviewed in Spanish and two-thirds in English, although respondents
sometimes switched back and forth from one language to the other. The
median age was thirty-nine, with ages ranging from the early twenties to
the mid-fifties. 49 percent of the sample reported having a blue-collar occupation while 51 percent had professional or managerial positions. All
but four of the men were working full-time, one participant was laid off,
and two worked part-time. Significantly, 73 percent of the participants'
wives also worked outside the home. With reference to language preference, 40 percent preferred English to Spanish, 34 percent preferred Spanish, and 24 percent reported no preference or that it depended on the
situation or social context. With regard to language preference at home,
10 percent identified as speaking only English at home, 49 percent as
speaking mostly English, 23 percent as speaking both English and Spanish equally, and only 17 percent said they spoke mostly Spanish or only
Spanish at home.

The vast majority of respondents were foreign-born: 93 percent were born
in Mexico, 3 percent reported Central America as their place of birth, and 4
percent had a country of origin other than Mexico or Central America.

About a third of the sample had completed twelfth grade or less of
school, 22 percent attended some college, and 45 percent completed four
years of college or more. While the sample had a relatively high educational
attainment, most came from working-class families with low educational
attainment, as 72 percent of the men reported mothers with an eighth grade
education or less, and only 3 percent had mothers who had completed
four years of college. Similarly, 72 percent had fathers with an eighth grade
education or less, and only 4 percent reported having fathers who had completed four years of college.

The interviews consisted of structured and open-ended questions that
tried to identify the core characteristics that are valued by Latino men. To
tap into these values, my questions focused on themes such as the type of
man that is "most respected or admired," special attributes that are most
and least respected in a man, the "worst" or "lowest" thing that a man can
do, and traits or characteristics that are generally valued in a son. Another
series of questions addressed the role of the father in the family and general
attitudes toward child-rearing and fathering, such as what is perceived as
a father's most important responsibility or duty to his children, whether
respondents saw themselves as being "good" fathers or not, what characteristics were associated with being a "good" or a "bad" father, the strengths
and weaknesses that respondents viewed in themselves as fathers, and basic
attitudes that the men held toward children and the role of the father in
child-rearing and childcare. Comparisons were made based on income,
level of education, language preference, and immigrant status.

MEN MOST RESPECTED OR ADMIRED

Respondents were first asked to list the man or men that they most respected and/or admired. Their responses ranged from family members to celebrities. To better understand the men's responses, I grouped them according to whether the person or persons listed were immediate family members (such as father, son, or brother), non-immediate family members (uncle or cousin), or a non-family member (such as friend, historical figure, politician, or celebrity). In my analysis, I found that the respondents differed by education. In comparison to men who had less education, those with higher levels of education were more likely to identify non-family members such as friends, teachers, historical figures like Emiliano Zapata, Pancho Villa, Martin Luther King, and President Kennedy, as well as contemporary celebrities or public figures, as the men they most respected or admired. And, surprisingly, although asked for examples of "a man or men most respected," some respondents actually listed women as being the person or persons they most respected or admired. Some of the women listed as being most respected or admired were La Virgen María, Joan of Arc, farm worker leader Dolores Huerta, and political leaders, like Diane Feinstein, and relatives or friends and acquaintances. These responses indicate that some Latino men have a more androgynous view of gender that incorporates women among the persons they most admire.

QUALITIES MOST AND LEAST RESPECTED IN A MAN

Responses to the question "What qualities do you most respect in a man?" were grouped into three categories. The three categories were: 1) personal qualities (e.g., "warmth," "affectionate," or "kind"); 2) respectful (e.g., "respects others," "respects self"); and 3) honest/ethical (e.g., "honest," "trustworthy," or "ethical").

Differences in the qualities "most respected" in a man varied substantially by immigrant status, income, education, and occupation. For example, immigrant fathers, and those with less education, were more likely than those born in the United States to see "honesty" or being "reliable" as the quality they most valued in a man, whereas non-immigrants and men with more education and higher incomes were more likely to identify being "respectful" rather than being "honest" as the quality they most respected in a man. This suggests that men who adhered to a more traditional conception of masculinity were more likely to value qualities in a man that related to how honest or trustworthy he was, whereas less traditional men were more likely to value respecting yourself and/or others and being honest or having integrity. Honesty, trustworthiness, and being respectful were apparently more salient traits for men with less education and lower incomes. One man reported what he most respected or admired, "*Un hombre que atiende a su familia. Que siempre les respeta. Hay gente que piensa que un hombre debe ser valiente, pero un hombre debe ser formal con su familia. Que no los desampare*" ("A man who looks after the family. Who understands the value of the family. Who always respects his family. There are people who think a man should be brave, but a man should be responsible relative to his family. He should never abandon them"). Better-educated men and those with higher incomes, on the other hand, were more likely to stress and value "respect."

The participants were also asked to respond to "what qualities are least respected in a man." Similarly, their responses were grouped into three distinct categories: 1) abuses, injures, or "uses" other people (e.g., abuses wife, children, or others); 2) does not respect self or others; and 3) selfish/irresponsible, or does not take care of family.

Both immigrant and low-income men were more likely than U.S.-born or higher-income men to identify being selfish or being self-centered as traits that were least respected or admired in a man. Interestingly, 34 percent of men born outside the United States identified *egoismo*, or "selfishness," as the trait least respected in a man. One immigrant respondent said he did not respect someone who was "a liar, unreliable, egotistical, and unwilling to bend, unemotional, uncaring, greedy, and selfish." Another man said that what he least respected was "a man who is lazy, irresponsible, like he is not supportive of his own family, and one who is selfish, or just thinks of himself."

Language preference (whether the interview was conducted in English or Spanish) also proved to be an important indicator. Respondents who opted to be interviewed in Spanish more often identified selfishness and irresponsibility as traits that were least respected or admired in a man. Only about 15 percent of the men who conducted the interview in English identified *egoismo* or selfishness as the trait that they least respected or admired in a man, compared to almost 40 percent of those interviewed in Spanish. On the other hand, those who conducted the interview in English were much more likely to list "not respecting" yourself and/or others as the quality least admired in a man. Some 71 percent of the English-speaking men said that "not respecting yourself or others" was the lowest or least respected quality in a man, as compared to only 56 percent of the Spanish-speaking men.

These findings are perhaps not surprising, since *egoísmo* or self-centeredness is often seen as a negative character trait in Mexico and other Latino cultures and among Spanish-speaking people. One of the respondents noted, for instance, that what he viewed as the most negative or despicable qualities in a man were things like "*El no respetar a la familia.*

No cumplir con deberes familiares y sociales" ("A lack of respect for the family. Not fulfilling familial and social obligations"). Another respondent said that what he least respected or admired was *"Pues, un hombre que no toma su obligación como debe ser"* ("Well, a man who does not accept his responsibilities, as he should").

WORST OR LOWEST THING A MAN CAN DO

The men were also asked, "What is the worst or lowest thing a man can do?" Their responses ranged from joking remarks by an attorney, of "not paying your lawyer," to killing, murdering, raping or giving AIDS to someone, or "being boastful" or arrogant. As before, the responses fell into three categories: 1) seriously harm/abuse someone; 2) use others (e.g., lie, or have no dignity or self-respect); and 3) abandon, not support, or "to put down one's family."

Once again, language preference was important. Respondents who were interviewed in English (as well as those with more education) were more apt to consider serious harm or abuse to be the worst or lowest thing a man can do. For one man, the worst or lowest thing a man could do was *"Un hombre realmente que tenga la familia en pobreza cuando no es necesario"* ("A man who keeps his family in poverty when it is not necessary"). 52 percent of those who were interviewed in English said that "injuring" or "abusing" others was the worst thing a man could do. However, only 30 percent of those interviewed in Spanish said that this was the worst or lowest thing that a man could do. Those interviewed in Spanish, as well as those with less education, saw abandoning the family as the worst or lowest thing that a man can do. Interestingly, there were minimal differences by income or occupation.

QUALITIES VALUED IN A SON

I also asked fathers, "If you had or have a son, what kind of a man would you like him to be when he grows up?" This question elicited a broad range of responses, which were grouped into three categories, including a son who: 1) is responsible/hard-working; 2) has integrity ("defends his beliefs and principles"); and 3) is honest/compassionate.

Immigrant men, and those who preferred to be interviewed in Spanish, more often mentioned being responsible and/or hard-working as preferred qualities in a son, while U.S.-born respondents and those interviewed in English were more likely to emphasize personal attributes such as being warm or honest.

MOST IMPORTANT FATHER
RESPONSIBILITY OR DUTY TO CHILDREN

When asked "What is your most important responsibility or duty to your children?" the men's responses grouped into two broad categories. The first group of responses stressed being a provider and taking care of their children's basic needs. The second category focused on providing love, affection, and moral guidance. There were generally nominal differences by socioeconomic status or region, and ironically those with less education were somewhat more likely to stress financial responsibility and taking care of the physical needs of children. In fact, more than half of the respondents with less than a high school education indicated that taking care of the financial and/or physical needs of their children was their most important responsibility, as compared with only one-third of those with a high school education or more education.

Both immigrant fathers and fathers interviewed in Spanish more often identified providing for children or taking care of their physical needs as their most important responsibility or duty to them. More than 50 percent of the men with less than a high school education felt that taking care of the financial or physical needs of children was their most important responsibility or duty as fathers. Also, 51 percent of those interviewed in Spanish said that taking care of the financial or physical needs of children was the most important responsibility or duty that they owed them, whereas only about 33 percent of those interviewed in English felt that this was their most important duty or responsibility. U.S.-born and English-speaking respondents, on the other hand, were more apt to focus on emotional or moral development as their most important duty or responsibility to children.

WHY DO YOU CONSIDER YOURSELF A GOOD FATHER?

A key question posed to the participants was whether they considered themselves to be a good father, and why. Not surprisingly, most respondents believed themselves to be good fathers. Their responses as to why they considered themselves good fathers were grouped into three categories, according to whether they saw themselves as good fathers because they: 1) provided for the needs of their children; 2) made time for or listened to their children; or 3) were nurturing ("loving," "affectionate") with children. There were modest regional and socioeconomic differences. For some reason, *Tejanos* (participants from Texas) and those in nonprofessional occupations more often stressed their loving and/or nurturing qualities, while northern Californians and professionals stressed making time for and "listening" to children, although the significance of these findings is not readily apparent.

Both immigrant men and those who preferred to be interviewed in Spanish were more likely to feel that they were good fathers because they provided for the needs of their children, whereas U.S.-born men, and those interviewed in English, more often said they were good fathers because they were "loving" and "affectionate." The response of one U.S.-born man illustrates the importance that non-immigrant men placed on being "loving and affectionate" as qualities that made them good fathers. He said he was a good father "because I put my love and affection for them above everything else." A Texas native similarly said he was a good father "because I spend a lot of time with my wife and children. I go to church with them. I get involved in their activities, like sports as a coach." A third non-immigrant respondent said,

> I think I try to be responsive to their needs and interests as much as possible. I think I'm taking very seriously their future needs, being sensitive and responsive to the different aspects that contribute to the children's growth and development. It's much more than putting food on the table. I try to empathize with their fears and concerns. I sure as hell wish that my dad would have taken me to Little League practice or come to my defense when there was a hassle at school.

Rather than focusing on listening or being attuned to the emotional needs of children, immigrant men, Spanish-dominant men, and working-class men were more likely to stress being responsible, being a good provider, "putting food on the table," and taking care of the basic needs of their children as qualities that made them good fathers and qualities they most respected or admired in a father. One man said that he was a good father *"porque yo me preocupo que a ellos no les falten comida y ropa. Y si tienen un problema que tengan confianza en mí"* ("because I make sure that they are not in need of food or clothing. And if they have a problem that they can count on me"). Another man similarly said, *"Porque cumplo con mis deberes de la casa. Cumplo con mis hijos"* ("Because I fulfill my household responsibilities. I take care of my children").

STRENGTHS AND WEAKNESSES AS A FATHER

Finally, respondents were asked to identify what they saw as their "strengths and weaknesses" as fathers. The perceived weaknesses were grouped into four categories: 1) not an adequate provider; 2) does not spend enough time with, or does not listen to, children; 3) is not as affectionate or loving as he would like; and 4) does not have any weaknesses. Men with less education and lower incomes and nonprofessionals were slightly more apt to see not being able to provide adequately as a weakness, or to say that they did not have any weaknesses, although these differences were not substantial. Thus, middle-class and more educated men were more often worried about having enough time to nurture children and/or to attend to their emotional needs, whereas working-class men and those with less education were more likely to focus on being able to fulfill the provider role, making sure that the children have adequate housing and clothing and are well fed.

Responses to perceived strengths as fathers were grouped into four categories: 1) a good provider; 2) a good listener; 3) heavily involved with children and their activities; and 4) affectionate and loving. Overall, working-class, less educated, and immigrant men, and those interviewed in Spanish, were again more likely to list being a good provider as the primary reason for thinking of themselves as good fathers, rather than spending a lot of time or being affectionate with children. Professionals and men with more education, and those born in the United States, however, more often said they were good fathers because they listened to their children and were involved in their activities.

DISCUSSION

While much has been written about "macho men" and obsessive masculinity in Latino cultures, until recently such generalizations were often based on limited or anecdotal evidence and served more to preserve and perpetuate prevailing racial/ethnic stereotypes and misconceptions than to inform academic scholarship on the subject. Despite the emergence of more sophisticated works on Latino masculinity and fatherhood (for examples, see Gutmann, 1996, 2003; Mirandé, 1997; González, 1996; and Coltrane, Parke, and Adams, 2004), we still know little about how Latino men acquire masculinity and traditional macho traits, or the role that Latino fathers play in their families.

These findings suggest that Latino men's perception and conceptions of masculinity and fatherhood are varied and complex and cannot be understood by using simple, one-dimensional stereotypical models. Contrary to these stereotypes, the Latino men I studied did not follow the dominant assimilation/acculturation hypothesis. Immigrant men and Spanish-dominant men were not necessarily more traditional or hyper-macho, but they were more likely than either U.S.-born or English-dominant Latino men to have a positive or favorable view of the word "macho," to associate being macho with positive traits such as being honorable or respectful of others, or to consider themselves macho.

The Spanish-speaking Latino immigrants I interviewed often stressed being responsible to their family and being a good provider as their major roles in the family. These qualities were valued over spending time with or "being a friend" to their children. The role of provider was such a core belief that being "selfish" (focusing on yourself and not your family) was viewed as one of the least respected qualities in a man.

Self-centeredness or *egoísmo* is a negative quality. As a result, immigrant men were generally less apt to say that "love and affection" was most important in how they were raised, or to see providing moral and emotional guidance as the most important responsibility or duty that they have to their children.

These findings suggest that there may be a distinct Latino cultural ethic surrounding masculinity and fatherhood that is radically different from dominant societal conceptions of masculinity and fatherhood. Accordingly, whether a man is considered to be successful or a good father is determined not so much by such external qualities as success, fame, or wealth but by such internal qualities as responsibility, selflessness, and moral character. According to this ethic, the worst or lowest thing that a man can do is to be irresponsible, to put his interests and welfare above those of the family, or to not take care of his family and children. This is a far different picture than the view of the macho male preoccupied with sexual conquest, aloofness, and being uninvolved with the family.

While the findings discussed here are preliminary and much more work needs to be done, they have important implications for understanding Latino masculinity and the role of the father in Latino culture, and Latino immigrant fathers. First, the discussion here clearly reveals that Latino men are incredibly diverse, such that internal differences among them may be as great as or greater than differences found between Latinos and non-Latinos. As a result, to fully understand the diversity of Latino men and fathers, we need to carefully examine the dimensions of language use, generational status, and education, as well as social class. Although these factors are interconnected, a thorough consideration is necessary to gain full insight into this complex population. Finally, the findings of this work call into question the acculturation/assimilation model, which posits that greater assimilation and exposure to the dominant culture is inevitably associated with greater gender equality and greater involvement of the man in the family and fathering.

The findings discussed here are consistent with the call in the recent research literature on fatherhood to look at the diversity among fathers and to replace the single or unitary view of fatherhood with broader and more inclusive dimensions (Cabrera, Tamis-Lemonda, Bradley, Hofferth, and Lamb 2000). Lamb, Pleck, Charnov, and Levine (1987) for example, implore researchers to distinguish among various critical dimensions of father involvement such as accessibility (presence and availability to the child), engagement (contact and shared interactions with the child), and responsibility (engaging in childcare and monitoring children's activities). Some researchers further suggest that responsibility, a dimension often neglected in survey research, may be a particularly important dimension of fatherhood (Cabrera et al., 2000).

Although the findings of this study are preliminary and are not generalizable to the entire Latino population, they suggest that providing and assuming responsibility for children is indeed a salient dimension of the father role for Latino men, particularly for immigrant fathers.

As we look at fatherhood in the twenty-first century, it is important that we take into account recent changes in the American family. Cabrera, Tamis-LeMonda, Bradley, Hofferth, and Lamb (2000) point to two changes that seem especially relevant for understanding contemporary fatherhood among Latinos. One of the changes is the increased number of women, including Latinas, entering the paid labor force and the enrollment of children under six years old in non-parental care. In 1950, 12 percent of married women with children were in the paid labor force, but by the turn of the century that figure had exceeded two-thirds (Cabrera et al., 2000).

The second change is the increase in father absence not only in the society at large but also among Latino families. In 1960, only 6 percent of the families in the United States were headed by women, but by 1998 that figure had risen to 24 percent (U.S. Bureau of the Census, 1998). It is estimated that the proportion of children who will live with only one parent at some point in their childhood will continue to exceed 50 percent in the near future (Cabrera et al., 2000). These trends suggest that in the future someone other than their biological parents will raise a larger and larger proportion of children. These changes increase the need to continue our study of Latino men and the impact that they have on their children and families.

REFERENCES

Behnke, B. A., and Taylor, A. (2005). Fathering across the border: Latino fathers in Mexico and the U.S. *Fathering, 22,* 99–120.
Cabrera, N., and Garcia-Coll, C. (2004). Latino fathers: Uncharted territory in need of much exploration. In M. E. Lamb (Ed.), *The role of the father in child development* (fourth ed., 98–120). New York: Wiley.
Cabrera, N. J., Tamis-LeMonda, C. S., Bradley, R. H., Hofferth, S., and Lamb, M. E. (2000). Fatherhood in the twenty-first century. *Child Development, 71,* 127–36.
Cisneros, S. (1998). The genius of creative flexibility. *Los Angeles Times,* February 28.
Coltrane, S. (2001). Stability and change in Chicano men's family lives. In M. Kimmel and M. Messner (Eds.), *Men's lives* (fifth ed., 451–66). New York: Macmillan.

Coltrane, S., Parke, R. D., and Adams, M. (2004). Complexity of father involvement in low-income Mexican American families. *Family Relations, 53*, 179–89.

González, R. (1996). *Muy macho: Latino men confront their manhood.* New York: Anchor Books.

Gutmann, M. C. (1996). *The meaning of macho.* Berkeley: University of California Press.

——. (2003). *Changing men and masculinity in Latin America.* Durham, NC: Duke University Press.

Hofferth, S. (2003). Race/ethnic differences in father involvement in two-parent families. *Journal of Family Issues, 24*, 185–216.

Lamb, M. E., Pleck, J. H., Charnov, E. L., and Levine, J. A. (1987). A biosocial perspective on paternal behavior and involvement. In U. G. Lancaster, J. Altman, A. S. Ross, and L. R. Sherroa (Eds.), *Parenting across the lifespan: Biosocial dimensions* (111–42). New York: University of Chicago Press.

Mirandé, A. (1997). *Hombres y machos: Masculinity and Latino culture.* Boulder, CO: Westview.

U.S. Bureau of the Census. (1998). Statistical Abstract of the United States 1998. Washington, DC: U.S. Department of Commerce.

Vigoya, M. V. (2003). Contemporary Latin American perspectives on masculinity. In M. C. Gutmann (Ed.), *Changing men and masculinity in Latin America* (27–57). Durham, NC: Duke University Press.

11

Breaking New Ground: Dominican, Mexican, and Chinese Fathers and Families

Catherine S. Tamis-LeMonda, Erika Y. Niwa,
Ronit Kahana-Kalman, and Hirokazu Yoshikawa

Fathers are no longer the forgotten parent. Research over the past several decades has yielded compelling evidence for the importance of fathers' social and economic investments for children's cognitive development, emotional regulation, social competence, school achievement, and well being during childhood and adolescence (Lamb, 1999, 2004; Tamis-LeMonda and Cabrera, 2002). Moreover, links between father involvement and children's outcomes persist after controlling for measures such as mother-child interactions and parental education, indicating that father involvement is directly linked to children's developmental achievements (Tamis-LeMonda, Shannon, Cabrera, and Lamb, 2004).

Nonetheless, researchers have only skimmed the surface in understanding the experiences of fathers from diverse ethnic backgrounds, both in terms of what fathers do in family life and in how they experience and think about their roles. In particular, *virtually nothing is known about immigrant fathers* from Latino (Dominican and Mexican) and Asian (especially Chinese) groups (but see Chao and Kim, 2000; Parke, Coltrane, Duffy, Buriel, Dennis, Powers, French, and Widaman, 2004). This gap is particularly noteworthy in light of recent demographic shifts in the United States. Approximately 20 percent of children were born in a foreign country or had at least one parent who was born outside of the United States in the year 2000 (Malone, Baluja, Costanzo, and Davis, 2003), with Chinese, Dominican, and Mexican families among the fastest growing populations of new immigrants (Hernandez and Denton, 2005).

Moreover, there is a need to better understand the factors that relate to father involvement in immigrant groups within and across developmental time. Although the vast majority of fathers are strongly committed to their

231

new role at their infants' births, there is enormous variation in the long-term trajectories of men's actual involvement with children and families. What enables certain men to sustain positive relationships with their young children, while others withdraw from their commitments to their children? Immigrant fathers in particular confront a range of social and economic barriers that may challenge their roles in the family, and studies are needed to understand the specific factors that may shape their roles in family life and child development.

In response to these gaps, the current chapter is structured around two core issues: 1) How should positive father involvement be conceptualized in the study of Mexican, Dominican, and Chinese immigrants?; and 2) What are the roles of family-level and human capital resources in father involvement in these groups? These three groups have been a central focus of our ongoing research at New York University's Center for Research on Culture, Development, and Education (NSF Grant # BCS0218159), where we are longitudinally following approximately three hundred infants and their families from birth through the preschool years. These families were recruited into our studies from three public hospitals in New York City within two days of the birth of infants. Longitudinal data are being gathered at infants' birth and at one, six, fourteen, twenty-four, and thirty-six months using multiple methods including surveys, semi-structured interviews, ethnographies, videotaped observations, and direct child assessments. The focus of this chapter is on early findings about these fathers and families during the first year of infants' lives.

THE CHANGING U.S. LANDSCAPE

According to 2000 U.S. Census figures, one out of every five children was born in a foreign country or has at least one parent who was born outside of the United States (i.e., is a first- or second-generation immigrant, respectively). Latino and Asian communities are expected to triple in size by 2050 and it is estimated that by 2040, the youth population of the United States will become half "majority" Caucasian and half "minority" (Bales, Christmas-Best, Diversi, McLaughlin, Silbereisen, and Youniss, 2002). These new waves of children in immigrant families are expected to follow different paths of assimilation and adaptation than prior waves who were of predominantly European descent (Oropesa and Landale, 2004; Portes and Rumbaut, 2001).

In terms of *Mexican immigrants*, in 2000, 20.6 million people of Mexican origin (58 percent of the total number of Latinos in the United States) resided in the United States. This represents an increase of over seven million Mexicans since 1990 alone (Ramirez, 2004). By 2030, the population of Mexican immigrants in the United States is expected to at least double. High rates of Mexican immigration are driven by high and chronic rates of underemployment in Mexico and the temptation of higher wages, and existing social networks in the United States. In New York City, Mexicans showed higher rates of population growth than any other Latino immigrant group during the 1990s (Smith, 2005). If the Mexican community continues to grow at the present rate, there will be more than half a million Mexicans living in New York City by 2010 (Smith, 2005). Some argue that these numbers are in fact lower than in actuality, as undocumented Mexicans are not accounted for in such calculations.

Dominican immigrants also represent a rapidly growing Latino immigrant community. Despite their relative absence from studies, Dominicans are the fourth largest Latino group in the United States after Mexicans, Puerto Ricans, and Cubans and are expected to become the largest Latino population in New York City within the next ten years (Hernandez and Denton, 2005). It is estimated that by 2010, Dominicans will become the third largest Latino group (overtaking Cubans) (Ramirez, 2004). While there has been a spread of immigration and settlement of Dominicans across the country, the state of New York continues to have the highest concentration of Dominicans in the United States. In 2000, the Dominican Republic was the single largest source of foreign-born New Yorkers (13 percent of the total NYC population).

In terms of *Chinese immigrants*, in the year 2000, there were over 2.4 million Chinese people living in the United States, making them the largest Asian ethnic group in the country. The majority of Chinese living in the United States (69 percent) are between the ages of eighteen and sixty-four years of age, but over 21 percent are children (under eighteen years of age) (Barnes and Bennett, 2002). In 2000, the largest Chinese population in the United States resided in the New York metropolitan area (although their concentration is higher in other cities, such as San Francisco). Further, 75 percent of Chinese residing in New York City in 2000 were foreign-born, and of those 27 percent were not citizens. In fact, China was the second largest source of foreign-born New Yorkers in the 2000 census (Asian American Federation of New York Census Information Center, 2004).

DIMENSIONS OF FATHER INVOLVEMENT

To date, the most widely cited taxonomy for describing aspects of father involvement is Lamb and colleagues' (Lamb, Pleck, Charnov, and Levine, 1987) multidimensional framework, which focuses on fathers' accessibility, engagement, and responsibility. *Accessibility* refers to a father's available time to the child, irrespective of the nature or extent of interactions between father and child. *Engagement* refers to a father's experience of direct contact and shared interactions with his child in the form of caretaking, play, or leisure, and the extent to which the quality of those engagements are supportive. Finally, *responsibility* refers to a father's financial provisioning and taking part in important decisions in a child's life (e.g., school choice). For purposes of this chapter, we limit our discussion to the financial aspects of father responsibility, and use the term "economic investment" in line with economic theorists (e.g., Becker, 1991).

Considering these forms of father involvement together advances the theory about the pathways through which fathers might affect children, and how those pathways might differ across cultural groups. We propose three such pathways (see figure 11.1). Father involvement might affect children through influences on mothers. That is, if a father is highly involved in the family system, mothers might feel better about the mother-father relationship and engage children in sensitive ways. Studies have revealed associations between supportive father-child interactions and mothers' involvement with children (e.g., Tamis-LeMonda et al., 2004), and studies with nonresident fathers find that child support payments influence mother-father relationships, which in turn affect children's well-being by increasing father-child contact and lessening conflict between parents (McLanahan and Sandefur, 1994; Yoshikawa, 1999).

Second, fathers' engagements with children might directly promote children's early development of skills, including language, cognition, and emotional regulation. This pathway aligns with developmental theories that highlight parents' direct role in facilitating children's learning (Vygotsky,

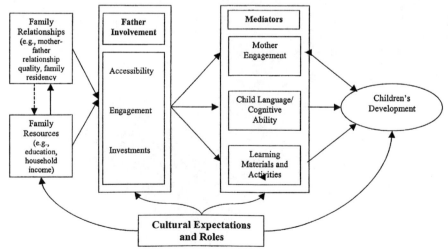

Figure 11.1.

1962). A growing body of literature supports this pathway by revealing positive associations among fathers' sensitivity, warmth, language use, and didactic stimulation and children's language development, cognitive status, problem solving, and cognitive competencies in children's first three years of life (Black et al., 1999; Easterbrooks and Goldberg, 1984; Shannon et al., 2006; Tamis-LeMonda et al., 2004).

Finally, fathers' economic investments in children might influence children's access to learning materials and resources. Family income in early childhood is strongly associated with children's school success when compared to later developmental periods (Morris, Duncan, and Clark-Kauffman, 2005), and fathers' wage rates in childhood predict children's outcomes in adulthood (Yeung et al., 2000). Moreover, parents' earnings and income have been shown to result in child access to cognitively stimulating materials in the home (e.g., Guo and Harris, 2000; Yeung, Linver, and Brooks-Gunn, 2002) (see figure 11.1).

Nonetheless, although Lamb and Pleck's (1987) taxonomy provides a valuable framework for conceptualizing involved fathering, its validity has yet to be tested in culturally diverse groups. What does it mean to be accessible, engaged, or responsible in Mexican, Dominican, and Chinese families? How do these different aspects of father involvement co-vary, and are patterns of covariance similar or different across these groups? Through which pathways might father involvement influence children's developmental outcomes? Unfortunately, little work has been done to unpackage the nature and meanings of accessibility, engagement, and economic investments in different immigrant groups.

Fathers' Accessibility in Different Communities

The extant research on father involvement in immigrant families, in combination with our work, suggests complex patterns of father accessibility in Mexican, Dominican, and Chinese families. Oftentimes, fathers' accessibility is compromised by the immigration process itself. For example, separation from one or both parents occurs for a high percentage of immigrant youth (Suárez-Orozco, Todorova, and Louie, 2002). Among youth born in the Dominican Republic in their sample, 25 percent were separated from their father only and 61 percent were separated from both parents for a length of time that stretched from six months to over five years.

Similarly, immigration is associated with family separation in Mexican families. One qualitative study examined Mexican parenting of both mothers and fathers within the context of transnationalism (when a parent migrates to one country leaving the child behind) (Dreby, 2006). Transnational Mexican migrant mothers and fathers living in the United States were interviewed about their experiences with being separated from their children still residing in Mexico. Mexican mothers and fathers had different emotional responses to the separation. Fathers most often left their wives and children in Mexico and migrated to the United States. Not surprisingly, separation placed stress on the marital relationship. However, even if separated, the fathers maintained contact and responsibility by calling and sending money. The only time fathers became distant from their children was when they were unable to fulfill the role as family breadwinner. Thus, being a good father was intimately linked to providing financial support.

Separations of children from their fathers and families have also been documented in Chinese families (Suárez-Orozco et al., 2002), as well as our own work with Chinese immigrant families in New York City (Gaytan, Xue, Yoshikawa, Tamis-LeMonda, and Kahana-Kalman, 2008). One of the unexpected patterns we have uncovered is the extent of transnational movement of Chinese infants soon after their birth. Our current sample of Chinese families is overwhelmingly Fujianese. Fujian province is now the province of China that sends the largest number of Chinese immigrants to the United States (Liang and Ye, 2001). We have found that over 70 percent of this group, largely undocumented and with low levels of human capital, send their three- to six-month-old infants back to China to their own parents for several years, with the intention of bringing their children back to the United States in time for school entry. The group of Chinese immigrant families in which we are observing this sending behavior is representative of Chinese immigrants to the United States as a whole (Suárez-Orozco et al., 2002). Even for those families whose infants were not sent back to China, fathers sometimes worked in different towns or cities near New York, only returning home on weekends. Long work hours and low wages, most often in Chinese restaurants, prevented these fathers from spending as much time with their infants as they would like, yet extended absence from their children was viewed to be necessary to supporting the family financially. In contrast, separations from fathers were more rare in Mexican and Dominican families. Only 1 percent of Mexican infants traveled to Mexico in the first six months of life. However, 22 percent of Dominican infants traveled to the Dominican Republic in the first six months of life (Gaytan et al., 2008). Parents from Dominican families were much more likely to give reasons for return involving seeing family and the homeland than Chinese families, who overwhelmingly gave economic reasons.

Fathers' Engagement in Different Communities

In addition to the varied forms of accessibility found in different immigrant communities, father engagement may also vary across immigrant groups due to different expectations about fathers' roles. Unfortunately, however, few research studies have focused on specific Latino or Asian groups, and there has been sharp criticism of the widespread use of pan-ethnic categories in the study of parenting.

Research on Dominican fathers is virtually nonexistent, although Dominican mothers are described as engaging in high levels of praise and physical affection and low levels of harsh, inconsistent, and punitive parenting behaviors (Calzada and Eyberg, 2002). In terms of teaching styles, Dominican mothers revealed that they frequently use directives, visual cues, and high levels of modeling (Planos, Zayas, and Busch-Rossnagle, 1995). This form of parenting may reflect the hierarchical nature of family relationships in which children are expected to be obedient and respectful of adults, and to learn through observation (Tamis-LeMonda, Way, Hughes, Yoshikawa, Kahana-Kalman, and Niwa, 2008).

In terms of Mexican American families, mothers have been observed to engage in high levels of nurturance and indulgence early in children's development (Zuniga, 1992). In contrast to traditional Mexican conceptions of motherhood as centered around caring for children, fatherhood was associated with providing economic resources for the family (Gutmann, 1996) and was closely bound with the notion of honor (Melhuus, 1996). Moreover, these traditional values also emphasized adherence to convention, respect for authority, identity with family (Romero, 1983), and the valuing of compliance (Holloway, Gorman, and Fuller, 1988). The emphasis on authority and compliance in immigrant Mexicans has been found to predict heightened authoritarian parenting when fathers' engagements with infants are coded (Varela, Vernberg, Sanchez-Sosa, Riveros, Mitchell, and Mashunkashey, 2004). Although Mexican mothers did not appear to differ in their behavior toward their male or female children, research on Mexican families, focusing on fathers in particular, is limited with the majority of studies on Mexican fathers focusing on those living in Mexico, as opposed to Mexican immigrant fathers. However, it has also been suggested that authoritarian parenting practices were in part the result of immigrating to the United States. Varela and colleagues (2004) found that Caucasian non-Hispanic families reported less authoritarian parenting than their Mexican American counterparts. Interestingly, though, there was no difference in authoritarian parenting between Caucasian non-Hispanic families in the United States and Mexican families residing in Mexico, while there was a difference between those Mexican families and Mexican immigrant or Mexican American families residing in the United States. This unexpected finding led Varela and colleagues (2004) to argue that ethnic minority status, as opposed to Mexican culture per se, may lead to a greater use of authoritarian parenting in Mexican families in the United States.

Nonetheless, stereotypes of Latino fathers generally (and Mexican fathers specifically) as authoritarian, controlling, emotionally distant, and dominant have been challenged. In one study, Mexican fathers were more playful, emotionally supportive, and affectionate than the stereotype (Fitzpatrick et al., 1999). Thus, although traditional father roles emerged in their qualitative study (e.g., in terms of provider and disciplinarian), they also found that fathers fulfilled roles that contradicted rigid stereotypes. In particular, they found that fathers were also conceived to be teachers of social skills and knowledge related to being part of a community. Fathers were also considered to be affectionate playmates to their children, as well as a source of emotional support. As further evidence for these qualitative findings, Mexican fathers were more playful with their children than were mothers.

Our research also revealed support for Mexican fathers' dual and seemingly paradoxical roles as disciplinarians and nurturers. For example, Mexican, Dominican, and African American mothers were interviewed about what they viewed to be characteristics of a "bad father" when their children were fourteen months. Significantly more Mexican than Dominican and African American mothers expressed concerns about father abuse and harsh punishment of children, a finding that accords with Mexican fathers as disciplinarians (Tamis-LeMonda, Kahana-Kalman, Kowalczyk, and Rojas, 2007). At the same time, however, interviews about daily routines with these same mothers when babies were one month of age revealed the affectionate side of Mexican fathers. During in-depth telephone interviews, mothers reported on the hour-by-hour activities of their one-month old infants, and for each activity, noted the person who was directly engaged with the infant. This study was based on a total sample of 380 Mexican, Dominican, Chinese, and African American families (Kahana-Kalman, Niwa, Kowalczyk, and Rojas, 2007). From these diaries we identified the types of activities that babies were engaged in (e.g., caregiving, play, outings) as well as the person who engaged in those activities (e.g., mothers, fathers, siblings). Findings revealed that Mexican fathers engaged in the highest levels of social play with their new babies when compared to Chinese, Dominican, and African American fathers. In fact, Mexican fathers still engaged in higher levels of social interaction when their infant was six months of age compared to their Chinese, Dominican, and African American counterparts.

Similar to characterizations of parenting in Mexican families, Chinese parenting is said to shift "from relative indulgence to strict socialization" (Bowes, Chen, San, and Yuan, 2004) when children reach the "age of understanding" which occurs around six years of age (Ho, 1986; Wu, 1996). Much of what has been deemed traditional child-rearing practice in China is attributed to Confucian principles, although some studies suggest that the parenting styles of urban Chinese families differ from more traditional Confucian-based ways of parenting (Bowes et al., 2004; Chen, Rubin, and Li, 1994; Lai, Zhang, and Wang, 2000; Wu, 1996).

Research on parenting views in Chinese populations living in mainland China, Taiwan, or Hong Kong highlighted the importance of obedience

(Berndt, Cheung, Lau, Hau, and Lew, 1993; Wu, 1996), respect for elders, and conciliation as opposed to conflict within the home (Bond, 1991; Wu, 1996). For Chinese immigrants in the United States, research has also noted the use of a combination of training and guidance in raising children (Chao and Kim, 2000).

In terms of Chinese fathering more specifically, Chinese fathers are traditionally described as being remote and severe toward children after early childhood (Berndt et al., 1993), and are more often perceived as the disciplinarian in the household who administers punishment (Ho, 1986). In support of these traditional father roles, Chinese adolescents from Hong Kong perceived fathers as relatively less responsive, less demanding, less concerned, and harsher than mothers (Shek, 1998). These findings support the popular Chinese saying, "strict father, kind mother," which paints fathers as the strict disciplinarians who are intent on propriety rather than feelings and should be feared by the child (Wilson, 1974). In contrast, mothers are characterized as affectionate, kind, protective, lenient, and indulgent. These traditional characterizations of Chinese maternal and paternal roles have been derived from Chinese families living in China.

Fathers' Investments in Different Communities

In terms of economic investments, the importance of fathers as breadwinners may be salient in immigrant Dominican, Mexican, and Chinese groups alike, given their larger context of relative poverty in the host country of the United States. Fathers in our study were generally working long hours for low wage work. 78 percent of Dominican fathers were working at infants' birth; over half were working more than forty hours per week, and 20 percent were working over fifty hours per week. For Mexican fathers, 94 percent were working; 65 percent were working over forty hours, and 40 percent were working over fifty hours per week. For Chinese fathers, 76 percent were working, but those working put in the longest hours of the three immigrant groups. More than 84 percent of Chinese fathers were working over fifty hours per week. These long hours, in the context of the relatively low household incomes of these families, indicated that fathers were placing much time each day into providing for their families' necessities. This time may come at a cost as it limits the time that these immigrant fathers have available to spend in everyday activities with their infants.

Covariation among Forms of Father Involvement

Not only is there a lack of information on the accessibility, engagement, and responsibility of fathers from different groups, but virtually nothing is known about the tradeoffs that might exist among these various forms of fathering. The literature on fathering implies that positive covariation among forms of fathering should be the norm, such that fathers who are more accessible and engaged are more likely to invest in their children as well. This view is found in both economic and developmental theoretical literatures. According to economic theory, a father's financial investments in children should predict greater father accessibility (in terms of time spent with child), especially for non-resident fathers who "check" that their support dollars are reaching children (Edin and Kefalas, 2005). Similarly, developmental theorists posit that fathers who are more emotionally committed to their roles as fathers are more likely to invest more time and money in their children compared to less invested fathers. In support of these speculations, a number of studies have revealed positive associations between father accessibility and fathers' economic and time investments in children (e.g., Arditti and Keith, 1993; Furstenberg, Nord, Peterson, and Zill, 1983; Seltzer, Schaeffer, and Charing, 1989; Sonenstein and Calhoun, 1990). However, correspondences among aspects of father involvement might not be straightforward, especially when models are tested in different immigrant groups. For example, fathers in immigrant families might be more likely to spend time separated from their children in efforts to maximize financial resources for children. (We found this to be true in our Chinese families.) In such instances, a father's strong commitment to getting food on the table and paying rent might result in less accessibility and less engagement.

SUMMARY

There is a dearth of literature on fathering in Dominican, Mexican, and Chinese families. The studies that do exist, however, suggest that immigrant children are often separated from their fathers (and sometimes mothers) for extended periods of time. These separations result from both the immigration process itself, as well as the fact that fathers are often the primary breadwinners in the family. When fathers' actual engagements with their children are studied, Mexican and Chinese fathers alike have been characterized as disciplinarians. However, whereas characterizations of the remote Chinese father dominate the literature, there is some suggestion that Mexican immigrant fathers are playful and emotionally expressive with their children, already in the first months of their infants' lives, and this finding is also reflected in our work. Finally, although no studies have directly examined covariation among forms of father involvement in immigrant fathers, there is reason to expect that in certain families *lower* levels of father accessibility will be associated with *greater* financial investments in children due to fathers' strong commitment to the breadwinner role and a father's need to separate from his family to achieve such aims. These trade-offs between financial resources and time might benefit the larger good of the family, yet whether and how they affect children's developmental outcomes remains unexamined.

PREDICTORS OF FATHER INVOLVEMENT

A question that continues to permeate much of the literature on father involvement concerns the determinants of fathering: Which factors support and which impede positive father involvement? How might these predictors of father involvement vary by ethnic group? Answers to these questions have enormous implications for programs and outreach to fathers and families.

We, and others, have found conflicted family relationships and lack of resources to predict declines in father involvement over time (e.g., Shannon, Tamis-LeMonda, and Margolin, 2005). Qualitative studies also highlight the central role that family relationships and human capital resources play in father involvement (e.g., Jarrett, Roy, and Burton, 2002; Nelson, Clampet-Lundquist, and Edin, 2002). In line with these findings, our research on the determinants of father involvement in immigrant families also emphasizes these two sets of predictors (as also depicted in figure 11.1).

Family Relationships

Under the broad umbrella of family relationships, our focus has been on fathers' prenatal commitment to the pregnancy, residency and marital status, the quality of the mother-father relationship, and fathers' and mothers' multi-partner fertility.

First, *father involvement during the prenatal period* has been shown to relate to fathers' involvement over the long term. In our research with low-income white, Latino, and African American fathers out of the Early Head Start national father consortium, close to 90 percent of fathers who were more involved during the prenatal period saw their children three times per week or more when children were five years of age, versus fewer than 30 percent of fathers who demonstrated low levels of prenatal involvement (Shannon, Tamis-LeMonda, and Cabrera, 2006).

In our research with Dominican, Mexican, and Chinese immigrant families, we interviewed mothers in postpartum hospital wards, where we asked about various forms of fathers' emotional and instrumental prenatal involvement. Emotional forms of prenatal involvement included talking to the baby, feeling the baby move, and talking with the mother about the pregnancy. Instrumental forms included accompanying the mother to a doctor visit, seeing an ultrasound, listening to the baby's heartbeat, and buying the baby things before its birth. Based on these indicators, the majority of Dominican, Mexican, and Chinese fathers were involved during the prenatal period, with over 80 percent of fathers engaging in emotional forms of involvement across all groups. In terms of instrumental forms of involvement, between 77 percent and 91 percent of fathers had visited the doctor with the mother, seen an ultrasound, heard the baby's heartbeat, or bought the baby things before its birth. Fewer fathers had attended Lamaze classes (between 15 and 28 percent). Even within these high overall rates of prenatal involvement, Chinese fathers scored highest on nearly all items, and significantly differed from the other groups on their levels of instrumental involvement. For all immigrant groups, prenatal involvement scores predicted fathers' accessibility and engagement with infants at one month based on time diary data (Kahana-Kalman et al., 2007) and their participation in learning activities with their infants at fourteen months (Tamis-LeMonda, Yoshikawa, Kahana-Kalman, Niwa, and Castellano, in preparation).

Second, *father residency* has been found to be one of the strongest predictors of father accessibility, engagement, and economic investments in children. Two-parent households, because of their generally higher incomes (McLanahan and Sandefur, 1994), are theorized to display greater expenditures on children. Entry into, or exits from, marriage or a relationship can alter levels of investment in children, as households often draw on combined income in relationships and marriages. Income from partners and spouses typically falls, for example, following separations and divorce (Amato, 1994). Changes in marital or relationship status can also alter fathers' accessibility to the child and support of learning during engagements. Transitions to single-parent status, for example, could result in less time engaging in learning activities if the parent works more and spends less time at home (Hetherington and Kelly, 2002).

In terms of the immigrant families we are studying, there were varied rates of father residency that generally paralleled trends identified in national statistics. For Dominicans, overall statistics reveal higher rates of father nonresidency than in the average population, and in our sample, Dominican fathers were less likely to reside with their infants than were Mexican or Chinese immigrants. Statistics for Dominicans in New York City reveal that of those families living in poverty, 38.2 percent reside in female-headed households with no spouse present, whereas only 22.1 percent of the overall city lives in such households. In our sample, at the birth of infants, 61 percent of Dominican fathers were residing with their children.

Mexicans' rates of single parenthood are lower (though higher than Euro-Americans') (Oropesa and Landale, 2004). Consistent with this finding, Mexicans in our study were more likely to reside with their infants than

Dominicans (87 percent), and rates of residency approached those of Chinese immigrants (95 percent). Chinese households also had higher rates of marriage, with 61 percent of all Chinese being both married and living in the same household. In our sample, 59 percent of Chinese immigrant fathers of newborns were married to their partners. Of the 41 percent who were not, most (91 percent) expressed intentions to soon marry.

Our research also revealed links between father residency and father involvement when daily time diaries were examined. Fathers who resided with their infants were more likely to be accessible to their infants and more likely to have engaged in caregiving or play with their infants. In Dominicans, for example (the group with the highest rates of father non-residency), the percentages of resident as compared to non-resident fathers who were accessible, engaged in caregiving, and engaged in play were 83 percent vs. 16 percent, 51 percent vs. 3 percent, and 52 percent vs. 11 percent, respectively, at one month of the infants' lives.

The *quality of the mother-father relationship* affected the roles fathers play in family life. Positive father influences were more likely to occur when fathers establish positive relationships with the mothers of their children. Warm and close mother-father relationships are linked to greater paternal involvement (McKenry, Price, Fine, and Serovich, 1992) as well as to positive child outcomes (Gable, Crnic, and Belsky, 1994). In contrast, unmarried fathers or those in unstable, conflicted, or hostile relationships with their child's mother are more likely to be uninvolved and to display negative involvement with their children (Coley and Chase-Lansdale, 1998; Cummings, Goeke-Morey, and Raymond, 2004).

Reciprocally, greater father involvement also predicted higher quality mother-father relationships, and these associations have also been identified in our work with immigrant families. Specifically, for Dominican, Mexican, and Chinese families alike, fathers who were more involved both prenatally and at one month (in terms of being more accessible, and engaging in more caregiving and play with their infants) were rated as more supportive by mothers, and were also rated as sharing a better quality relationship with mothers. These associations between prenatal and perinatal involvement and ratings of the mother-father relationship persisted after co-varying a number of other factors, including fathers' income and education. In fact, fathers' prenatal involvement was the strongest predictor of mothers' ratings of the mother-father relationship, beyond fathers' contributions to household income, education, or other demographic characteristics.

Finally, *father involvement may vary with obligations to children outside the family system*, yet few studies have carefully examined the role of multi-partner fertility in father involvement. In our research, both Mexican and Dominican immigrant fathers and mothers reported relatively high levels of multi-partner fertility. Specifically, 41 percent of Dominican men and 24 percent of Mexican men had had children by another mother. Similarly, 26 percent and 22 percent of Dominican and Mexican mothers, respectively, had had children by another father. In contrast, only 2 percent of Chinese fathers had children outside the present household.

These families were therefore likely to experience competing demands for time and resources that might have affected parenting and children's development. Our research provides tentative support for inverse associations between multi-partner fertility and father involvement. For example, in infants' first year, both mothers' and fathers' multi-partner fertility was negatively related to father accessibility and engagement with infants. Specifically, in comparing fathers who did versus did not have children with other partners on daily diary measures of father involvement when infants were one month of age, 56 percent vs. 62 percent of fathers were accessible, 25 percent vs. 40 percent engaged in caregiving, and 33 percent vs. 40 percent played with their infants.

Family Resources

Family resources are a second major influence on father involvement. To the extent that family resources positively predict father involvement, Dominican, Mexican, and Chinese immigrant groups, who experience disproportionately low incomes, fewer years of education, and higher rates of unemployment relative to whites, might be vulnerable to threats to father involvement.

Dominicans

Dominican immigrants in the United States struggle with high levels of non-employment, with about 64 percent of Dominican men working and 53 percent of Dominican women working in 2000, substantially lower than labor force participation in the general American population. These levels of unemployment may be tied to declines in Dominicans being employed in manufacturing jobs, as has been the case for all demographic groups over the last several decades, including the 1990s. Only 17 percent of all Dominicans in the United States hold managerial, professional, or technical jobs, reducing the capacity for increased wages (Hernandez and Denton, 2005).

In our sample of lower-income immigrant fathers, however, Dominicans held a greater variety of positions than Mexicans or Chinese fathers. Although a fairly high percentage of fathers were working in low-skilled, non-managerial jobs such as deliveries, stocking shelves in stores, in factories, or as porters in hotels (26 percent), sizable groups worked higher-skill jobs such as mechanic, carpenter, or electrician (12 percent), better-paying jobs such as construction (9 percent), and some managerial/supervisor positions (7 percent). There were scattered other positions in the police department, as professional sports players, and in the music business, suggesting a more diversified employment picture than for either our Mexican or Chinese fathers. This may be due to the fact that there was a small percentage of second-generation parents in our sample among the Dominicans, but not the Mexicans.

In line with low levels of employment and wages, Dominicans remain as a relatively low-income community. In 1999, the average annual per-capita household income for Dominicans in the United States was $11,065, which is half of the per-capita income of the average American household that year. It was also significantly lower than the income of the average black/African American household and lower than the income of the average Latino household (Hernandez and Denton, 2005). Additionally, the educational attainment of Dominican immigrants is one of the lowest across the United States. In 2000, 49 percent of Dominican immigrants over twenty-five years of age had not completed high school and only 11 percent had completed college, far below levels of the general American population. These trends change somewhat for second-generation, U.S.-born Dominicans, who as a community have been steadily increasing their human capital over the past two decades.

Mexicans

In a pattern similar to that found among Dominicans, rates of poverty are higher for Mexican American immigrants than for whites and African Americans (Oropesa and Landale, 2004). Moreover, Mexican American immigrant children and youth attend lower quality and more segregated schools than their white or African American peers (Crosnoe, 2005; Suárez-Orozco and Suárez-Orozco, 2001).

Findings from our research with Mexicans indicate that Mexican immigrant parents are younger, have lower levels of human capital, and live in more overcrowded housing than parents from Chinese and Dominican groups living in New York City. In interviews with these families it became apparent that the high crowding in Mexican households was largely due to co-residence among multiple families and consequently a greater number of adults residing in households. Sharing dwellings was an intentional strategy that enabled these families to cover the household expenses. At the same time, though, children of Mexican immigrants are also more likely to live in intact families with one or more working parent(s). Further, they tend to be members of well-established and supportive communities.

In terms of work, Mexicans are more likely to work either part-time or seasonally. Mexican immigrants in New York City generally work in the unskilled labor sectors of manufacturing, construction, and service. Our data show that they also report working in jobs with significantly lower levels of occupational complexity, when compared to Dominicans, Chinese, and African American parents (Yoshikawa, Lugo-Gil, and Tamis-LeMonda, 2006). This corroborates other research finding more generally that undocumented immigrants work in lower-status, lower-paying jobs than documented immigrants (Passel, 2005). Mexican fathers in our sample were most likely to work in the food industry, as busboys, line cooks, or kitchen aides in restaurants and delis (51 percent), or in stores or doing deliveries for stores (28 percent). Only a small percentage (12 percent) engaged in more highly skilled work such as mechanic, carpenter, or printer. A small percentage (8 percent) worked in construction, and an even smaller percentage (7 percent) were self-employed or working as managers or business owners (Yoshikawa and Longo, 2007).

Mexicans in the United States tend to have low levels of parental education. Mirroring national trends, Mexicans in New York City have an average educational attainment level of approximately nine years, as opposed to the average thirteen years for New Yorkers overall (Smith, 2005). This disparity is partly explained by the low levels of schooling and educational attainment among Mexican migrants, of whom almost one-third have only an elementary school education. The states of origin of Mexican migrants to New York—chiefly Puebla and Guerrero—are among the poorest states in Mexico, with relatively low levels of educational attainment (Consejo Nacional de Población, 2000; Yoshikawa, McCartney, et al., 2007). Additionally, Mexican teens have the lowest high school retention rates in New York City (Smith, 2005).

As immigration and transnationalism create unique stressors and contexts for father involvement, some research has examined how economic stressors affect parenting among Mexican immigrants. Parke and colleagues (2004) found that economic hardship in Mexican immigrants was associated with economic pressures that were consequently linked to depressive symptoms among both mothers and fathers, regardless of ethnicity. Those depressive symptoms were then linked to both hostile parenting and marital problems, and marital problems in turn were linked to child adjustment problems.

Further, the intersection of socioeconomic status and parenting has emerged. For example, among Mexican mothers of young children, mothers from higher socioeconomic status had higher developmental expectations for their children, used less frequent discipline, and used more frequent nurturing practices than their counterparts from lower socioeconomic statuses (Solis-Camara and Fox, 1996). The impact of immigration can be felt in multiple parts of Mexican families' lives, including through the experience of separations related to the immigration process (see Dominican section for explanation). In Suárez-Orozco et al.'s study (2002), 42 percent of Mexican adolescents had lived separately from parents.

Other comparative research examined Mexican fathers living in Mexico and Euro-American fathers living in the United States (Fox and Solis-Camara, 1997). This study found that Mexican and American fathers did not significantly differ with regard to their parental practices and developmental expectations. However, when accounting for socioeconomic status, in both countries, fathers who were from families with lower socioeconomic status engaged in less nurturing behaviors and used discipline more frequently than their higher SES counterparts.

Chinese

Examinations of the 2000 census have highlighted the vastly different experiences of Chinese New Yorkers as compared to New Yorkers overall. In comparison to New Yorkers overall, Chinese New Yorkers had less education—42 percent had not graduated from high school. Further, 31 percent of Chinese adults in New York City had less than a ninth-grade education, which is more than double the rate for all adult New Yorkers. More than 60 percent of New York City's Chinese residents had limited English proficiency in 2000. In addition, 22 percent of Chinese lived below the poverty line, as compared to 21 percent of the general population. The average annual per-capita income of Chinese immigrants is $16,700. However, 27 percent of Chinese children lived under the poverty line, which is lower than children in New York City overall. As with the Mexican population, however, Chinese households are likely to be two-parent households: in 2000, 80 percent of Chinese children living in poverty lived in two-parent homes, compared to 34 percent of all city children in poverty (Asian American Federation Census Information Center, 2004). As for education, while a high proportion of Chinese over the age of twenty-five have earned at least a bachelor's degree (48 percent), an estimated 23 percent have not graduated from high school (Asian American Federation Census Information Center, 2004; Barnes and Bennett, 2002).

Based on the research in our lab, low-income Chinese immigrants in our New York sample are employed primarily in the restaurant business (a whopping 90 percent of our sample of Chinese fathers worked in restaurants). Our sample of relatively young fathers of infants, for the most part, did not run restaurants (only 5 percent did). Due most likely to the variety of roles required of workers in Chinese restaurants (from cooking to serving to reception to delivery), the average occupational complexity of the Chinese workers' jobs was higher than that of Mexicans (Yoshikawa and Longo, 2007).

Relations between Resources and Parenting in Immigrant Groups

Associations between family resources (e.g., employment, household income, access to public resources), father involvement, and parenting are complex and may vary depending on the form of father involvement as well as by immigrant group. In our data, households in which both mothers and fathers (or any other adults) had bank accounts or credit cards, for example, experienced both higher levels of economic hardship and lower levels of parent-child activities involving resources such as toys, books, or games (Yoshikawa, Godfrey, et al., 2006). Isolation from financial and public institutions, often associated with undocumented status, may be responsible for these associations.

Access to resources can differentially shape paternal involvement. In fact, increased maternal employment, periods of economic decline, joint work schedules, flexible hours, irregular work schedules, part-time employment, job sharing, and home-based work are all examples of resource-based issues that may increase the likelihood that children will be cared for by their father, and for longer durations (Casper and O'Connell, 1998; Hsueh and Yoshikawa, 2007; Presser, 1995). Fathers are also more likely to care for their children when family income is low and work schedules are non-overlapping (Casper and O'Connell, 1998). In addition, in hard times the more income a wife has relative to her husband, the more likely the husband is to care for his children. Thus, changes in economic conditions affect the interplay of father care, work schedules, and family income (Brayfield, 1995; Casper and O'Connell, 1998). In immigrant families, decreased resources might actually be associated with greater father accessibility, particularly if families do not have access to childcare benefits and are separated from extended kin who might otherwise assist with childcare.

GENERAL DISCUSSION

There has been an unprecedented amount of research on fathers within the past thirty years as researchers and policy makers come to better understand the important influences that fathers have on children's development (Tamis-LeMonda and Cabrera, 2002). Although recent research has generated new information on the national demographics of fatherhood, fathering behaviors, and the role of fathers in children's development, gaps still exist on the experiences of fathers from diverse ethnic and socioeconomic backgrounds in the United States. In particular, little research exists on the experiences of immigrant fathers from Dominican, Mexican, and Chinese backgrounds (Cabrera and Garcia-Coll, 2004; Roopnarine, 2002; Shwalb, Nakazawa, Yamamoto, and Hyun, 2004), and our work at New York University's CRCDE aims to address this gap. These groups are among the fastest growing immigrant populations in the United States, and confront numerous economic and social challenges as they adjust to the demands of the new society.

The central premise of this chapter was that the forms and influences of father involvement must be placed in the context of cultural expectations and norms. Parents create "cultural niches" for children's development (Super and Harkness, 1986), which include what, how, when, and with whom a child learns, the routines and settings of daily life, and the roles that fathers play in children's development. Cultural expectations or prescriptions about appropriate ways of thinking and acting profoundly affect how men and women view their roles within family systems and sociocultural communities. These cultural views in turn shape parenting practices in ways that channel children's behaviors toward what is expected (Tamis-LeMonda, 2004; Tamis-LeMonda et al., 2008).

Specific to fathering, cultural norms and values shape expectations of what it means to be a "good" and "bad" father, thereby feeding into both the roles fathers play and the pathways through which fathers affect children's development. Lamb's widely used taxonomy (Lamb et al., 1987) proposes three main forms of father involvement: engagement, availability, and responsibility. Future studies should examine the extent to which this taxonomy generalizes to fathers and families from Chinese, Mexican, and Dominican backgrounds, and how different groups might vary in their emphasis on the different forms of father involvement. For example, breadwinning and financial security may be of paramount importance in certain families and communities, whereas emotional support might be prioritized in others. Moreover, additional attention is needed to the pathways through which father involvement shapes children's development. Here, we proposed three pathways that we believe apply to fathers from all backgrounds: 1) father involvement might affect children through fathers' influence on mothers, 2) father engagement might directly promote children's developing skills, and 3) economic investments by fathers might influence children's access to learning materials and resources, thus bolstering development.

Finally, the study of fathering in a cultural context calls for attention to within-group variation, and variation in fathering across settings, developmental time, and life circumstances. That is, cultural values and norms (and in turn expectations about fathering) are not static, but rather vary with the immigration experience, changes to household income and employment, children's age, and so forth (Tamis-LeMonda, 2003; Tamis-LeMonda et al., 2008). As father involvement is explored across shifting cultural contexts, covariation among forms of father involvement may change as well (e.g., a father's accessibility might relate to fathers' economic investments in children in one group, but not in another, or at one point in time, but not another). As we have shown, father involvement in immigrant families is related to factors such as family relationships (including prenatal involvement, father residency, and the quality of the mother-father relationship) and family resources (including father education, income, and employment), and to the extent that these are changing, fathering might change as well. Therefore, future studies of father involvement should attend to the intersections among cultural, economic, and social factors as they shape the roles that fathers play and the influences they have on their children's development.

REFERENCES

Amato, P. R. (1994). Life-span adjustment of children to their parents' divorces. *The Future of Children*, 4, 143–64.

Arditti, J. A., and Keith, T. Z. (1993). Visitation frequency, child support payment, and the father-child relationship postdivorce. *Journal of Marriage and the Family*, 55, 699–712.

Asian American Federation of New York Census Information Center. (2004). *Census Profile: New York City's Chinese American Population*. Data derived from analysis by the Asian American Federation Census Information Center. Retrieved March 1, 2007, from the Asian American Federation Census Information Center website: http://www.aafny.org/cic/briefs/chinese.pdf.

Bales, S., Christmas-Best, V., Diversi, M., McLaughlin, M., Silbereisen, R., and Youniss, J. (2002). Youth civic engagement in the twenty-first century. *Journal of Research on Adolescence*, 12, 121–48.

Barnes, J. S., and Bennett, C. E. (2002). *The Asian Population: 2000*. U.S. Census Bureau.

Becker, G.S. (1991). *A treatise on the family: Enlarged edition*. Cambridge, MA: Harvard University Press.

Berndt, T. J., Cheung, P. C., Lau, S., Hau, K., and Lew, L. (1993). Perceptions of parenting in mainland China, Taiwan, and Hong Kong: Sex differences and societal differences. *Developmental Psychology*, 29, 156–64.

Black, M. M., Dubowitz, H., and Starr, R. H. (1999). African American fathers in low-income, urban families: Development, behavior, and home environment of their three-year-olds. *Child Development*, 70, 967–78.

Bond, M. H. (1991). *Beyond the Chinese face*. Hong Kong: Oxford University Press.

Bowes, J. M., Chen, M-J., San, L. Q., and Yuan, L. (2004). Reasoning and negotiation about child responsibility in urban Chinese families: Reports from mothers, fathers, and children. *International Journal of Behavioral Development*, 28, 48–58.

Brayfield, A. (1995). Juggling jobs and kids: The impact of employment schedules on fathers' caring for children. *Journal of Marriage and the Family*, 57, 321–32.

Cabrera, N. J., and Garcia-Coll, C. (2004). Latino fathers: Uncharted territory in need of much exploration. In M. E. Lamb (Ed.), *The role of the father in child development* (fourth ed., 98–120). New York: Wiley.

Calzada, E. J., and Eyberg, S. M. (2002). Self-reported parenting practices in Dominican and Puerto Rican mothers of young children. *Journal of Clinical Child and Adolescent Psychology, 31*, 354–63.

Casper, L. M., and O'Connell, M. (1998). Work, income, the economy, and married fathers as child care providers. *Demography, 35*, 243–50.

Chao, R. K., and Kim, K. (2000). Parenting differences among immigrant Chinese fathers and mothers in the United States. *Journal of Psychology in Chinese Societies, 1*, 71–91.

Chen, X., Rubin, K. H., and Li, B. S. (1994). Only children and sibling children in urban China: A reexamination. *International Journal of Behavioral Development, 17*, 413–21.

Coley, R. L., and Chase-Lansdale, P. L. (1998). Adolescent pregnancy and parenthood. *American Psychologist, 53*, 152–66.

Consejo Nacional de Población (CONAPO). (2000). *Marginación por entidad federativa*. Mexico City: Consejo Nacional de Población.

Crosnoe, R. (2005). Double disadvantage or signs of resilience? The elementary school contexts of children from Mexican immigrant families. *American Educational Research Journal, 42*, 269–303.

Cummings, E. M., Goeke-Morey, M. C., and Raymond, J. (2004). Fathers in family context: Effects of marital quality and marital conflict. In M. E. Lamb (Ed.), *The role of the father in child development* (fourth ed., 196–221). Hoboken, NJ: Wiley.

Dreby, J. (2006). Honor and virtue: Mexican parenting in the transnational context. *Gender & Society, 20*, 32–59.

Easterbrooks, M. A., and Goldberg, W. A. (1984). Toddler development in the family: Impact of father involvement and parenting characteristics. *Child Development, 55*, 740–52.

Edin, K., and Kefalas, M. (2005). *Promises I can keep: Why poor women put motherhood before marriage*. Berkeley: University of California Press.

Fitzpatrick, J., Calder, Y. M., Pursley, M., and Wampler, K. (1999). Hispanic mother and father perceptions of fathering: A qualitative analysis. *Family & Consumer Sciences Research Journal, 28*, 133–66.

Fox, R. A., and Solis-Camara, P. (1997). Parenting of young children by fathers in Mexico and the United States. *Journal of Social Psychology, 137*, 489–95.

Furstenberg, F. F. Jr., Nord, C. W., Peterson, J. L., and Zill, N. (1983). The life course of children of divorce. *American Psychological Review, 48*, 656–68.

Gable, S., Crnic, K., and Belsky, J. (1994). Coparenting within the family system: Influences on children's development. *Family Relations, 43*, 380–86.

Gaytan, F., Xue, Q., Yoshikawa, H., Tamis-LeMonda, C. S., and Kahana-Kalman, R. (2008). Transnationalism in infancy: Patterns and predictors of early childhood travel to immigrant mothers' native countries. In H. Yoshikawa and N. Way (Eds.), *From peers to policy: Understudied social contexts of children's development in immigrant families*. New Directions in Child and Adolescent Development.

Guo, G., and Harris, K. M. (2000). The mechanisms mediating the effects of poverty on children's intellectual development. *Demography, 37*, 431–47.

Gutmann, M. C. (1996). Imaginary fathers, genuine fathers. In M. C. Guttman (Ed.), *The meaning of being macho: Being a man in Mexico City* (50–88). Thousand Oaks, CA: Sage.

Hernandez, D. J., and Denton, N. A. (2005). Resources and challenges for immigrant families with young children. In H. Yoshikawa (Chair), *The development of young children in immigrant families.* Symposium presented at the biennial meeting of the Society for Research in Child Development, Atlanta, GA.

Hetherington, E. M., and Kelly, J. (2002). *For better or for worse: Divorce reconsidered.* New York: Norton.

Ho, D. Y. F. (1986). Chinese patterns of socialization: A critical review. In M. H. Bond (Ed.), *The psychology of Chinese people* (1–37). Hong Kong: Oxford University Press.

Holloway, S. D., Gorman, K. S., and Fuller, B. (1988). Child-rearing beliefs within diverse social structures: Mothers and day-care providers in Mexico. *International Journal of Psychology, 23,* 303–17.

Hsueh, J., and Yoshikawa, H. (2007). Working nonstandard schedules and variable shifts in low-income families: Associations with parental psychological well-being, family functioning, and child well-being. *Developmental Psychology, 43,* 620–32.

Jarrett, R. L., Roy, K. M., and Burton, L. M. (2002). Fathers in the "hood": Insights from qualitative research on low-income African-American men. In C. S. Tamis-LeMonda and N. Cabrera (Eds.), *Handbook of father involvement: Multidisciplinary perspectives* (211–48). Mahwah, NJ: Erlbaum.

Kahana-Kalman, R., Niwa, E. Y., Kowalczyk, M., and Rojas-Zambrano, P. (2007). *Daily routines of infants from ethnically diverse backgrounds during the first year.* Paper presented at the biennial meeting of the Society for Research in Child Development, Boston.

Lai, A. C., Zhang, Z.-X., and Wang, W.-Z. (2000). Maternal child-rearing practices in Hong Kong and Beijing Chinese families: A comparative study. *International Journal of Psychology, 35,* 60–66.

Lamb, M. E. (Ed.). (1999). *Parenting and child development in nontraditional families.* Mahwah, NJ: Erlbaum.

———. (2004). *The role of the father in child development* (fourth ed.). Hoboken, NJ: Wiley.

Lamb, M. E., Pleck, J. H., Charnov, E. L., and Levine, J. A. (1987). A biosocial perspective on paternal behavior and involvement. In J. B. Lancaster, J. Altman, A. S. Rossi, and L. R. Shorroa (Eds.), *Parenting across the lifespan: Biosocial dimensions* (111–42). New York: Aldine de Gruyter.

Liang, Z., and Ye, W. (2001). From Fujian to New York: Understanding the new Chinese immigration. In D. Kyle and R. Koslowski (Eds.), *Global human smuggling: Comparative perspectives* (187–215). Baltimore: Johns Hopkins University Press.

Malone, N., Baluja, K. F., Costanzo, J. M., and Davis, C. J. (2003). *The foreign-born population: 2000.* U.S. Census Bureau.

McKenry, P. C., Price, S. J., Fine, M. A., and Serovich, J. (1992). Predictors of single, noncustodial fathers' physical involvement with their children. *Journal of Genetic Psychology, 153,* 305–19.

McLanahan, S. S., and Sandefur, G. (1994). *Growing up with a single parent: What hurts, what helps.* Cambridge, MA: Harvard University Press.

Melhuus, M. (1996). Power, value and the ambiguous meanings of gender. In M. Melhuus and K. A. Stolen (Eds.), *Machos, mistresses, madonnas: Contesting the power of Latin American gender imagery* (230–59). London: Verso.

Morris, P., Duncan, G. J., and Clark-Kauffman, E. (2005). Child well-being in an era of welfare reform: The sensitivity of transitions in development to policy change. *Developmental Psychology, 41,* 919–32.

Nelson, T. J., Clampet-Lundquist, S., and Edin, K. (2002). Sustaining fragile fatherhood: Father involvement among low-income, noncustodial African-American fathers in Philadelphia. In C. S. Tamis-LeMonda and N. Cabrera (Eds.), *Handbook of father involvement: Multidisciplinary perspectives* (525–54). Mahwah, NJ: Erlbaum.

Oropesa, R. S., and Landale, N. S. (2004). The future of marriage and Hispanics. *Journal of Marriage and Family, 66,* 901–20.

Parke, R. D., Coltrane, S., Duffy, S., Buriel, R., Dennis, J., Powers, J., French, S., and Widaman, K. (2004). Economic stress, parenting, and child adjustment in Mexican American and European American families. *Child Development, 75,* 1632–56.

Passel, Jeffrey S. (2005). Unauthorized Migrants: Numbers and Characteristics. Washington, DC: Pew Hispanic Center. Available at http://pewhispanic.org/files/reports/46.pdf.

Planos, R., Zayas, L. H., and Busch-Rossnagle, N. A. (1995). Acculturation and teaching behaviors of Dominican and Puerto Rican mothers. *Hispanic Journal of Behavioral Sciences, 17,* 225–36.

Portes, A., and Rumbaut, R. G. (2001). *Legacies: The story of the second generation.* Berkeley: University of California Press.

Presser, H. B. (1995). Job, family, gender: Determinants of nonstandard work schedules among employed Americans in 1991. *Demography, 32,* 577–98.

Ramirez, R. R. (2004). *We the people: Hispanic in the United States.* Census 2000 Special Reports, U.S. Census Bureau.

Romero, A. (1983). The Mexican American child: A sociological approach to research. In G. Powell, J. Yamanato, A. Romero, and A. Morales (Eds.), *The psychosocial development of minority group children* (538–72). New York: Brunner/Mazel.

Roopnarine, J. L. (2002). Father involvement in English-speaking Caribbean families. In C. S. Tamis-LeMonda and N. Cabrera (Eds.), *Handbook of father involvement: Multidisciplinary perspectives* (279–302). Mahwah, NJ: Erlbaum.

Seltzer, J. A., Schaeffer, N. C., and Charing, H.-W. (1989). Family ties after divorce: The relationship between visiting and paying child support. *Journal of Marriage and the Family, 51,* 1013–31.

Shannon, J., Tamis-LeMonda, C., and Margolin, A. (2005). Father involvement in infancy: Influences of past and current relationships. *Infancy, 8,* 21–41.

Shannon, J. D., Tamis-LeMonda, C. S., and Cabrera, N. J. (2006). Fathering in infancy: Mutuality and stability between 8 and 16 months. *Parenting: Science and Practice, 6,* 167–88.

Shek, D. T. L. (1998). Adolescents' perceptions of paternal and maternal parenting styles in a Chinese context. *Journal of Psychology: Interdisciplinary and Applied, 132,* 527–37.

Shwalb, D. W., Nakazawa, J., Yamamoto, T., and Hyun, J.-H. (2004). Fathering in Japanese, Chinese, and Korean cultures: A review of the research literature. In M. E. Lamb (Ed.), *The role of the father in child development* (fourth ed., 146–81). New York: Wiley.

Smith, R. (2005). *Mexican New York: Transnational lives of new immigrants.* Berkeley: University of California Press.

Solis-Camara, P., and Fox, R. A. (1995). Parenting among mothers with young children in Mexico and the United States. *Journal of Social Psychology, 135*, 591–99.

Sonenstein, F. L., and Calhoun, C. A. (1990). Determinants of child support: A pilot study of absent parents. *Contemporary Policy Issues, 8*, 75–94.

Suárez-Orozco, C., and Suárez-Orozco, M. (2001). *Children of immigration* (first ed.). Cambridge, MA: Harvard University Press.

Suárez-Orozco, C., Todorova, I. L. G., and Louie, J. (2002). Making up for lost time: The experience of separation and reunification among immigrant families. *Family Process, 41*, 625–43.

Super, C. M., and Harkness, S. (1986). The developmental niche: A conceptualization at the interface of child and culture. *International Journal of Behavioral Development. Special Issue: Cross-cultural human development, 9*, 545–69.

Tamis-LeMonda, C. S. (2003). Cultural perspectives on the "What?" and "Whys?" of parenting. *Human Development, 46*, 319–27.

———. (2004). Conceptualizing fathers' roles: Playmates and more. *Human Development, 47*, 220–27.

Tamis-LeMonda, C., and Cabrera, N. (2002). Multidisciplinary perspectives on fatherhood: An introduction. In C. S. Tamis-LeMonda and N. Cabrera (Eds.), *Handbook of father involvement: Multidisciplinary perspectives* (xi–xvii). Mahwah, NJ: Erlbaum.

Tamis-LeMonda, C. S., Kahana-Kalman, R., Kowalczyk, M., and Rojas, P. (2007). Cultural beliefs and practices at the transition to parenting: Dominican, Mexican, American, and Chinese families. Invited talk, Columbia University, March 2007.

Tamis-LeMonda, C. S., Shannon, J. D., Cabrera, N., and Lamb, M. E. (2004). Fathers and mothers at play with their 2- and 3-year olds. *Child Development, 75*, 1806–1820.

Tamis-LeMonda, C. S., Way, N., Hughes, D., Yoshikawa, H., Kahana-Kalman, R., and Niwa, E. Y. (2008). Parents' goals for children: The dynamic co-existence of individualism and collectivism in cultures and individuals. *Social Development, 17*, 183–209.

Tamis-LeMonda, C. S., Yoshikawa, H., Kahana-Kalman, R., Niwa, E., and Castellano, J. (in preparation). Fathers' prenatal involvement and activities with infants: Predictors of the mother-father relationship. To appear in *Sex Roles*.

Varela, R. E., Vernberg, E. M., Sanchez-Sosa, J. J., Riveros, A., Mitchell, M., and Mashunkashey, J. (2004). Parenting style of Mexican, Mexican American, and Caucasian-non-Hispanic families: Social context and cultural influences. *Journal of Family Psychology, 18*, 651–57.

Vygotsky, L. S. (1962). *Thought and language* (E. Hanfmann and G. Vakar, Trans.). New York: MIT Press and Wiley. (Original work published 1934.)

Wilson, R. W. (1974). *The moral state: A study of the political socialization of Chinese and American children.* New York: Free Press.

Wu, D. Y. H. (1996). Chinese childhood socialization. In M. H. Bond (Ed.), *The handbook of Chinese psychology* (143–54). New York: Oxford University Press.

Yeung, W. J., Duncan, G. J., and Hill, M. S. (2000). Putting fathers back in the picture: Parental activities and children's adult outcomes. *Marriage & Family Review. Special Issue: Fatherhood: Research interventions and policies, 29*, 97–113.

Yeung, W. J., Linver, M. R., and Brooks-Gunn, J. (2002). How money matters for young children's development: Parental investment and family processes. *Child Development, 73*, 1861–79.

Yoshikawa, H. (1999). Welfare dynamics, support services, mothers' earnings, and child cognitive development: Implications for contemporary welfare reform. *Child Development, 70*, 779–801.

Yoshikawa, H., Godfrey, E., Rivera, A., and Tamis-LeMonda, C. S. (2006, November). *Institutional and policy exclusion among low-income immigrant families: Implications for economic hardship and parenting activities.* Paper presented at the annual meeting of the Association for Public Policy Analysis and Management, Madison, WI.

Yoshikawa, H., and Longo, F. (2007). Occupations of low-income immigrant parents. Unpublished data.

Yoshikawa, H., Lugo-Gil, J., and Tamis-LeMonda, C. (2006). How lower-income immigrant parents in New York City navigate U.S. programs and policies for children. Manuscript in preparation.

Yoshikawa, H., McCartney, K., Myers, R., Bub, K., Lugo-Gil, J., Knaul, F., and Ramos, M. (2007). *Preschool education in Mexico: Expansion, Quality Improvement, and Curricular Reform.* Florence, Italy: UNICEF Innocenti Research Centre Working Paper. Available at http://www.unicef-irc.org/publications/pdf/iwp_2007_03.pdf.

Zuniga, M. E. (1992). Families with Latino roots. In E. W. Lynch and M. J. Hanson (Eds.), *Developing cross-cultural competence: A guide for working with young children and their families* (151–79). Baltimore: Paul H. Brookes Publishing.

12

Studying Immigrant Fathering: Methodological and Conceptual Challenges

Joseph H. Pleck

This chapter analyzes challenges in studying immigrant fathering in the United States. The issues discussed concern: 1) sampling and recruitment, 2) research design and analysis, and 3) fathering constructs and dynamics. Some of the research challenges discussed are unique to investigations of immigrant fathers while others arise in fatherhood research more generally.

The sampling and recruitment issues considered here include: defining exactly who immigrant fathers are, and recruiting them. The challenges in research design and analysis discussed are: employing fathers, mothers, or both as informants about fathering; using comparative data about mothering; analyzing the pros and cons of immigrant-only and immigrant/non-immigrant designs; analyzing the pros and cons of national survey datasets for studying immigrant fathering; and addressing the interrelationships among immigrant status, race-ethnicity, and SES. Particular attention is given to the fathering constructs and dynamics investigated in research on immigrant fathers. Considered here are challenges in assessing the applicability of existing constructs in fathering research, especially father involvement, to immigrant fathers; developing new fathering constructs based on the experience of immigrant fathers; and assessing the relevance of fathering dynamics studied in existing fathering research to immigrant fathers, and exploring additional dynamics. Each of these challenges provides new directions and opportunities for immigrant father research.

SAMPLING AND RECRUITMENT

Defining Immigrant Fathers

Before a researcher can draw a sample of immigrant fathers, exactly who "immigrant fathers" are needs to be defined. The definition used by U.S. Census demographers is that immigrant fathers are those fathers who live with their dependent children (biological or step), and 1) who themselves were born outside the United States, and/or 2) who live with a foreign-born wife (Hernandez and Brandon, 2004). By this definition, immigrant fathers constitute about 20 percent of U.S. fathers with resident children in 1999, a percentage likely to many to be surprisingly high. Considering this definition in some detail can help researchers clarify how the definition of immigrant fathers for purposes of their particular studies may need to differ from it. National origin is undoubtedly the single most important aspect of diversity among immigrant fathers. But reflecting on the census definition calls attention to other potentially important facets of immigrant fathers' diversity that researchers should consider in defining immigrant fathers in a specific study.

The Hernandez-Brandon definition is a reasonable one, but it does exclude some subgroups that might be considered to be immigrant fathers in some research contexts. First, this definition concerns only fathers who are currently coresident with their minor children. Immigrant fathers with only adult children in the United States are not included. Immigrant fathers whose minor children are not living with them because the fathers immigrated first themselves and plan to bring their children at a later time are excluded. Also excluded are fathers whose minor children are residing elsewhere in the United States, due to disruption of the father-mother relationship or other reasons. Likewise, fathers born and living abroad whose children reside in the United States are not included. In addition, the definition's criterion 2 concerns native-born fathers with foreign-born wives. Other native-born fathers may reside with children of a foreign-born resident female partner who is not their wife, and are therefore not included. Thus, for some research purposes (e.g., investigating fathers whose children are adults, fathers whose children will come to the United States at a later time, relationships with children of divorced/separated fathers, unmarried fathers), the Hernandez-Brandon definition is too restrictive.

It is also important to recognize that the Hernandez-Brandon definition contains subgroups whose experience may vary from each other in important ways. Foreign-born fathers may or may not be the biological fathers of the minor children in their households. Likewise, foreign-born fathers with minor resident children may or may not have a resident co-parent, whom they may be married to or not. Another example is that the definition includes both fathers who are immigrants themselves (criterion 1) as well as native-born fathers whose wives are immigrants (criterion 2). Men meeting criterion 1 only, vs. criterion 2 only, vs. both, may differ from each other in ways that have implications for their role with the children. Also, within criterion 2, there are many different pathways by which native-born men form marital unions with foreign-born partners, likewise potentially influencing the native-born father's behavior and identity with his children. In addition, for men considered immigrant fathers because they meet criterion 2 only, their foreign-born wives may or may not be the biological mothers of the father's children. Perhaps most important, immigrant fathers include both those whose children are born outside the United States, those whose children are born inside the United States, and those with some of each.

Of course, the potential implications of immigration for fathering do not stop with the father born outside the United States (or with a foreign-born wife) himself. U.S.-born fathers, one or both of whose parents were born outside the United States, are also touched by the immigration experience. Expanding the definition of immigrant fathers to include this additional group would dramatically increase the estimate of the proportion of U.S. fathers classified as immigrants, to likely at least 40 percent. Study of the impact of paternal immigration across more than one generation necessarily has to go beyond the Hernandez-Brandon definition.

Thus, for purposes of a particular study, defining who immigrant fathers are requires that the researchers explicitly decide whether any of the groups noted above who fall outside the Hernandez-Brandon definition (e.g., unmarried fathers) are included. Investigators should also decide whether any of the subgroups noted above who do fall within the definition (e.g., U.S.-born fathers whose wives are immigrants) should be excluded from the study.

Finally, going beyond the issues of sample inclusion and exclusion raised by the Hernandez-Brandon definition, a number of special subgroups of fathers are receiving increasing attention in mainstream fatherhood research, such as teen fathers, incarcerated or formerly incarcerated fathers, gay fathers, fathers of children with special needs and fathers with special needs themselves, and primary caregiving fathers. Those studying immigrant fathers should be explicit about whether or not their samples include these subgroups.

Recruiting Immigrant Fathers

Some of the challenges in sample recruitment in immigrant father research are shared with fatherhood research in general, while others are more specific to immigrant fathers. In the former category, it is endemic to family research that fathers are harder to recruit than mothers (Costigan and Cox, 2001). Further, in most research, fathers are recruited through mothers. When this is the case, paternal selection bias (i.e., the fathers who participate not being representative of all eligible fathers) can occur for several different reasons. If the biological father is non-resident, the mother may not know where he is, and in some cases may not even know who he is. If she knows where he is, she may not have a routine way of contacting him. If she has a routine way of contacting him, she may decline to pass on recruiting materials, or allow him to be contacted for recruitment, because of conflict in the co-parental relationship, or because she has a new resident or non-resident partner who is functioning as a social father to the children and who is not comfortable with her contacting the biological father. In this situation, it may not be clear to the researcher whom to consider the child's "father": the biological father, the social father, or both.

Even when the biological father (or a step or other social father) is co-resident with the mother, she may simply decline to assist in recruiting him for a variety of reasons. Also, some resident fathers are raising children alone, and thus are not recruitable through the usual procedure of working through resident mothers. Finally, when successfully reached for recruitment, fathers themselves may simply decline. It would be valuable to study the extent to which father selection bias is greater or less in immigrant than in non-immigrant families, and if so, which of the above factors promoting it occur more or less frequently.

My experience in the Healthy Families/Healthy Fathers project, conducted in 2005 with Brent McBride and Aaron Ebata, illustrates some of the general difficulties in recruiting fathers as well as barriers more unique to recruiting immigrant fathers. The project's objective was to develop a needs assessment of the service and program needs of the fathers of children in at-risk families whose mothers were currently receiving home visiting and/or group services from an Illinois social service agency, of whom an estimated 20 percent were immigrant families from Mexico. The protocol involved conducting focus groups and interviews with both mothers and fathers. Because the families were receiving social services, they were a vulnerable population from a human subjects (IRB) perspective, and in addition, HIPAA (Health Insurance Portability and Accountability Act of 1996) rules applied. Our recruiting procedure was that the family service worker, while on a routine service visit, briefly described the study to the mother, and if she wanted to learn more, offered the mother a release of information form to sign so that her name and address could be released to a project recruiter who would accompany the worker on the next service visit. At this later visit, the project recruiter would accompany the family service worker, and while the family service worker went to another room, discuss the study with the mother, have the mother sign an informed consent if she agreed to participate, and offer the mother a paternal recruiting flyer to pass on to the father.

There were three respects in which recruiting immigrant Latino fathers was more difficult than other fathers. First, the majority of the Latino mothers in the program were minors whose parents were in Mexico. Thus, there was no realistic way to get written parental consent for these mothers' participation. Even though the fathers of their children were not minors, by being thus ineligible to participate themselves, these mothers were unlikely to help recruit their partners. Second, Latino adult mothers seemed to feel less comfortable inviting their partners to participate than did other mothers. Third, Latino fathers were more likely than other fathers to hold multiple jobs, decreasing the likelihood of their participation even if interested in the study. Given that our recruiting entry point was the group of mothers who were already receiving services, we did not directly observe legal status as a barrier in father recruitment. Nonetheless, it likely had an indirect negative impact on immigrant father recruitment by limiting mothers' program access. Only one father was successfully recruited for the project, and thus mothers were the primary informants for our assessment of fathers' service needs.

RESEARCH DESIGN AND ANALYSIS

Who Provides the Data about Fathering?

In designing a study of immigrant fathers, one of the first choices a researcher has to make is: from whom will the data about fathers and their fathering be collected? The three main options are fathers only, mothers only, and both fathers and mothers. (In studies of father-child relationships with adolescent or adult children, the child is, of course, another potential informant.) In making the design choice regarding fathers and/or mothers as informants, two kinds of potential bias are at issue—selection bias and reporting bias.

Selection bias (those actually participating in a study not being representative of those eligible) is usually substantial if fathers are the sole informants about fathering. In a particularly comprehensive analysis, Costigan and Cox (2001) reported that fathers who participated in research underrepresented those who were racial-ethnic minorities and who were working-class, as well as those with less education, in more ambivalent marriages, with partners with more traditional childrearing beliefs, in families with less optimal parenting environments, and with infants who were unplanned, had more difficult temperaments, and were less healthy.

Reporting bias is also a potential problem. Fathers may overreport their level of involvement because it is considered socially desirable by most people. Several studies, however, have found fathers' reports of their involvement to be unrelated to measures of social desirability response set

(De Luccie, 1996; Palkovitz, 1984). Nonetheless, in light of the potential for fathers' overreporting bias, combined with selection bias, it might seem that using mothers as informants about fathering is generally the best design choice. If mothers are the informants, then data can be collected about fathering even for fathers who do not or would not participate in the research themselves.

However, although using mothers as informants avoids potential paternal overreporting bias and leads to samples that are more representative of the sample frame, some scholars have expressed the concern that mothers may have reporting biases of their own, specifically, that they may *underreport* paternal involvement (Coley and Morris, 2002). One solution is, of course, to collect data from both mother and father, and combine these data in some way. This strategy minimizes or at least addresses reporting bias. Unfortunately, however, restricting analysis to families in which both parents' reports are available leads to the same selection bias that occurs when fathers are used as the only informants. Thus, while the multi-informant approach may reduce reporting bias, it does so at the cost of increasing selection bias.

Although the father-mother multiple informant design has the problem of selection bias, data from studies using this design provide information helpful in deciding to what extent reporting bias by either parent is a potential difficulty. Of course, one should be clear at the outset that these data cannot be used to determine how "accurate" either fathers or mothers are in reporting father involvement. Such data can show the accuracy of, for example, fathers only if one assumes mothers' reports are completely accurate, a "gold standard" against which fathers' reports can be compared—an untenable assumption. Nonetheless, these data are informative.

Several studies using father-mother pairs have found high agreement between fathers' reports of their involvement and wives' assessments (Pleck and Masciadrelli, 2004; Wical and Doherty, 2005). The father-mother correlations in these studies appear higher than those reported in past studies for father-child agreement about father acceptance, rejection, discipline, and closeness (Marsiglio, Amato, Day, and Lamb, 2000). When differences exist, fathers rate their participation higher than mothers do, but the differences are small (Coley and Morris, 2002; Deutsch, Lozy, and Saxon, 1993). Importantly, though, fathers' and mothers' reports of paternal involvement may differ more in divorced families (Braver et al., 1993; but see Coley and Morris, 2002) as well as in high-conflict relationships (Coley and Morris, 2002).

For researchers who elect to collect data about father involvement from only one parent, these findings have two implications. First, if data from only fathers are collected, these data are likely to be relatively concordant with data from mothers had such data been collected. However, the researcher should note that the results obtained might not be as generalizable to fathers in high-conflict relationships as to other fathers.

Second, if data from only mothers are collected, the same qualification needs to be made but even more strongly. Recall that because of fathers' low participation rates in research, one of the major potential benefits of using maternal reports is obtaining data about more fathers, and from a more representative proportion of eligible families, than if the researcher used data collected only directly from fathers themselves. That is, the main "value added" by using data from mothers only is getting assessments about those fathers who would not have provided data about themselves. But how valid are mothers' reports about these additional fathers likely to be? As already noted, families in which the father declines to participate in research have higher conflict than those in which he does. In samples in which data from both parents are available, discrepancies are greater in the higher-conflict relationships. Thus, although using data from mothers adds to the number of fathers about whom data is collected, the data about these additional fathers is less likely to be concordant with fathers' own reports, had they been collected. In essence, using data from mothers alone (compared to from fathers alone, or from both parents) does increase the sample, but in doing so disproportionately increases the number of cases in which mothers' data about father involvement are discrepant from fathers' actual or potential data.

Overall, deciding whether to collect data about fathering from fathers only, mothers only, or both fathers and mothers involves weighing the relative importance of minimizing selection bias and reporting bias. Costigan and Cox (2001) conclude that self-selection bias is a greater threat to validity in fathering research than is reporting bias, thus recommending mothers as informants. But their conclusion assumes that the relatively high similarity between mother and father reports in studies where both parents' data are available shows that reporting bias is minimal. However, as argued above, when mothers are used as informants in order to reduce selection bias, mothers' reporting bias may greater than it is in the samples on which the finding of high mother-father reporting similarity and the conclusion of low maternal reporting bias is based. Thus, it is difficult to determine whether, in general, selection or reporting bias is the greater threat. In selecting informant(s) about fathering, researchers need to weigh the risks of each kind of bias in their particular research context.

Finally, an additional consideration influencing the decision about father or mother as informant is the issue of same-informant bias (i.e., data being related simply because they are collected from the same person). If the data collected about fathering will be compared to other data collected from fathers themselves (e.g., in a study of the father characteristics that predict father involvement), collecting the data about fathering from mothers will avoid same-informant bias.

Using Comparative Data about Mothering

In addition to deciding whom to collect data about fathers *from*, researchers face another critical design choice: whether to collect data *about* fathers only, or about both fathers and mothers. These "father-only" and "comparative father-mother" designs each have strengths and weaknesses. In father-only designs, a key limitation is that the researcher cannot determine whether any results obtained are unique to fathers, or might apply to mothers as well. For example, if a father-only study finds that fathers' control predicts good child outcomes, we cannot know whether this shows a unique paternal effect (father control but not mother control influences the outcomes) or a generic parental effect (father control predicts the outcomes, but mother control does as well).

This issue is especially important in studies of the association between child outcomes and father involvement, since father involvement and mother involvement with the child are usually moderately correlated. If maternal involvement with the child is not controlled for, apparent associations between paternal involvement and child outcomes do not establish a direct linkage between the two because they do not establish that paternal involvement has a linkage with the outcomes *independent* of maternal involvement (Pleck, 1997; Pleck and Masciadrelli, 2004)

Comparative father-mother designs do make it possible to determine whether particular associations between fathering and other variables show something unique to fathering rather than generic to parenting. These designs also provide coparental context, making possible an understanding of fathering and mothering as part of the broader process of coparenting. One cost of this design is that because research resources are finite, collecting data from mothers inevitably reduces the amount of data collected from fathers. Perhaps the principal concern about this design, however, is that collection of data about both fathers and mothers inherently may imply a "deficit model" of fathering. That is, mothers' behavior, attitudes, and values may implicitly be considered a benchmark against which fathers are compared. For a discussion of this issue, see Pleck and Stueve (2001).

Analyzing the Pros and Cons of Immigrant-Only and Immigrant/Non-Immigrant Designs in Smaller-Scale Studies

A third important design question is whether or not to employ a comparison group of non-immigrant fathers, a question raising some of the same issues as whether or not to include a comparison group of mothers. On the one hand, being able to make comparisons has potential value. On the other hand, it potentially implies a deficit model in which non-immigrant fathers are considered the normative group in comparison to which immigrant fathers are viewed as variant, even deviant—by consumers of the research even if not by the researchers themselves. In addition, collecting data from non-immigrant fathers reduces resources available for data collection from immigrant fathers themselves.

Whether an immigrant-only or immigrant/non-immigrant design is used, researchers can choose to study only one immigrant group or multiple immigrant groups. Subgroups with varying acculturation levels, or varying SES, or located in different sites, may or may not be employed. The design tradeoff here is obtaining greater depth of information for one immigrant group, or subpopulation within that group, vs. being able to make comparisons across groups, acculturation level, SES, or site.

Analyzing the Pros and Cons of Using National Survey Datasets

Nationally representative or other large-scale national datasets such as the National Longitudinal Surveys of Youth (NLSY79, NLSY97), the National Survey of Families and Households (NSFH), the National Longitudinal Survey of Adolescent Health (Add Health), the Child Development Supplement of the Panel Study of Income Dynamics (CDS-PSID), the Early Childhood Longitudinal Study—Birth Cohort (ECLS-B), the Fragile Families and Child Well-Being (FFCW) study, Early Head Start (EHS), and the National Survey of Adolescent Males (NSAM) offer opportunities for analyses of fatherhood (Cabrera et al., 2002). Since information about immigrant status is available and racial-ethnic minorities are overrepresented, these and similar datasets provide particular opportunities for research on immigrant fathers.

Use of these datasets presents a tradeoff. On the one hand, the data come from large samples of known representativeness, are easily available to researchers, and are already used by many scholars so that findings from different analyses can be compared to and build on each other. The disadvantages are that they do not have large subsamples of specific national origin groups, and do not have the breadth and depth of measures necessary for many research purposes. In addition, in the longitudinal component of nationally representative datasets, immigration subsequent to the first wave makes each follow-up wave less representative of the current U.S. population in terms of the inclusion of recent immigrants. To address this problem, at later follow-up waves some survey programs such as the PSID add an "immigrant refresher" subsample to the core sample (in later waves, adding a subsample of immigrants to reflect recent immigration, so that the sample better represents the current U.S. population). This certainly helps, although measures needed for a particular research purpose may have been collected only in waves prior to the immigrant refresher.

Addressing the Interrelationships among Immigrant Status, Race-Ethnicity, and SES

Immigrant status, race-ethnicity, and socioeconomic status (SES) are interrelated. Hernandez and Brandon (2004) provide results from the census's 1999 Current Population Survey detailing the extent of these associations at the national level. For example, fathers in different racial-ethnic groups varied in the proportion who were immigrants: 65.9 percent of Hispanic fathers and 75.5 percent of other race, non-Hispanic fathers (primarily Asian) were immigrants, compared to 12.5 percent of black, non-Hispanic fathers and 8.3 percent of white, non-Hispanic fathers. Likewise, immigrant fathers were more likely to be Hispanic or of other race than to be white or black non-Hispanics, although the proportion of immigrant fathers who were white is higher than some might have expected: 44.5 percent of immigrant fathers in 1999 were Hispanic, 19.4 percent of other race, 30.7 percent white, and 5.4 percent black (calculated from Hernandez and Brandon, 2004, table 2.3). Levels of completed education also vary markedly by combinations of race-ethnicity and immigrant status (table 2.7). Of course, since immigration patterns have changed markedly over recent decades and are likely to continue to change, the degree and nature of the interrelationships among immigrant status, race-ethnicity, and socioeconomic indicators such as education may shift over time.

The confounds potentially introduced by these interrelationships are particularly evident in research using national datasets, but arise in smaller-scale purposive samples as well, especially samples of a single immigrant group who are relatively homogeneous in race-ethnicity and SES. Analyzing the conceptual issues in addressing these interrelationships is beyond the scope of this chapter (but see Bornstein and Bradley, 2003; Bornstein and Cote, 2006; Mahalingam, 2006), but one important practical concern can be discussed briefly.

An issue frequently arising in analyses of large-scale datasets concerns whether immigrant status and Latino or Hispanic ethnicity can be used simultaneously as predictor variables in multivariate models. The usual practice is to assume that they are so highly correlated that both cannot be used at the same time because there would be substantial multicollinearity, causing the estimates of the two variables' effects to be unstable. Analysts almost always give priority to Latino ethnicity, omitting immigrant status. When effects are found for Hispanic ethnicity, analysts often (but not always) note its potential confound with immigrant status.

A recent analysis of predictors of traditional beliefs about masculinity using data from the 1988 National Survey of Adolescent Males (NSAM), conducted with my colleague Arik Marcel, has led me to reconsider this standard analytical practice (Marcel, Sonenstein, and Pleck, 2006). In the weighted 1988 national representative sample of fifteen- to nineteen-year-old males, 9.3 percent were Hispanic, and 6 percent were born outside of the United States. Marcel, whose background is in adolescent medicine and public health, did not "know" that one cannot include both Latino ethnicity and immigrant status as simultaneous predictors in a regression model. When I learned that both had been included in the initial analyses, we performed the tests for multicollinearity (the tolerance test, and the variable inflation factor [VIF] test). Although some other predictors did show multicollinearity, these two did not. The association between the two may have been relatively weak in the 1988 NSAM (and weaker than in some other datasets) because in the late 1980s cohort of U.S. teenagers, immigration by Hispanics (compared to non-Hispanics) had been relatively low compared to later cohorts. In bivariate analyses, masculinity beliefs were not significantly associated with either Hispanic ethnicity (vs. Euro-American) or immigrant status. However, in multivariate analyses including both these and additional demographic and substantive variables, being foreign-born had a significant association with more traditional beliefs about masculinity (and Hispanic ethnicity did not). If immigrant status had not been included in the model, its association to masculinity beliefs would have been overlooked.

Hofferth and Fitzgerald's (2004) analysis using the 1997 Child Development Supplement (CDS) of the Panel Study of Income Dynamics (PSID) illustrates another approach to analyzing immigrant status and race-ethnicity simultaneously. The sample used in the analysis included, first, 179 first- and second-generation immigrant children (child born outside the United States; child born in the United States of parents born outside the United States) in the 1997 immigrant refresher CDS subsample. Another three hundred children in the analysis sample included all families of Hispanic origin in the main CDS sample, and a random group of other race-ethnicities from the main sample, selected to maintain comparable sample sizes with those in the immigrant refresher sample. The 179 immigrant children included 132 first- or second-generation Hispanic children, thirty-six Asian first- or second-generation children, and eleven other first- or second-generation children. Dummy variables representing these three groups, together with a dummy variable representing third-generation Hispanic children in the main sample (both child and parents born in the United States, grandparents born abroad), were used in multivariate analyses of the primary caregiver's warmth, emotional support, cognitive stimulation, activities with the child, and monitoring. Analyses found, for example, that parents of Hispanic first- and second-generation children were significantly lower on monitoring than white parents, while parents of Hispanic third-generation children differed little. Further analyses showed that first- and second-generation Hispanic parents' lower monitoring was mediated by socioeconomic factors, family structure, and parental values.

Thus, in national datasets it is recommended not to simply assume that immigrant status is too confounded with race-ethnicity and SES to conduct analyses by immigrant status. Given the fluctuating nature of immigration to the U.S., researchers need to be cautious of overreiying on accepted analytical conventions such as not analyzing race-ethnicity and immigrant status simultaneously. Researchers should actually perform formal tests for multicollinearity before dropping immigrant status, or create pattern variables combining race-ethnicity and immigrant status.

FATHERING CONSTRUCTS

Assessing the Applicability of Existing Constructs in Fathering Research, Especially Father Involvement

In human development and family studies research, researchers have sometimes applied constructs that were developed on white, often only middle-class samples to other groups in an uncritical way. Parental style research presents an especially relevant example. When research on parental style was extended to diverse race-ethnic groups, it was found that the most frequent parental style in Asian American parents was authoritarian. However, this finding was problematic in that numerous prior studies in Euro-American samples had shown that the authoritative style is associated with the best academic and psychosocial outcomes in children and adolescents. Yet Asian American adolescents, whose parents were typically authoritarian, showed higher average academic performance than did adolescents from Euro-American and African American families, in which the authoritative style was the most prevalent. Further, within African American families, academic performance was higher among children whose parents were authoritarian rather than authoritative (Chao, 1994; Steinberg, Dornbusch, and Brown, 1999). These findings presented a considerable challenge to the parenting education field, since promoting authoritative parenting has traditionally been central to parenting programs.

For the last two decades, "father involvement" (Lamb, Pleck, Charnov, and Levine, 1985; Pleck, Lamb, and Levine, 1985) has been a foundational construct in fathering research. The nature of the samples from which the construct was developed, and the extent to which it may overlook aspects of fatherhood that are more important in racial-ethnic minority fathers, non-middle-class fathers, and by extension immigrant fathers, will therefore be briefly assessed. The section then reviews the ways that father involvement is conceptualized and operationalized in recent research, followed by discussion of other important current fathering constructs and their potential applicability to immigrant fathers.

On Whose Experience Was the Father Involvement Construct Based?

It is sometimes thought that the father involvement construct was developed using data from only white, middle-class fathers, therefore overlooking aspects of fatherhood potentially more important in racial-ethnic minority fathers, non-middle-class fathers, and by extension immigrant fathers. In particular, some have been concerned that the application of the involvement construct to non-white, lower SES, and immigrant fathers could lead to the erroneous conclusion that these fathers are less involved, and therefore "deficient" (Palkovitz, 1997).

Actually, the primary data for Lamb and Pleck's formulation of paternal involvement came from time diary and other time use studies with large representative national samples in which race-ethnic minorities were overrepresented. Use of these samples made it possible to characterize levels of involvement for diverse groups. Although data on diverse subgroups were not emphasized in the publications first presenting the involvement construct (Lamb et al., 1985; Pleck et al., 1985), they are discussed elsewhere (Pleck, 1983, 1985, 1997).

Concern that the involvement construct entails a deficit perspective on fathers who are not white and middle-class appears to assume that when the construct *is* applied to those fathers, the data will give the misleading impression that non-white, non-middle-class fathers are less involved with their children. However, in the data available for two-parent families, majority fathers and racial-ethnic minority fathers either show no differences in average level of involvement, or the differences found favor minority fathers. The same pattern holds true for comparisons by educational level, income, and occupational prestige (Pleck, 1997; Pleck and Masciadrelli, 2004). Thus, in light of the samples on which the construct was developed as well as the data available about it in diverse groups, use of the involvement construct does not appear to inherently entail a deficit perspective on non-white, non-middle-class fathers (Pleck and Stueve, 2001).

Father Involvement: Current Conceptualization and Operationalization

There has been debate about what the construct of father involvement as originally formulated by Lamb and Pleck *did* include, as well as debate about what the construct *should* include (Pleck and Stueve, 2001). Rather than review this debate, it is more valuable here to consider what the construct actually *does* include in current research. After giving an overview, an illustrative example of a recent study exploring father involvement in diverse racial-ethnic groups will be considered.

Lamb and Pleck (Lamb et al., 1985; Pleck et al., 1985) formulated paternal involvement as consisting of engagement (direct interaction with the child), accessibility (being available to the child), and responsibility (doing things for the child, and making sure the child is cared for). In later reviews, Pleck (1997; Pleck and Masciadrelli, 2004) noted that the conceptualization and operationalization of father involvement have evolved in later research in ways differing somewhat from the original conception. Of the engagement, accessibility, and responsibility components formulated by Lamb and Pleck, most attention has been given to engagement and responsibility (but see Yeung, Sandberg, Davis-Kean, and Hofferth, 2001).

First, the engagement component has continued to be assessed with time diaries, corresponding to Lamb and Pleck's original formulation. In particular, a time diary measure of paternal engagement is available in an important public-use national dataset, the 1997 Child Development Supplement (Child Development Supplement, 2006). However, engagement has most often been operationalized in recent research with measures of the frequency of specific activities such as play, reading, and having conversations (Hofferth et al., 2002; Marsiglio, 1991). The activities included are typically ones that promote development. Thus, the focus of engagement measures has shifted from only time spent to participation in positive, development-promoting activities with the child.

Second, paternal warmth or responsiveness to the child is increasingly included as an important aspect of paternal involvement, consistent with research showing their contribution to positive child outcomes. Evidence has accumulated that positive qualitative features such warmth and closeness are significantly correlated with frequency of positive engagement activities (Pleck and Masciadrelli, 2004). In addition, Pleck and Masciadrelli (2004) document how several measures now combine warmth or responsiveness with father's activity frequency. For example, Amato (1987) developed a summary "paternal support" variable combining frequency of positive paternal activities with the child's report of the father being a favorite person to have talks with, and the person in the family the child tells if he or she is really worried.

A final shift in the involvement construct concerns the responsibility component. In the original Lamb and Pleck formulation, responsibility included process responsibility (ensuring that the child's needs are being met, involving monitoring and coordinating), and indirect care (deciding about things and doing things for the child that do not involve direct interaction with the child) (Pleck and Stueve, 2001; Pleck and Masciadrelli, 2004). In recent father involvement research, fathers' monitoring of and decision-making about the child, which can be considered aspects of process responsibility, have received the most attention. There is some confirmation that monitoring is significantly correlated with frequency of engagement activities (Toth and Xu, 1999). In summary, current research is increasingly operationalizing father involvement with assessments of positive engagement activities rather than simply engagement time spent, of warmth and responsiveness, and of monitoring and decisionmaking.

Race-Ethnic Comparisons in Father Involvement: An Illustration

A study by Hofferth (2003) provides a good example of how recent research investigates paternal involvement, as well as provides illustrative findings on how diverse race-ethnic groups compare with each other. The analysis used the sample of two-parent families in the 1997 Child Development Supplement, a national representative sample in which African American and Hispanic families, as well as immigrants, were overrepresented. The study assessed paternal engagement time with a time diary measure, corresponding to Lamb and Pleck's original formulation of engagement. However, involvement was additionally operationalized with measures of paternal warmth, monitoring, and responsibility.

80 percent of the Hispanic fathers arrived in the United States in 1968 or later, with 75 percent of these of Mexican descent, and most of the remainder from Central America and a few from South America. In multivariate analyses with other variables controlled, black and Hispanic fathers did not differ significantly from whites in engagement. Immigrant status was not investigated directly as a potential predictor (as it was in Hofferth and Fitzgerald, 2004), but the lack of a significant difference associated with Hispanic ethnicity makes it unlikely that Hispanic immigrant fathers were less involved than other fathers in these data. On other involvement dimensions, black fathers were significantly less warm and more controlling than white fathers. Hispanic fathers were significantly warmer and more responsible than white fathers. Fathers of other races did not differ from white fathers on any of the four fathering components. In addition, with race-ethnicity controlled, fathers' education was not significantly related to the four involvement measures. The mixed pattern of differences and similarities among different racial ethnic groups does not appear to be interpretable as indicating that non-white groups show a "deficit" in father involvement compared to whites.

We now consider available engagement and responsibility measures in more detail. These measures are highlighted here because they are less well known than the measures available to assess warmth and responsiveness, and monitoring and decisionmaking, that are also currently used in fathering research.

Engagement Measures: Four Types

Researchers using the engagement component of involvement employ one or more of four different kinds of measures. The first is *time diaries*. In Hofferth (2003), primary caregivers (almost always mothers) completed time diaries for a target child aged zero to twelve in their family. For each activity, the caregiver reported "who was doing the activity with the child," "who (else) was there but not directly involved in the activity" and "what else was the child doing at the same time." Paternal engagement is coded as children's time in activities in which the father is listed as doing the activity with the child. In addition, paternal accessibility is coded as children's time in activities in which the father is noted as being present, but not directly involved in the child's activity. Table 12.1 includes an excerpt from a sample diary about a seven-year-old child (Child Development Supplement, 2006). In this example, the father would be coded as spending fifty-five minutes engaged with the child (5:30–6:25 p.m.), and an additional sixty-five minutes accessible to the child (6:25–7:30). In addition to coding total engagement and total accessibility time, it is of course possible to code for specific types of engagement activities.

A second approach is *time estimates*. This approach simply asks fathers to estimate how much time they spend in child-related tasks or activities. For example, the 1987–1988 National Survey of Families and Households (NSFH) asked parents with children under five "about how many hours in a typical day do you spend taking care of (child's) needs, including feeding, bathing, dressing, and putting him/her to bed?" (Blair and Hardesty, 1994). Time estimate measures produce considerably higher figures for engagement time than diary measures. Many researchers today regard time estimate

Table 12.1.   Excerpt from the Sample Diary of a Seven-Year-Old Child in the 1997 Child Development Supplement

What did your child do?	Time Began	Time Ended	Who was doing . . . with child?	Who else there . . . not directly involved with the child?
watching TV	5:30pm	6:00	father, cousin	mother
eating dinner	6:00	6:25	father, mother, cousin	
reading book	6:25	7:00		cousin, mother, father
computer games	7:00	7:30	cousin	mother, father

measures as imprecise measurements of the amount of time an individual parent spends with his or her children (Pleck, 1985; Sandberg and Hofferth, 2001). At the same time, correlations between time diary and time estimate measures of engagement are relatively high (e.g., .62 in Canada's 1988 General Social Survey, higher than the parallel diary-estimate correlations for work and for housework) (Zuzanek, 2000). Engagement time estimates are often converted to proportional measures (i.e., father's proportion of the total time spent by both parents). Since the exact wording may vary in time estimate questions, converting the results to proportions makes it possible to compare results across studies. Respondents could be asked to estimate their accessibility time, but existing research has rarely done this.

The third assessment approach is *activity frequency measures*. Here, fathers are asked to report how frequently they engage in specific activities. For example, in the 1987–1988 NSFH fathers with preschool children were asked about the frequency of three activities with their child or children: outings away from home (e.g., parks, zoos, museums), playing at home, and reading, with six response categories ranging from never to almost every day. Men with school-aged (five to eighteen) children reported the frequency of leisure activities, working on projects or playing at home, private talks, and helping with reading and doing homework (Marsiglio, 1991). Other examples include the caregiving subscale of Bruce and Fox's (1997; Fox and Bruce, 2001) paternal involvement scale, and the thirteen-item parental activity scale in the 1997 CDS (Hofferth et al., 2002). It is important to realize that the specific activities included in these measures are not necessarily intended to represent engagement activities proportional to their frequency of occurrence. As suggested by the examples above, items focus on more interactive or "quality" engagement (i.e., forms of engagement likely to promote development). Finally, Radin's (1994) Paternal Index of Child Care Involvement (PICCI) contains an accessibility subscale that actually includes some engagement items (e.g., how often father has breakfast during the week with children and family).

The fourth approach is *relative engagement measures*. These measures ask fathers (or mothers) how engagement activities with the child are divided with the child's other parent. Common response categories are father entirely, father more than mother, equal, mother more than father, or mother entirely. Examples include the subscales assessing childcare and child socialization engagement in Radin's (1994) PICCI. Like frequency measures, these relative engagement measures tend to focus on "quality" engagement activities.

Thus, four general strategies to assess paternal engagement are available for use in research on immigrant fathers. Activity frequency and relative engagement measures have been used far more often than time diaries and time estimates. Recent research employing time use measures generally supplements them with activity frequency and relative engagement measures. Each strategy has advantages and disadvantages. The first two time-oriented engagement measures may be more appropriate in research concerning time trends in engagement and accessibility, and concerning the parental division of labor and its consequences for wives and marital dynamics. The latter frequency and relative engagement measures focus on more interactive forms of engagement, and thus may have greater value in research on the consequences of paternal engagement for children and for fathers themselves. Both sets of measures may have value in the exploration of sources of involvement.

Responsibility

The responsibility component of paternal involvement has been operationalized in more diverse ways than engagement or accessibility (Pleck and Stueve, 2001). Lamb et al.'s (1985, 884) definition included two subcomponents: "making sure that the child is taken care of" (process responsibility) and "arranging for resources to be available for the child" (indirect care). Two measures available clearly focus on process responsibility by asking parents to rate tasks in terms of who remembers, plans, and schedules them, regardless of who actually ends up doing them. McBride and Mills (1993) use this format for a set of indirect care tasks. Baruch and Barnett's (1986) measure employs a similar format for both indirect and direct care activities as well as housework.

The majority of existing measures intended to assess responsibility, however, do so by asking "who usually does" a list of activities, thus not addressing process in terms of taking initiative, monitoring, and planning. To be consistent with at least the second part of Lamb and Pleck's definition, only indirect care tasks should be included, e.g., the "executive functions" subscale of Bruce and Fox's (1997) paternal involvement scale. However, some other measures labeled as assessing responsibility actually focus on who does direct care activities, thus assessing engagement instead of responsibility. An example is Radin's (1994) PICCI subscales labeled "child care responsibility" and "socialization responsibility," which ask who usually does tasks like feeding the child and helping the child to learn. Other measures intended to assess responsibility ask who usually does both direct and indirect care activities. For example, Hofferth's (2003) responsibility scale asks parents to report who usually performs five indirect care tasks, but also includes direct care activities such as bathing, playing with, and disciplining children (cf. Hossain, 2001; Hwang and Lamb, 1997; Sanderson and Sanders-Thompson, 2002). Researchers on immigrant fathers who wish to explore paternal responsibility in Lamb and Pleck's sense should decide whether they will investigate responsibility as process responsibility, as indirect care, or both, and then use or modify existing measures.

Other Fathering Constructs Available for Use in Immigrant Father Research

Many other constructs from existing fatherhood research are available for use in studies of immigrant fathers. Paternal breadwinning or economic support is of course a central construct (Amato, 1998; Maurer and Pleck, 2006; Maurer, Pleck, and Rane, 2001). Paternal warmth and paternal monitoring have already been noted in Hofferth's (2003) CDS analysis. Other concepts important in existing fatherhood research include: attitudes about fatherhood (Palkovitz, 1984; Hofferth, 2003); paternal identity (Maurer et al., 2001; Rane and McBride, 2000; Stueve and Pleck, 2001); paternal generativity (Hawkins and Dollahite, 1997; Snarey, 1993; Snarey and Pleck, 1993); paternal investment (Whiteside-Mansell, Bradley, and Rakow, 2000); paternal ideology (Auerbach, Silverstein, and Zizi, 1997); paternal visions (Marsiglio et al., 2000); and paternal social capital (Pleck, 2007).

Paternal Identity and Constructions of the Paternal Role

Of these additional constructs just noted, paternal identity may have particular utility in immigrant father research. Paternal identity, framed in a symbolic interactionist perspective, can be viewed as a broader disposition that motivates involvement. In one approach, paternal identity is interpreted as broad and multidimensional, e.g., Ihinger-Tallman et al.'s (1993) operationalization of paternal identity as a composite of role satisfaction, self-perceived competence, investment (wanting to learn more about fathering), and role salience (the importance of fatherhood compared to other roles). However, these different components have differential empirical relationships with behavioral involvement (Minton and Pasley, 1996). In addition, paternal role satisfaction and competence are independent, theoretically established concepts in their own right, and the value of subsuming them within a broader construct of identity is not clear. A second body of research operationalizes paternal identity more narrowly as the importance of fatherhood to the individual, especially as compared to other roles, labeled with terms such as identity salience, identity commitment, or identity centrality. Perhaps surprisingly, the direct linkage between these narrower assessments of paternal identity and measures of fathers' behavioral involvement is actually disconfirmed (Maurer et al., 2001; McBride and Mills, 1993; Rane and McBride, 2000; Minton and Pasley, 1996; Sanderson and Sanders-Thompson, 2002) more often than it is confirmed (Fox and Bruce, 2001; Hossain and Roopnarine, 1994).

Future research on the problematic link between paternal identity and involvement needs to address several theoretical issues. Fathering (and parenting) includes multiple domains, for example, Stueve and Pleck's (2001) conceptualization of five domains: caregiving, promoting development, arranging and planning, breadwinning, and positive emotional relationship with the child. This multifaceted nature of fathering may account for why assessment of paternal identity as a father's rating of the importance of "fathering" to him does not have consistent associations with paternal behavior. Two fathers may both rate fathering as extremely important to them, but one may be thinking of caregiving while the other is focusing on breadwinning. If the behavioral measure being linked to identity focuses, for example, only on caregiving, it is not surprising that the association between importance of "fathering" and caregiving is weak, since not all respondents necessarily interpret "fathering" as emphasizing caregiving. By contrast, when research assesses identity salience at the domain level (e.g., caregiving), associations with the corresponding paternal behaviors are more consistent (Maurer, Pleck, and Rane, 2003).

In addition, the gender-incongruent nature of paternal involvement has theoretical implications for its link to identity. For example, behavior in gender-incongruent domains may have stronger association to the perceived expectations of others than to identity because identity in gender-incongruent roles is less clearly established. Consistent with this hypothesis, in Maurer et al.'s (2001) multivariate models, although paternal caregiving was not related to the level of fathers' own paternal caregiving identity, it was related to their perceptions of their wives' expectations about their caregiving.

The realization that paternal identity is most usefully conceptualized not as the importance to the father of "fathering" as a whole, but as the importance of particular fathering domains, has implications for future investigation of paternal identity. It suggests that an alternate approach to paternal identity is to assess the pattern or profile of the importance that the father attributes to various parenting domains. For example, one typical profile may ascribe much higher importance to breadwinning than to all other domains. Another profile may emphasize promotion of development, and arrangement and planning, and so forth. The concept of paternal identity as the father's "domain importance profile" may be of value in immigrant father research.

Developing New Fathering Constructs Based on the Experience of Immigrant Fathers

When researchers conduct research with groups previously unstudied or understudied, in addition to assessing and utilizing existing constructs, they should also develop new constructs derived from the experience of the group under investigation. A good illustration of this approach in prior research on immigrant parenting is Chao's (1994) work on Asian American parenting. As noted earlier, research on parental style was challenged by the apparent paradox that authoritarian style is the most frequent among Asian American parents, yet Asian American youth show higher average academic performance than other youth whose parents' modal style was authoritative. Based on an analysis of Chinese ideas about parenting, Chao argued that the Chinese concept of parental "training" (*guan*) has features that distinguish it from the authoritarian concept, in particular that it is not intended to dominate the child, that parents are responsible for providing positive models for the child, and that training occurs in the context of a supportive relationship with the child. Sample items in Chao's attitude scale for this construct included "the parent must train the child to work hard and be disciplined," and "parents express love by helping their child succeed."

In a sample of Chinese American and Euro-American mothers, Chao found that training is moderately correlated with standard measures of authoritarian parental style. But Chao then demonstrated that *guan* is nonetheless distinct from authoritarian parental style. She compared the subgroups within Chinese American and within Euro-American mothers who were classified as authoritarian. Although the two groups were matched on authoritarianism, the Chinese mothers scored significantly higher on training. This finding suggested that training is a distinct aspect of Chinese parenting, not identical to authoritarianism. Chao argued that Chinese parents' emphasis on training might account for children's school success.

Caughy et al.'s (2002) study of racial socialization in African American families provides another precedent for developing new parenting constructs based on the unique experience of a racial-ethnic group. Based on interviews and focus groups, the investigators conceptualized five aspects of African American parents' racial socialization: promotion of mistrust (of whites), preparation for bias, ethnic/racial pride, spirituality, and having an Africentric home environment. In structural equation modeling using data from two hundred families from thirty-nine Baltimore neighborhoods, parents' provision of an Africentric home environment was associated with their children having greater problem-solving skills and knowledge. In addition, parents' promotion of ethnic/racial pride was linked to their children having fewer problem behaviors.

Immigrant father research should develop new or revised fathering constructs based on the experience of immigrant fathers. For example, immigration itself may emerge as an important fathering construct (i.e., immigrant fathers may experience migration as a specifically paternal act to improve children's life chances). Another example is that generativity may need to be formulated in new and unique ways for immigrant fathers. Qualitative and mixed method research will clearly be important sources of new constructs.

The Relevance of Fathering Dynamics

Distinct from fatherhood constructs assessed at the level of the individual father are fathering *dynamics*, that is, the broad patterns of factors influencing fathering, and other relationships between fathering and other variables. Several dynamics explored in existing fatherhood research may be particularly relevant to immigrant fathers. In addition, their application to immigrant fathers may assist in the refinement or revision of our understanding of these dynamics in other fathering contexts. An admittedly incomplete list might include the following three dynamics.

Influence of Kin Networks on Fathering

Parents' social network is conceptualized as a major influence on parenting in Belsky's (1984) process model of parenting. Lamb and Pleck's four-factor model of the sources of father involvement (Lamb et al., 1985; Pleck et al., 1985) likewise includes social support as a central predictor. Empirical research on linkages between fathers' connections to their kin networks and their fathering, however, has been surprisingly limited (but see Riley, 1990; Bost et al., 2002). The influence of immigrant fathers' kin networks on their fathering is well worth study. On the one hand, immigrant fathers may have closer links to their kin networks than native-born fathers. On the other hand, some of their kin are still in their country of origin, which may or may not reduce their influence. Members of immigrant fathers' kin networks in the United States will also vary in their degree of acculturation, which may complicate how kinship influence operates.

Religious Influence on Fathering

The role of religion in fathering is starting to receive more attention (Silverstein, Auerbach, Grieco, and Dunkel, 1999; Wilcox, 2002; see also review in Pleck and Masciadrelli, 2004). Religion is often extremely important in immigrant families. An excellent example of research exploring the role of religion in immigrant fathering is Auerbach, Silverstein, and Zizi's (1997) analysis of how Haitian Americans used religious beliefs as a "facilitating ideology" to help them bridge the gap between the bicultural gender role strain concerning their ambivalence about the traditional Haitian father and a more gratifying definition of fatherhood.

Coparenting

Originally developed to describe parenting following divorce, the coparenting construct is now being applied to two-parent residential families (McHale et al., 2002). Coparenting has been variously defined as the extent to which parents cooperate as a team in rearing offspring (McHale, 1997), the quality of coordination between adults in their parental roles (McHale, Kuersten, Lauretti, and Rasmussen, 2000), and the relationship between adults in the family as coparents (Schoppe-Sullivan, Manglesdorf, Frosch, and McHale, 2004). Coparenting is conceptually close to Cohen and Weissman's (1984) concept of parenting alliance, which includes each parent investing in the child, each parent valuing the importance of the other parent, each parent respecting and valuing the judgments of the other parent, and ongoing means of communication between the parents. Stueve and Pleck's (2001; Pleck and Stueve, 2004) concept of parental identity "conjointness" can be interpreted as the manifestation of coparenting at the identity level. This construct refers to the balance between "self-as-parent" and "self-as-coparent" in a parent's identity, as expressed in parents' narratives.

The concept of coparenting is not without controversy. Some have questioned the value of distinguishing coparenting from the broader concept of marital (or relationship) quality. Proponents of the coparenting concept argue that although measures of coparenting are correlated with relationship quality measures, coparenting measures nonetheless account for unique variance in child outcomes beyond that predicted by broader measures of marital quality. They further hold that a family systems view of child development in family context conceptually fosters the use of coparenting as a construct distinct from the marital relationship (McHale et al., 2002; Schoppe-Sullivan et al., 2004).

The coparenting perspective provides a new "frame" in which to understand and link together a number of topics important in current fathering research previously studied in isolation. One such topic is the level of father involvement compared to mother involvement. The coparenting framework views this parental division of labor in parenting as just one element in a broader set of coparental processes. Another topic important in fatherhood research is the association between father involvement and parents' relationship quality. Some studies assume that involvement is the independent variable and relationship quality is the dependent variable, while others assume the opposite (Pleck, 1997; Pleck and Masciadrelli, 2004). In the coparenting perspective, both processes are part of a larger whole.

A final important fatherhood research topic that could benefit by being understood in a broader coparenting perspective is the proposition that father involvement is, in some deep and fundamental way, ultimately "mediated" by mothers (Ihinger-Tallman et al., 1993). The most obvious supporting evidence is that when the father-mother relationship is weakened, as in divorce, on average father involvement decreases markedly. The concept of maternal "gate keeping" (Allen and Hawkins, 1999; Fagan and Barnett, 2003) can be viewed as a more specific form of maternal mediation of paternal involvement.

Although there is evidence for maternal mediation and maternal gate keeping for divorced fathers (Maccoby, Mnookin, Depner, and Peters, 1992), the evidence is less clear in two-parent families. In particular, in large representative samples there is no association between father involvement and mothers' attitudes about fathering (Pleck and Masciadrelli, 2004). In any event, maternal mediation and gate keeping can be reframed as aspects of broader coparental process. Doing so would have brought attention earlier to the obverse process that Parke (2002) suggested, maternal "gate opening" (i.e., that some mothers actively facilitate fathers' involvement with their children). The coparenting perspective makes researchers alert to the possibility that fathers may likewise either facilitate or inhibit mothers' involvement.

These and other coparenting dynamics have not as yet received much attention in immigrant father research. As a historical note, it is intriguing to recall how immigrant status was explored as an influence of the marital division of labor in one of the foundational monographs in family studies, Blood and Wolfe's (1960) *Husbands and Wives*. In one of the study's central arguments, Blood and Wolfe held that the marital division of labor in household tasks and in decisionmaking is *not* determined by gender norms, but only by husbands' and wives' having differential "resources" such as time. To support this proposition, the researchers compared different subgroups in their Detroit-area sample, which they posited held more traditional or less traditional gender norms (which had not been directly assessed at the individual level). The groups they assumed had more traditional gender norms (and which they found did not show more traditional marital division of labor in either housework tasks or decisionmaking) included rural (vs. urban) families, and Catholic (vs. other) families—a not atypical view of Catholics in that era. Notable, though, among these comparisons was a table comparing immigrant vs. other families. No difference in marital division of labor was found. Blood and Wolfe's conclusion from their data was not that immigrant families did not in fact hold more traditional gender norms, but rather that immigrant families' presumed more traditional gender norms simply did not influence their behavior. This historical example illustrates how past research rather uncritically interpreted immigrant status as a proxy for "traditional" gender norms that potentially influence marital division of labor, and by extension coparental division of labor.

Future research should explore processes related to kinship networks, religion, and coparenting in immigrant fathers. As with the development of new fathering constructs, qualitative and mixed method research will clearly be important sources of new understanding of how these dynamics function in immigrant fathers. In addition, these research methods should explore dynamics arising more uniquely out of the experience of immigrant fathers (e.g., how children being more acculturated than their fathers influences the father-child relationship).

SUMMARY

Conducting research on immigrant fathers presents numerous challenges as well as opportunities. In sampling and recruiting, researchers must first define who immigrant fathers are for purposes of their studies. The U.S. Census definition, men living with dependent children, and who are foreign-born themselves and/or live with a foreign born wife, both excludes some groups who researchers might want to include in a particular study (e.g., non-resident fathers) as well as includes diverse subgroups, not all of whom may be appropriate to sample for a particular study (e.g., native-born fathers with foreign-born wives). Considering the census definition in some detail can serve to clarify how a researcher's definition of immigrant fathers for purposes of a particular study may need to differ from it. Researchers also need to be explicit about whether or not their sample includes special subgroups of fathers receiving increasing attention in mainstream father-hood research such as incarcerated or formerly incarcerated fathers, gay fa-thers, fathers of children with special needs, fathers with special needs, and primary caregiving fathers. In recruiting immigrant fathers, the researcher faces the challenges of recruiting fathers in general (e.g., their participation rate is lower than mothers, and they are typically recruited via mothers), as well as such additional challenges as legal status and mothers' comfort in helping recruit fathers.

Two major design choices arise in any study of fathering: whether fathers, mothers, or both will be informants about fathering, and whether com-parative data will be collected about mothers. Deciding on the fathering informant(s) involves weighing the relative risks of selection bias and report-ing bias, and deciding which is the more important to minimize for a particu-lar research purpose. Collecting comparative data about mothers provides context for understanding fathers, but since research resources are always limited, inevitably reduces the depth of data collection from fathers them-selves. In addition to these generic design questions in fathering research, im-migrant father studies face choices about whether or not to include compara-tive samples of non-immigrants. Again, costs and benefits of either decision need to be analyzed in the context of the study's objectives. Immigrant father research also has to address the interrelationships among immigrant status, race-ethnicity, and socioeconomic status that potentially confound analysis. Some models exist for doing so, and some analytical conventions (e.g., in national datasets, race-ethnicity and immigrant status cannot simultaneously be analyzed as predictor variables) may need reconsideration, especially in light of the fluctuating nature of recent U.S. immigration.

The extent to which existing constructs in fathering research are appropri-ate in research on immigrant fathers needs careful consideration. In spite of some concerns about the application of the foundational construct of father involvement to immigrant and other non-majority fathers, the evidence available suggests it both has utility and does not inherently entail a deficit perspective on fathers who are not white, middle-class, and native-born. Researchers using the involvement construct should be aware of how the conceptualization and operationalization of father involvement have evolved since Lamb and Pleck's initial formulation. They should also familiarize themselves with the range of different measures available assessing engagement and responsibility, as well as the measures of warmth and responsiveness and of monitoring and decisionmaking that are increasingly included in father involvement studies. In addition, other important constructs in current fathering research such as attitudes about fatherhood, paternal identity, paternal generativity, paternal ideology, paternal visions, and paternal social capital may have value in studies of immigrant fathers. New constructs more specifically relevant to immigrant fathering should be developed based on the experience of immigrant fathers themselves. Distinct from fathering constructs, several domains of fathering dynamics studied in non-immigrant fathers (such as the role of kinship networks, religion, and coparenting processes) could be usefully applied in immigrant father research. Qualitative and mixed method research is likely to reveal new fathering dynamics more unique to the experience of immigrant fathers.

In conclusion, this chapter has identified many avenues for "next steps" in immigrant father studies. There are so many, in fact, that selecting some as especially promising inevitably reflects an author's own specific interests. Nonetheless, I suggest that future research give particular attention to four broad areas. The first is deeper exploration of immigrant fathers' paternal identities. Second, more investigation of immigrant fathers' experience of coparenting should be undertaken. Third, diversity among immigrant fathers needs much greater attention. This of course includes diversity by national origin, but in addition includes nonresident and divorced fathers, teen fathers, incarcerated or formerly incarcerated fathers, gay fathers, fathers of children with special needs and fathers with special needs themselves, and primary caregiving fathers. Finally, immigrant father research will benefit especially from the development of new fathering-relation constructs and dynamics derived from the experience of immigrant fathers themselves.

AUTHOR NOTE

The work reported here was supported by the Cooperative State Research, Education and Extension Service, U.S. Department of Agriculture, under Project No. ILLU-45-0366 to Joseph H. Pleck.

The author thanks the editors for their helpful comments on earlier drafts of this chapter.

REFERENCES

Allen, S., and Hawkins, A. (1999). Maternal gatekeeping: Mothers' beliefs and behaviors that inhibit greater father involvement in family work. *Journal of Marriage and the Family, 61,* 199–212.

Amato, P. (1987). *Children in Australian families: The growth of competence.* New York: Prentice-Hall.

———. (1998). More than money? Men's contribution to their children's lives. In A. Booth and A. Crouter (Eds.), *Men in families: When do they get involved? What difference does it make?* (241–78). Mahwah, NJ: Erlbaum.

Auerbach, C., Silverstein, L. B., and Zizi, M. (1997). The evolving structure of fatherhood among Haitian Americans. *Journal of African-American Male Studies, 25,* 59–85.

Baruch, G., and Barnett, R. (1986). Consequences of fathers' participation in family work: Parents' role strain and well-being. *Journal of Personality and Social Psychology, 51,* 983–92.

Belsky, J. (1984). The determinants of parenting: A process model. *Child Development, 55,* 83–96.

Blair, S., and Hardesty, C. (1994). Parental involvement and the well-being of fathers and mothers of young children. *Journal of Men's Studies, 3,* 49–68.

Blood, R., and Wolfe, D. (1960). *Husbands and wives: The dynamics of married living.* Glencoe, IL: Free Press.

Bornstein, M., and Bradley, R. (2003). *Socioeconomic status, parenting, and child development.* Mahwah, NJ: Erlbaum.

Bornstein, M., and Cote, L. (2006). *Acculturation and parent-child relationships: Measurement and development.* Mahwah, NJ: Erlbaum.

Bost, K., Cox, M., Burchinal, M., and Payne, C. (2002). Structural and supportive change in couples' family and friendship networks across the transition to parenthood. *Journal of Marriage and the Family, 64,* 517–31.

Braver, S., Wolchik, S., Sandler, I., Sheets, V., Fogas, B., and Bay, R. (1993). A longitudinal study of noncustodial parents: Parents without children. *Journal of Family Psychology, 7,* 9–23.

Bruce, C., and Fox, G. (1997, November). *Measuring father involvement among lower-income White and African-American populations.* Presented at the National Council on Family Relations, Crystal City, VA.

Cabrera, N., Brooks-Gunn, J., Moore, K., West. J., Boller, K., and Tamis-LeMonda, C. (2002). Bridging research and policy: Including fathers of young children in national studies. In C. Tamis-LeMonda and N. Cabrera (Eds.), *Handbook of father involvement: Multidisciplinary perspectives* (489–524). Mahwah, NJ: Erlbaum.

Caughy, M., O'Campo, P., Randolph, S., and Nickerson, K. (2002). The influence of racial socialization practices on the cognitive and behavioral competence of African American preschoolers. *Child Development, 73,* 1611–25.

Chao, R. (1994). Beyond parental control and authoritarian parenting style: Understanding Chinese parenting through the cultural notion of training. *Child Development, 65*, 1111–19.

Child Development Supplement. (2006). Retrieved from http://psidonline.isr.umich.edu/CDS/questionnaires/cds-i/english/Tdiary.pdf.

Cohen, R., and Weissman, S. (1984). The parenting alliance. In R. Cohen, B. Cohler, and S. Weissman (Eds.), *Parenthood: A psychodynamic perspective* (33–49). New York: Guilford.

Coley, R., and Morris, J. (2002). Comparing father and mother reports of father involvement among low-income minority families. *Journal of Marriage and the Family, 64*, 982–97.

Costigan, C., and Cox, M. (2001). Fathers' participation in family research: Is there a self-selection bias? *Journal of Family Psychology, 15*, 706–20.

De Luccie, M. F. (1996). Predictors of paternal involvement and satisfaction. *Psychological Reports, 79*, 1351–59.

Deutsch, F., Lozy, J., and Saxon, S. (1993). Taking credit: Couples' reports of contributions to child care. *Journal of Family Issues, 14*, 421–37.

Fagan, J., and Barnett, M. (2003). Mothers' attitudes about the father role, and father involvement. *Journal of Family Issues, 24*, 1030–43.

Fox, G., and Bruce, C. (2001). Conditional fatherhood: Identity theory and parental investment theory as alternative sources of explanation of fathering. *Journal of Marriage and the Family, 63*, 394–403.

Hawkins, A., and Dollahite, D. (1997). *Generative fathering: Beyond deficit perspectives*. Thousand Oaks, CA: Sage.

Hernandez, D., and Brandon, P. (2004). Who are the fathers of today? In C. Tamis-LeMonda and N. Cabrera (Eds.), *Handbook of father involvement: Multidisciplinary perspectives* (33–62). Mahwah, NJ: Erlbaum.

Hofferth, S. (2003). Race/ethnic differences in father involvement in two-parent families: Culture, context, or economy? *Journal of Family Issues, 24*, 185–216.

Hofferth, S. L., Cabrera, N., Carlson, M., Coley, R., Day, R., and Schindler, H. (2002). Resident father involvement and social fathering. In S. Hofferth and L. Casper (Eds.), *Handbook of measurement issues in family research* (335–69). Mahwah, NJ: Erlbaum.

Hofferth, S. L., and Fitzgerald, M. (2004, November). *Generational and ethnic differences in parenting across Hispanic, Asian, Black, and White families.* Presented at the National Council on Family Relations, Orlando, FL.

Hossain, Z. (2001). Division of household labor and family functioning in off-reservation Navajo Indian families. *Family Relations, 50*, 255–61.

Hossain, Z., and Roopnarine, J. L. (1994). African-American fathers' involvement with infants: Relationship to their functioning style, support, education, and income. *Infant Behavior and Development, 17*, 175–84.

Hwang, C., and Lamb, M. E. (1997). Father involvement in Sweden: A longitudinal study of its stability and correlates. *International Journal of Behavioral Development, 21*, 621–32.

Ihinger-Tallman, M., Pasley, K., and Buehler, C. (1993). Developing a middle-range theory of father involvement postdivorce. *Journal of Family Issues, 14*, 550–71.

Lamb, M., Pleck, J., Charnov, E., and Levine, J. (1985). Paternal behavior in humans. *American Zoologist, 25,* 883–94.

Maccoby, E., Mnookin, R., Depner, C., and Peters, H. E. (1992). *Dividing the child: Social and legal dilemmas of custody.* Cambridge, MA: Harvard University Press.

Mahalingam, R. (2006). *Cultural psychology of immigrants.* Mahwah, NJ: Erlbaum.

Marcel, A., Sonenstein, F., and Pleck, J. (2006, March). *Adolescent males' masculinity ideology: Testing a conceptual framework.* Presented at the Society for Adolescent Medicine, Boston.

Marsiglio, W. (1991). Paternal engagement activities with minor children. *Journal of Marriage and the Family, 53,* 973–86.

Marsiglio, W., Amato, P., Day, R. L., and Lamb, M. E. (2000). Exploring fatherhood diversity: Implications for conceptualizing father involvement. *Journal of Marriage and the Family, 62,* 1173–91.

Maurer, T., and Pleck, J. (2006). Fathers' caregiving and breadwinning: A gender congruence analysis. *Psychology of Men and Masculinity, 73,* 101–12.

Maurer, T., Pleck, J., and Rane, T. (2001). Parental identity and reflected appraisals: Measurement and gender dynamics. *Journal of Marriage and the Family, 63,* 309–21.

———. (2003). Methodological considerations in measuring paternal identity. *Fathering: A Journal of Research, Theory, and Practice about Men as Fathers, 14,* 117–29.

McBride, B., and Mills, G. (1993). A comparison of mother and father involvement with their preschool age children. *Early Childhood Research Quarterly, 8,* 457–77.

McHale, J. (1997). Overt and covert coparenting process in the family. *Family Process, 36,* 183–210.

McHale, J., Khazan, I., Erera, P., Rotman, T., DeCourcey, W., and Connell, M. (2002). Coparenting in diverse family systems. In M. Bornstein (Ed.), *Handbook of parenting, Vol. 3: Being and becoming a parent* (second ed., 76–108). Mahwah, NJ: Erlbaum.

McHale, J., Kuersten, R., Lauretti, A., and Rasmussen, J. (2000). Parental reports of coparenting and observed coparenting behavior during the toddler period. *Journal of Family Psychology, 14,* 220–37.

Minton, C., and Pasley, K. (1996). Fathers' parenting role identity and father involvement: A comparison of nondivorced and divorced, nonresident fathers. *Journal of Family Issues, 17,* 26–45.

Palkovitz, R. (1984). Parental attitudes and fathers' interactions with their 5-month-old infants. *Developmental Psychology, 20,* 1054–60.

———. (1997). Reconstructing "involvement": Expanding conceptualizations of men's caring in contemporary families. In A. Hawkins and D. Dollahite (Eds.), *Generative fathering: Beyond deficit perspectives* (200–216). Thousand Oaks, CA: Sage.

Parke, R. D. (2002). Fathers and families. In M. H. Bornstein (Ed.), *Handbook of parenting, Vol. 3: Being and becoming a parent* (second ed., 27–73). Mahwah, NJ: Erlbaum.

Pleck, J. H. (1983). Husbands' paid work and family roles: Current research issues. In H. Lopata and J. H. Pleck (Eds.), *Research in the interweave of social roles: Vol. 3. Families and jobs* (231–333). Greenwich, CT: JAI Press.

―――. (1985). *Working wives, working husbands*. Beverly Hills, CA: Sage.

―――. (1997). Paternal involvement: Levels, sources, and consequences. In M. Lamb (Ed.), *The role of the father in child development* (third ed., 66–103). New York: Wiley.

―――. (2007). Why could father involvement benefit children? Theoretical perspectives. *Applied Developmental Science, 11*, 1–7.

Pleck, J. H., Lamb, M. E., and Levine, J. (1985). Facilitating future change in men's family roles. *Marriage and Family Review, 9*, 11–16.

Pleck, J. H., and Masciadrelli, B. P. (2004). Paternal involvement in U.S. residential fathers: Levels, sources, and consequences. In M. E. Lamb (Ed.), *The role of the father in child development* (fourth ed., 222–71). New York: Wiley.

Pleck, J. H., and Stueve, J. (2001). Time and paternal involvement. In K. Daly (Ed.), *Minding the time in family experience: Emerging perspectives and issues* (205–26). Oxford: Elsevier Science.

―――. (2004). A narrative approach to paternal identity: The importance of parental identity "conjointness." In R. R. Day and M. E. Lamb (Eds.), *Conceptualizing and measuring paternal involvement* (83–107). Mahwah, NJ: Erlbaum.

Radin, N. (1994). Primary-caregiving fathers in intact families. In A. Gottfried and A. Gottfried (Eds.), *Redefining families: Implications for children's development* (55–97). New York: Plenum.

Rane, T., and McBride, B. (2000). Identity theory as a guide to understanding fathers' involvement with their children. *Journal of Family Issues, 21*, 347–66.

Riley, D. (1990). Network influence on father involvement in childrearing. In M. Cochran, M. Larner, D. G. Riley, L. Henderson, and C. Henderson (Eds.), *Extending families: The social networks of parents and their children* (131–53). Cambridge: Cambridge University Press.

Sandberg, J., and Hofferth, S. (2001). Changes in children's time with parents: United States, 1981–1997. *Demography, 38*, 423–36.

Sanderson, S., and Sanders-Thompson, V. L. T. (2002). Factors associated with perceived paternal involvement in childrearing. *Sex Roles, 46*, 99–111.

Schoppe-Sullivan, S., Manglesdorf, S., Frosch, C., and McHale, J. (2004). Coparenting, family process, and family structure: Implications for preschoolers' externalizing behavior problems. *Journal of Family Psychology, 18*, 194–207.

Silverstein, L., Auerbach, C., Grieco, L., and Dunkel, F. (1999). Do promise keepers dream of feminist sheep? *Sex Roles, 40*, 665–88.

Snarey, J. S. (1993). *How fathers care for the next generation: A four-decade study*. Cambridge, MA: Harvard University Press.

Snarey, J., and Pleck, J. H. (1993). Consequences of fathers' care-giving for fathers themselves: Middle-adult love, work, and societal generativity. In J. S. Snarey (Ed.), *How fathers care for the next generation: A four-decade study* (84–119). Cambridge, MA: Harvard University Press.

Steinberg, L., Dornbusch, S., and Brown, R. (1999). Ethnic differences in adolescent achievement: An ecological perspective. *American Psychologist, 47*, 723–29.

Stueve, J., and Pleck, J. H. (2001). "Parenting voices": Solo parent identity and coparent identities in married parents' narratives of meaningful parenting experiences. *Journal of Social and Personal Relationships, 18*, 691–708.

Toth, J., and Xu, X. (1999). Ethnic and cultural diversity in fathers' involvement: A racial/ethnic comparison of African American, Hispanic, and White fathers. *Youth and Society, 31*, 76–99.

Whiteside-Mansell, L., Bradley, R., and Rakow, E. (2000). Similarities and differences in parental investment for mothers and fathers. *Journal of Family Issues, 22*, 63–83.

Wical, K., and Doherty, W. (2005). How reliable are fathers' reports of involvement with their children? A methodological report. *Fathering: A Journal of Research, Theory, and Practice about Men as Fathers, 3*, 81–93.

Wilcox, W. (2002). Religion, convention, and paternal involvement. *Journal of Marriage and the Family, 64*, 780–92.

Yeung, W. J., Sandberg, J. F., Davis-Kean, P. E., and Hofferth, S. L. (2001). Children's time with fathers in intact families. *Journal of Marriage and the Family, 64*, 780–92.

Zuzanek, J. (2000). *The effects of time use and time pressure on child-parent relationships.* Waterloo, Ontario: Otium Publications.

13

Imagining the Future of Immigrant Fathers

Ross D. Parke, Eric Vega, Jeffrey Cookston,
Norma Perez-Brena, and Scott Coltrane

> This country was put together not only by bloodlines, kin and tradition, but by tides of newcomers of every stock, creed and persuasion.
>
> —Peter C. Newman, 1997 (Canadian journalist, Halifax, Nova Scotia, Immigration Museum)

This quote about Canada can apply equally to the United States and many countries in Europe and reminds us that immigration is a natural phenomenon, not a novel or pathology-inducing event. In fact, one could argue that citizens of many countries are in fact only immigrants with seniority (Bryant, 1997). In this chapter we speculate about the future status of immigrant fathers and provide some guidelines for theory development and research in the coming decade.

THE HISTORICAL CONTEXT OF IMMIGRATION

Several assumptions guide our thinking about the issues associated with parenting, immigration, and child development that suggest the need to examine the historical context of immigration in recognition of the diversity of immigrant fathers. To fully appreciate how immigrant fathers adapt to their new geographic and cultural milieus, the historical time period in which these groups migrate needs to be recognized. For example, the pattern of acculturation that characterized immigrant groups in the United States at the turn of the twentieth century was one of relatively rapid assimilation into the mainstream culture and where homogenous ethnic enclaves bound ethnic orientations. In contrast, the current wave of immigration that is occurring a century later is less likely to promote an abandonment or bounded expression of the cultural heritage of one's country of origin and more likely to encourage biculturalism and mutual accommodation.

To use cultural brokering as an example, it is clear that earlier historical immigrant populations faced linguistic issues, although it is not clear to what degree children acted as the liaisons between their parents and the social context outside the home and their ethnic communities. For children to act as cultural brokers for their parents, they must be more adept in the use of the English language, possibly as a function of a historical trend in which more immigrant children are participating in public schooling and becoming more facile in their second language acquisition. Research on the prevalence of cultural brokering notes the importance of conditions that necessitate communication between immigrant populations and the host country, where strategies including brokering are influenced by ethnic discrimination and the degree of self-sufficiency that immigrant communities establish (Zhou, 2001). Could the meaning, consequences, and utility of child cultural brokering be the same within different historical periods? Within the past twenty years, opportunities to interact with the U.S. culture have emerged independent of the school context, including the availability and accessibility of personal computers, the Internet, cell phones, and other technological devices that are commonly used by children (and never quite as well by their parents). To fully appreciate how the changing historical context modifies this phenomenon requires a detailed historical examination of form, frequency, and consequences of brokering in different points in our history. A similar opportunity is present with the patterns of worker migration from Eastern to Western Europe; this issue could benefit from U.S.-European comparisons with both viewed through a historically informed perspective.

Moreover, the demographic context of immigration in North America has important implications for the experience of the immigrant. In the United States, immigration patterns have shifted radically over the last century. Seventy to eighty years ago, the U.S. population was 9.7 percent African American and 1.7 percent other racial minorities (U.S. Census Bureau, 1933). In other words, 90 percent of the population was white. In contrast, according to recent Census figures (U.S. Census Bureau, 2003), the demographic picture has changed radically. In 2003, 31 percent of the population belonged to a racial or ethnic minority group—a threefold increase in the minority population since the 1930s. Trends suggest that in parts of the United States some ethnic groups, such as Latinos, will be a majority by the year 2030. This shift in demographic proportional representation will have profound implications for economic opportunities, political influence, and social policy decisions that will alter the role of fathers as well as the socioemotional adjustments of fathers and their families. If Latino fathers are part of the majority in some regions, for example, then economic status may increase and social services may be more available; in turn, fathers may have more time for children, may suffer less discrimination and prejudice and, in turn, their children may be afforded more opportunities to be better adjusted. As such, it appears important to track rates and changes in cohorts of immigrant fathers to describe and evaluate the changing demographic context of immigrant fathers in North America. In Canada, by contrast, immigration patterns appear to be following a different path but a similarly compelling one. Whereas it took seventy to eighty years for the ethnic minority proportion of the population in the United States to increase threefold, a similar threefold pattern has been observed in Canada between 1981 and 2001 (Statistics Canada, 2003). In 1981, only 1.1 million individuals in Canada (4.7 percent of the total population) were ethnic minority, compared to the 3.2 million who identified themselves as minority in 2001 (11.2 percent). By 2016 it is projected that one-fifth of the populace of Canada will identify as ethnic minority. In view of these demographic shifts in North America, there is both an opportunity to evaluate the generalizability of our assumptions about developmental processes and a moral obligation to better understand a large segment of our population.

BEYOND A SINGLE SNAPSHOT OF THE IMMIGRANT FATHER: FROM SNAPSHOTS TO VIDEO

There is no single likeness of immigrant fathers but many portraits. Progress will only be made if we recognize the heterogeneity of immigrant fathers. Immigrants come to a new country for very different reasons. Some are asylum seekers or refugees who wish to avoid religious, political, or ethnic prosecution. Others seek new economic opportunities. Combining immigrants who arrive for vastly different reasons will make our task of unraveling the puzzle of immigrant fathers more difficult. Rather we need to know how motivations to immigrate explain and alter fathering behaviors.

Reasons for immigration are not independent of legal/illegal status. While asylum seekers and/or refugees may often be legal immigrants, many economic-opportunity-oriented immigrants may be illegal residents. Undocumented fathers are likely influenced by their perceived need for secrecy and by a lack of trust in official institutions. Although this lack of trust is to be expected given fears of deportation, does this mistrust lead to more social isolation from others in the community and from the resources that are available to aid families, such as social service, educational, and health agencies? To what extent have fathers forged alternative relationships with "non-official, non-reporting" kinship groups or faith-based organizations and how have these networks influenced fathering practices and notions of fatherhood?

Welfare reforms enacted in 1996 excluded many non-citizens from eligibility for public programs, leading some immigrant parents to refrain from seeking public benefits for their children, who were eligible for such benefits if born in the United States (Hernandez, 2004). It is clear that immigrant children are less likely to be insured or use mental health services than U.S.-born children (Huang, Yu, and Ledsky, 2006), and the children of undocumented immigrants are using services at greater rates than their parents. Over half of the children in immigrant families live in mixed-status households (where at least one household member is not a U.S. citizen), and this poses new challenges for service providers (Hernandez, 2004). Non-citizen parents may not know that their children are eligible for important services or may be afraid that they will be deported if they contact government agencies.

These dilemmas raise new questions for researchers studying immigrant families. Are economically motivated fathers more likely to return to their home country after establishing a degree of economic resources than refugees who are less able to safely travel between the United States and their country of origin? Are they more or less likely to transplant their family from one country to another strictly based on earnings that are easily transferred across borders? Variations in long-term commitment to the host country will have profound impacts on attitudes toward new customs, norms, and language. Rates of assimilation, for example, will vary depending on the prospect of staying permanently or returning to a home country as a long-term goal. It is possible that religious and political refugees are more likely to focus on these opportunities and instill these interests in their children. As such, are economic refugees more likely to involve their children in family economic work? Although early involvement in work outside the home has been associated with problematic development for native-born children (Greenberger and Steinberg, 1986), considerably less attention has been paid to the effects of such employment for foreign-born children.

How do the family structures of different types of immigrants vary? Sojourner fathers (or mothers) who immigrate for relatively brief periods of time in order to take advantage of seasonal or periodic job opportunities may have very different family contact patterns than permanent immigrants (Glenn, 1992; Hondagneu-Sotelo and Avila, 1997). Sojourners may move temporarily without their families who stay in the country of origin in contrast to permanent immigrants who may come as a family unit. We know little about the impact of these alternative contact patterns on household authority patterns. Do fathers who are absent experience more difficulty in asserting their authority relative to mothers or extended kin, who are stable figures in children's lives? Do marital problems increase as a result of the patterns of intercountry mobility? Do these outcomes shift with duration of absence and/or the degree of contact between fathers and their families? As free-market, neo-liberal economic agents create increasing economic disparities in semi-periphery and periphery countries (Chase-Dunn, 1998; Volker and Chase-Dunn, 1985), decisions to migrate internationally for work are becoming increasingly necessary. In the future, with the increasingly widespread availability of new communication technologies such as the Internet for transmission of photos, video phones, and other advances, the impact of these separations on fathers may shift. However, immigrant families are often too poor to have access to the new technologies. Moreover families in the country of origin may have limited access to computers as well (Suárez-Orozco and Suárez-Orozco, 2001). As Sanger (1999) found, access varies across ethnic groups: Asian Americans have more access to these new modes of communication than Latinos or African Americans.

Finally, immigrants tend to reside in different types of communities. Sojourners, for example, often live in highly homogeneous work-based community facilities oriented toward unmarried or unaccompanied workers with few family-centered housing opportunities. In contrast, permanent immigrants tend to cluster—at least initially—in ethnically homogeneous communities that are often more family-oriented. Others, due to economic constraints, may reside in ethnically mixed communities and high-risk neighborhoods (Coltrane, Melzer, Vega, and Parke, 2005). Tracking how these community characteristics alter fathering behaviors is a major challenge.

As the title of this section suggests, we need to recognize the dynamic character of the immigration process and move beyond the metaphor of snapshots that are cross-sectional and time-bound to a more contemporary "video" metaphor (Pomerantz, Ruble, and Bolger, 2003) that is longitudinal and is able to capture change across time. Documenting the changes across time for the diverse types of immigrant fathers is critical for progress in this area.

THE CONTINUING INTERPLAY BETWEEN WORK AND IMMIGRATION

In this section we consider a variety of issues that will confront immigrant fathers and their families, including economic challenges, educational barriers, and language obstacles. Although many men leave their country of origin to improve their economic situation, economic hardship remains a significant problem for many immigrants. Immigrants continue to work in low-paying jobs that require long hours to make a living wage. As our recent work (Coltrane, Parke, and Adams, 2004; Parke, Coltrane, Duffy, Buriel, Dennis, Powers, et al., 2004) illustrates, immigrant fathers who experience economic hardship show similar patterns of adjustment problems as their Euro-American counterparts, namely, increases in depression and marital problems, higher levels of harsh parenting, and, in turn, higher levels of internalizing and externalizing problems among their children.

Our quantitative findings are reflected in the qualitative interviews with Mexican American fathers. When asked, "What would you change in your parenting?" one father talked about how work-related stress can lead to harsh and explosive reactions to his children[1]:

> I get upset quickly, I get frustrated. Maybe it's because I'm so tired, I don't know, but I get upset, I get frustrated. (thirty-six-year-old first-generation Mexican immigrant father)

A thirty-year-old first-generation immigrant father, in response to the query about what he would like to change said "change my temper":

> I would change my character a little, my character because of work, or financial worries, because of it I'm a bit demanding. (thirty-year-old first-generation Mexican immigrant father)

Moreover, economic stress takes its toll on immigrant fathers' availability to their children as well. Some of these fathers lament the lack of time with their children caused by work demands:

> Well, play with him more because we don't have time to play with him. Work doesn't let me, I even work on Sundays. (thirty-year-old first-generation Mexican immigrant father)

As these quotes illustrate, economic conditions play a major role in shaping the quality and quantity of father involvement.

However, focusing too narrowly on economically disadvantaged immigrant fathers presents a distorted view of immigrant family life. As Suárez-Orozco and Suárez-Orozco (2001) noted,

> An emerging feature of the new economic landscape—the increasing "hourglass" shape of the opportunity structure—is of central relevance to the lives and future of immigrants and their children. On one end of the hourglass, high-skilled immigrants are moving into well-remunerated knowledge–intensive industries at an unprecedented rate (e.g., Silicon Valley jobs where 32 percent are immigrants). On the other end of the hourglass economy, large numbers of low-skilled immigrants are entering poorly paid and uninsured service–sector jobs. (61)

Where our focus as a field has been on the lower half of the hourglass, in the future we need to describe in more detail the lives of immigrant fathers at the top end of the hourglass. Do they still, in spite of economic success, experience discrimination and prejudice? How is their fathering different from that of economically deprived fathers? Do the demands of high prestige and time-demanding jobs make them less available as fathers? Can we learn lessons from these successful immigrants for improving economic success of impoverished immigrants? A note of caution—there are clear confounds between economic success and country of origin that need to be addressed in this area. While many Mexican and Latino immigrants are often poor and relatively limited in their education, Asian and Indian immigrants are often better educated and are able to move to the United States legally as a result of their job skills and corporate sponsorship. Do these fathers move with their families more frequently than less educated immigrant fathers who often leave their families behind? Such differences underscore our need to recognize and learn from the diversity that characterizes immigrant fathers. There are many types of economic experiences that immigrant fathers face and we need to pay more attention to this diversity of economic opportunities and assess its impact on fathering.

IMPACT OF THE EDUCATIONAL DISPARITY BETWEEN IMMIGRANT FATHERS AND THEIR CHILDREN

Another consequence of the differential opportunities available to immigrant parents and children is the resulting inability of many immigrant fathers to serve as educational tutors and guides for their children. Not only does this impede the eventual academic attainment of their children, but it may be a further source of intergenerational conflict and cause of heightened emotional distance between fathers and their children. It may also lessen the child's respect for the father due to awareness of his educational limitations. Children even take advantage of parents' linguistic limitations and their lack of knowledge about the educational system. For example, Suárez-Orozco and Suárez-Orozco (2001) reported that "a thirteen-year-old Mexican boy admitted to us that he had told his parents that the F on his report card stood for 'fabulous'" (74). From our own work with Mexican American families, we find that fathers are painfully aware of how their limitations in English interfere with their ability to help their children with their homework, as illustrated below:

> I wouldn't change much. Actually I would try to help more in her school work because I really have not been able to help them in that because of the

English barrier and because I'm not good at school. (thirty-three-year-old first-generation Mexican immigrant father)

Or consider the problems immigrant fathers with limited English proficiency face when trying to deal with schools. We asked fathers the following question: How have you handled problems that your child has had at school?

Well to plan all the time to try to be, if we go to school that there is someone that talks to me in Spanish. Yes, yes because . . . I normally understand a little, a little English but not a lot. No his . . . to speak it I don't know how to speak it, darn. Like sometimes he . . . sometimes I tell him, I mean that they are talking to me in English I tell him to tell me what he is saying, I mean he doesn't know how to tell me, like I know . . . how do you say . . . he gets, he gets embarrassed and at the end he doesn't know how to say what it is that they are saying in English. (forty-seven-year-old first-generation Mexican immigrant father)

Another father answered as follows:

I would say, try to help on her homework when she says she doesn't understand. I do all I can although sometimes it's difficult because of the language. She will help *me* understand what it says in English. (forty-eight-year-old first-generation Mexican immigrant father)

Or consider this father who recognizes that his child has advanced beyond his own level of educational achievement:

My oldest entered, got to eighth grade, high school. I tried to explain some equations from first grade, second grade and I felt very good when she assimilated them even though I had to go through all of the bibliography and all of the textbooks that she used. I remember, I tried to explain and she understood, and she has gotten very good grades in mathematics, and now well, now it's like she speaks to me in Chinese because she is taking analytic trigonometry, analytic geometry that I don't understand, but she's advancing. (forty-three-year-old first-generation Mexican immigrant father)

Finally, some immigrant fathers may simply be unaware of the rules and routes through the educational system such as the courses that are needed to enter college, the potential sources of financial aid, or the availability of career counseling services. This lack of information may limit their ability to offer guidance and help to their children as they traverse the education maze and may result in premature departure from the school system.

"Do you think it is harder for kids whose parents did not go to school here as opposed to the kids whose parents did go to school here?" was another question that we posed to immigrant fathers.

One father stated:

> I think it is. Because she sometimes wants us to help and sincerely we can't. We can't even help in the language. Unfortunately, we can't even explain it to her in our language, no we can't. Well sometimes one does feel bad. That wants to help but can't. (forty-eight-year-old first-generation Mexican immigrant father)

Another father responded:

> Well, I think so. Well, for example, the guys at least speak the language and they have studied. For example, that I am still doing high school here like it is, I cannot give an explanation to her. There are homeworks that they get now, and I see that she is complaining. If I could, well, I would help her but unfortunately I don't have an idea to help her. Yes, that is the hardest. (forty-eight-year-old first-generation Mexican immigrant father)

These examples illustrate the problems that many immigrant fathers face as they seek to support their children's educational progress. Therefore, we need to be aware of the diversity of educational attainment across fathers from different countries of origin. The relatively high success rate of Asian and white immigrants, for example, reminds us that we cannot generalize easily across immigrant groups (Vernez and Abrahamse, 1996). Clearly, more attention to how different ethnic groups negotiate the educational system and support their children's learning is needed.

RECOGNITION OF THE DYNAMIC INTERPLAY BETWEEN IMMIGRANT FATHERS, FAMILIES, AND HOST COUNTRY

As Berry (this volume) and others (Phinney, 2006) have argued, we need to move beyond unidirectional conceptions that focus on the changes that occur for the immigrant fathers and explore the changes that occur for members of the host country as a result of contact with immigrants. Such considerations will shift the dialogue from a focus on the negative implications of immigrants on the host culture to a more balanced view that recognizes the positive effects of immigrants on members of the host culture. In particular, we posit several factors that may influence the impact of immigrant fathers on host fathers. First, the degree of exposure to immigrant fathers and their families is a major determinant; this is likely to vary across different areas of the United States with residents in traditional immigration sites such as New York, Florida, Texas, Arizona, and California being most likely to have high exposure to recent immigrants. As we know, contact per se is unlikely to result in positive perceptions (Dixon, Durrheim, and Tredoux, 2005).

Indeed, the nature of the interpersonal experience between immigrants and host individuals needs to be measured as well. Together, the amount of contact and the positive/negative valence of the experience are important determinants of whether there is openness or dismissal of lessons offered by immigrant fathers.

In the current historical context, perception of economic threat in terms of reduction of job opportunities will have a major influence on attitudes of members of the host culture toward immigrants. Variations across social class and education levels will be likely, with lower SES and more poorly educated host country fathers being most threatened by immigrants of color (Rubin, 1994). On the other hand, as the recent film *A Day without a Mexican* so dramatically documents, many middle-class families depend on an immigrant workforce to fulfill needs for gardeners, housekeepers, day care providers, and nannies. The hotel, travel, entertainment, service, and manufacturing sectors of the economy are increasingly dependent on immigrant labor in all regions of the United States, and agricultural production is still heavily dependent on immigrants as a source of inexpensive labor for planting and harvesting. According to occupational analysis from the Bureau of Labor Statistics, two-thirds of all U.S. jobs do not require formal education or experience, a trend expected to continue for another decade (Nightingale and Fix, 2004). Although the labor practices in many employment sectors disadvantage immigrant workers, the heavy dependence on the labor of immigrants could lead many managers and business owners to develop positive attitudes toward immigrants.

Similarly, host acceptance is likely to depend upon perceptions of the educational impact of immigrants on their own children's educational experiences and opportunities. Some host fathers may view exposure to other cultural and linguistic groups as opportunities for teaching attitudes about acceptance of diversity and broadening of children's cultural learning. Others may view bilingual classrooms or other educational accommodations to immigrants as threats to educational quality of host country children. Perceptions of the impact of immigrant families on availability and cost of medical and local services will be a further factor that will shape attitudes of host country fathers. Children of Asian immigrants tend to do better in school and achieve higher college attendance rates than host country children (with the exception of Southeast Asians; see Yang, 2004), leading some host country parents to react negatively to all Asian groups. Anti-immigrant initiatives denying services to non-citizens and requiring the use of English have been applied to all immigrant groups, though in the American Southwest, they were motivated by a rapidly growing Latino population and the formerly dominant Anglo majority feeling threatened (Wilson, 2001). On the positive side, host fathers may benefit from the strengths of immigrant families in terms of their family values—familism in Latino families—indicating commitment to the involvement of extended families in rearing children. Such practices can provide alternate models of family functioning that can be contrasted with an individualistic style inherited from northern European forebears.

How will fathers' roles in the host country change as a consequence of both exposure to and attitudes toward immigrant fathers? How fathers' engagement, accessibility, and responsibility for children shift as a function of exposure to immigrant fathers is a topic ripe for further analysis. Will American fathers' focus on playful interaction shift in response to exposure to alternative models of fatherhood? For example, siblings and mothers rather than fathers often serve as play partners for younger children in Mexican culture (Zukow-Goldring, 2002). Similarly, will host fathers seek more contact and support from extended family members as a result of this exposure? Clearly, fathers in the United States have much to gain from exposure to alternative fathering models (Parke, Coltrane, and Schofield, 2007); to what extent they will be influenced remains an open question.

ACCULTURATION: WHO, HOW, AND WHEN

Acculturation is another factor that needs to be considered if we are to increase our understanding of immigrant fathers. Different individuals in the family acculturate at different rates and therefore we need to move toward a more differentiated model of acculturation in which acculturation trajectories of different family members are recognized. For example, mothers, fathers, and children acculturate at different rates due to varied educational and work experiences. Children learn English at a faster rate than adults while fathers' and mothers' rates of acculturation may vary as a function of the type of employment settings in which they work. Parents who stay at home or who work in ethnically homogeneous groups (e.g., hotel maids, garment workers, construction workers, gardeners) acculturate more slowly than those who are exposed to a wider range of ethnicities in the workplace (e.g., schools, banks, and other white-collar occupations). How do the resulting discrepancies in rates of acculturation influence fathering roles and marital relationships?

From our own work (Parke, Coltrane, Duffy, Buriel, Dennis, Powers, et al., 2004) with Mexican American families, acculturation was associated with less use of harsh discipline on the part of parents. At the same time, marital problems increased as women acculturated to the host country and began to expect more equality within the marriage (and between the parents and children) than did their husbands. Moreover, the empowerment that may come as a result of children's linguistic and cultural (host) competence may increase child-parent conflict due to children's push for autonomy and greater decisionmaking within the family. Similarly, conflict between parents and children may increase as a result of children's adoption of norms and beliefs based on their experience in the host culture. Issues of dress codes, curfew, and activities with peers are likely to produce conflict with parents (Raffaelli and Ontai, 2004). In our own studies (Vega, Coltrane, Pyke, and Parke, 2006) we see these conflicts increase most dramatically for Mexican-born fathers as they attempt to control their adolescent daughters more tightly than their adolescent sons. Below is an excerpt from a father who discusses his worries about his daughter.

> I take her and bring her [to and from school]. And she tells me, "Don't go for me, I will walk," but I tell her, "I don't want you flirting," understand. She is old now and with any little thing that you do they are going to steal you. I tell her, "If you don't want any problems with any one, don't go walking if someone bothers you, that says you know, do you want a friendship, or a ride, or whatever." Tell them, "My dad is coming and he brings me and takes me so I don't need anything from no one." (fifty-two-year-old first-generation Mexican immigrant father)

In past studies, little attention had been given to the possible differences in acculturation that can occur between siblings and how immigrant fathers might respond. It is expected that differential acculturation styles may affect family dynamics and in particular the father-child relationships. This is important because the siblings' levels of acculturation have been related to how comfortable and connected each child feels with their parents and extended family members (Pyke, 2005). When language was an issue, it was also found that one sibling needed to translate for a more acculturated sibling when intergenerational interaction was in order. It will be important for future research to focus on differential sibling acculturation and how this can occur in relation to their age at immigration, birth order, and gender. By further studying how these different factors affect acculturation within a family, we can better understand the outcomes related to immigrant families' environments.

It is likely that siblings of different ages will acculturate at different rates due to the age at which they are exposed to a new language and culture and the family's differential treatment of each child (Pyke, 2005). For example, Newport (1990) has shown that children who are exposed to a new language before puberty will acquire the new language faster and speak with a less pronounced accent than those who are exposed to a new linguistic environment only after the onset of puberty. Siblings who arrive before and after adolescence may have differential language proficiencies, which, in turn, may result in different patterns of sibling relationships.

In addition, depending on the age at immigration, the new school climate may differ substantially from the school system in the country of origin. In California, children of parents whose primary language is not English are tested for English proficiency and referred to mandatory English instruction as needed. Following the goals of the "English-only" proposition (CA Prop 227) children are placed in "immersion" (English-only) classrooms where only English is spoken and provided with special English-language development instruction. A child with limited English proficiency is eligible, upon parent request, to be placed in a bilingual program, with the goal of full immersion within a year (California Education Code 300–340). Because the manner in which mainstream society accepts multiculturalism has an effect on acculturation outcomes and ethnic identity (Phinney, Horenczyk, Liebkin, and Vedder, 2001), it is expected that school experiences will have an effect on children's acculturation and ethnic identity. Therefore, siblings of different ages may have a substantially different school experience and feel different pressures to assimilate into the new environment.

As previous research has found, language is significantly related to social competence (Damico and Damico, 1993). If siblings enter into the mainstream school system at different ages, not only may their English-language skills and accent differ (Newport, 1990), but their social competence may differ as well (Damico and Damico, 1993). If one child has a less pronounced accent and is more comfortable with the English language, social activity with children of different cultural and linguistic competencies may occur more frequently and fluidly, thus facilitating further acculturation. On the other hand, another sibling with limited English skills may feel more comfortable interacting with their parents and peers from the same ethnic background, thus limiting their enculturation opportunities.

Another aspect of the sibling relationship that has been alluded to is the issue of birth order. Researchers have found that older siblings have a stronger grasp of the native culture as they have had more experience in the native country and have more direct contact with their parents (Pyke, 2005). Also, as more children enter into the family, the family's time and resources may be further strained and the younger child may be raised with fewer opportunities to be enculturated by the family (Cheng and Kuo, 2000). The less time children have with their parents, or family members with a strong connection to the native culture, the less they are able to establish a strong cultural foundation. And as siblings acculturate differently and at different rates their relationship with their parents may also be different.

Finally, we must also look at gender as a source of differential treatment within the family. As sibling structure differs between families, so will the dynamics of the family. For example, it has been found that all-male sibling groups have higher intimacy with parents, and being a female in a mostly male sibling group is associated with less intimacy. In such a sibling structure, the fathers may feel less intimate with their daughters because they may feel pressured to socialize the boys first and foremost (Lawson and Brossart, 2004). In terms of acculturation, it stands to reason that the sibling structure will affect the manner in which each child is pressured to maintain the native culture, and how close the children feel toward their parents, and in turn their connections to the native culture.

As we have stated, a number of conditions may lead to differential acculturation among siblings. It is necessary to understand how such conditions relate to one another to gain further knowledge of how the father role may change as a consequence of the differential acculturation rates. Pyke's (2005) finding that translation between siblings and parents was sometimes necessary has implications for father-child dynamics. For example, a father may have less authority within the family, as he must depend on one child to translate for him in order to talk to another child. One child may feel pressure to be the disciplinarian for his father, as the other child may never experience discipline directly from the father. In addition, as siblings acculturate differently they may form distinct ideas of what a father must be. Therefore in order to be an effective father, in his children's eyes, he must parent each child differently in order to fulfill the distinct needs. How connected a father is to his children, and how well his behavior maps onto what his children feel he is doing, may have a substantial effect on later developmental and behavioral outcomes, and for this reason it merits attention.

CULTURAL BROKERS

Recent work on children who serve as "brokers" between parents and the wider culture illustrates the richness of this cultural variation for understanding not only family dynamics in immigrant groups but also the dynamic and bi-directional nature of the parent-child relationship. Children often act as cultural brokers on behalf of the family in part due to the linguistic limitations of the parents:

> With responsibility as interpreters of the new culture and language, immigrant parents are often in a position with no one to translate or interpret for them. Traditional intergenerational authority relationships change and the child also becomes involved in the worries and concerns of the family, such as hassles with landlords, arranging for medical care, and dealing with the legal system. (Olsen and Chen, 1988, 31)

As Buriel, Chao, and their colleagues (Buriel, Perez, DeMent, Chavez, and Moran, 1998; Chao, 2001) have discovered, these natural experiments of migration (cultural brokering) produce parent-child role reversal, shifts in generational power, and increases in responsibility taking. While these experiences may be maturity enhancing as well as stressful for children, they may be threatening to the father's authority in the family and a potential source of conflict between parents and children. As such, they provide unique opportunities to test our assumptions about the capabilities of children to manage developmentally off-time challenges and about how families cope and adapt to the obstacles of entering a new culture. The unique situation of cultural brokering has important implications for children's socioemotional and academic development and also gives us insight into how father roles shift under these changes in family power dynamics.

RESEARCH DIRECTIONS

In this section, we explore future directions that research on immigrant fathers might take, including a multidisciplinary focus, the endorsement of multilevel models of analysis, and innovations in sampling and design.

Multidisciplinary Orientation

First, multiple disciplines are necessary if we are to fully understand immigrant fathers. *Historians* are necessary to remind us of prior immigration experiences and to show how historical shifts shape fathering roles. Did the immigrant fathers of the late 1800s experience the same issues as immigrant fathers of 2005 and 2020? *Demographers* remind us that demographic trends are important contexts for our understanding and interpretation of fathering roles, opportunities, and behaviors. Tracing the demographic trend lines is a critical task to understand how fathering is modified by shifts in the relative percentages of different immigrant groups relative to the host culture. *Anthropologists* remind us that concepts of intercultural contact are derived from classic anthropological studies (Redfield, Linton, and Herskovits, 1936) and that ethnographic methods are critical tools to employ in this process. *Sociologists* remind us that societal structures, in terms of class and race/ethnicity, shape attitudes, opportunities, and access to societal resources and services and are, thus, critical considerations for understanding fathers. *Economists* remind us that economic opportunity is a critical determinant of the variations in immigrant fathering behavior. Fathers' perceptions of their roles as "provider" will be altered by vocational circumstances, and the family's level of financial stress and security will be determined, in part, by economic opportunities for fathers (and mothers). *Political scientists* remind us that the political power and influence acquired by different immigrant groups will have major effects on social policies, which will directly impact the level and cultural appropriateness of social services as well as economic opportunities. *Psychologists* remind us that a variety of psychological processes merit examination at various phases of the immigration experience, including coping strategies, social support availability and utilization, and interpersonal relationships among family members.

Theoretical Considerations

What kind of theoretical framework is needed to understand immigrant fathers? What are the new techniques that are available that will help us better understand fathers in general and immigrant fathers in particular? We should proceed from a multilevel framework as a guide and consider the techniques that may be available for assessing individual, dyadic, familial, social, and cultural levels of analysis. Finally, a transactional model and multilevel framework are necessary to understand immigrant fathers and their impact on children's development.

Individual Level

Individual level differences in social and psychological characteristics of fathers in terms of attitudes toward involvement, motivation for fathering, skill and competence, and gender-based attitudes toward fathering have long been recognized (Lamb, 2004). However, there has been interest recently in the biological basis of fathering with the recognition that hormonal changes occur in response to the transition to fatherhood. For example, Storey, Walsh, Quinton, and Wynne-Edwards (2000) found that men experienced significant pre-, peri-, and postnatal changes in each of three hormones (prolactin, cortisol, and testosterone)—a pattern of results that was similar to that of the women in their study. Specifically, prolactin levels were higher for both men and women in the late prenatal period than in the early postnatal period and cortisol levels increased just before and decreased in the postnatal period. Perhaps of greater interest is the fact that men who are highly involved with their partners during pregnancy are more likely to show lower levels of testosterone in the postnatal period. In turn, this may increase their responsiveness to infant cues during the postnatal period.

What are the hormonal changes associated with the transition to fatherhood among immigrant fathers of different types? For example, are sojourner immigrant fathers who are absent for part of the prenatal pregnancy period less likely to show hormonal shifts that have been found for fathers who are available and involved with their partners during pregnancy? And what are the long-term implications of these different patterns of hormonal changes? Studies of these questions not only offer new insights into immigrant father processes, but also explore natural experimental tests of variation in father availability and biological responses to becoming a father.

Dyadic Level Processes

At the dyadic level father-child, father-mother, and coparenting relationships are recognized as important aspects of fathering. At present, we are in a better position to evaluate and measure dyadic level processes than previously (Kenny, Mohr, and Levesque, 2001) by being able to evaluate actor, partner, or dyad level contributions to relationships. How do these components shift across time in response to the transition and the degree and type of acculturative experiences various family dyads have, such as parent-child (father-child; mother-child) and husband-wife dyads? Do the individual level components become more important as a result of: 1) entry into a more individualistically oriented culture from a more collectivist culture, and 2) different rates of acculturation to the host culture on the part of different partners in the parent-child or marital dyads?

Family Level Processes

Does the commitment and expression of familism change as a result of the immigration experience? Again, new techniques for assessment of family level variables will be helpful in moving this level of analysis from metaphor to measurement. Recent work by Cook and Kenny (2004) on assessment of family level variables could be usefully applied to families of immigrant fathers. Other family level assessments, such as looking at routines and rituals (Fiese, 2006), are useful indices of family organization and functioning. Assessment of how these change across time or are a consequence of immigration would be useful not only to gauge family relationships but also to measure of how families adapt to new cultural contexts. The film *What's Cooking?* is an excellent illustration of how a Vietnamese, a Latino, an African American, and a Jewish family incorporated both culture-specific and American elements into their celebration of the Thanksgiving dinner ritual: All cooked a turkey but collard greens, rice, latkes, and tamales were central parts of the feast for the respective families. This, in fact, may be an example of the concept of creolization— a creative mélange of values of the traditional culture (Chinese, Mexican, etc.) and U.S. cultural norms (see Auerbach, Silverstein, and colleagues, this volume).

Community Level

Fathers are affected not only by individual, dyadic, and family level factors but by whether they are embedded in a network of community level influences as well. New techniques for the assessment of community level influences such as neighborhoods are becoming available, including census tract measures, community surveys, and systematic social observation (Leventhal and Brooks-Gunn, 2000; Sampson, 2005). Another promising methodological tool for neighborhood level assessments is geographical information systems (GIS), also termed computer mapping, which allows pictorial maps that depict variations in the distributions of groups, services, crime levels, and other community level indicators (Cadora, Swartz, and Gordon, 2003). These new neighborhood level approaches will allow us to better characterize the qualities of different communities in terms of their ethnic variation and/or homogeneity, the economic opportunity structure, the availability of services, the levels of social capital, as well as the levels of violence—all factors that may have an influence on fathering behavior. For example, immigrant fathers in neighborhoods that are characterized by high levels of perceived danger may be more authoritarian than fathers in less threatening contexts (Dodge, McLoyd, and Lansford, 2005). In our studies of Mexican American families, we have found that immigrant fathers who live in rough neighborhoods are more likely to monitor and control their children's activities, but that they also rely on support from kin and co-ethnics who live nearby (Coltrane et al., 2005). In the tradition of ecological systems theory (Bronfenbrenner and Morris, 1998), the task will be to describe the ways in which shifts in these various levels of analysis occur over time as a result of acculturation and new waves of immigration, and to determine how these shifts affect fathers' roles and levels of involvement.

Methodological Issues in Research on Immigrant Fathers

As the research base in the area of immigrant fathers accumulates evidence, there will likely be related methodological innovations that will inform the study of immigrant fathers. As has been urged elsewhere, it is imperative for future studies to include multiple waves of measurement (Phinney, 2006), with data gathered using mixed methods from multiple reporters (Patterson and Yoerger, 1993). However, we focus here on other innovations that should be considered in research studies. In other work we outlined some of the barriers to research with Latino fathers (e.g., recruitment, attrition, measurement equivalence; Parke, Coltrane, Duffy, Powers, Adams, Fabricius, et al., 2004), and in this section we offer recommendations for the future of research on immigrant fathers.

Qualitative and Quantitative Approaches Are Both Useful

Developmentalists (and other social scientists) are often prone to binary thinking. This applies to methodological preferences as well as to a variety of conceptual issues (Parke, Coltrane, Duffy, Powers, Adams, Fabricius, et al., 2004). In no case is this more evident than in the division between those who endorse qualitative approaches and those who endorse quantitative approaches. Although most child developmentalists are trained in quantitative methods, as our research agenda has broadened, the need for analysis of qualitative data is increasingly recognized. Qualitative approaches such as focus groups and ethnographies are commonly used in other disciplines but have less often been used by child developmentalists (García-Coll and Magnuson, 1999). Focus groups are excellent forums in which to explore as well as to examine similarities and differences across gender, socioeconomic classes, and ethnic groups. These groups provide a unique opportunity for parents and children to articulate their concerns, values, and goals in a context that is less constrained than the usual interview format. This technique is important in the early stages of research with understudied populations and is important in the study of immigrant fathers (see Parke, Coltrane, Duffy, Powers, Adams, Fabricius, et al., 2004, for examples of this approach in the study of Latino fathers). However, this approach is useful at the data interpretation stage, as well. For example, Cooper (1999) used follow-up focus groups to aid in interpretation of paradoxical findings. Cooper found that although Chinese American and Vietnamese American students hold strong family values and respect their parents a great deal, they do not necessarily involve them in decisions or discussions about their college majors or sexual orientations. Focus groups helped Cooper resolve the paradox: students did not communicate with their parents about such sensitive topics out of deference, not lack of respect.

However, qualitative studies are not without limitations. For example, many qualitative studies do not generalize to larger populations, and most qualitative studies lack the analytic ability to test complex theories of family processes. Also, qualitative studies are time-intensive and difficult to replicate; thus, there may be a long delay between a study being conducted and the dissemination of the results. Finally, because many qualitative studies employ methods that are unique to that particular study, they are oftentimes not published in top-tier peer-reviewed journals (e.g., only one qualitative study, Wassenberg, Feron, and Kessels, 2005, was published in *Child Development* between 2001 and 2005), and policymakers and academics oftentimes overlook qualitative studies. As a result, we urge researchers to conduct qualitative studies as an essential first step, but also recommend that future studies employ large samples using a combination of quantitative and qualitative approaches.

Innovations in Sampling

The field needs to entertain approaches beyond traditional random sampling procedures because such methods are unlikely to yield representative samples of immigrant families (Brown, Long, Gould, Weitz, and Milliken, 2000). Alternatively, there are a number of methods that promote recruitment, curb attrition, and facilitate participation among marginalized groups. Specifically, researchers of immigrant fathers may want to consider employing either participant action research methods (Gilmore, Krantz, and Ramirez, 1986) or respondent-driven sampling methods (Heckathorn, 1997, 2002).

Participant action research (PAR) is by no means new (Lewin, 1946), but involves allowing researchers to collaborate closely with the individuals they study. One study of adolescent students that employed PAR methods involved selecting a diverse group of students, training them in research methods, informing them of the project goals and methods, eliciting their input about the plan, and adapting the recruitment strategies given their input (Fine et al., 2005). PAR methods enable "learning by doing" and can be employed when researchers wish both to study and to affect a phenomenon in short order (Gilmore et al., 1986). Like qualitative methods, PAR demands a good deal of time and energy expenditure by researchers to develop relationships within communities. It also requires the researcher to give up control when it comes to recruitment and interviewing. However, PAR does not presume that established research measures and methods will not be employed once the sample is obtained.

Respondent-driven sampling (RDS)—a method of deriving population parameter estimates based on snowball sampling methods—allows for the identification and recruitment of populations for which knowledge of group membership (e.g., undocumented immigrant status) may have associated risk or stigma (e.g., deportation). This approach is useful in situations where it is not possible to randomly sample a population that is underground or hidden due to their fear of the consequences of identification (i.e., in case of undocumented immigrants). Through the use of appropriate incentives and rigorous controls, RDS accounts for the problematic biases that are present in existing chain-referral methods (e.g., snowball sampling) by statistically modeling the chain of referral in a manner that allows for unbiased population estimates (Heckathorn, 1997, 2002). RDS uses group-mediated social control processes (Heckathorn, 1997) to reward participants twice: once for their involvement in the study and again when they recruit other participants. In a study of referrals for mental health treatment, Asian Americans were more frequently voluntarily referred by friends, loved ones, and organizations than members of other ethnic groups, in which coercive referrals were more common (Takeuchi and Cheung, 1998). It is possible that similar socially mediated group referral processes can be profitably employed in future studies of immigrant father populations.

Construct Validity in Research on Immigrant Fathers

There is a need for additional construct validity studies of measurement equivalence among immigrant populations. Conducting research with immigrant families tends to involve preliminary qualitative work to determine the scope of the research question and to explore the usefulness of research measures, followed by subsequent large-scale studies in which established research measures are adapted and used (Knight and Hill, 1998). However, many widely employed measures of adjustment and stress have not been validated with ethnic minority and immigrant populations. The Child Behavior Checklist (Achenbach and Edelbrock, 1983) is an exception, with validity studies published from samples in a wide range of countries in Europe and Asia (Achenbach and Rescorla, 2007). In addition, studies have determined the cross-ethnic equivalence of measures of health outcomes (Lubetkin, Jia, and Gold, 2004), acculturation (Zea, Asner-Self, and Birman, 2003), intelligence (Te Nijenhuis, Tolboom, and Resing, 2004), and intercultural adjustment (Matsumoto, LeRoux, and Ratzlaff, 2001). We encourage researchers to conduct, and disseminate the results from, construct validity studies. In addition, editors need to include such studies in their journals. Publishing these findings will enable others to employ established research measures in their own studies, which will allow for replication and eventually a more credible body of knowledge.

Advances in the Measurement of Context

There is a growing body of evidence suggesting that the experiences of immigrant families are linked both to the contexts in which they live (Guerra and Smith, 2006) and to their perceptions of those contexts (Greenberger, Chen, and Beam, 2000). In addition, regardless of whether one actually lives and works near immigrants, perceptions of the number of immigrants in the United States are changing, such that non-immigrants overestimate the number of immigrants in the country (Alba, Rumbaut, and Marotz, 2005). However, creating an operational definition of context is a complex task. By asking participants to provide their zip codes, it is possible to use census tract estimates to obtain information on neighborhood characteristics such as household structure, income, and employment. Although these census-based approaches to context are widely used, they may capture only part of the important variation in contexts such as neighborhoods (Parke et al., at press). Alternatively, non-census-based measures of context that may be relevant to the experiences of immigrant fathers include state laws regarding legal and undocumented immigration, access to public transportation, and public school policies. A greater focus on the role of context as a determinant of immigrant father attitudes and behaviors may be useful in explaining which immigrant fathers thrive and which fathers have difficulty adapting to the host culture (Coltrane et al., 2005).

Increased Focus on Within-Group Variability

Researchers of immigrant families have tended to report mean level differences between different immigrant groups (e.g., comparing Mexican and Chinese immigrants) or mean differences between immigrants and non-immigrants. However, a focus on mean level differences tends to overlook the variability within groups (Parke and Buriel, 2006; Parke, Coltrane, Duffy, Buriel, Dennis, Powers, et al., 2004). This could be especially salient for research on immigrant fathers for a number of reasons. First, mean differences between immigrant and non-immigrant fathers may not reflect true score differences but instead may be a function of measurement variability. Second, although it is reasonable to hypothesize differences between groups, such differences are only meaningful if they explain unique rates of adjustment over time. Third, too many studies group immigrants from different countries and compare them to non-immigrants. Whereas such grouping methods may be useful in terms of offering insights about policy, researchers ought to focus narrowly on a particular national heritage to demonstrate important processes within groups (Sue, Sue, Sue, and Takeuchi, 1995). For example, immigrant fathers from both China and the Philippines may value filial piety and believe family members should avoid shame for the family. However, the political and economic differences in these two countries that motivated their decisions to immigrate might differentially explain how such values translate into patterns of behavior and processes within families.

Conceptualizing Father Involvement among Immigrant Fathers

Considerable theoretical work has sought to describe the components of father involvement. Two decades ago, Lamb, Pleck, Charnov, and Levine (1987) urged that father involvement be assessed as a multidimensional construct comprised of accessibility, engagement, and responsibility. This framework has proved a useful guide for conceptualizing father involvement. However, the applicability of this conceptual scheme for understanding immigrant father involvement remains untested, and alternative theoretical conceptualizations of father involvement in the context of immigrant experiences have begun to appear (Cabrera and Garcia-Coll, 2004). A well-conceived conceptualization of immigrant father involvement is needed to guide research in this domain. This theoretical conceptualization needs to go beyond a narrow focus on status predictors such as generation of immigration and instead include resources and vulnerabilities within groups.

Ethical Treatment of Immigrant Fathers as Research Participants

As interest in immigrant fathers flourishes, so too will the number of studies on immigrant families increase. In our growing efforts to collect information from these families, it will be important to ensure that participants are included in studies in a manner that is ethical and appropriately adjusted to their cultural expectations. Immigrants who have come to the United States as refugees may experience distress in response to questions about the decision to leave their native countries (Suárez-Orozco and Suárez-Orozco, 2001). As a result, it is important to develop demographic measures of the pre-immigration history using surveys and interview techniques that accurately capture those life experiences without unnecessarily upsetting the reporter. As methods for gathering this information become more prevalent, researchers may wish to consider standardizing collection of this data to elicit information without evoking emotional reactions. In addition, researchers ought to be trained to offer extensive opportunities for participants to be debriefed to minimize their distress. Finally, we urge researchers who recruit low-income participants to be sensitive to perceived economic pressures associated with large amounts of monetary compensation. If a compensation amount is too large, some immigrant fathers may feel compelled to participate, despite privacy concerns that might otherwise prevent them from being involved.

Researchers in This Area Need Community

Today's technologies offer remarkable opportunities for the establishment of a like-minded academic community, allowing access to information, long-distance collaboration, and dissemination of knowledge. The Special Interest Group on Studying Immigrant Families (SIG-SIF) and the Immigrant Families Scholars List are interactive online forums for discussion and dissemination of knowledge and opportunities in this area (see http://www.education.wisc.edu/edpsych/imfamsig).

Use Continuous Measures to "Fill the Cells"

One challenge facing investigations of immigrant family experiences concerns the difficulty of gathering participants in a way that allows for meaningful within-group comparisons. For example, we are currently conducting a study of the social construction of fatherhood among 393 families using a 2×2 design based on ethnicity (Euro-American vs. Mexican American) and type of family structure (biological fathers in intact families vs. stepfathers in remarried families). In our data, we have 118 first-generation immigrant fathers and, thus, can explore variability between our first- and second-generation fathers; however, we have no other ethnicities in our sample or any families with never-married parents, or single-mother families.

Although it is implausible that a single research project could resolve all of the questions related to a phenomenon, we hope methodological advances will permit us not only to answer questions at the group level but also to use continuous measures of group status. Returning to the example study above, generation of immigration is a group variable that could be quantified in terms of number of years in the United States. Similarly, stepfather presence could be quantified in terms of number of years that the stepfather was in the home. By moving away from status, we may be able to more readily account for within-group variability that does not require assignment of cases to cells only on the basis of group status criteria.

In this section we have suggested methodological innovations that future researchers of immigrant fathers may wish to consider in order to further understanding of this critical issue.

Policy Implications

Few areas of scholarship are as relevant to policy as work on immigrant fathers. As the current national debate in the United States continues about the status and rights of immigrant fathers as well as mothers, children, and other relatives, research is needed to guide the policymaking process. More attention to the economic contributions of immigrant fathers and their families to the national welfare is needed in addition to efforts to quantify the costs of providing health care and education to families and their children. What are the rights of native-born children when they are born to undocumented parents? Although the focus of the current debate is on the short-term economic costs and benefits, imagining the future requires a longer-term perspective. For example, population replacement rates are declining in many countries, which threatens long-term economic tax bases and the supply of work force participants. As Tierney (2006) recently noted,

> The fertility rate of native-born Americans in many states, including California, has fallen to near or below the replacement rate, as it has in European countries that are struggling to support their aging populations. Worried European leaders have been trying to reverse the decline by offering subsidies to parents. . . . But America is in better shape than Europe. Its population is still growing robustly, partly because of the arrival of adult immigrants, and partly because immigrants don't have to be bribed to have children. Their higher fertility rate helps off-set the natives', bringing the overall national rate just about up to the replacement level. . . . Now that birthrates are low and retirees are living so long, America needs immigrants more than ever. If there were a moratorium on legal immigration, the Social Security deficit would rise by nearly a third over the next 50 years (Anderson, 2005). Even illegal immigrants help the system's finances because when they give employers bogus Social Security numbers, the taxes paid on their behalf end up in the trust fund. With fewer immigrants, we'd have to either raise taxes or cut retiree benefits. And who would do the work they're now doing? (A23)

In sum, in the longer view it is possible that immigration—as it has in the past—benefits not just the immigrants but the members of the host country as well. At the same time, predicting the future is a hazardous endeavor. As Robert Coles (1999) reminds us, "Time holds its mysteries and the future resists our easy grasp, however anxious we be to assert it conclusively" (17).

FINAL MESSAGE

By recognizing that fathering, including immigrant fathering, is a dynamic concept open to historical, cultural, and technological influences, we will be better positioned to understand the inevitable changes that will take place for future immigrant fathers, and we will be better able to design policies and programs for immigrant fathers in this new millennium.

NOTE FROM THE AUTHOR

1. Each of the quotes that appear in this article was provided by participants in Spanish and translated for use in this chapter. For space, the original Spanish quotes were removed but can be obtained at http://devpsych.sfsu.edu/PAYS/PAYS_presentations.htm. The work in this chapter was supported by NIMH grant MH54154 and NIMH/NICHD grant MH64829.

REFERENCES

Achenbach, T. M., and Edelbrock, C. (1983). *Manual for the Child Behavior Checklist and Revised Child Behavior Profile*. Burlington: University of Vermont Department of Psychiatry.

Achenbach, T. M., and Rescorla, L. A. (2007). *Multicultural understanding of child and adolescent psychopathology: Implications for mental health assessment*. New York: Guilford.

Alba, R. D., Rumbaut, R. G., and Marotz, K. (2005). A distorted nation: Perceptions of racial/ethnic group sizes and attitudes toward immigrants and other minorities. *Social Forces, 84*, 901–19.

Anderson, S. (2005). The contribution of legal immigration to the Social Security system. Arlington, VA: National Foundation of American Policy.

Auerbach, C. F., Silverstein, L. B., Zlotnick-Woldenberg, C., Peguero, A., and Tacher-Roffe, S. (this volume).

Berry, J. W. (this volume).

Berry, J. W., Phinney, J. P., Sam, D. L., and Vedder, P. (2006). *Immigrant youth in cultural transition: Acculturation, identity, and adaptation across national contexts*. Mahwah, NJ: Erlbaum.

Bronfenbrenner, U., and Morris, P. (1998). The ecology of developmental processes. In W. Damon (Series Ed.) and R. M. Lerner (Vol. Ed.), *Handbook of child psychology: Vol. 1. Theoretical models of human development* (993–1028). New York: Wiley.

Brown, B. A., Long, H. L., Gould, H., Weitz, T., and Milliken, N. (2000). A conceptual model for the recruitment of diverse women into research studies. *Journal of Women's Health & Gender-Based Medicine, 9*, 625–32.

Bryant, E. (1997). Quote on wall of Nova Scotia Immigration Museum, Halifax, N. S.

Buriel, R., Perez, W., DeMent, L., Chavez, D., and Moran, V. (1998). The relationship of language brokering to academic performance, biculturalism and self-efficacy among Latino adolescents. *Hispanic Journal of Behavioral Sciences, 20*, 283–97.

Cabrera, N. J., and Garcia-Coll, C. T. (2004). Latino fathers: Uncharted territory in need of much exploration. In M. E. Lamb (Ed.), *The role of the father in child development* (98–120). New York: Wiley.

Cadora, E., Swartz, C., and Gordon, M. (2003). Criminal justice and health and human services: An exploration of overlapping needs, resources and interests in Brooklyn neighborhoods. In J. Travis and M. Waul (Eds.), *Prisoners once removed* (285–312). Washington, DC: Urban Institute Press.

California Education Code 300–340. Retrieved on June 20, 2006 from http://caselaw.lp.findlaw.com/cacodes/edc.html.

Chao, R. (2001). Extending research on the consequences of parenting style for Chinese Americans and European Americans. *Child Development, 72*, 1832–1843.

Chase-Dunn, C. (1998). *Global formation: Structures of the world-economy.* Lanham, MD: Rowman & Littlefield.

Cheng, S. H., and Kuo, W. H. (2000). Family socialization of ethnic identity among Chinese American pre-adolescents. *Journal of Comparative Family Studies, 31*, 463–84.

Coles, R. (1999, October 17). Make room for daddies. *New York Times.*

Coltrane, S., Melzer, S., Vega, E., and Parke, R. D. (2005). Mexican American fathering in neighborhood context. In W. Marsiglio, K. Roy, and G. L. Fox (Eds.), *Situated fathering: A focus on physical and social spaces* (277–98). Boulder, CO: Rowman & Littlefield.

Coltrane, S., Parke, R. D., and Adams, M. (2004). Complexity of father involvement in low-income Mexican American families. *Family Relations, 53*, 179–89.

Cook, W. L., and Kenny, D. A. (2004). Application of the Social Relations Model to family assessment. *Journal of Family Psychology, 18*, 361–71.

Cooper, C. R. (1999). Cultural perspectives on individuality and connectedness in adolescent development. In A. S. Masten (Ed.), *Cultural processes in child development, Vol. 29* (25–57). Mahwah, NJ: Erlbaum.

Damico, J. S., and Damico, S. K. (1993). Language and social skills from a diversity perspective: Considerations for the speech-language pathologist. *Language, Speech, and Hearing Services in Schools, 24*, 236–43.

Dixon, J., Durrheim, K., and Tredoux, C. (2005). Beyond the optimal contact strategy: A reality check for the contact hypothesis. *American Psychologist, 60*, 697–711.

Dodge, K. A., McLoyd, V. C., and Lansford, J. E. (2005). The cultural context of physically disciplining children. In V. C. McLoyd, N. E. Hill, and K. A. Dodge

(Eds.), *African American family life: Ecological and cultural diversity* (245–63). New York: Guilford Press.

Fiese, B. (2006). *Family routines and rituals.* New Haven, CT: Yale University Press.

Fine, M., Bloom, J., Burns, A., Chajet, L., Guishard, M., Payne, Y., Perkins-Munn, T., and Torre, M. A. (2005). Dear Zora: A letter to Zora Neale Hurston 50 years after Brown. *Teachers College Record, 107*(3), 496–528.

García-Coll, C. T., and Magnuson, K. (1999). Cultural influences on child development: Are we ready for a paradigm shift? In A. Masten (Ed.), *Minnesota symposium on child psychology, Vol. 29* (1–24). Mahwah, NJ: Erlbaum.

Gilmore, T., Krantz, J., and Ramirez, R. (1986). Action-based modes of inquiry and the host-researcher relationship. *Consultation, 5,* 160–75.

Glenn, E. N. (1992). From servitude to service work: Historical continuities in the racial division of paid reproductive labor. *Signs, 18,* 1–43.

Greenberger, E., Chen, C., and Beam, M. (2000). The perceived social context of adolescents' misconduct: A comparative study of youths in three cultures. *Journal of Research on Adolescence, 10,* 365–88.

Greenberger, E., and Steinberg, L. D. (1986). *When teenagers work: The psychological and social costs of adolescent employment.* New York: Basic Books.

Guerra, N. G., and Smith, E. P. (Eds.). (2006). Preventing youth violence in a multicultural society. Washington, DC: APA Books.

Heckathorn, D. D. (1997). Respondent-driven sampling: A new approach to the study of hidden populations. *Social Problems, 44,* 174–99.

———. (2002). Respondent-driven sampling II: Deriving valid population estimates from chain-referral samples of hidden populations. *Social Problems, 49,* 11–34.

Hernandez, D. J. (2004). Demographic change and the life circumstances of immigrant families. *The Future of Children, 14,* 17–47.

Hondagneu-Sotelo, P., and Avila, E. (1997). "I'm here but I'm there": The meanings of Latina transnational motherhood. *Gender & Society, 11,* 548–71.

Huang, Z. J., Yu, S. M., and Ledsky, R. (2006). Health status and health service access and use among children in U.S. immigrant families. *American Journal of Public Health, 96,* 634–40.

Kenny, D. A., Mohr, C., and Levesque, M. (2001). A social relations variance partitioning of dyadic behavior. *Psychological Bulletin, 127,* 128–41.

Knight, G. P., and Hill, N. E. (1998). Measurement equivalence in research involving minority adolescents. In C. McLoyd and L. Steinberg (Eds.), *Studying minority adolescents: Conceptual, methodological, and theoretical issues* (183–210). Mahwah, NJ: Erlbaum.

Lamb, M. E. (Ed.). (2004). *The role of the father in child development* (fourth ed.). Hoboken, NJ: Wiley.

Lamb, M. E., Pleck, J. H., Charnov, E. L., and Levine, J. A. (1987). A biosocial perspective on paternal behavior and involvement. In J. B. Lancaster, J. Altmann, A. S. Rossi, and L. R. Sherrod (Eds.), *Parenting across the life span: Biosocial dimensions* (111–42). New York: Aldine De Gruyter.

Lawson, D. M., and Brossart, D. F. (2004). Association between current intergenerational family relationships and sibling structure. *Journal of Counseling & Development, 82,* 472–82.

Leventhal, T., and Brooks-Gunn, J. (2000). The neighborhoods they live in: The effects of neighborhood residence on child and adolescent outcomes. *Psychological Bulletin, 126*, 309–37.

Lewin, K. (1946). Action research and minority problems. *Journal of Social Issues, 2*, 34–46.

Lubetkin, E. I., Jia, H., and Gold, M. R. (2004). Construct validity of the EQ-5D in low-income Chinese American primary care patients. *Quality of Life Research: An International Journal of Quality of Life Aspects of Treatment, Care & Rehabilitation, 13*, 1467.

Matsumoto, D., LeRoux, J., and Ratzlaff, C. (2001). Development and validation of a measure of intercultural adjustment potential in Japanese sojourners: The Intercultural Adjustment Potential Scale (ICAPS). *International Journal of Intercultural Relations, 25*, 483–510.

Newport, E. L. (1990). Maturational constraints on language learning. *Cognitive Science, 14*, 11–28.

Nightingale, D. S., and Fix, M. (2004). Economic and labor market trends. *The Future of Children, 14*, 49–59.

Olsen, L., and Chen, M. T. (1988). *Crossing the schoolhouse border: Immigrant students and California public schools.* San Francisco: California Tomorrow.

Parke, R. D., and Buriel, R. (2006). Socialization in the family: Ethnic and ecological perspectives. In W. Damon and R. M. Lerner (Editors-in-chief) and N. Eisenberg (Vol. Ed.), *The handbook of child psychology, Vol. 3* (429–504). New York: Wiley.

Parke, R. D., Coltrane, S., Duffy, S., Buriel, R., Dennis, J., Powers, J., et al. (2004). Economic stress, parenting and child adjustment in Mexican American and European American families. *Child Development, 75*, 1–25.

Parke, R. D., Coltrane, S., Duffy, S., Powers, J., Adams, M., Fabricius, W., et al. (2004). Assessing father involvement in Mexican American families. In R. Day and M. Lamb (Eds.), *Conceptualizing and measuring father involvement* (17–38). Mahwah, NJ: Erlbaum.

Parke, R. D., Coltrane, S., and Schofield, T. (2007). New Americans, new families. *Greater Good* (Fall), 22–26. Berkeley, CA: UC Center for Peace and Well Being.

Parke, R. D., Lio, S., Schofield, T., Tuthill, L., Vega, E., and Coltrane, S. (at press). Neighborhood environments: A multi-measure, multi-level approach. In L. C. Mayes and M. Lewis (Eds.), *The environment of human development: A handbook of theory and measurement.* New York: Cambridge University Press.

Patterson, G. R., and Yoerger, K. (1993). Developmental models for delinquent behavior. In S. Hodgins (Ed.), *Mental disorder and crime* (140–72). Thousand Oaks, CA: Sage.

Phinney, J. (2006). Ethnic identity exploration in emerging adulthood. In J. J. Arnett and J. L. Tanner (Eds.), *Emerging adults in America: Coming of age in the 21st century* (117–34). Washington, DC: American Psychological Association.

Phinney, J. S., Horenczyk, G., Liebkin, K., and Vedder, P. (2001). Ethnic identity, immigration, and well-being: An interactional approach. *Journal of Social Issues, 57*, 493–510.

Pomerantz, E. M., Ruble, D. N., and Bolger, N. (2003). Supplementing the snapshots with video footage: Taking a developmental approach to understanding social-psychological phenomena. In C. Sansone, C. C. Morf, and A. T. Panter (Eds.), *The Sage handbook of methods in social psychology* (405-25). New York: Sage.

Pyke, K. (2005). "Generational Deserters" and "Black Sheep": Acculturative differences among siblings in Asian immigrant families. *Journal of Family Issues, 26*, 491-517.

Raffaelli, M., and Ontai, L. L. (2004). Gender socialization in Latino/a families. *Sex Roles, 50*, 287-99.

Redfield, R., Linton, R., and Herskovits, M. J. (1936). Memorandum for the study of acculturation. *American Anthropologist, 38*, 149-52.

Rubin, L. (1994). *Families on the fault-line: America's working class speaks about the family, economy and ethnicity.* New York: Harper Collins.

Sampson, R. J. (2005). How does community context matter? Social mechanisms and the explanation of crime. In W. Per-Olof and R. J. Sampson (Eds.), *The explanation of crime: Context, mechanisms, and development.* New York/Cambridge: Cambridge University Press.

Sanger, D. E. (1999). *Report shows increase in digital divide. National Telecommunications and Information Administration.* Retrieved on June 22, 2006, from http://www.ntia.doc.gov/ntiahome/digitaldivide/.

Storey, A. E., Walsh, C. J., Quinton, R., and Wynne-Edwards, K. E. (2000). Hormonal correlates of paternal responsiveness in new and expectant fathers. *Evolution and Human Behavior, 21*, 79-95.

Statistics Canada. (2003). 2001 Census: Analysis series. Canada's ethnocultural portrait: The changing mosaic. Retrieved December 3, 2006, from http://www12.statcan.ca/english/census01/products/analytic/companion/etoimm/pdf/96F0030XIE2001008.pdf.

Suárez-Orozco, C., and Suárez-Orozco, M. (2001). *Children of immigration.* Cambridge, MA: Harvard University Press.

Sue, S., Sue, D. W., Sue, L., and Takeuchi, D. T. (1995). Psychopathology among Asian Americans. *Cultural Diversity and Mental Health, 1*, 39-54.

Takeuchi, D. T., and Cheung, M. (1998). Coercive and voluntary referrals: How ethnic minority adults get into mental health treatment. *Ethnicity & Health, 3*, 149-58.

Te Nijenhuis, J., Tolboom, E., and Resing, W. (2004). Does cultural background influence the intellectual performance of children from immigrant groups? The RAKIT Intelligence Test for immigrant children. *European Journal of Psychological Assessment, 20*, 10-26.

Tierney, J. (2006, May 27). No más immigrants, no more care? Why baby boomers need foreign aides. *New York Times*, A23.

U.S. Census Bureau. (1933). *Fifteenth Census of the United States: 1930; Population Volume II: General Report/Statistical Subjects* (25). Washington, DC: U.S. Government Printing Office. Retrieved June 20, 2006, from http://www.census.gov/.

——. (2003). 2002 Economics and Statistics Census, The Hispanic Population in the United States. Washington, DC: U.S. Government Printing Office. Retrieved March 19, 2008, from http://www.census.gov/prod/2003pubs/p20-545.pdf.

Vega, E., Coltrane, S., Pyke, K., and Parke, R. D. (2006). Voices of immigrant Mexican American families. Unpublished manuscript, University of California, Riverside.

Vernez, G., and Abrahamse, A. (1996). How immigrants fare in U.S. education. Santa Monica, CA: RAND.

Volker, B., and Chase-Dunn, C. (1985). *Transnational corporations and underdevelopment.* New York: Praeger.

Wassenberg, R., Feron, F. J. M., and Kessels, A. G. H. (2005). Relationship between cognitive and motor performance in 5- to 6-year-old children: Results from a large-scale cross-sectional study. *Child Development, 76,* 1092–1103.

Wilson, T. C. (2001). Americans' views on immigration policy: Testing the role of threatened group interests. *Sociological Perspectives, 44,* 485–501.

Yang, K. (2004). Southeast Asian American children: Not the "model minority." *The Future of Children, 14,* 127–33.

Zea, M. C., Asner-Self, K. K., and Birman, D. (2003). The abbreviated multidimensional acculturation scale: Empirical validation with two Latino/Latina samples. *Cultural Diversity & Ethnic Minority Psychology, 9,* 107–26.

Zhou, M. (2001). Contemporary immigration and the dynamics of race and ethnicity. In N. Smelser, W. J. Wilson, and F. Mitchell (Eds.), *America becoming, Vol. 1: Racial trends and their consequences* (200–42). Washington, DC: National Academy Press.

Zukow-Goldring, P. (2002). Sibling caregiving. In M. H. Bornstein (Ed.), *Handbook of parenting, Vol. 3: Being and becoming a parent* (253–86). Mahwah, NJ: Erlbaum.

Author Index

Subject Index

absolute levels (of father involvement). *See* time diaries

academic achievement/attainment, 94, 96–97, 106, 144, 161, 231, 268, 277, 298, 303; African American families, 268; Asian, Asian Americans, 155, 164–66, 168, 276, 298; Euro-Americans, 268; expectations, 186; father support, 156, 185, 187, 191, 295; parenting, 155–56, 185–86, 191, 268, 276–77; test scores, 161, 165, 167–68

acculturation, adaptation, 17–18, 40–41, 126, 198, 299–302; biculturation, 290; cultural, 133, 135, 145; definition, 32, 34, 197–98; differential, 289, 299–302; framework, 32–35, 198; influences on, 136, 147, 299, 301; integration, 126; intergenerational, 18–15, 189–90; level of, 34, 135, 168, 265, 278, 300; mutual accommodation, 290; patterns, 289; process of, 25, 32–33, 35, 42; psychological, 32–33; rates of, 289, 292, 299, 305; strategies, 25, 34

adolescence: adjustment, 3, 152, 154–57, 160, 163–64, 167–68, 185, 187, 189; autonomy, 154, 180, 184, 185; delinquency, 155, 160; externalizing behavior, 160–61, 165, 194; independence, 185, 202; internalizing behavior, 160–61, 165, 194; respect for parents, 164, 168

affluence, 29, 36–38, 40–41; African American fathers, 214; class of worker distribution, 117; employment stability, 111; employment status, 111; families, 241, 245–46, 268, 271, 277; involvement, 238; parental practices and beliefs, 238, 241

Africentric home environment, 277

Afro-Caribbean and Caribbean fathers, 49, 60, 113, 116, 117, 200; class of worker distribution, 117; employment stability, 116; employment status, 112, 116

agriculture groups, 16

Aka, 9, 15–16

anthropolgists, 26, 30, 198, 303

anthropolgy, 26

anti-immigrants, 298

Asian. *See* Chinese

Asian fathers, 109

Asian immigrant. *See* Chinese

329

About the Editors

Dr. Susan S. Chuang is currently an Assistant Professor in the Department of Family Relations and Applied Nutrition at the University of Guelph, Ontario, Canada. She received her baccalaureate in Criminology and Sociology at the University of Toronto, Ontario. At the University of Rochester, New York, U.S., she received a Masters of Science in Elementary Education, and a Masters of Science and Ph.D. in Human Development. She then received post-doctoral training under Dr. Michael E. Lamb at the Institute of Child Health and Human Development, Maryland, U.S. Her research focuses on parenting of young children among immigrant and mainland Chinese families. Her second line of research examines adolescent mental health among various socio-cultural contexts. She is currently co-editing special issues in *Sex Roles*, the *International Journal of Behavioral Development*, and the *Journal of Family Psychology* which all focus on issues and challenges that immigrant children, youth, and families face. She has published in various journals such as *Child Development, International Journal of Behavioral Development*, and *Social Development*.

Dr. Robert P. Moreno is currently an Associate Professor in the Department of Child and Family at Syracuse University, New York, U.S. He received his baccalaureate in psychology at UCLA, and his Ph.D. in Child and Adolescent Development from Stanford University. He is also a National Academy of Education/Spencer Postdoctoral Fellowship recipient. His research examines familial and cultural influences on children's learning and academic achievement among Latinos and low-income families. His publications include a special issue of the *Hispanic Journal of Behavioral Sciences* entitled "Conversations within Mexican Descent Families: Diverse

Contexts for Language Socialization and Learning" (co-edited with Deanne R. Pérez-Granados and Christi A. Cervantes). He also has a chapter entitled "Chicano Families and Schools: Myths, Knowledge, and Future Directions for Understanding" appearing in *Chicano School Failure and Success: Past, Present and Future,* edited by Richard R. Valencia.

List of Contributors

Carl F. Auerbach (Yeshiva University)

James D. Bachmeier (University of California, Irvine)

John W. Berry (Queen's University)

Louise Bordeaux Silverstein (Yeshiva University)

Ruth K. Chao (University of California, Riverside)

Susan S. Chuang (University of Guelph)

Scott Coltrane (University of California, Riverside)

Jeffrey Cookston (San Francisco State University)

Roberto M. De Anda (Portland State University)

Nancy A. Denton (University at Albany, SUNY)

Uwe P. Gielen (St. Francis College)

Donald J. Hernandez (University at Albany, SUNY)

Ronit Kahana-Kalman (New York University)

Akira Kanatsu (University of California, Riverside)

Eunjung Kim (University of Washington)

Michael E. Lamb (University of Cambridge)

Suzanne E. Macartney (University at Albany, SUNY)

Alfredo Mirandé (University of California, Riverside)

Robert P. Moreno (Syracuse University)

Erika Y. Niwa (New York University)

Ross D. Parke (University of California, Riverside)

Aris Peguero (Yeshiva University)

Norma Perez-Brena (San Francisco State University)

Joseph H. Pleck (University of Illinois, Urbana-Campaign)

Yanjie Su (Peking University)

Sara Tacher-Rosse (Yeshiva University)

Catherine S. Tamis-LeMonda (New York University)

Eric Vega (University of California, Riverside)

Hirokazu Yoshikawa (Harvard University)

Carrie Zlotnick-Woldenberg (Yeshiva University)